Elizabethan Lyrics

ELIZABETHAN LYRICS

from the original texts

chosen, edited and arranged
by
NORMAN AULT

faber and faber
LONDON · BOSTON

First published in 1925 by
Longmans, Green and Company Limited London
Revised and corrected edition published in 1949
by William Sloane Associates New York
This edition published in 1986
by Faber and Faber Limited
3 Queen Square London WC1N 3AU

Printed in Great Britain by
Butler & Tanner Ltd
Frome and London

Purchased 02 July 1992

British Library Cataloguing in Publication Data

Elizabethan Lyrics
1. English poetry—Early modern, 1500–1700
I. Ault, Norman
821'.3'08   PR1205
ISBN 0-571-13929-9

The Printer to the Reader

You that in music do delight
   Your minds for to solàce,
This little book of sonnets may
   Well like you in that case.
Here may you have such pretty things
   As women much desire:
Here may you have of sundry sorts
   Such songs as you require.
Wherefore, my friend, if you regard
   Such songs to read or hear,
Doubt not to buy this pretty Book,
   The price is not so dear.   *Jones (?)*

'*A Handful of Pleasant Delights,*' 1584.*

PREFACE

THE opportunity provided by the printing of a new edition of this work has enabled me to revise it in the light of such textual and bibliographical discoveries as have been recorded since it was first published. Thus six short poems of the original six hundred and forty have been replaced by other pieces, and changes have been made in the attributed authorship of some half-dozen more. In addition, modern scholarship has also made possible a closer approximation to the elusive dates of a number of other lyrics, particularly amongst those taken from the plays. Moreover, the consequent shifting of the chronological position of these pieces has, in turn, promoted a further rearrangement for convenience of reference—the poems within each year's group being now placed in the alphabetical order of their authors' names, followed by the anonymous pieces. It should also be noted that, for a like reason, an appendix of brief biographies of the chief poets of the period is now included. In all essentials, however, in plan, scope and selection, the third edition of *Elizabethan Lyrics* remains identical with that which first appeared twenty-four years ago.

Similarly unchanged remains my appreciation of the numerous kindnesses I received during the compilation of the work, my formal thanks for which I am happy to reprint.

First I must acknowledge the unfailing courtesy and assistance of the Librarians and Staffs of the Bodleian and the British Museum, where most of my researches were carried out; and also of the Librarians of The Queen's College, and

Christ Church, Oxford; Trinity College, Emmanuel College, and the University Library, Cambridge; and Sion College, and the Royal College of Music, London—where I have also worked.

I owe an expression of special gratitude for the following: a generous gift by the Librarian of the Henry E. Huntington Library, California, of photostats of nearly twenty pages from unique first editions now in that library; literal transcripts or collations of texts from MSS. or rare first editions in their charge by the Librarians of Eton College; Trinity College, Dublin; Chetham Library, Manchester; the Marquis of Salisbury's Library, Hatfield; the Duke of Devonshire's Library, Chatsworth; the National Museum of Antiquities, and the University Library, Edinburgh; the State and University Library, Hamburg; and also by Mr. W. A. White of New York from rare books in his possession; a fresh collation by Mr. F. Lewis Payne, from the only known copy of a book in York Cathedral; the loan to the Bodleian on my behalf by the Earl of Macclesfield of a MS. from Shirburn Castle; the kind consent of Dr. W. W. Greg to my use of a text from his and Dr. McKerrow's reprint (Mal. Soc.) of a play, the original of which is no longer available; and, finally, the permission accorded me by the Governing Body of Christ Church, Oxford, to include four poems from MSS. in their Library, three of which have never before been printed.

To these acknowledgements must now be added my gratitude for more recent kindnesses; for I cannot end without thanking all those friends, both here and in the United States, who have helped me in the preparation of the present edition of *Elizabethan Lyrics*.

N. A.

Oxford, 1925—1949

CONTENTS

INTRODUCTION

THIS Anthology is compiled on a new plan. Its purpose is to present the lyric poetry of the Elizabethan Age as a living literary movement, the evolution of which can best be seen, not in the piecemeal study of individual writers, but only when their collective work is viewed chronologically and as an organic whole. Consequently the poems are neither placed in the order of the birthdays of the authors, nor grouped under various subjects; but arranged year by year, according to the dates at which each poem first became known to the public for whom the author wrote. This plan renders it possible to follow step by step the development of the lyric, and its many fashions and phases, throughout the entire Elizabethan period; to see each poem in relation to its proper historical background of contemporary song, and thus to estimate its comparative as well as its actual quality; and, in the case of the better-known poets (who are, of course represented by more numerous selections), to study in chronological sequence the development of the work of the individual author. Ordinarily the date to which a poem is assigned is that of the first printed edition; but occasionally, where printing was long delayed—famous instances being Donne's *Poems* and Shakespeare's *Sonnets*—the poems are placed according to the approximate time at which they were written, began first to circulate in manuscript among the poet's acquaintance, or, in the case of songs taken from plays, the date of first performance.

To carry out my plan I felt compelled to undertake a

fresh survey at first hand of the whole field of Elizabethan
verse, entailing a careful search through upwards of two
thousand printed books, and nearly three hundred manu-
scripts of the sixteenth and early seventeenth centuries. Out
of a preliminary selection of some 2300 lyrics I have chosen
640, which seemed in some special way to be illustrative,
either of the lyric movement of the period as a whole, or of
its highest achievement. In such a selection, while the best-
known poets are necessarily represented by those miracles of
song which no familiarity can stale, many less well-known
but no less exquisite examples of their work find a place. But
my researches also brought to light numerous unexpected
treasures by other poets little known, long since forgotten, or
anonymous,—poets whose whole work has in not a few in-
stances come down to us in one solitary copy. Of the pieces
which I have taken from such books, many have never been
set up in type since the first and only edition was struck, more
than three centuries ago, on the old wooden screw-presses of
a Colwell or a Jones; and most of them now appear in an an-
thology for the first time. Wherever practicable I have gone
back to the original MSS., and not infrequently I have been
rewarded by the discovery of older versions or better texts
of poems already known to the literary world. I found, too,
that the searcher in old music books and other MSS. of the
period may still occasionally light upon poems of genuine
merit which have escaped the vigilance of editors, and no
less than ten of the lyrics included in this volume are, I be-
lieve, now printed for the first time: these being indicated
by the dagger (†) in the Index of First Lines.

In making my selection I have aimed at representing not
only the poets, but also the diverse form and content of
Elizabethan lyrical poetry. Of necessity love poetry predom-
inates; but war, travel and exploration, town life and country

life, birds, beasts and flowers, court and cottage, work and play, feasting, drinking and smoking, lullabies, marriage songs and elegies, religion and superstition, classical learning and local folk-lore, philosophy and madness, humour, parody, and even sheer nonsense, are all mirrored here, and combine their myriad patterns and colours to form an ever-changing picture of English social life during the reign of the great Queen.

Some pieces are included, not only for their intrinsic merit, but also because they were so popular in their day that they provided the dramatists of the period with endless topical quotations, humorous and otherwise. Twelve of these are of special interest to the Shakespearean student, and where this is so I have appended the necessary references to his plays; as regards at least two of them the connection with Shakespeare has never, I believe, been noticed before. I have also included specimens (pp. 85, 100, 141, 340) of the much execrated 'classical metre craze,' the complete exclusion of which—except for Campion's *Laura*—from previous anthologies of this period is difficult to justify from the point of view of the student of literature. I would also submit that these little-known metrical experiments do attain a measure of beauty which should qualify to some extent the usual wholesale condemnation of them. The work of the elder Scots poets I have purposely excluded, both because their vocabulary presents too great difficulties to the English reader, and because they can hardly be called Elizabethan in any sense of the term. But the younger Scots poets, who, frequenting the Court after 1603, entered into the English lyric tradition, are fully represented.

It is usual to begin the study of Elizabethan verse with Wyatt, the first writer of modern English poetry. With this custom I comply, not only because it is convenient to start from an accepted date, but because of the influence of Wyatt on his successors. His best work would seem to have been written when Elizabeth was a child, but nothing of his was printed until Tottel's famous Miscellany appeared in 1557 on the eve of her accession. The book leapt into instant and enduring popularity, so that he and Surrey, its chief contributors, may be said to have become Elizabethan by adoption. To another accepted convention I must, however, demur: I mean to the judgement which summarizes the early history of the Elizabethan lyric in the sentence 'After Wyatt and Surrey nothing, then Sidney and the giants.' In this volume I have printed more than eighty examples taken from no less than thirty-six poets (not counting anonymous writers) belonging to this neglected period. Any one who studies them will, I think, be inclined to appraise very differently the lyrical activity of these little-known years and its standard of achievement.

For the lower limit of the Elizabethan period I have decided to take the year 1620. Of course, no date that can be fixed upon to divide 'Elizabethan' from 'Seventeenth Century' poetry can be other than arbitrary. But it seems to me that the year 1620 may approximately be deemed to mark the turn of the tide; since the change in the mental attitude of the poets (first heralded by Donne at the end of the previous century), and the change in the cadence of their verse (first heard in Ayton's lyrics a few years later), are otherwise hardly perceptible before 1620, whereas after that date they become increasingly evident and general. The choice of 1620 means, of course, that the later lyrics of the few surviving Elizabethans are excluded. For these I may perhaps refer the reader to my more recent volume, *Seventeenth Century Lyrics*. Since that begins with the year 1621, belated Elizabethan lyrics appear there alongside the work of the late Jacobean and the Caroline poets, in their chronological order, and with their proper historical background.

At the foot of each poem I have appended the source from which the text has been taken. I hope that by this device, without detracting from the appeal of the book to the general reader—who asks only for a collection of the finest lyrics of the greatest age of English letters—I may have been able to provide the student of literature with what is really a bibliography of the best lyric poetry of the period. With the source is normally supplied the date of the poem; but, as is well known, the dates both of the composition and first performance of many plays of the time—including several of Shakespeare's—are still in dispute. I have, therefore, in all doubtful cases followed the chronology of *The Elizabethan Stage* by Sir E. K. Chambers; but, to save much repetition and space, have done so silently. For all established dates I have referred as briefly as possible to the authoritative evidence, either below the poems or in the notes. I should also add in conclusion that when a play or poem cannot be more precisely dated than by a period of several years (*e.g.* 1598–1601), the lyric concerned is placed under the year first mentioned.

The Texts

The essential beauty of a lyric lies in the melody of the oral word—sung, intoned, or spoken; it has nothing whatever to do with the orthography of the written word. The Elizabethans, poets and printers alike, appreciated this fact more truly than do some modern scholars; they cared little how a word was spelt, so long as it was readily recognizable as the written symbol of the spoken word. Thus frequently in the same poem, sometimes in the same verse, a word is spelt in three or four different ways. But these variations being all familiar, the word for them remained always the same word, just because a rigid standardized orthography had not yet

been evolved. For us, however, the spoken word is repre-
sented by one immutable symbol, a particular collocation of
letters, so well known that any modification of it may fail to
suggest at once the sound it represents. Consequently, when
we read an Elizabethan lyric in an original text, the unfamiliar
and changing orthography of necessity checks in a greater or
lesser degree the limpid flow of the words which is vital to
the music of the poem; and by its very strangeness evokes in
our mind thoughts foreign—often even antipathetic—to the
mood of the verse. Since, then, the very essence of the lyric
dwells in the spoken word and not in its printed symbol, I
hold, in spite of the contrary opinion of a few experts—who
seem to me to sacrifice aesthetic to antiquarian and philolog-
ical considerations—that in a book of this kind it is more
'scholarly' in the true sense of that word to employ modern
spelling, and, with it, modern punctuation.

The Elizabethans frequently varied their pronunciation,
often within the same poem; and they pronounced many
words differently from us. Sometimes a vowel sounded by
them has now become mute, or has vanished altogether; such
vowels I have indicated by a diaeresis, thus: affectïon, soür
(spelt 'sower'), prayër, willës, turnëd. Sometimes a word was
pronounced with a stress different from the modern; these I
have shown, though only when it is not obvious, by an ac-
cent, thus: Jùly, persèver, envỳ. A few words, to judge from
their place in a rhyme scheme and their spelling, we may be
fairly sure carried a quite different vowel sound from ours;
and these, together with archaic words, I have printed as
originally spelt, but have glossed them, where necessary, in a
footnote.

The occasional elision in Elizabethan typography of the
final vowel in the definite article and some pronouns and
prepositions before a word beginning with a vowel was prob-

be no possible doubt, I have made the necessary correction silently. Otherwise I print no emendation, nor alternative reading, without giving the earliest authority for it and the date (or, where I am myself responsible for it, my own initials) either in a footnote, or in the 'Notes' at the end of the volume, together with the unemended reading. Thus the student is never at the mercy of the subjective judgements of editors past or present, but always has before him the actual text of the MS. or that of the printed edition which is either the first or the oldest extant, or which represents the author's own final revision.

ELIZABETHAN
LYRICS

FORGET NOT YET

Forget not yet the tried intent
Of such a truth as I have meant;
My great travail so gladly spent,
        Forget not yet!

Forget not yet when first began
The weary life ye know, since whan
The suit, the service, none tell can;
        Forget not yet!

Forget not yet the great assays,
The cruel wrong, the scornful ways,
The painful patience in denays,
        Forget not yet!

Forget not yet, forget not this—
How long ago hath been, and is,
The mind that never meant amiss,
        Forget not yet!

denays] denies, *i.e.* denials.

Forget not then thine own approved,
The which so long hath thee so loved,
Whose steadfast faith yet never moved:
Forget not this!   *Wyatt.*

B.M. Add. MS. 17492. (Poem written before 1533.)*

THE LOVER COMPARETH HIS STATE TO A SHIP
IN PERILOUS STORM TOSSED ON THE SEA

My galley, chargëd with forgetfulness,
Thorough sharp seas in winter nights doth pass
'Tween rock and rock; and eke my foe, alas,
That is my lord, steereth with cruelness;
And every hour, a thought in readiness,
As though that death were light in such a case;
An endless wind doth tear the sail apace
Of forcëd sighs, and trusty fearfulness;
A rain of tears, a cloud of dark disdain,
Hath done the wearied cords great hinderance;
Wreathëd with error and eke with ignorance,
The stars be hid that led me to this pain.
Drownëd is reason that should me comfòrt,
And I remain, despairing of the port.   *Wyatt.*

B.M. Egerton MS. 2711. (Poem in Tottel, 1557; written before 1533.)

AND WILT THOU LEAVE ME THUS?

And wilt thou leave me thus?
Say nay, say nay, for shame!

---

my foe] 1557; mine enemy, MS.

To save thee from the blame
Of all my grief and grame.
And wilt thou leave me thus?
Say nay! say nay!

And wilt thou leave me thus,
That hath loved thee so long
In wealth and woe among?
And is thy heart so strong
As for to leave me thus?
Say nay! say nay!

And wilt thou leave me thus,
That hath given thee my heart
Never for to depart
Neither for pain nor smart:
And wilt thou leave me thus?
Say nay! say nay!

And wilt thou leave me thus,
And have no more pity
Of him that loveth thee?
Alas, thy cruelty!
And wilt thou leave me thus?
Say nay! say nay!   *Wyatt.*

B.M. Add. MS. 17492. (Poem written before 1533.)

A PRAISE OF HIS LADY

Give place, you ladies, and be gone!
Boast not yourselves at all!

---

grame] sorrow, vexation.

For here at hand approacheth one
   Whose face will stain you all.

The virtue of her lively looks
   Excels the precious stone;
I wish to have none other books
   To read or look upon.

In each of her two crystal eyes
   Smileth a naked boy;
It would you all in heart suffice
   To see that lamp of joy.

I think Nature hath lost the mould
   Where she her shape did take;
Or else I doubt if Nature could
   So fair a creature make.

She may be well compared
   Unto the Phoenix kind,
Whose like was never seen or heard,
   That any man can find.

In life, she is Diana chaste;
   In troth, Penelope;
In word and eke in deed steadfast:
   What will you more we say?

If all the world were sought so far,
   Who could find such a wight?
Her beauty twinkleth like a star
   Within the frosty night.

stain] shame.

Her rosial colour comes and goes
    With such a comely grace,
More redier too than doth the rose,
    Within her lively face.

At Bacchus' feast none shall her meet,
    Ne at no wanton play;
Nor gazing in an open street,
    Nor gadding as a stray.

The modest mirth that she doth use
    Is mixed with shamefastness;
All vice she doth wholly refuse,
    And hateth idleness.

O Lord, it is a world to see
    How virtue can repair
And deck in her such honesty,
    Whom Nature made so fair!

Truly she doth as far exceed
    Our women nowadays,
As doth the gillyflower a weed;
    And more, a thousand ways.

How might I do to get a graff
    Of this unspotted tree?
For all the rest are plain but chaff,
    Which seem good corn to be.

This gift alone I shall her give:
    When death doth what he can,
Her honest fame shall ever live
    Within the mouth of man. *John Heywood.*

Tottel's *Songs and Sonnets*, 1557. (Poem written 1535 ?)*
repair] resort to.

THE LOVER COMPLAINETH THE UNKINDNESS
OF HIS LOVE

My lute, awake! perform the last
Labour that thou and I shall wast,
   And end that I have now begun;
For when this song is sung and past,
   My lute, be still, for I have done.

As to be heard where ear is none,
As lead to grave in marble stone,
   My song may pierce her heart as soon:
Should we then sigh, or sing, or moan?
   No, no, my lute, for I have done.

The rocks do not so cruelly
Repulse the waves continually,
   As she my suit and affectïon;
So that I am past remedy:
   Whereby my lute and I have done.

Proud of the spoil that thou hast got
Of simple hearts thorough Love's shot,
   By whom, unkind, thou hast them won;
Think not he hath his bow forgot,
   Although my lute and I have done.

Vengeance shall fall on thy disdain,
That makest but game on earnest pain:
   Think not alone under the sun
Unquit to cause thy lover's plain,
   Although my lute and I have done.

---

wast] waste.   to grave] to engrave.

Perchance thee lie withered and old
The winter nights that are so cold,
    Plaining in vain unto the moon:
Thy wishes then dare not be told:
    Care then who list, for I have done.

And then may chance thee to repent
The time that thou hast lost and spent
    To cause thy lover's sigh and swoon:
Then shalt thou know beauty but lent,
    And wish and want as I have done.

Now cease, my lute! this is the last
Labour that thou and I shall wast,
    And ended is that we begun:
Now is this song both sung and past—
    My lute, be still, for I have done.   *Wyatt.*

B.M. Egerton MS. 2711. (Poem in Tottel, 1557; written before 1536.)

THE LOVER SHOWETH HOW HE IS FORSAKEN
OF SUCH AS HE SOMETIME ENJOYED

They flee from me that sometime did me seek,
    With naked foot stalking within my chamber:
Once have I seen them gentle, tame, and meek,
    That now are wild, and do not once remember
That sometime they have put themselves in danger
To take bread at my hand: and now they range,
    Busily seeking in continual change.

nights] 1557; night, MS.

Thankèd be fortune, it hath been otherwise
   Twenty times better; but once especïal,
In thin array, after a pleasant guise,
   When her loose gown did from her shoulders fall,
And she me caught in her arms long and small,
And therewithal so sweetly did me kiss,
   And softly said, 'Dear heart, how like you this?'

It was no dream; for I lay broad awaking:
   But all is turned now, through my gentleness,
Into a bitter fashion of forsaking;
   And I have leave to go of her goodnèss;
And she also to use new-fangleness.
But since that I unkindly so am served,
   'How like you this?'—what hath she now deserved?

                          Wyatt.

Tottel's *Songs and Sonnets*, 1557. (Poem written before 1536.)

TO A LADY TO ANSWER DIRECTLY WITH YEA OR NAY

Madam, withouten many words,
   Once, I am sure, ye will or no:
And if ye will, then leave your bords
   And use your wit and show it so:
And with a beck ye shall me call;
   And if of one, that burneth alway,
Ye have any pity at all,
   Answer him fair with yea, or nay.
If it be yea, I shall be fain;
   If it be nay, friends as before;

bords] jests, games.

Ye shall another man obtain,
And I mine own and yours no more.   *Wyatt.*

B.M. Egerton MS. 2711. (Poem in Tottel, 1557; written before 1536.)

WITH SERVING STILL

With serving still
   This have I won:
For my goodwill
   To be undone.

And for redress
   Of all my pain,
Disdainfulness
   I have again.

And for reward
   Of all my smart,
Lo, thus unhard
   I must depart!

Wherefore all ye
   That after shall
By fortune be
   As I am, thrall,

Example take
   What I have won:
Thus for her sake
   To be undone!   *Wyatt.*

B.M. Add. MS. 17492. (Poem written before 1536.)

unhard] unheard.

O DEATH, ROCK ME ASLEEP

O Death, O Death, rock me asleep,
　　Bring me to quiet rest;
Let pass my weary guiltless ghost
　　Out of my careful breast.
　　　　Toll on, thou passing bell;
　　　　Ring out my doleful knell;
　　　　Thy sound my death abroad will tell,
　　　　　For I must die:
　　　　　There is no remedy.

My pains, my pains, who can express?
　　Alas, they are so strong!
My dolours will not suffer strength
　　My life for to prolong.
　　　　Toll on, thou passing bell, &c.

Alone, alone in prison strong
　　I wail my destiny:
Woe worth this cruel hap that I
　　Must taste this misery!
　　　　Toll on, thou passing bell, &c.

Farewell, farewell, my pleasures past!
　　Welcome, my present pain!
I feel my torment so increase
　　That life can not remain.
　　　　Cease now, thou passing bell,
　　　　Ring out my doleful knoll,
　　　　For thou my death dost tell:
　　　　Lord, pity thou my soul!

Cease now, thou] N. A.; Cease now then, MS.

Death doth draw nigh,
Sound dolefully:
For now I die,
I die, I die.   *Rochford*(?)

B.M. Add. MS. 26737. (Poem written 1536.)* Quoted, 2 *King Henry IV.*,
II. iv. 211.

BLAME NOT MY LUTE

Blame not my lute! for he must sound
    Of this or that as liketh me;
For lack of wit the lute is bound
    To give such tunes as pleaseth me;
Though my songs be somewhat strange,
And speaks such words as touch thy change,
        Blame not my lute!

My lute, alas! doth not offend,
    Though that perforce he must agree
To sound such tunes as I intend
    To sing to them that heareth me;
Then though my songs be somewhat plain,
And toucheth some that use to feign,
        Blame not my lute!

My lute and strings may not deny,
    But as I strike they must obey;
Break not them then so wrongfully,
    But wreak thyself some other way;
And though the songs which I indite
Do quit thy change with rightful spite,
        Blame not my lute!

quit] requite.

Spite asketh spite, and changing change,
  And falsëd faith must needs be known;
The faults so great, the case so strange,
  Of right it must abroad be blown;
Then since that by thine own desart
My songs do tell how true thou art,
        Blame not my lute!

Blame but thyself that hast misdone,
  And well deservëd to have blame;
Change thou thy way, so evil begun,
  And then my lute shall sound that same;
But if till then my fingers play
By thy desart their wonted way,
        Blame not my lute!

Farewell, unknown! for though thou break
  My strings in spite with great disdain,
Yet have I found out, for thy sake,
  Strings for to string my lute again:
And if, perchance, this foolish rhyme
Do make thee blush at any time,
        Blame not my lute!   *Wyatt.*

B.M. Add. MS. 17492. (Poem written c. 1537.)

IF IN THE WORLD THERE BE MORE WOE

If in the world there be more woe
  Than I have in my heart,
Whereso it is, it doth come fro,
And in my breast there doth it grow,

For to increase my smart.
Alas! I am receipt of every care,
And of my life each sorrow claims his part.
　Who list to live in quietness
　　By me let him beware,
　　For I by high disdain
　　Am made without redress,
　And ùnkindness, alas, hath slain
My poor true heart, all comfortless.　　　　　　*Wyatt.*

B.M. Egerton MS. 2711. (Poem written before 1542.)

IF LOVE, FOR LOVE OF LONG TIME HAD

If love, for love of long time had,
　May join with joy, and care hence cast,
Then may remembrance make me glad,
　Days, weeks, and years, in all time past
My Love hath loved me so lovingly,
And I will love her as trulỳ.

And as we twain have ḷ̣ṿed and do,
　So be we fixed to love even still;
The law of love hath made us two
　To work two willës in one will:
My Love will love me so lovingly,
And I will love her as trulỳ.

Ye lovers all in present place
　That long for love continual,
I wish to you like pleasant case

For to] Foxwell, 1913; From to, MS.

As ye perceive by me doth fall,
And yours to love as lovingly.

John Heywood.

B.M. Add. MS. 15233, [c. 1545].*

All a green willow, willow, willow,
All a green willow is my garland.

Alas! by what mean may I make ye to know
The unkindness for kindness that to me doth grow?
That one who most kind love on me should bestow,
Most unkind unkindness to me she doth show,
      For all a green willow is my garland.

To have love and hold love, where love is so sped,
Oh, delicate food to the lover so fed!
From love won to love lost, where lovers be led,
Oh, desperate dolour, the lover is dead!
      For all a green willow is his garland.

She said she did love me, and would love me still,
She sware above all men I had her good will;
She said and she sware she would my will fulfil:
The promise all good, the performance all ill;
      For all a green willow is my garland.

Could I forget thee, as thou canst forget me,
That were my sound fault, which cannot nor shall be;
Though thou, like the soaring hawk, every way flee,
I will be the turtle most steadfast to thee,
      And patiently wear this green willow garland.

All ye that have had love, and have my like wrong,
My like truth and patïence plant you among;
When feminine fancies for new love do long,
Old love cannot hold them, new love is so strong,
     For all a green willow is your garland.

                                        John Heywood.

B.M. Add. MS. 15233, [c. 1545].* The earliest of the 'Willow' songs;
cf. *Othello*, IV. iii.

THE MEANS TO ATTAIN HAPPY LIFE

My friend, the things that do attain
     The happy life be these, I find:
The riches left, not got with pain;
     The fruitful ground, the quiet mind;

The equal friend; no grudge, no strife;
     No charge of rule, nor governance;
Without disease the healthy life;
     The household of continuance;

The mean dièt, no dainty fare;
     Wisdom joinëd with simpleness;
The night dischargëd of all care,
     Where wine the wit may not oppress;

The faithful wife, without debate;
     Such sleeps as may beguile the night:
Content thyself with thine estate,
     Neither wish death, nor fear his might.   *Surrey.*

W. Baldwin's *Treatise of Moral Philosophy*, 1547. (Variant in Tottel, 1557.
Poem written before 1547.)

A PRAISE OF HIS LOVE, WHEREIN HE REPROVETH
THEM THAT COMPARE THEIR LADIES WITH HIS

Give place, ye lovers, here before
    That spent your boasts and brags in vain;
My lady's beauty passeth more
    The best of yours, I dare well sayen,
Than doth the sun the candle-light,
Or brightest day the darkest night.

And thereto hath a troth as just
    As had Penelope the fair;
For what she saith, ye may it trust,
    As it by writing sealèd were:
And virtues hath she many moe
Than I with pen have skill to show.

I could rehearse, if that I would,
    The whole effect of Nature's plaint,
When she had lost the perfect mould,
    The like to whom she could not paint:
With wringing hands, how she did cry,
And what she said, I know it, I.

I know she swore with raging mind,
    Her kingdom only set apart,
There was no loss by law of kind
    That could have gone so near her heart;
And this was chiefly all her pain—
She could not make the like again.

Sith Nature thus gave her the praise,
    To be the chiefest work she wrought;

In faith, methink, some better ways
   On your behalf might well be sought,
Than to compare, as ye have done,
To match the candle with the sun.   *Surrey.*

Tottel's *Songs and Sonnets*, 1557. (Poem written before 1547.)

COMPLAINT OF THE ABSENCE OF HER LOVER
BEING UPON THE SEA

O happy dames! that may embrace
   The fruit of your delight,
Help to bewail the woeful case
   And eke the heavy plight
Of me, that wonted to rejoice
The fortune of my pleasant choice:
Good ladies, help to fill my mourning voice.

In ship, freight with rememberance
   Of thoughts and pleasures past,
He sails that hath in governance
   My life while it will last:
With scalding sighs, for lack of gale,
Furthering his hope, that is his sail,
Toward me, the sweet port of his avail.

Alas! how oft in dreams I see
   Those eyes that were my food;
Which sometime so delighted me,
   That yet they do me good:
Wherewith I wake with his return,
Whose absent flame did make me burn:
But when I find the lack, Lord, how I mourn!

When other lovers in arms across
   Rejoice their chief delight,
Drownëd in tears, to mourn my loss
   I stand the bitter night
In my window, where I may see
Before the winds how the clouds flee:
Lo! what a mariner love hath made me!

And in green waves when the salt flood
   Doth rise by rage of wind,
A thousand fancies in that mood
   Assail my restless mind:
Alas! now drencheth my sweet foe,
That with the spoil of my heart did go,
And left me; but, alas! why did he so?

And when the seas wax calm again
   To chase fro me annoy,
My doubtful hope doth cause me plain:
   So dread cuts off my joy.
Thus is my wealth mingled with woe,
And of each thought a doubt doth grow;
Now he comes! Will he come? Alas, no, no!

Surrey.

Tottel's *Songs and Sonnets*, 1557. (Poem written before 1547.)

DESCRIPTION OF SPRING, WHEREIN EACH THING RENEWS, SAVE ONLY THE LOVER

The soote season, that bud and bloom forth brings,
With green hath clad the hill and eke the vale:
The nightingale with feathers new she sings;

---

drencheth] drowneth.   plain] mourn, complain.   soote] sweet.

The turtle to her make hath told her tale.
Summer is come, for every spray now springs:
The hart hath hung his old head on the pale;
The buck in brake his winter coat he flings;
The fishes float with new repairèd scale;
The adder all her slough away she slings;
The swift swallow pursueth the flies smale;
The busy bee her honey now she mings;
Winter is worn that was the flowers' bale.
    And thus I see among these pleasant things
    Each care decays; and yet my sorrow springs.

Surrey.

Ibid.

A COMPLAINT BY NIGHT OF THE LOVER
NOT BELOVED

Alas! so all things now do hold their peace;
Heaven and earth disturbèd in no thing:
The beasts, the air, the birds their song do cease;
The nightès chare the stars about doth bring:
Calm is the sea; the waves work less and less:
So am not I, whom love, alas, doth wring,
Bringing before my face the great increase
Of my desires, whereat I weep and sing,
In joy and woe, as in a doubtful ease:
For my sweet thoughts sometime do pleasure bring;
But by and by, the cause of my disease
Gives me a pang, that inwardly doth sting,
    When that I think what grief it is again,
    To live and lack the thing should rid my pain.

Surrey.

Ibid.

make] mate.   head] antlers.   smale] small.   mings] mingles, mixes.
chare] car.   disease] dis-ease.

HOW NO AGE IS CONTENT WITH HIS OWN ESTATE

Laid in my quiet bed, in study as I were,
I saw within my troubled head a heap of thoughts
    appear.
And every thought did show so lively in mine eyes,
That now I sighed, and then I smiled, as cause of
    thought doth rise.
I saw the little boy in thought how oft that he
Did wish of God to scape the rod, a tall young man
    to be.
The young man eke that feels his bones with pains
    oppressed,
How he would be a rich old man, to live and lie at
    rest.
The rich old man that sees his end draw on so sore,
How he would be a boy again, to live so much the
    more.
Whereat full oft I smiled, to see how all these three,
From boy to man, from man to boy, would chop
    and change degree.   *Surrey.*

Tottel's *Songs and Sonnets*, 1557. (Poem written before 1547.)*

VOW TO LOVE FAITHFULLY, HOWSOEVER
HE BE REWARDED

Set me whereas the sun doth parch the green,
Or where his beams do not dissolve the ice;
In temperate heat, where he is felt and seen;
In presence prest of people, mad, or wise;
Set me in high, or yet in low degree;
In longest night, or in the shortest day;
In clearest sky, or where clouds thickest be;
In lusty youth, or when my hairs are gray:

---

prest] close at hand.

Set me in heaven, in earth, or else in hell,
In hill, or dale, or in the foaming flood;
Thrall, or at large, alive whereso I dwell,
Sick, or in health, in evil fame or good,
    Hers will I be; and only with this thought
    Content myself, although my chance be nought.

Ibid.   *Surrey.*

I SEE MY PLAINT

I see my plaint, with open ears
    Is heard, alas, and laughing eyes;
I see that scorn beholds my tears,
    And all the harm hap can devise;
I see my life away so wears
    That I myself myself despise;
And most of all wherewith I strive
Is that I see myself alive.   *Harington(?)*

B.M. Add. MS. 36529. (Poem written 1547.)*

CHRIST TO HIS SPOUSE

Lo, thou, my Love, art fair;
Myself have made thee so:
Yea, thou art fair indeed,
Wherefore thou shalt not need
In beauty to despair;
For I accept thee so,
        For fair.

For fair, because thine eyes
Are like the culvers' white,
Whose simpleness in deed
All others do exceed:

---

culvers' white] *i.e.* white culvers' (doves') eyes.

> Thy judgement wholly lies
> In true sense of sprite
> Most wise.   *Baldwin.*

The Canticles or Ballads of Solomon, 1549.

CHRIST, MY BELOVED

> Christ, my Beloved which still doth feed
> Among the flowers, having delight
> Among his faithful lilies,
> Doth take great care for me indeed,
> And I again with all my might
> Will do what so his will is.
>
> My Love in me and I in him,
> Conjoined by love, will still abide
> Among the faithful lilies
> Till day do break, and truth do dim
> All shadows dark and cause them slide,
> According as his will is.   *Baldwin.*

Ibid.

A SONNET MADE ON ISABELLA MARKHAM, WHEN I FIRST THOUGHT HER FAIR, AS SHE STOOD AT THE PRINCESS'S WINDOW IN GOODLY ATTIRE, AND TALKED TO DIVERS IN THE COURT-YARD

> Whence comes my love? O heart, disclose!
> 'Twas from cheeks that shame the rose,

shame] Park, 1804; shamed, 1769.

From lips that spoil the ruby's praise,
From eyes that mock the diamond's blaze.
Whence comes my woe? as freely own.
Ah, me! 'twas from a heart like stone.

The blushing cheek speaks modest mind;
The lips, befitting words most kind.
The eye does tempt to love's desire,
And seems to say 'tis Cupid's fire.
Yet all so fair, but speak my moan,
Since nought doth say the heart of stone.

Why thus, my love, so kind bespeak
Sweet lip, sweet eye, sweet blushing cheek,
Yet not a heart to save my pain?
O Venus! take thy gifts again;
Make not so fair to cause our moan,
Or make a heart that 's like our own!   *Harington.*

Nugae Antiquae, 1769. (Poem written c. 1549.)*

THOU SLEEPEST FAST

Thou sleepest fast, and I with woeful heart
    Stand here alone sighing and cannot fly:
Thou sleepest fast, when cruel Love his dart
    On me doth cast, alas, so painfully!
Thou sleepest fast, and I, all full of smart,
    To thee, my foe, in vain do call and cry:
And yet, methinkës, though thou sleepest fast
Thou dreamest still which way my life to wast.

                                           Anon.

Trin. Coll. Dublin MS. 160, [c. 1550].

though thou] See Note.   wast] waste.

LOVE ME AGAIN

Alas, dear heart! what hope had I
　　If that I might your grace attain!
And since I love you faithfully,
　　Why should ye not love me again?

Methinks of right ye should me love,
　　For well ye know I do not feign,
Nor never shall ye other prove:
　　Therefore, sweetheart, love me again.

I dare well say if that ye knew
　　How long that I have suffered pain,
Ye would not change me for no new,
　　But, even of right, love me again.

For as your own ye may be sure
　　Ye have my heart still to remain:
It lieth in you me to recure,
　　Therefore, sweetheart, love me again.

In hope I live, and have done long,
　　Trusting yet still for to obtain;
And sure, methinks, I have great wrong
　　If that I be not loved again.   *Anon.*

Trin. Coll. Dublin MS. 160, [c. 1550].*

OF YOUTH HE SINGETH

In a herber green asleep whereas I lay,
The birds sang sweet in the middes of the day;

---

herber] arbour.　　middes] middle.

I dreamèd fast of mirth and play:
    In youth is pleasure, in youth is pleasure.

Methought I walked still to and fro,
And from her company I could not go;
But when I waked it was not so:
    In youth is pleasure, in youth is pleasure.

Therefore my heart is surely pight
Of her alone to have a sight,
Which is my joy and heart's delight:
    In youth is pleasure, in youth is pleasure.

Lusty Juventus, [n.d.]. (Written before 1553.)*   *Weever.*

I MUN BE MARRIED A SUNDAY

I mun be married a Sunday;
I mun be married a Sunday;
Whosoever shall come that way,
I mun be married a Sunday.

Roister Doister is my name;
Roister Doister is my name;
A lusty brute I am the same;
I mun be married a Sunday.

Christian Custance have I found;
Christian Custance have I found;
A widow worth a thousand pound;
I mun be married a Sunday.

---

pight] fixed.

Custance is as sweet as honey;
Custance is as sweet as honey;
I her lamb, and she my coney;
I mun be married a Sunday.

When we shall make our wedding feast,
When we shall make our wedding feast,
There shall be cheer for man and beast,
I mun be married a Sunday.
   I mun be married a Sunday, &c. *Udall.*

Ralph Roister Doister, [n.d.]. (Registered 1566–7; written before 1553.)*
Quoted, *Taming of the Shrew*, II. i. 300, 326.

A MINION WIFE

Whoso to marry a minion wife
 Hath had good chance and hap,
Must love her and cherish her all his life,
 And dandle her in his lap.

If she will fare well, if she will go gay,
 A good husband ever still—
Whatever she lust to do or to say—
 Must let her have her own will.

About what affairs soever he go,
 He must show her all his mind;
None of his counsel she may be kept fro,
 Else is he a man unkind. *Udall.*
Ibid.

minion] pet, darling.

ELEGY WROTE IN THE TOWER, 1554

The life is long that loathsomely doth last,
  The doleful days draweth slowly to their date;
The present pangs and painful plagues forepast,
  Yields grief aye green to stablish this estate:
So that I feel in this great storm and strife
The death is sweet that short'neth such a life.

The pleasant years that soon so swiftly run,
  The merry days to end so fast that flit,
The joyful nights of which day dawns so soon,
  The happy hours which mo do miss than hit,
Doth all consume as snow against the sun,
And death makes end of all that life begun.

Death is a port whereby we pass to joy,
  Life is a lake that drowneth all in pain;
Death is so sweet it ceaseth all annoy,
  Life is so lewd it yieldeth all in vain;
And as by life to bondage man was brought,
Even so likewise by death was freedom wrought.

Harington.

Bodley MS. Ashm. 48. (MS. *temp.* Mary.)*

THE AGED LOVER RENOUNCETH LOVE

I loathe that I did love,
  In youth that I thought sweet,
As time requires for my behove,
  Methinks they are not meet.

---

fast that] Tottel, 1557; fast they, MS.   so likewise by] Tottel, 1557; so by,
MS.

My lusts they do me leave,
   My fancies all be fled,
And tract of time begins to weave
   Grey hairs upon my head.

For age with stealing steps
   Hath clawed me with his crutch,
And lusty life away she leaps
   As there had been none such.

My Muse doth not delight
   Me as she did before;
My hand and pen are not in plight,
   As they have been of yore.

For reason me denies
   This youthly idle rhyme;
And day by day to me she cries,
   'Leave off these toys in time.'

The wrinkles in my brow,
   The furrows in my face,
Say, limping age will lodge him now
   Where youth must give him place.

The harbinger of death,
   To me I see him ride,
The cough, the cold, the gasping breath
   Doth bid me to provide

A pickaxe and a spade,
   And eke a shrouding sheet,

crutch] 1565; cowche, 1557.   lodge] 1565; hedge, 1557.

A house of clay for to be made
   For such a guest most meet.

Methinks I hear the clark
   That knolls the careful knell,
And bids me leave my woeful wark,
   Ere nature me compel.

My keepers knit the knot
   That youth did laugh to scorn,
Of me that clean shall be forgot
   As I had not been born.

Thus must I youth give up,
   Whose badge I long did wear;
To them I yield the wanton cup
   That better may it bear.

Lo, here the barëd skull,
   By whose bald sign I know
That stooping age away shall pull
   Which youthful years did sow.

For beauty with her band
   These crooked cares hath wrought,
And shippëd me into the land
   From whence I first was brought.

And ye that bide behind,
   Have ye none other trust:
As ye of clay were cast by kind,
   So shall ye waste to dust.   *Vaux.*

Tottel's *Songs and Sonnets*, 1557. (Poem written before 1556.)
Quoted, *Hamlet,* v. i. 79–82, 102–5.

NO PLEASURE WITHOUT SOME PAIN

How can the tree but waste and wither away
    That hath not sometime comfort of the sun?
How can that flower but fade and soon decay
    That always is with dark clouds over-run?
Is this a life? Nay, death you may it call
That feels each pain and knows no joy at all.

What foodless beast can live long in good plight?
    Or is it life where senses there be none?
Or what availeth eyes without their light?
    Or else a tongue to him that is alone?
Is this a life? Nay, death you may it call
That feels each pain and knows no joy at all.

Whereto serve ears if that there be no sound?
    Or such a head where no device doth grow
But all of plaints, since sorrow is the ground
    Whereby the heart doth pine in deadly woe?
Is this a life? Nay, death you may it call
That feels each pain and knows no joy at all.   *Vaux.*

The Paradise of Dainty Devices, 1576. (Poem written before 1556.)*

OF A CONTENTED MIND

When all is done and said, in the end thus shall you find,
He most of all doth bathe in bliss that hath a quiet
    mind:
And, clear from worldly cares, to deem can be
    content
The sweetest time in all his life in thinking to be spent.

He most] Mod. eds.; The most, 1576.

The body subject is to fickle fortune's power,
And to a million of mishaps is casual every hour:
And death in time doth change it to a clod of clay;
Whenas the mind, which is divine, runs never to
　　decay.

Companion none is like unto the mind alone;
For many have been harmed by speech; through
　　thinking, few or none.
Fear oftentimes restraineth words, but makes not
　　thoughts to cease;
And he speaks best that hath the skill when for to
　　hold his peace.

Our wealth leaves us at death; our kinsmen at the
　　grave;
But virtues of the mind unto the heavens with us we
　　have.
Wherefore, for virtue's sake, I can be well content
The sweetest time of all my life to deem in thinking
　　spent.   *Vaux.*

Ibid.

A TRUE LOVE

What sweet relief the showers to thirsty plants we see,
What dear delight the blooms to bees, my true Love
　　is to me!
As fresh and lusty Ver foul winter doth exceed,
As morning bright, with scarlet sky, doth pass the
　　evening's weed,
As mellow pears above the crabs esteemëd be,—

Fear] Mod. eds.; Fewe, 1576.

So doth my Love surmount them all, whom yet I hap
   to see.
The oak shall olives bear, the lamb the lion fray,
The owl shall match the nightingale in tuning of her lay,
Or I my Love let slip out of mine èntire hert,
So deep reposëd in my breast is she for her desert.
For many blessëd gifts, O happy, happy land!
Where Mars and Pallas strive to make their glory most
   to stand!
Yet, land, more is thy bliss, that, in this cruel age,
A Venus' imp thou hast brought forth, so steadfast
   and so sage:
Among the Muses nine, a tenth if Jove would make,
And to the Graces three, a fourth her would Apollo
   take.
Let some for honour hunt, and hoard the massy gold:
With her so I may live and die, my weal can not be told.

Tottel's *Songs and Sonnets*, 1557.   *Grimald.*

AGAINST WOMEN EITHER GOOD OR BAD

A man may live thrice Nestor's life,
   Thrice wander out Ulysses' race,
Yet never find Ulysses' wife:
   Such change hath chancëd in this case.

Less age will serve than Paris had,
   Small pain—if none be small enough—
To find good store of Helen's trade:
   Such sap, the root doth yield the bough.

For one good wife Ulysses slew
   A worthy knot of gentle blood;

---

fray] make afraid.   hert] heart.

For one ill wife Greece overthrew
   The town of Troy. Sith bad and good
Work mischief, Lord, let be thy will
To keep me free from either ill!   *Norton.*

B. M. Cotton MS. Tit. A. xxiv. (Also in Tottel, 1557.)

THE LADY PRAYETH THE RETURN OF HER LOVER
ABIDING ON THE SEAS

Shall I thus ever long, and be no whit the near?
And shall I still complain to thee, the which me will
    not hear?
Alas! say nay! say nay! and be no more so dumb,
But open thou thy manly mouth, and say that thou
    wilt come:
Whereby my heart may think, although I see not thee,
That thou wilt come—thy word so sware—if thou a
    live man be.
The roaring hugy waves they threaten my poor ghost,
And toss thee up and down the seas, in danger to be
    lost:
Shall they not make me fear that they have swallowed
    thee?
But as thou art most sure alive, so wilt thou come to me.
Whereby I shall go see thy ship ride on the strand,
And think and say 'Lo where he comes,' and 'Sure
    here will he land';
And then I shall lift up to thee my little hand,
And thou shalt think thine heart in ease, in health to
    see me stand.
And if thou come indeed—as Christ thee send to do!—

Sith] 1557; Both, MS.   near] nearer.   live man] Mod. eds.; lives man,
1557.

Those arms which miss thee now, shall then embrace
    thee too:
  Each vein to every joint the lively blood shall spread,
Which now, for want of thy glad sight, doth show full
    pale and dead.
  But if thou slip thy troth, and do not come at all,
As minutes in the clock do strike, so call for death I shall;
    To please both thy false heart, and rid myself from
    woe,
That rather had to die in troth than live forsaken so.

Anon.

Tottel's *Songs and Sonnets*, 1557.

THE LOVER IN LIBERTY SMILETH AT THEM IN THRALDOM, THAT SOMETIME SCORNED HIS BONDAGE

At liberty I sit and see
  Them, that have erst laughed me to scorn,
Whipped with the whip that scourgëd me:
  And now they ban that they were born.

I see them sit full soberly
  And think their earnest looks to hide;
Now, in themselves, they cannot spy
  That they or this in me have spied.

I see them sitting all alone,
  Marking the steps, each word and look;
And now they tread where I have gone,
  The painful path that I forsook.

or this] ere this.

Now I see well I saw no whit
   When they saw well, that now are blind;
But happy hap hath made me quit,
   And just judgemènt hath them assigned.

I see them wander all alone,
   And tread full fast, in dreadful doubt,
The self-same path that I have gone:
   Blessèd be hap that brought me out!

At liberty all this I see,
   And say no word but erst among,
Smiling at them that laughed at me:
   Lo, such is hap! Mark well my song!   *Anon.*

Ibid.

THE PROMISE OF A CONSTANT LOVER

As laurel leaves that cease not to be green,
From parching sun, nor yet from winter's threat,
As hardened oak that fear'th no sword so keen,
As flint for tool in twain that will not fret,
As fast as rock or pillar surely set,—
So fast am I to you, and aye have been,
Assurèdly whom I can not forget,
For joy, for pain, for torment, nor for teen,
For loss, for gain, for frowning, nor for threat:
But ever one,—yea, both in calm and blast,—
Your faithful friend, and will be to my last.   *Anon.*

Ibid.

calm and blast] 1565; calm or blast, 1557.   teen] grief, trouble.

THE UNCERTAIN STATE OF A LOVER

Like as the rage of rain
  Fills rivers with excess,
And as the drought again
  Doth draw them less and less,
So I both fall and climb
With 'no' and 'yea' sometime.

As they swell high and high,
  So doth increase my state;
As they fall dry and dry,
  So doth my wealth abate;
As 'yea' is mixed with 'no,'
So mirth is mixed with woe.

As nothing can endure,
  That lives and lacks relief;
So nothing can stand sure
  Where change doth reign as chief:
Wherefore I must intend
To bow when others bend;

And when they laugh, to smile;
  And when they weep, to wail;
And when they craft, beguile;
  And when they fight, assail;
And think there is no change
Can make them seem too strange.

Oh, most unhappy slave!
  What man may lead this course—
To lack he would fainest have,
  Or else to do much worse?

These be rewards for such
As live and love too much.   *Anon.*

Tottel's *Songs and Sonnets*, 1557.

THAT EACH THING IS HURT OF ITSELF

Why fearest thou thy outward foe,
    When thou thyself thy harm dost feed?
Of grief, or hurt, of pain, or woe,
    Within each thing is sown the seed.

So fine was never yet the cloth,
    No smith so hard his iron did beat,—
But th' one consumèd was with moth,
    Th' other with canker all to fret.

The knotty oak and wainscot old,
    Within doth eat, the silly worm:
Even so a mind in envy rolled
    Always within itself doth burn.

Thus every thing that nature wrought,
    Within itself his hurt doth bear:
No outward harm need to be sought,
    Where en'mies be within so near.   *Anon.*

Ibid.

IF EVER I MARRY, I'LL MARRY A MAID

If ever I marry, I'll marry a maid;
    To marry a widow, I am sore afraid:

---

or woe] 1565 and 1574 edns; of woe, 1557.

For maids they are simple, and never will grutch,
But widows full oft, as they say, know too much.

A maid is so sweet, and so gentle of kind,
That a maid is the wife I will choose to my mind:
A widow is froward, and never will yield;
Or if such there be, you will meet them but seeld.

A maid ne'er complaineth, do what so you will;
But what you mean well, a widow takes ill:
A widow will make you a drudge and a slave,
And, cost ne'er so much, she will ever go brave.

A maid is so modest, she seemeth a rose
When it first beginneth the bud to unclose;
But a widow full-blowen full often deceives,
And the next wind that bloweth shakes down all
    her leaves.

The widows be lovely, I never gainsay,
But too well all their beauty they know to display;
But a maid hath so great hidden beauty in store,
She can spare to a widow, yet never be poor.

Then, if ever I marry, give me a fresh maid,
If to marry with any I be not afraid;
But to marry with any, it asketh much care;
And some bachelors hold they are best as they are.

                                                    Anon.

Ballad registered 1557–8. (J. P. Collier's MS., *temp.* James I.)*
grutch] grudge.   seeld] seldom.

> *The proverb reporteth, no man can deny,*
> *That wedding and hanging is destiny.*

I am a poor tiler in simple array,
And get a poor living, but eightpence a day,
My wife as I get it doth spend it away,
    And I cannot help it, she saith; wot we why?
    For wedding and hanging is destiny.

I thought, when I wed her, she had been a sheep,
At board to be friendly, to sleep when I sleep;
She loves so unkindly, she makes me to weep;
    But I dare say nothing, God wot! wot ye why?
    For wedding and hanging is destiny.

Besides this unkindness whereof my grief grows,
I think few tilers are matched with such shrows:
Before she leaves brawling, she falls to deal blows
    Which, early and late, doth cause me cry
    That wedding and hanging is destiny.

The more that I please her, the worse she doth like me;
The more I forbear her, the more she doth strike me;
The more that I get her, the more she doth glike me;
    Woe worth this ill fortune that maketh me cry
    That wedding and hanging is destiny.

If I had been hangèd when I had been married,
My torments had ended, though I had miscarried;
If I had been warnèd, then would I have tarried;

---

glike] flout, scoff.

But now all too lately I feel and cry
That wedding and hanging is destiny.

Anon.

Tom Tyler and His Wife. An excellent old Play, as it was Printed and Acted about a hundred years ago, 1661. (Song registered 1558–9.) Cf. Merchant of Venice, II. ix. 82–3.

IMPORTUNE ME NO MORE

When I was fair and young, and favour gracëd me,
Of many was I sought, their mistress for to be:
But I did scorn them all, and answered them therefore,
    'Go, go, go, seek some otherwhere!
        Importune me no more!'

How many weeping eyes I made to pine with woe,
How many sighing hearts, I have no skill to show:
Yet I the prouder grew, and answered them therefore,
    'Go, go, go, seek some otherwhere!
        Importune me no more!'

Then spake fair Venus' son, that proud victorious boy,
And said, 'Fine Dame, since that you be so coy,
I will so pluck your plumes that you shall say no more,
    'Go, go, go, seek some otherwhere!
        Importune me no more!'

When he had spake these words, such change grew in
   my breast
That neither night nor day since that, I could take
   any rest.
Then, lo! I did repent that I had said before,
    'Go, go, go, seek some otherwhere!
        Importune me no more!'

Queen Elizabeth.

Bodley MS. Rawl. Poet. 85. (Poem written c. 1561 ?)*

LULLABY

Lullaby baby, lullaby baby,
Thy nurse will tend thee, as duly as may be.

Be still, my sweet sweeting, no longer do cry;
  Sing lullaby, lullaby, lullaby baby:
Let dolours be fleeting, I fancy thee, I,
  To rock and to lull thee, I will not delay me.
    Lullaby baby, lullaby baby, &c.

What creature now living would hasten thy woe?
  Sing lullaby, lullaby, lullaby baby:
See for thy relieving, the time I bestow
  To dance and to prance thee, as prett'ly as may be.
    Lullaby baby, lullaby baby, &c.

The gods be thy shield, and comfort in need;
  Sing lullaby, lullaby, lullaby baby:
They give thee good fortune, and well for to speed,
  And this to desire, I will not delay me.
    Lullaby baby, lullaby baby,
    Thy nurse will tend thee, as duly as may be.

                                                    Phillip.

*Patient and meek Grissill.** (Registered 1565-6. Written before 1562.)

OF JOLLY GOOD ALE AND OLD

Back and side go bare, go bare,
  Both foot and hand go cold;
But, belly, God send thee good ale enough,
  Whether it be new or old.

I cannot eat but little meat,
  My stomach is not good;

But sure I think that I can drink
    With him that wears a hood.
Though I go bare, take ye no care,
    I am nothing a-cold;
I stuff my skin so full within
    Of jolly good ale and old.
        Back and side go bare, go bare, &c.

I love no roast but a nutbrown toast,
    And a crab laid in the fire;
A little bread shall do me stead,
    Much bread I not desire.
No frost nor snow, no wind, I trow,
    Can hurt me if I would,
I am so wrapt, and throughly lapt
    Of jolly good ale and old.
        Back and side go bare, go bare, &c.

And Tib my wife, that as her life
    Loveth well good ale to seek,
Full oft drinks she, till ye may see
    The tears run down her cheek.
Then doth she troll to me the bowl,
    Even as a maltworm should;
And saith, 'Sweetheart, I took my part
    Of this jolly good ale and old.'
        Back and side go bare, go bare, &c.

Now let them drink, till they nod and wink,
    Even as good fellows should do;
They shall not miss to have the bliss
    Good ale doth bring men to.
And all poor souls that have scourèd bowls,

Or have them lustily trolled,
God save the lives of them and their wives,
Whether they be young or old.
    Back and side go bare, go bare,
    Both foot and hand go cold;
    But, belly, God send thee good ale enough,
    Whether it be new or old.

                          Stevenson(?)

Gammer Gurton's Needle, 1575. (Registered 1562–3 ?)*

COMING HOMEWARD OUT OF SPAIN

O raging seas, and mighty Neptune's reign!
  In monstrous hills that throwest thyself so high,
That with thy floods dost beat the shores of Spain,
  And break the cliffs that dare thy force envỳ,
Cease now thy rage, and lay thine ire aside.
  And thou that hast the governance of all,
O mighty God! grant weather, wind, and tide,
  Till on my country coast our anchor fall.

                          Googe.

Eclogues, Epitaphs, and Sonnets, 1563.

OF MONEY

Give money me; take friendship whoso list!
  For friends are gone, come once adversity;
When money yet remaineth safe in chest,
  That quickly can thee bring from misery.
Fair face show friends, when riches do abound;
  Come time of proof, farewell, they must away!
Believe me well, they are not to be found
  If God but send thee once a louring day.

Gold never starts aside; but, in distress,
Finds ways enough to ease thine heaviness.   *Googe.*

Eclogues, Epitaphs, and Sonnets, 1563.

OUT OF SIGHT, OUT OF MIND

The oftener seen, the more I lust,
   The more I lust, the more I smart,
The more I smart, the more I trust,
   The more I trust, the heavier heart,
The heavy heart breeds mine unrest,
Thy absence therefore like I best.

The rarer seen, the less in mind,
   The less in mind, the lesser pain,
The lesser pain, less grief I find,
   The lesser grief, the greater gain,
The greater gain, the merrier I,
Therefore I wish thy sight to fly.

The further off, the more I joy,
   The more I joy, the happier life,
The happier life, less hurts annoy,
   The lesser hurts, pleasure most rife,
Such pleasures rife shall I obtain
When distance doth depart us twain.   *Googe.*

Ibid.

WINTER

The wrathful winter, 'proaching on apace,
   With blust'ring blasts had all ybared the treen:
And old Saturnus, with his frosty face,

With chilling cold had pierced the tender green,
The mantles rent, wherein enwrappëd been
    The gladsome groves that now lay overthrown,
    The tapets torn, and every bloom down blown.

The soil, that erst so seemly was to seen,
    Was all despoilëd of her beauty's hue;
And soot fresh flowers, wherewith the summer's
        queen
    Had clad the earth, now Boreas' blasts down blew:
    And small fowls flocking, in their song did rue
        The winter's wrath, wherewith each thing
            defaced
        In woeful wise bewailed the summer past.

Hawthorn had lost his motley livery,
    The naked twigs were shivering all for cold,
And dropping down the tears abundantly.
    Each thing, methought, with weeping eye me told
    The cruel season, bidding me withhold
        Myself within; for I was gotten out
        Into the fields, whereas I walked about. . . .

And sorrowing I, to see the summer flowers,
    The lively green, the lusty leas, forlorn;
The sturdy trees so shattered with the showers,
    The fields so fade, that flourished so beforne:
    It taught me well, all earthly things be born
        To die the death; for nought long time may last:
        The summer's beauty yields to winter's blast.

                                                        Sackville.

A Mirror for Magistrates, 1563. (Opening stanzas of the *Induction*.)*

tapets] tapestry, *i.e.* foliage.   soot] sweet.

AMANTIUM IRAE

In going to my naked bed, as one that would have slept,
I heard a wife sing to her child, that long before had
    wept;
She sighëd sore, and sang full sweet to bring the babe
    to rest,
That would not rest but criëd still, in sucking at her
    breast.
She was full weary of her watch, and grievëd with her
    child,
She rockëd it and rated it, until on her it smiled.
Then did she say, 'Now have I found this proverb
    true to prove,
The falling out of faithful friends, renewing is of love.'

Then took I paper, pen, and ink, this proverb for to
    write,
In register for to remain of such a worthy wight.
As she proceeded thus in song unto her little brat
Much matter uttered she of weight, in place whereas
    she sat:
And provëd plain there was no beast, nor creature
    bearing life
Could well be known to live in love, without discord
    and strife.
Then kissëd she her little babe, and sware, by God above,
The falling out of faithful friends, renewing is of love.

She said that neither king, ne prince, ne lord could
    live aright,
Until their puissance they did prove, their manhood,
    and their might:

---

sweet] 1578 and 1580; sore, 1576.

When manhood shall be matchëd so, that fear can
    take no place,
Then weary works make warriors each other to embrace,
And leave their force that failëd them, which did
    consume the rout
That might by force with love have lived the term of
    nature out.
Then did she sing, as one that thought no man could
    her reprove,
The falling out of faithful friends, renewing is of love.

She said she saw no fish, ne fowl, nor beast within her
    haunt
That met a stranger in their kind, but could give it a
    taunt.
Since flesh might not endure, but rest must wrath
    succeed,
And force the fight to fall to play in pasture where
    they feed,
So noble Nature can well end the work she hath begun,
And bridle well that will not cease her tragedy in some.
Thus in her song she oft rehearsed, as did her well
    behove,
The falling out of faithful friends, renewing is of love.

'I marvel much, pardy,' quoth she, 'for to behold the rout,
To see man, woman, boy, and beast, to toss the world
    about;
Some kneel, some crouch, some beck, some check, and
    some can smoothly smile,
And some embrace others in arms, and there think
    many a wile;

That might . . . out] See Note.

Some stand aloof at cap and knee, some humble, and
    some stout,
Yet are they never friends in deed until they once
    fall out!'
Thus ended she her song, and said, before she did
    remove,
The falling out of faithful friends, renewing is of love.

Edwards.

The Paradise of Dainty Devices, 1576. (Poem written before 1566.)

OF WOMEN

When women first Dame Nature wrought,
'All good,' quoth she, 'none shall be nought:
All wise shall be, none shall be fools,
For wit shall spring from women's schools.
In all good gifts they shall excel;
Their nature all, no tongue can tell.'
Thus Nature said. I heard it, I:
I pray you, ask them if I do lie.

By Nature's grant, this must ensue—
No woman false, but all are true;
None sow debate, but love maintain;
None joys to see her lover's pain:
As turtles true, their chosen one
They love, and pine where he is gone.
This is most true, none can deny:
I pray you, ask them if I do lie.

No lamb so meek as women be;
Their humble hearts from pride are free:
Rich things they wear, and wot you why?

renewing is] 1578 and 1580; is the renewing, 1576.

Only to please their husband's eye.
They never strive their wills to have;
Their husband's love, nought else, they crave;
Vain talk in them none can espy:
I pray you, ask them if I do lie.

If vice the earth should overcome,
And no wight left under the sun;
If wealth would wring the poor; and might,
With open force, would sùppress right;
If no rule were left on the ground,
In woman yet it might be found.
The star of goodness in them doth lie:
I pray you, ask them if I do lie.

The eagle with his piercing eye
Shall burn and waste the mountains high;
Huge rocks shall fleet as ship with sail;
The crab shall run; swim shall the snail;
Springs shall return from whence they came;
Sheep shall be wild, and tigers tame,
Or these my words false you shall try·
Ha, ha! methinks I make a lie.   *Edwards.*

B.M. Cotton MS. Tit. A. xxiv. (Poem written before 1566.)

Fain would I have a pretty thing
   To give unto my lady:
I name no thing, nor I mean no thing,
   But as pretty a thing as may be.

Twenty journeys would I make,
   And twenty ways would hie me,

Or these] Ere these.

To make adventure for her sake
  To set some matter by me.
    But I would fain have a pretty thing, &c.

Some do long for pretty knacks,
  And some for strange devices:
God send me that my lady lacks,
  I care not what the price is.
    Thus fain would I have a pretty thing, &c.

Some go here and some go there
  Where gazes be not geason;
And I go gaping everywhere,
  But still come out of season.
    Yet fain would I have a pretty thing, &c.

I walk the town and tread the street,
  In every corner seeking:
The pretty thing I cannot meet
  That 's for my lady's liking.
    Fain would I have a pretty thing, &c.

The mercers pull me going by;
  The silk-wives say, 'What lack ye?'
'The thing you have not,' then say I,
  'Ye foolish fools, go pack ye!'
    But fain would I have a pretty thing, &c.

It is not all the silk in Cheape,
  Nor all the golden treasure,
Nor twenty bushels on a heap,
  Can do my lady pleasure.
    But fain would I have a pretty thing, &c.

geason] uncommon.

The gravers of the golden shows
   With jewels do beset me;
The shemsters in the shops, that sews,
   They do nothing but let me.
     But fain would I have a pretty thing, &c.

But were it in the wit of man
   By any means to make it,
I could for money buy it than,
   And say, 'Fair lady, take it!'
     Thus fain would I have a pretty thing, &c.

O lady, what a luck is this—
   That my good willing misseth
To find what pretty thing it is
   That my good lady wisheth!
     Thus fain would I have had this pretty thing
       To give unto my lady:
     I said no harm, nor I meant no harm,
       But as pretty a thing as may be.   Anon.

A Handful of Pleasant Delights, 1584. (Ballad written before 1566–7?)*

SONG

Farewell, adieu, that court-like life!
   To war we 'tend to go:
It is good sport to see the strife
   Of soldiers on a row:
     How merrily they forward march
       Their enemies to slay!
     With hey trim and trixy too
       Their banners they display.

shemsters] sempstresses.   let] hinder.   than] then.   Their enemies]
See Note.

Now shall we have the golden cheats
    When others want the same;
And soldiers have full many feats
    Their enemies to tame:
        With cucking here and boming there
           They break their foe's array;
        And lusty lads amid the fields
           Their ensigns do display.

The drum and flute play lustily,
    The trumpet blows amain,
And vent'rous knights courageously
    Do march before their train,
        With spear in rest so lively dressed
           In armour bright and gay,
        With hey trim and trixy too
           Their banners they display.   *Pickering.*

The History of Horestes, 1567.

THE LOVER TO THE THAMES OF LONDON TO FAVOUR HIS LADY PASSING THEREON

Thou stately stream that with the swelling tide
'Gainst London walls incessantly dost beat,
Thou Thames, I say, where barge and boat doth ride,
And snow-white swans do fish for needful meat:

When so my Love, of force or pleasure, shall
Flit on thy flood as custom is to do,
Seek not with dread her courage to appal,
But calm thy tide, and smoothly let it go,
As she may joy, arrived to siker shore,
To pass the pleasant stream she did before.

want] lack.   siker] secure.

To welter up and surge in wrathful wise,
As did the flood where Helle drenchëd was,
Would but procure defame of thee to rise:
Wherefore let all such ruthless rigour pass,
So wish I that thou may'st with bending side
Have power for aye in wonted gulf to glide.

Epitaphs, Epigrams, Songs, and Sonnets, 1567.   *Turberville.*

THE LOVER ABUSED RENOUNCETH LOVE

Was never day came on my head
Wherein I did not sue for grace;
Was never night but I in bed
Unto my pillow told my case,
   Baining my breast, my breast,
    For want of rest,
With tears oppressed; yet remedy none
Was to be found for all my moan.

If she had deignëd my good will
And recompensed me with her love,
I would have been her vassal still,
And never once my heart remove:
   I did pretend, pretend
    To be her friend
Unto the end; but she refused
My loving heart, and me abused.

But since I see her stony heart
Cannot be pierced with pity's lance,
Since nought is gained but woeful smart,
I do intend to break the dance,
   And quite forgo, forgo

Baining] Bathing.

My pleasant foe
That pains me so, and thinks in fine
To make me like to Circe's swine.

I clean defy her flattering face,
I quite abhor her luring looks:
As long as Jove shall give me grace
She never comes within my books;
   I do detest, detest
   So false a guest
That breeds unrest, where she should plant
Her love, if pity did not want.

Let her go seek some other fool,
Let her enrage some other dolt:
I have been taught in Plato's school
From Cupid's banner to revolt,
   And to forsake, forsake
   As fearful snake,
Such as do make a man but smart
For bearing them a faithful heart.   *Turberville.*

Epitaphs, Epigrams, Songs, and Sonnets, 1567. (An excerpt.)*

TO HIS RING, GIVEN TO HIS LADY, WHEREIN WAS GRAVEN THIS VERSE, 'MY HEART IS YOURS'

Though thou, my ring, be small,
   And slender be thy price,
Yet hast thou in thy compass couched
   A lover's true device;
And though no ruby red,
   Ne turquoise, trim thy top,

Nor other jewel that commends
   The golden Vulcan's shop;
Yet may'st thou boldly vaunt,
   And make a true report
For me that am thy master yet,
   In such a semblant sort,
That aye 'my heart is hers;'
   Of thee I ask no more;
My pen and I will show the rest
   Which yet I keep in store.
Be mindful of thy charge,
   And of thy master's case:
Forget not that 'my heart is hers'
   Though I be not in place.
When thou hast told thy tale
   Which is but short and sweet,
Then let my Love conject the rest
   Till she and I do meet.
For as 'my heart is hers,'
   So shall it be for aye:
My heart, my hand, my life, my limbs,
   Are hers till dying day.
Yea, when the spirit gives up
   And body breathes his last,
Say naytheless 'my heart is hers'
   When life and all is past.   *Turberville.*

*Ibid.**

MY DEAR LADY

Am not I in blessèd case,
   Treasure and pleasure to possess?
I would not wish no better place

If I may still have wealthiness;
And to enjoy in perfect peace,
    My lady, lady,
My pleasant pleasure shall increase,
    My dear lady.

Helen may not comparëd be,
    Nor Cressida that was so bright;
These cannot stain the shine of thee,
    Nor yet Minerva of great might;
Thou passest Venus far away,
    Lady, lady;
Love thee I will, both night and day,
    My dear lady.

My mouse, my nobs, and coney sweet,
    My hope and joy, my whole delight;
Dame Nature may fall at thy feet,
    And may yield to thee her crown of right.
I will thy body now embrace,
    Lady, lady;
And kiss thy sweet and pleasant face,
    My dear lady.   *Anon.*

The Trial of Treasure, 1567.

A RELIGIOUS USE OF TAKING TOBACCO

The Indian weed witherëd quite,
Green at morn, cut down at night,
    Shows thy decay;
    All flesh is hay:
Thus think, then drink Tobacco.

And when the smoke ascends on high,
Think thou behold'st the vanity

Of worldly stuff,
Gone with a puff:
Thus think, then drink Tobacco.

But when the pipe grows foul within,
Think of thy soul defiled with sin.
And that the fire
Doth it require:
Thus think, then drink Tobacco.

The ashes that are left behind,
May serve to put thee still in mind
That into dust
Return thou must:
Thus think, then drink Tobacco.   *Wisdome.*

Trin. Coll. Dublin MS. G. 2. 21. (Poem written before 1568.)*

WHO WOULD HAVE THOUGHT

Who would have thought that face of thine
Had been so full of doubleness?
Or else within those crystal eyne
Had rest so much unstableness?
Thy face so fair, thy look so strange,
Who would have thought so full of change?

New Sonnets and Pretty Pamphlets, [1567–8].*   *T. Howell.*

TO MISTRESS ANNE CECIL, UPON MAKING HER A NEW YEAR'S GIFT, JANUARY 1, 1567–8

As years do grow, so cares increase;
And time will move to look to thrift:
Though years in me work nothing less,

Yet, for your years, and New Year's gift.
This housewife's toy is now my shift!
  To set you on work, some thrift to feel,
  I send you now a Spinning Wheel.

But one thing first, I wish and pray,
  Lest thirst of thrift might soon you tire,
Only to spin one pound a day,
  And play the rest, as time require:
  Sweat not! (oh fie!) fling rock in fire!
    God send, who send'th all thrift and wealth,
    You, long years; and your father, health!

                                                Burleigh.

B.M. Lansdowne MS. 104.

OF MISERY

Corpse, clad with carefulness;
Heart, heaped with heaviness;
Purse, poor and penniless;
Back, bare in bitterness;
Lips, laid with loathsomeness;
Oh, get my grave in readiness;
Fain would I die to end this stress,
          Remèdiless.   *T. Howell.*

The Arbor of Amitie, 1568.*

WHEN HE THOUGHT HIMSELF CONTEMNED

O heart, why dost thou sigh, and wilt not break?
  O doleful chance, thou hast a cause thereto,
For thy reward in love and kindness sake
  Is recompensed by hate and deadly woe.

---

rock] distaff.   Corpse] Body.

Have I so plight my heart and mind to thee,
　　Have I been bent so whole unto thy hand,
And others now obtain the fruit from me?
　　Thou art unkind forsooth, such foe to stand.

O doleful heart, thus plunged in pinching pain,
　　Lament no more, but break! thy truth to try:
For where thy comfort was and joy did reign
　　Now hate returns no news, O heart, now die!

T. Howell.

Ibid.*

THE ROSE

　　Whenas the mildest month
　　　　Of jolly June doth spring,
And gardens green with happy hue
　　　　Their famous fruits do bring,
　　When eke the lustiest time
　　　　Reviveth youthly blood,
Then springs the finest featured flower
　　　　In border fair that stood:
　　Which moveth me to say,
　　　　In time of pleasant year,
Of all the pleasant flowers in June
　　　　The red rose hath no peer.   *T. Howell.*

Ibid.*

THERE WAS A MAID

There was a maid came out of Kent,
　　Dainty love, dainty love;
There was a maid came out of Kent,

plight] plighted.

Dangerous be:
There was a maid came out of Kent,
Fair, proper, small and gent,
As ever upon the ground went,
    For so should it be.   *Anon.*

W. Wager's *The longer thou livest, the more fool thou,* [n.d.]. (Registered
1568–9.)

THAT HE FINDETH OTHERS AS FAIR, BUT NOT
SO FAITHFUL AS HIS FRIEND

I sundry see, for beauty's gloss,
    That with my mistress may compare:
But few I find for true good-will
    That to their friends so friendly are.

Look, what she says I may assure
    Myself thereof; she will not feign:
What others speak is hard to trust,
    They measure all their words by gain.

Her looks declare her loving mind;
    Her count'nance and her heart agree:
When others laugh they look as smooth
    But love not half so well as she.

The grief is hers when I am griped,
    My finger's ache is her disease:
With me though others mourn to sight,
    Yet are their hearts at quiet ease.

So that I mark in Cupid's court
    Are many fair and fresh to see:

disease] dis-ease.

Each where is sown Dame Beauty's seed,
But fair and faithful few there be.   *Turberville.*

Tragical Tales, 1576. (Text 1587. Poem written c. 1569.)*

LOVE ME LITTLE, LOVE ME LONG

Love me little, love me long,
Is the burden of my song.
Love that is too hot and strong
 Burneth soon to waste:
Still, I would not have thee cold,
Not too backward, nor too bold;
Love that lasteth till 'tis old
 Fadeth not in haste.
  Love me little, love me long,
  Is the burden of my song.

If thou lovest me too much,
It will not prove as true as touch;
Love me little, more than such,
 For I fear the end:
I am with little well content,
And a little from thee sent
Is enough, with true intent
 To be steadfast friend.
  Love me little, love me long, &c.

Say thou lov'st me while thou live;
I to thee my love will give,
Never dreaming to deceive
 Whiles that life endures:
Nay, and after death, in sooth,
I to thee will keep my truth,

As now, when in my May of youth;
    This my love assures.
        Love me little, love me long, &c.

Constant love is moderate ever,
And it will through life persèver:
Give me that, with true endeavour
    I will it restore.
A suit of durance let it be
For all weathers that for me,
For the land or for the sea,
    Lasting evermore.
        Love me little, love me long, &c.

Winter's cold, or summer's heat,
Autumn's tempests, on it beat,
It can never know defeat,
    Never can rebel:
Such the love that I would gain,
Such the love, I tell thee plain,
Thou must give, or woo in vain:
    So to thee, farewell!
        Love me little, love me long,
        Is the burden of my song.   *Anon.*

Ballad registered 1569–70. (J. P. Collier's MS., *temp.* James I.)*

SONG

How can that tree but withered be,
    That wanteth sap to moist the root?
How can that vine but waste and pine,
    Whose plants are trodden under foot?
How can that spray but soon decay,
    That is with wild weeds overgrown?

How can that wight in aught delight,
   Which shows and hath no good-will shown?
Or else how can that heart, alas,
But die, by whom each joy doth pass?   *Anon.*

Sir Clyomon and Sir Clamydes, 1599. (Written c. 1570.)

NOW THAT THE TRUTH IS TRIED

Now that the truth is tried
Of things that be late past,
I see, when all is spied,
That words are but a blast,
   And promise great
   Is but a heat
If not performed at last.   *Whythorne.*

Songs of 3, 4, and 5 voices, 1571.

THE LULLABY OF A LOVER

Sing lullaby, as women do,
   Wherewith they bring their babes to rest;
And lullaby can I sing too,
   As womanly as can the best.
With lullaby they still the child;
And, if I be not much beguiled,
Full many wanton babes have I,
Which must be stilled with lullaby.

First, lullaby my youthful years,
   It is now time to go to bed;
For crooked age and hoary hairs
   Have won the haven within my head.

With lullaby, then, youth, be still!
With lullaby content thy will!
Since courage quails and comes behind,
Go sleep, and so beguile thy mind!

Next, lullaby my gazing eyes,
    Which wonted were to glance apace;
For every glass may now suffice
    To show the furrows in my face.
With lullaby, then, wink awhile!
With lullaby your looks beguile!
Let no fair face, nor beauty bright,
Entice you eft with vain delight.

And lullaby my wanton will;
    Let reason's rule now reign thy thought,
Since all too late I find by skill
    How dear I have thy fancies bought.
With lullaby now take thine ease!
With lullaby thy doubts appease!
For trust to this, if thou be still,
My body shall obey thy will.

Eke lullaby my loving boy;
    My little Robin, take thy rest!
Since age is cold and nothing coy,
    Keep close thy coin, for so is best.
With lullaby be thou content!
With lullaby thy lusts relent!
Let others pay which have mo pence,
Thou art too poor for such expense.

Thus, lullaby my youth, mine eyes,
    My will, my ware, and all that was:

I can no mo delays devise;
  But welcome pain, let pleasure pass.
With lullaby now take your leave!
With lullaby your dreams deceive!
And when you rise with waking eye,
Remember then this lullaby!   *Gascoigne.*

A Hundreth Sundry Flowers, 1572. (Text from *Posies*, 1575.)

THE LOOKS OF A LOVER ENAMOURED

Thou, with thy looks, on whom I look full oft,
And find therein great cause of deep delight,
Thy face is fair, thy skin is smooth and soft,
Thy lips are sweet, thine eyes are clear and bright,
And every part seems pleasant in my sight;
Yet wote thou well, those looks have wrought my woe,
Because I love to look upon them so.

For first those looks allured mine eye to look,
And straight mine eye stirred up my heart to love;
And cruel love, with deep deceitful hook,
Choked up my mind, whom fancy cannot move,
Nor hope relieve, nor other help behoove
But still to look; and though I look too much,
Needs must I look because I see none such.

Thus in thy looks my love and life have hold;
And with such life my death draws on apace:
And for such death no med'cine can be told
But looking still upon thy lovely face,
Wherein are painted pity, peace, and grace.
Then though thy looks should cause me for to die,
Needs must I look, because I live thereby.

Since then thy looks my life have so in thrall
As I can like none other looks but thine,
Lo, here I yield my life, my love, and all
Into thy hands, and all things else resign
But liberty to gaze upon thine eyen:
Which when I do, then think it were thy part
To look again, and link with me in heart.   *Gascoigne.*

A Hundreth Sundry Flowers, 1572.

AND IF I DID, WHAT THEN?

'And if I did, what then?
Are you aggrieved therefore?
The sea hath fish for every man,
And what would you have more?'

Thus did my mistress once
Amaze my mind with doubt;
And popped a question for the nonce,
To beat my brains about.

Whereto I thus replied:
'Each fisherman can wish
That all the seas at every tide
Were his alone to fish;

And so did I, in vain;
But since it may not be,
Let such fish there as find the gain,
And leave the loss for me.

And with such luck and loss
I will content myself,

Till tides of turning time may toss
Such fishers on the shelf.

And when they stick on sands,
That every man may see,
Then will I laugh and clap my hands,
As they do now at me.'   *Gascoigne.*

Ibid.

FOR THAT HE LOOKED NOT UPON HER

You must not wonder, though you think it strange,
To see me hold my louring head so low;
And that mine eyes take no delight to range
About the gleams which on your face do grow.
The mouse which once hath broken out of trap,
Is seldom 'ticëd with the trustless bait,
But lies aloof for fear of more mishap,
And feedeth still in doubt of deep deceit.
The scorchëd fly, which once hath 'scaped the flame,
Will hardly come to play again with fire:
Whereby I learn that grievous is the game
Which follows fancy dazzled by desire:
    So that I wink or else hold down my head,
    Because your blazing eyes my bale have bred.
                                                                Gascoigne.

Ibid.

UPON THE AUTHOR'S FIRST SEVEN YEARS' SERVICE

Seven times hath Janus ta'en new year by hand,
Seven times hath blust'ring March blown forth his power
To drive out April's buds, by sea and land,

---

louring] sorrowful.

For minion May to deck most trim with flower.
Seven times hath temperate Ver like pageant played,
And pleasant Aestas eke her flowers told;
Seven times Autumnës heat hath been delayed
With Hyem's boist'rous blasts and bitter cold.
Seven times, the thirteen moons have changëd hue,
Seven times, the sun his course hath gone about,
Seven times, each bird her nest hath built anew,
Since first time you to serve I chosëd out.
   Still yours am I, though thus the time hath passed,
   And trust to be so long as life shall last.   *Tusser.*

Five hundreth points of good Husbandry, 1573.

FIE, PLEASURE, FIE!

Fie, pleasure, fie! thou cloyest me with delight;
   Thou fill'st my mouth with sweetmeats overmuch;
I wallow still in joy both day and night:
   I deem, I dream, I do, I taste, I touch
No thing but all that smells of perfect bliss,
Fie, pleasure, fie! I cannot like of this.

To taste, sometimes, a bait of bitter gall,
   To drink a draught of soür ale, some season,
To eat brown bread with homely hands in hall,
   Doth much increase men's appetites, by reason,
And makes the sweet more sugared that ensues,
Since minds of men do still seek after news.

It might suffice that Love hath built his bower
   Between my lady's lively shining eyes;
It were enough that beauty's fading flower

news] new things.

Grows ever fresh with her in heavenly wise;
It had been well that she were fair of face,
And yet not rob all other dames of grace.

To muse in mind, how wise, how fair, how good,
  How brave, how frank, how courteous, and how
    true
My lady is, doth but inflame my blood
  With humours such as bid my health adieu:
Since hap always when it is clomb on high,
Doth fall full low, though erst it reached the sky.

Lo, pleasure, lo! lo, thus I lead a life
  That laughs for joy and trembleth oft for dread;
Thy pangs are such as call for change's knife
  To cut the twist, or else to stretch the thread,
Which holds yfeer the bundle of my bliss:
Fie, pleasure, fie! I dare not trust to this.   *Gascoigne.*

Posies, 1575.*

A NOSEGAY ALWAYS SWEET, FOR LOVERS TO SEND
FOR TOKENS OF LOVE AT NEW YEAR'S TIDE,
OR FOR FAIRINGS

A Nosegay, lacking flowers fresh,
  To you now I do send;
Desiring you to look thereon,
  When that you may intend:
For flowers fresh begin to fade,
  And Boreas in the field
Even with his hard congealëd frost
  No better flowers doth yield.

yfeer] together.

But if that winter could have sprung
   A sweeter flower than this,
I would have sent it presently
   To you withouten miss:
Accept this then as time doth serve,
   Be thankful for the same,
Despise it not, but keep it well,
   And mark each flower his name.

Lavender is for lovers true,
   Which evermore be fain,
Desiring always for to have
   Some pleasure for their pain;
And when that they obtainëd have
   The love that they require,
Then have they all their perfect joy,
   And quenchëd is the fire.

Rosemary is for remembrance
   Between us day and night;
Wishing that I might always have
   You present in my sight.
And when I cannot have
   As I have said before,
Then Cupid with his deadly dart
   Doth wound my heart full sore.

Sage is for sustenance,
   That should man's life sustain;
For I do still lie languishing
   Continually in pain,
And shall do still until I die,
   Except thou favour show:
My pain and all my grievous smart
   Full well you do it know.

Fennel is for flatterers,
    An evil thing it is sure:
But I have always meant truly,
    With constant heart most pure;
And will continue in the same
    As long as life doth last,
Still hoping for a joyful day
    When all our pains be past.

Violet is for faithfulness
    Which in me shall abide;
Hoping likewise that from your heart
    You will not let it slide;
And will continue in the same
    As you have now begun,
And then for ever to abide,
    Then you my heart have won.

Thyme is to try me,
    As each be trïed must,
Letting you know while life doth last
    I will not be unjust;
And if I should I would to God
    To hell my soul should bear,
And eke also that Belzebub
    With teeth he should me tear.

Roses is to rule me
    With reason as you will,
For to be still obedient
    Your mind for to fulfil;
And thereto will not disagree
    In nothing that you say,
But will content your mind truly
    In all things that I may.

Gillyflowers is for gentleness,
    Which in me shall remain,
Hoping that no sedition shall
    Depart our hearts in twain.
As soon the sun shall lose his course,
    The moon against her kind
Shall have no light, if that I do
    Once put you from my mind.

Carnations is for graciousness,
    Mark that now by the way,
Have no regard to flatterers,
    Nor pass not what they say:
For they will come with lying tales
    Your ears for to fulfil:
In any case do you consent
    Nothing unto their will.

Marigolds is for marriage,
    That would our minds suffice,
Lest that suspicion of us twain
    By any means should rise:
As for my part, I do not care,
    Myself I will still use
That all the women of the world
    For you I will refuse.

Pennyroyal is to print your love
    So deep within my heart,
That when you look this Nosegay on
    My pain you may impart;
And when that you have read the same,
    Consider well my woe,
Think ye then how to recompense
    Even him that loves you so.

Cowslips is for counsel,
  For secrets us between,
That none but you and I alone
  Should know the thing we mean:
And if you will thus wisely do,
  As I think to be best,
Then have you surely won the field
  And set my heart at rest.

I pray you keep this Nosegay well,
  And set by it some store:
And thus farewell! the gods thee guide
  Both now and evermore!
Not as the common sort do use,
  To set it in your breast,
That when the smell is gone away,
  On ground he takes his rest.   *Hunnis(?)*

A Handful of Pleasant Delights, 1584. (Poem written before 1576?) * Quoted,
Hamlet, iv. v.176–84.

LOOK OR YOU LEAP

If thou in surety safe wilt sit,
  If thou delight at rest to dwell,
Spend no more words than shall seem fit,
  Let tongue in silence talk expel:
    In all things that thou seest men bent,
    See all! say nought! hold thee content!

In worldly works degrees are three,
  Makers, doers, and lookers-on:
The lookers-on have liberty
  Both the others to judge upon:

LOOK OR] LOOK ERE.

Wherefore, in all, as men are bent,
See all! say nought! hold thee content!

The makers oft are in fault found;
The doers doubt of praise or shame;
The lookers-on find surest ground,
They have the fruit, yet free from blame:
This doth persuade in all here meant,
See all! say nought! hold thee content!

The proverb is not south and west,
Which hath been said long time ago,
'Of little meddling cometh rest,
The busy man never wanteth woe':
The best way is, in all worlds sent,
See all! say nought! hold thee content!

Jasper Heywood.

The Paradise of Dainty Devices, 1576.

PAINS AND GAINS

The labouring man, that tills the fertile soil
And reaps the harvest fruit, hath not in deed
The gain, but pain; and if for all his toil
He gets the straw, the lord will have the seed.

The manchet fine falls not unto his share,
On coarsest cheat his hungry stomach feeds;
The landlord doth possess the finest fare,
He pulls the flowers; the other plucks but weeds.

---

manchet] finest wheaten bread.   cheat] coarse bread of poorer quality.

The mason poor, that builds the lordly halls,
    Dwells not in them; they are for high degree;
His cottage is compact in paper walls,
    And not with brick or stone as others be.

The idle drone, that labours not at all,
    Sucks up the sweet of honey from the bee:
Who worketh most, to their share least doth fall;
    With due desert reward will never be.

The swiftest hare unto the mastiff slow
    Oft-times doth fall, to him as for a prey;
The greyhound thereby doth miss his game, we know,
    For which he made such speedy haste away.

So he that takes the pain to pen the book,
    Reaps not the gifts of goodly golden Muse,
But those gain that, who on the work shall look
    And from the sour the sweet by skill doth choose.
For he that beats the bush the bird not gets,
But who sits still and holdeth fast the nets.   *Oxford.*

T. Bedingfield's *Cardanus' Comfort*, 1576.

OF LOVE

Love all the senses doth beguile
    And bleareth all our eyes;
It cuts off freedom of the mind
    And makes us gape for flies.
I think some furious fiend of hell

The heart doth thus inflame,
And bringeth quite the same a-down
    From lofty reason's frame:
Ne is this Love a god in deed,
    But lies and bitter bane.   *Sandford.*

The Mirror of Madness, 1576.

GIVE ME MY WORK

Give me my work, that I may sit and sew,
And so escape the trains of trustless men:
I find too true, by witness of my woe,
How that fair words with faithless works they blen,
    Much syren-like, with sweet enticing call,
    We silly dames to witch and wray in thrall.

O cruel friend, whose false of faith I rue,
Thou forcest me to count all men unjust;
For if that vow or oath might make one true
Thou usëdst such as might well force to trust:
    But I, betrayed by too far trusting thee,
    Will henceforth take fair words even as they be.

I will be deaf, though thousands sue for grace,
My sight as dim, if sights in silence plead;
Salt tears no ruth within my heart shall place,
For this shall be my song and daily rede—
    Poor I, that lived in thraldom linked of yore,
    Unbound at length, will learn to love no more.
                                                  Whetstone.

The Rock of Regard, 1576.

thus] N.A.; this, 1576.   blen] blend.   wray] bewray, betray.
rede] resolve.

BEING FORSAKEN OF HIS FRIEND HE
COMPLAINETH

Why should I longer long to live
   In this disease of fantasy?
Since Fortune doth not cease to give
   Things to my mind most còntrary;
And at my joys doth lour and frown
Till she hath turned them upsidown.

A friend I had, to me most dear,
   And of long time faithful and just;
There was no one my heart so near,
   Nor one in whom I had more trust;
Whom now of late, without cause why,
Fortune hath made my enemy.

The grass, methinks, should grow in sky,
   The stars unto the earth cleave fast;
The water-stream should pass awry,
   The winds should leave their strength of blast;
The sun and moon by one assent
Should both forsake the firmament;

The fish in air should fly with fin,
   The fowls in flood should bring forth fry;
All things, methinks, should erst begin
   To take their course unnaturally
Afore my friend should alter so,
Without a cause to be my foe.

But such is Fortune's hate, I say,
   Such is her will on me to wreak,

---

disease] dis-ease.

Such spite she hath at me alway,
    And ceaseth not my heart to break:
With such despite of cruelty,
    Wherefore then longer live should I?   E. S.

The Paradise of Dainty Devices, 1576.

A FAREWELL TO A FONDLING

The heat is past that did me fret,
    The fire is out that nature wrought;
The plants of love, which youth did set,
    Are dry and dead within my thought:
The frost hath killed the kindly sap
    Which kept the heart in lively state;
The sudden storms and thunder clap
    Hath turnëd love to mortal hate.

The mist is gone that bleared mine eyes,
    The louring clouds I see appear:
Although the blind eats many flies,
    I would she knew my sight is clear.
Her sweet, deceiving, flattering face
    Did make me think the crow was white:
I muse how she had such a grace
    To seem a hawk, and be a kite.   *Churchyard.*

Churchyard's Charge, 1580. (Also with extra stanzas in *A Gorgeous Gallery
of Gallant Inventions*, 1578.)

HOW TIME CONSUMETH ALL EARTHLY THINGS

Ay me, ay me! I sigh to see the scythe a-field;
    Down goeth the grass, soon wrought to withered hay:

Ay me, alas! ay me, alas! that beauty needs must yield,
  And princes pass, as grass doth fade away.

Ay me, ay me! that life can not have lasting leave,
  Nor gold take hold of everlasting joy:
Ay me, alas! ay me, alas! that time hath talents to receive,
  And yet no time can make a suer stay.

Ay me, ay me! that wit can not have wishëd choice,
  Nor wish can win that will desires to see:
Ay me, alas! ay me, alas! that mirth can promise no rejoice,
  Nor study tell what afterward shall be.

Ay me, ay me! that no sure staff is given to age,
  Nor age can give sure wit that youth will take:
Ay me, alas! ay me, alas! that no counsel wise and sage
  Will shun the show that all doth mar and make.

Ay me, ay me! come, Time, shear on and shake thy hay,
  It is no boot to balk thy bitter blows:
Ay me, alas! ay me, alas! come, Time, take every thing away,
  For all is thine, be it good or bad, that grows.

Proctor(?)*

A Gorgeous Gallery of Gallant Inventions, 1578.

I WOULD I WERE ACTAEON

I would I were Actaeon, whom Diana did disguise.
To walk the woods unknown whereas my lady lies:
A hart of pleasant hue I wish that I were so,
So that my lady knew alone me and no mo.

suer] sure, as a disyllable.

To follow thick and plain, by hill and dale alow,
To drink the water fain, and feed me with the sloe;
I would not fear the frost, to lie upon the ground,
Delight should quite the cost, what pain so that I found.

The shaling nuts and mast that falleth from the tree
Should serve for my repast, might I my lady see;
Sometime that I might say when I saw her alone,
'Behold thy slave, alone, that walks these woods
    unknown!'   *Anon.*

A Gorgeous Gallery of Gallant Inventions, 1578.*

OF PERFECT FRIENDSHIP

True friendship unfeignëd
Doth rest unrestrainëd,
    No terror can tame it:
Not gaining, nor losing,
Nor gallant gay glosing,
    Can ever reclaim it.
In pain, and in pleasure,
The most truest treasure
    That may be desirëd,
Is loyal love deemëd,
Of wisdom esteemëd
    And chiefly requirëd.   *Cheke(?)**

The Forest of Fancy, 1579.

A ROUNDELAY

Perigot. It fell upon a holy eve,
Willie.   Hey, ho, holiday!
Per. When holy fathers wont to shrieve;
Wil.   Now ginneth this roundelay.

---

quite] requite.   glosing] flattery, deceit.

Per. Sitting upon a hill so high,
Wil.   Hey, ho, the high hill!
Per. The while my flock did feed thereby;
Wil.   The while the shepherd self did spill;
Per. I saw the bouncing Bellibone,
Wil.   Hey, ho, Bonibell!
Per. Tripping over the dale alone,
Wil.   She can trip it very well!
Per. Well deckèd in a frock of gray,
Wil.   Hey, ho, gray is greete!
Per. And in a kirtle of green saye,
Wil.   The green is for maidens meet.
Per. A chapelet on her head she wore,
Wil.   Hey, ho, chapelet!
Per. Of sweet violets therein was store,
Wil.   She sweeter than the violet.
Per. My sheep did leave their wonted food,
Wil.   Hey, ho, silly sheep!
Per. And gazed on her as they were wood,
Wil.   Wood as he that did them keep!
Per. As the bonilasse passèd by,
Wil.   Hey, ho, bonilasse!
Per. She roved at me with glancing eye,
Wil.   As clear as the crystal glass:
Per. All as the sunny beam so bright,
Wil.   Hey, ho, the sun beam!
Per. Glanceth from Phoebus' face forthright,
Wil.   So love into thy heart did stream:
Per. Or as the thunder cleaves the clouds.
Wil.   Hey, ho, the thunder!
Per. Wherein the lightsome levin shrouds,
Wil.   So cleaves thy soul asunder:

---

spill] destroy, injure. greete] mourning. saye] fine cloth. wood] mad.
roved] shot, as with an arrow.   thy heart] 1611; my heart, 1579.
levin] lightning.

Per. Or as Dame Cynthia's silver ray,
Wil.   Hey, ho, the moonlight!
Per. Upon the glittering wave doth play,
Wil.   Such play is a piteous plight.
Per. The glance into my heart did glide;
Wil.   Hey, ho, the glider!
Per. Therewith my soul was sharply gryde.
Wil.   Such wounds soon waxen wider.
Per. Hasting to raunch the arrow out,
Wil.   Hey, ho, Perigot!
Per. I left the head in my heart-root,
Wil.   It was a desperate shot.
Per. There it rankleth, ay more and more,
Wil.   Hey, ho, the arrow!
Per. Ne can I find salve for my sore:
Wil.   Love is a cureless sorrow.
Per. And though my bale with death I bought,
Wil.   Hey, ho, heavy cheer!
Per. Yet should thilk lass not from my thought,
Wil.   So you may buy gold too dear.
Per. But whether in painful love I pine,
Wil.   Hey, ho, pinching pain!
Per. Or thrive in wealth, she shall be mine,
Wil.   But if thou can her obtain.
Per. And if for graceless grief I die,
Wil.   Hey, ho, graceless grief!
Per. Witness she slew me with her eye,
Wil.   Let thy folly be the prief.
Per. And you, that saw it, simple sheep,
Wil.   Hey, ho, the fair flock!
Per. For prief thereof, my death shall weep,
Wil.   And moan with many a mock.

---

gryde] pierced.   raunch] pull, pluck.   cureless] Collier, 1862; careless, 1579.
prief] proof.

    Per.   So learned I love on a holy eve,
    Wil.   Hey, ho, holiday!
    Per.   That ever since my heart did grieve,
    Wil.   Now endeth our roundelay.   *Spenser.*

The Shepherd's Calendar, 1579.

FOR SOLDIERS

Ye buds of Brutus' land, courageous youths, now play your
    parts!
Unto your tackle stand! Abide the brunt with valiant hearts!
For news is carried to and fro, that we must forth to warfare
    go:
Men muster now in every place, and soldiers are pressed
    forth apace.
Faint not, spend blood, to do your Queen and country good!
Fair words, good pay, will make men cast all care away.

The time of war is come: prepare your corslet, spear, and
    shield!
Methinks I hear the drum strike doleful marches to the field;
Tantarà! tantarà! the trumpets sound, which makes our
    hearts with joy abound.
The roaring guns are heard afar, and every thing denounceth
    war.
Serve God! Stand stout! Bold courage brings this gear about.
Fear not! Forth run! Faint heart fair lady never won.

Ye curious carpet knights, that spend the time in sport and
    play,
Abroad, and see new sights! your country's cause calls you
    away;
Do not, to make your ladies' game, bring blemish to your
    worthy name!

Away to field and win renown, with courage beat your
    enemies down!
Stout hearts gain praise, when dastards sail in Slander's seas.
Hap what hap shall, we sure shall die but once for all.

Alarm methinks they cry. Be packing, mates, be gone with
    speed!
Our foes are very nigh; shame have that man that shrinks at
    need!
Unto it boldly let us stand, God will give right the upper
    hand.
Our cause is good, we need not doubt. In sign of courage
    give a shout!
March forth! Be strong! Good hap will come ere it be long.
Shrink not! Fight well! For lusty lads must bear the bell.

All you that will shun evil, must dwell in warfare every day;
The world, the flesh, and devil, always do seek our souls'
    decay,
Strive with these foes with all your might, so shall you fight
    a worthy fight.
That conquest doth deserve most praise, where vice do yield
    to virtue's ways.
Beat down foul sin, a worthy crown then shall ye win:
If we live well, in heaven with Christ our souls shall dwell.

Gifford.

A Posie of Gilloflowers, 1580.

SONG

A woman's face is full of wiles,
    Her tears are like the crocadill:
With outward cheer on thee she smiles,
    When in her heart she thinks thee ill.

Her tongue still chats of this and that,
    Than aspen leaf it wags more fast;
And as she talks she knows not what,
    There issues many a truthless blast.

Thou far dost take thy mark amiss
    If thou think faith in them to find;
The weathercock more constant is,
    Which turns about with every wind.

Oh, how in pity they abound!
    Their heart is mild, like marble stone:
If in thyself no hope be found
    Be sure of them thou gettest none.

I know some pepper-nosèd dame
    Will term me fool, and saucy jack,
That dare their credit so defame
    And lay such slanders on their back:

What though on me they pour their spite?
    I may not use the glozer's trade,
I cannot say the crow is white,
    But needs must call a spade a spade.   *Gifford.*

Ibid.

IAMBICUM TRIMETRUM

Unhappy Verse, the witness of my unhappy state,
    Make thyself flutt'ring wings of thy fast flying
        Thought, and fly forth unto my Love, wheresoever
        she be:
Whether lying restless in heavy bed, or else

Sitting so cheerless at the cheerful board, or else
  Playing alone careless on her heavenly virginals.
If in bed, tell her that my eyes can take no rest;
  If at board, tell her that my mouth can eat no meat;
  If at her virginals, tell her I can hear no mirth.
Askëd, why? say: Waking love suffereth no sleep;
  Say that raging love doth appal the weak stomach;
  Say that lamenting love marreth the musical.
Tell her that her pleasures were wont to lull me asleep;
  Tell her that her beauty was wont to feed mine eyes;
  Tell her that her sweet tongue was wont to make me
    mirth.
Now do I nightly waste, wanting my kindly rest;
  Now do I daily starve, wanting my lively food;
  Now do I always die, wanting thy timely mirth.
And if I waste, who will bewail my heavy chance?
  And if I starve, who will record my cursëd end?
  And if I die, who will say, 'This was Immerito'?

Spenser.

Two other very commendable Letters, 1580.

A NEW COURTLY SONNET OF THE LADY
GREENSLEEVES

Greensleeves was all my joy,
  Greensleeves was my delight;
Greensleeves was my heart of gold,
  And who but Lady Greensleeves.

Alas, my Love! ye do me wrong
  To cast me off discourteously:
And I have lovëd you so long,
  Delighting in your company.
    Greensleeves was all my joy, &c.

I have been ready at your hand,
  To grant whatever you would crave.
I have both wagëd life and land,
  Your love and goodwill for to have.
    Greensleeves was all my joy, &c.

I bought thee kerchers to thy head,
  That were wrought fine and gallantly:
I kept thee both at board and bed,
  Which cost my purse well favouredly.
    Greensleeves was all my joy, &c.

I bought thee petticoats of the best,
  The cloth so fine as fine might be:
I gave thee jewels for thy chest,
  And all this cost I spent on thee.
    Greensleeves was all my joy, &c.

Thy smock of silk, both fair and white,
  With gold embroidered gorgeously:
Thy petticoat of sendal right:
  And thus I bought thee gladly.
    Greensleeves was all my joy, &c.

Thy girdle of gold so red,
  With pearls bedeckëd sumptuously:
The like no other lasses had,
  And yet thou wouldst not love me.
    Greensleeves was all my joy, &c.

Thy purse and eke thy gay gilt knives,
  Thy pincase gallant to the eye,
No better wore the burgess wives,
  And yet thou wouldst not love me.
    Greensleeves was all my joy, &c.

Thy crimson stockings all of silk,
  With gold all wrought above the knee;
Thy pumps as white as was the milk,
  And yet thou wouldst not love me.
    Greensleeves was all my joy, &c.

Thy gown was of the grossie green,
  Thy sleeves of satin hanging by,
Which made thee be our harvest queen,
  And yet thou wouldst not love me.
    Greensleeves was all my joy, &c.

Thy garters fringëd with the gold,
  And silver aglets hanging by,
Which made thee blithe for to behold,
  And yet thou wouldst not love me.
    Greensleeves was all my joy, &c.

My gayest gelding I thee gave,
  To ride wherever likëd thee;
No lady ever was so brave,
  And yet thou wouldst not love me.
    Greensleeves was all my joy, &c.

My men were clothëd all in green,
  And they did ever wait on thee:
All this was gallant to be seen,
  And yet thou wouldst not love me.
    Greensleeves was all my joy, &c.

They set thee up, they took thee down,
  They served thee with humility;
Thy foot might not once touch the ground,
  And yet thou wouldst not love me.
    Greensleeves was all my joy, &c.

For every morning when thou rose,
   I sent thee dainties orderly,
To cheer thy stomach from all woes,
   And yet thou wouldst not love me.
     Greensleeves was all my joy, &c.

Thou couldst desire no earthly thing
   But still thou hadst it readily:
Thy music still to play and sing,
   And yet thou wouldst not love me.
     Greensleeves was all my joy, &c.

And who did pay for all this gear
   That thou didst spend when pleasëd thee?
Even I that am rejected here,
   And thou disdain'st to love me.
     Greensleeves was all my joy, &c.

Well, I will pray to God on high,
   That thou my constancy may'st see,
And that yet once before I die
   Thou wilt vouchsafe to love me.
     Greensleeves was all my joy, &c.

Greensleeves, now farewell! adieu!
   God I pray to prosper thee:
For I am still thy lover true—
   Come once again and love me.
     Greensleeves was all my joy,
       Greensleeves was my delight;
     Greensleeves was my heart of gold,
       And who but Lady Greensleeves.   **Anon.**

A Handful of Pleasant Delights, 1584. (Poem registered 1580.)*

SONNETS

Lock up, fair lids, the treasure of my heart;
Preserve those beams, this age's only light:
To her sweet sense, sweet sleep, some ease impart—
Her sense too weak to bear her spirit's might.
And while, O sleep, thou closest up her sight—
Her sight where Love did forge his fairest dart—
Oh, harbour all her parts in easeful plight;
Let no strange dream make her fair body start.
But yet, O dream, if thou wilt not depart
In this rare subject from thy common right,
But wilt thyself in such a seat delight,
Then take my shape, and play a lover's part:
   Kiss her from me, and say unto her sprite,
   Till her eyes shine I live in darkest night.

Sidney.

Arcadia, 3rd Ed. 1598. (Written 1580–81.)*

My true Love hath my heart, and I have his,
By just exchange one for the other given:
I hold his dear, and mine he cannot miss;
There never was a better bargain driven.
His heart in me keeps me and him in one,
My heart in him his thoughts and senses guides:
He loves my heart, for once it was his own;
I cherish his because in me it bides.
His heart his wound receivëd from my sight,
My heart was wounded with his wounded heart;

---

sprite] 1629; spirit, 1598.

For as from me, on him his hurt did light,
So still methought in me his hurt did smart.
  Both, equal hurt, in this change sought our bliss:
  My true Love hath my heart, and I have his.

Sidney.

Ibid.

RURAL POESY

O words, which fall like summer dew on me!
  O breath, more sweet than is the growing bean!
O tongue, in which all honeyed liquors be!
  O voice, that doth the thrush in shrillness stain!—
    Do you say still this is her promise due,
    That she is mine, as I to her am true.

Gay hair, more gay than straw when harvest lies!
  Lips, red and plump as cherry's ruddy side!
Eyes fair and great, like fair great ox's eyes!
  O breast, in which two white sheep swell in pride!—
    Join you with me to seal this promise due,
    That she be mine, as I to her am true.

But thou white skin, as white as curds well pressed,
  So smooth as, sleek-stone like, it smooths each part!
And thou dear flesh, as soft as wool new dressed,
  And yet as hard as brawn made hard by art!—
    First four but say, next four their saying seal;
    But you must pay the gage of promised weal.

Sidney.

Ibid.

stain] shame, disgrace.

TO STELLA

Doubt you to whom my Muse these notes intendeth,
Which now my breast, o'ercharged, to music lendeth?
   To you! to you! all song of praise is due:
Only in you my song begins and endeth.

Who hath the eyes which marry state with pleasure?
Who keeps the key of Nature's chiefest treasure?
   To you! to you! all song of praise is due:
Only for you the heaven forgat all measure.

Who hath the lips where wit in fairness reigneth?
Who womankind at once both decks and staineth?
   To you! to you! all song of praise is due:
Only by you Cupid his crown maintaineth.

Who hath the feet, whose step all sweetness planteth?
Who else, for whom Fame worthy trumpets wanteth?
   To you! to you! all song of praise is due:
Only to you her sceptre Venus granteth.

Who hath the breast whose milk doth passions nourish?
Whose grace is such, that when it chides doth cherish?
   To you! to you! all song of praise is due:
Only through you the tree of life doth flourish.

Who hath the hand which without stroke subdueth?
Who long dead beauty with increase reneweth?
   To you! to you! all song of praise is due:
Only at you all envy hopeless rueth.

Who hath the hair which loosest fastest tieth?
Who makes a man live then glad when he dieth?

staineth] shameth.

To you! to you! all song of praise is due:
Only of you the flatterer never lieth.

Who hath the voice which soul from senses sunders?
Whose force but yours the bolts of beauty thunders?
    To you! to you! all song of praise is due:
Only with you not miracles are wonders.

Doubt you to whom my Muse these notes intendeth,
Which now my breast, o'ercharged, to music lendeth?
    To you! to you! all song of praise is due:
Only in you my song begins and endeth.   *Sidney.*

Astrophel and Stella, 1598. (Poem written c. 1581?)

SONNETS

In truth, O Love, with what a boyish kind
Thou dost proceed in thy most serious ways,
That when the heaven to thee his best displays,
Yet of that best thou leav'st the best behind!
For, like a child, that some fair book doth find,
With gilded leaves or coloured vellum plays,
Or, at the most, on some fine picture stays,
But never heeds the fruit of writer's mind;
So, when thou saw'st, in Nature's cabinet,
Stella, thou straight look'st babies in her eyes;
In her cheeks' pit thou didst thy pitfold set,
And in her breast, bo-peep or couching, lies,
    Playing and shining in each outward part;
    But, fool, seek'st not to get into her heart.   *Sidney.*

Ibid.

With how sad steps, O Moon, thou climb'st the skies!
How silently, and with how wan a face!
What, may it be that even in heavenly place
That busy archer his sharp arrows tries?
Sure, if that long-with-love-acquainted eyes
Can judge of love, thou feel'st a lover's case—
I read it in thy looks; thy languished grace,
To me, that feel the like, thy state descries.
Then, even of fellowship, O Moon, tell me,
Is constant love deemed there but want of wit?
Are beauties there as proud as here they be?
Do they, above, love to be loved, and yet
    Those lovers scorn whom that love doth possess?
    Do they call virtue, there, ungratefulness?   *Sidney.*

Astrophel and Stella, 1598. (Poem written c. 1581?)

ONLY JOY! NOW HERE YOU ARE

Only Joy! now here you are,
Fit to hear and ease my care,
Let my whispering voice obtain
Sweet reward for sharpest pain:
Take me to thee, and thee to me.
No, no, no, no, my Dear, let be.

Night hath closed all in her cloak,
Twinkling stars love-thoughts provoke,
Danger hence good care doth keep,
Jealousy itself doth sleep:
Take me to thee, and thee to me.
No, no, no, no, my Dear, let be.

call virtue, etc.] *i.e.* call ungratefulness virtue.

Better place no wit can find,
Cupid's knot to loose or bind;
These sweet flowers on fine bed too,
Us in their best language woo:
Take me to thee, and thee to me.
No, no, no, no, my Dear, let be.

This small light the moon bestows
Serves thy beams but to disclose;
So to raise my hap more high,
Fear not else, none can us spy;
Take me to thee, and thee to me.
No, no, no, no, my Dear, let be.

That you heard was but a mouse,
Dumb sleep holdeth all the house:
Yet asleep, methinks they say,
'Young folks, take time while you may':
Take me to thee, and thee to me.
No, no, no, no, my Dear, let be.

Niggard Time threats, if we miss
This large offer of our bliss,
Long stay, ere he grant the same:
Sweet, then, while each thing doth frame,
Take me to thee, and thee to me.
No, no, no, no, my Dear, let be.

Your fair mother is a-bed,
Candles out and curtains spread;
She thinks you do letters write;
Write, but first let me indite:

knot] 1591; yoke, 1598.

'Take me to thee, and thee to me.'
No, no, no, no, my Dear, let be.

Sweet, alas, why strive you thus?
Concord better fitteth us;
Leave to Mars the force of hands,
Your power in your beauty stands:
Take me to thee, and thee to me.
No, no, no, no, my Dear, let be.

Woe to me! and do you swear
Me to hate, but I forbear?
Cursëd be my destines all,
That brought me so high to fall!
Soon with my death I will please thee.
No, no, no, no, my Dear, let be.   *Sidney.*

Astrophel and Stella, 1598. (Poem written c. 1581?)

SONNETS

Come, Sleep! O Sleep, the certain knot of peace,
The baiting-place of wit, the balm of woe,
The poor man's wealth, the prisoner's release,
The indifferent judge between the high and low;
With shield of proof shield me from out the prease
Of those fierce darts Despair at me doth throw:
Oh, make in me those civil wars to cease;
I will good tribute pay, if thou do so.
Take thou of me smooth pillows, sweetest bed,
A chamber deaf to noise and blind to light,
A rosy garland and a weary head:

but I forbear] except I forbear.   destines] destinies.   prease] press.

And if these things, as being thine in right,
    Move not thy heavy grace, thou shalt in me,
    Livelier than elsewhere, Stella's image see.

Sidney.

Ibid.

Highway, since you my chief Parnassus be,
And that my Muse, to some ears not unsweet,
Tempers her words to trampling horses' feet
More oft than to a chamber-melody,
Now blessèd you bear onward blessèd me
To her, where I my heart, safe-left, shall meet;
My Muse and I must you of duty greet
With thanks and wishes, wishing thankfully:
Be you still fair, honoured by public heed;
By no encroachment wronged, nor time forgot;
Nor blamed for blood, nor shamed for sinful deed;
And, that you know I envy you no lot
    Of highest wish, I wish you so much bliss,—
    Hundreds of years you Stella's feet may kiss!

Sidney.

Ibid.

WHO IS IT THAT THIS DARK NIGHT

'Who is it that this dark night
Underneath my window plaineth?'
    It is one who from thy sight
Being, ah, exiled, disdaineth
    Every other vulgar light.

'Why, alas, and are you he?
Be not yet those fancies changèd?'

Dear, when you find change in me,
Though from me you be estrangëd,
   Let my change to ruin be.

   'Well, in absence this will die;
Leave to see, and leave to wonder.'
   Absence, sure, will help, if I
Can learn how much myself to sunder
   From what in my heart doth lie.

   'But time will these thoughts remove;
Time doth work what no man knoweth.'
   Time doth as the subject prove;
With time still the affection groweth
   In the faithful turtle-dove.

   'What if you new beauties see,
Will not they stir new affection?'
   I will think they pictures be,
(Image-like, of saints' perfection)
   Poorly counterfeiting thee.

   'But your reason's purest light
Bids you leave such minds to nourish.'
   Dear, do reason no such spite:
Never doth thy beauty flourish
   More than in my reason's sight.

   'But the wrongs Love bears will make
Love at length leave undertaking.'
   No, the more fools it do shake,
In a ground of so firm making
   Deeper still they drive the stake.

'Peace! I think that some give ear,
Come, no more, lest I get anger.'
   Bliss! I will my bliss forbear,
Fearing, sweet, you to endanger;
   But my soul shall harbour there.

   'Well, be gone; be gone, I say!
Lest that Argus' eyes perceive you.'
   Oh, unjust is Fortune's sway,
Which can make me thus to leave you;
   And from lowts to run away.   *Sidney.*

Astrophel and Stella, 1598. (Poem written c. 1581?)

NEW BROOMS

New brooms, green brooms, will you buy any?
Come, maidens, come quickly, let me take a penny.

My brooms are not steepèd,
   But very well bound:
My brooms be not crooked,
   But smooth-cut and round.
I wish it should please you
   To buy of my broom,
Then would it well ease me
   If market were done.

Have you any old boots,
   Or any old shoon,
Pouch-rings, or buskins,
   To cope for new broom?

---

harbour there] 1629; harbour thee, 1598 and 1613.   lowts] servants.

If so you have, maidens,
　　I pray you bring hither,
That you and I friendly
　　May bargain together.

New brooms, green brooms, will you buy any?
Come, maidens, come quickly, let me take a penny.

Wilson.

The Three Ladies of London, 1584.* (Written c. 1581.)

A PRAYER TO THE TRINITY

In English Sapphic Verse

Trinity blessëd, deity coequal,
Unity sacred, God one eke in essence,
Yield to thy servant pitifully calling,
　　　　Merciful hearing.

Virtuous living did I long relinquish,
Thy will and precepts miserably scorning;
Grant to me, sinful, patïent repenting,
　　　　Healthful amendment.

Blessëd I judge him, that in heart is healëd:
Cursëd I know him, that in health is harmëd:
Thy physic, therefore, to me, wretch unhappy,
　　　　Send, my Redeemer.

Glory to God the Father, and his only
Son, the protector of us earthly sinners,
Thee, sacred Spirit, labourers refreshing,
　　　　Still be renownëd.　　　　　*Stanyhurst.*

The First Four Books of Virgil, 1582.*

COME, GENTLE DEATH!

Come, gentle Death! *Who calls?* One that 's oppressed.
What is thy will? That thou abridge my woe
By cutting off my life. *Cease thy request,*
I cannot kill thee yet. Alas! why so?
　Thou want'st thy heart. Who stole the same away?
　Love, whom thou serv'st. Intreat him, if thou may.

Come, come, come, Love! *Who calleth me so oft?*
Thy vassal true, whom thou shouldst know by right.
What makes thy cry so faint? My voice is soft
And almost spent by wailing day and night.
　Why then, what 's thy request? That thou restore
　To me my heart, and steal the same no more.

And thou, O Death! when I possess my heart,
Dispatch me then at once. *Why so?*
By promise thou art bound to end my smart.
Why, if thy heart return, then what 's thy woe?
　That, brought from cold, it never will desire
　To rest with me, which am more hot than fire.

Watson.

Hecatompathia, [1582].

HERE LIETH LOVE

Resolved to dust, intombed here lieth Love,
Through fault of her, who here herself should lie;
He struck her breast, but all in vain did prove
To fire the ice: and doubting by and by
　His brand had lost his force, he gan to try
　Upon himself; which trial made him die.

In sooth no force; let those lament that lust;
I 'll sing a carol-song for obsequy;
For tòwards me his dealings were unjust,
And cause of all my passëd misery:
    The Fates, I think, seeing what I had passed,
    In my behalf wrought this revenge at last.

But somewhat more to pacify my mind,
By illing him, through whom I lived a slave,
I 'll cast his ashes to the open wind,
Or write this epitaph upon his grave—
    'Here lieth Love, of Mars the bastard son,
    Whose foolish fault to death himself hath done.'

                                Watson.

Hecatompathia, [1582].

EXCEPT I LOVE

Except I love, I cannot have delight,
    It is a care that doth to life belong;
For why I hold that life in great despite
    That hath not soür mixed with sweet among.
    And though the torments which I feel be strong,
Yet had I rather thus for to remain
Than laugh, and live, not feeling lover's pain.

                                Parry (?)

The Mirror of Knighthood, II. 1583.*

SONG

    Shepherd, who can pass such wrong,
    And a life in woes so deep,

For why] Because.   soür] a disyllable; sower, 1583.

Which to live is too too long,
　　As it is too short to weep?

Grievous sighs in vain I waste,
　　Leesing my affiance, and
I perceive my hope at last
　　With a candle in the hand.

What time then to hope among
　　Bitter hopes that ever sleep,
When this life is too too long,
　　As it is too short to weep?

This grief, which I feel so rife,
　　Wretch, I do deserve as hire;
Since I came to put my life
　　In the hands of my desire.

Then cease not my plaints so strong;
　　For, though life her course doth keep,
It is not to live so long,
　　As it is too short to weep.   *Young.*

Diana, 1598. (Written 1583.)*

WHEREAT EREWHILE I WEPT, I LAUGH

Whereat erewhile I wept, I laugh;
　　That which I feared, I now despise;
My victor once, my vassal is;
　　My foe constrained, my weal supplies:
　　　　Thus do I triumph on my foe,
　　　　I weep at weal, I laugh at woe.

My care is cured, yet hath none end;
 Not that I want, but that I have;
My chance was change, yet still I stay,
 I would have less, and yet I crave:
  Ay me, poor wretch! that thus do live,
  Constrained to take, yet forced to give.

She whose delights are signs of death,
 Who when she smiles, begins to lour,
Constant in this that still she change,
 Her sweetest gifts time proves but sour:
  I live in care, crossed with her guile,
  Through her I weep, at her I smile.

Greene.

Arbasto, 1584.

CUPID AND CAMPASPE

Cupid and my Campaspe played
At cards for kisses—Cupid paid:
He stakes his quiver, bow and arrows,
His mother's doves, and team of sparrows;
Loses them too; then down he throws
The coral of his lip, the rose
Growing on 's cheek (but none knows how);
With these, the crystal of his brow,
And then the dimple of his chin:
All these did my Campaspe win.
At last he set her both his eyes,
She won, and Cupid blind did rise.
 O Love! has she done this to thee?
 What shall, alas, become of me?

Lyly (?)

Alexander and Campaspe, 1584. (Text 1632.)*

WHAT BIRD SO SINGS

What bird so sings, yet so does wail?
Oh, 'tis the ravished nightingale.
Jug, jug, jug, jug, tereu! she cries,
And still her woes at midnight rise.
Brave prick-song! who is 't now we hear?
None but the lark so shrill and clear;
How at heaven's gates she claps her wings!—
The morn not waking till she sings.
Hark, hark, with what a pretty throat
Poor robin redbreast tunes his note!
Hark how the jolly cuckoos sing
Cuckoo! to welcome in the spring!
Cuckoo! to welcome in the spring!   *Lyly* (?)

*Ibid.**

VULCAN'S SONG

My shag-hair Cyclops, come let 's ply
Our Lemnian hammers lustily!
        By my wife's sparrows,
        I swear these arrows
        Shall singing fly
        Through many a wanton's eye.
These headed are with golden blisses,
These silver ones feathered with kisses;
        But this of lead
        Strikes a clown dead,
        When in a dance
        He falls in a trance,
To see his black-brow lass not buss him,
And then whines out for death to untruss him.
So, so; our work being done, let 's play:
Holiday, boys! cry holiday!   *Lyly* (?)

Sappho and Phao, 1584. (Text 1632.)

I SERVE A MISTRESS

I serve a mistress whiter than the snow,
  Straighter than cedar, brighter than the glass,
Finer in trip and swifter than the roe,
  More pleasant than the field of flowering grass;
More gladsome to my withering joys that fade
Than winter's sun or summer's cooling shade.

Sweeter than swelling grape of ripest wine,
  Softer than feathers of the fairest swan,
Smoother than jet, more stately than the pine,
  Fresher than poplar, smaller than my span,
Clearer than beauty's fiery-pointed beam,
Or icy crust of crystal's frozen stream.

Yet is she curster than the bear by kind,
  And harder-hearted than the agèd oak,
More glib than oil, more fickle than the wind,
  Stiffer than steel, no sooner bent but broke.
Lo, thus my service is a lasting sore;
Yet will I serve, although I die therefore.   *Munday* (?)

Two Italian Gentlemen, [1584].

FAIR AND FAIR

Oenone.   Fair and fair, and twice so fair,
                 As fair as any may be;
               The fairest shepherd on our green,
                 A Love for any lady.
Paris.   Fair and fair, and twice so fair,
                 As fair as any may be;
               Thy Love is fair for thee alone,
                 And for no other lady.
Oenone.   My Love is fair, my Love is gay,

As fresh as bin the flowers in May;
And of my Love my roundelay,
My merry, merry, merry roundelay
  Concludes with Cupid's curse,—
They that do change old love for new,
  Pray gods they change for worse.

Together. They that do change old love for new,
    Pray gods they change for worse.

Oenone. Fair and fair, and twice so fair,
    As fair as any may be;
  The fairest shepherd on our green,
    A Love for any lady.

Paris. Fair and fair, and twice so fair,
    As fair as any may be;
  Thy Love is fair for thee alone,
    And for no other lady.

Oenone. My Love can pipe, my Love can sing,
  My Love can many a pretty thing,
  And of his lovely praises ring
  My merry, merry, merry roundelays.
    Amen to Cupid's curse,—
  They that do change old love for new,
    Pray gods they change for worse.

Together. They that do change old love for new,
    Pray gods they change for worse.

                      Peele.

The Arraignment of Paris, 1584.

O GENTLE LOVE

O gentle Love, ungentle for thy deed,
    Thou makest my heart
    A bloody mark

With piercing shot to bleed.
Shoot soft, sweet Love, for fear thou shoot amiss,
            For fear too keen
            Thy arrows been,
And hit the heart where my belovëd is.
Too fair that fortune were, nor never I
            Shall be so blessed,
            Among the rest,
That Love shall seize on her by sympathy.
Then since with Love my prayërs bear no boot,
            This doth remain
            To cease my pain,
I take the wound, and die at Venus' foot.   *Peele.*

The Arraignment of Paris, 1584.

OENONE'S COMPLAINT

Melpomene, the Muse of tragic songs,
With mournful tunes, in stole of dismal hue
Assist a silly nymph to wail her woe,
And leave thy lusty company behind.

Thou luckless wreath! becomes not me to wear
The poplar tree for triumph of my love:
Then as my joy, my pride of love, is left,
Be thou unclothëd of thy lovely green;

And in thy leaves my fortune written be,
And them some gentle wind let blow abroad,
That all the world may see how false of love
False Paris hath to his Oenone been.   *Peele.*

Ibid.

DIRGE

Welladay, welladay, poor Colin, thou art going to the
        ground,
    The love whom Thestylis hath slain,
    Hard heart, fair face, fraught with disdain,
Disdain in love a deadly wound.
        Wound her, sweet Love, so deep again,
        That she may feel the dying pain
        Of this unhappy shepherd's swain,
And die for love as Colin died, as Colin died.

Peele.

Ibid.

TAKE HEED OF GAZING OVERMUCH

Take heed of gazing overmuch
    On damsels fair, unknown:
For oftentimes the snake doth lie
    With roses overgrown;
        And under fairest flowers
            Do noisome adders lurk;
        Of whom take heed, I thee areed,
            Lest that thy cares they work.

What though that she doth smile on thee?
    Perchance she doth not love;
And though she smack thee once or twice,
    She thinks thee so to prove;
        And when that thou dost think
            She loveth none but thee,
        She hath in store, perhaps, some more
            Which so deceivèd be.

Trust not therefore the outward show;
   Beware in any case;
For good conditions do not lie
   Where is a pleasant face:
      But if it be thy chance
         A lover true to have,
         Be sure of this, thou shalt not miss
            Each thing that thou wilt crave.

And when as thou, good Reader, shalt
   Peruse this scroll of mine,
Let this a warning be to thee;
   And say a friend of thine
      Did write thee this of love,
         And of a zealous mind,
         Because that he, sufficiently,
            Hath tried the female kind.   *Richardson.*

A Handful of Pleasant Delights, 1584. (An excerpt from *A proper new
Song*.)*

UPON SIR FRANCIS DRAKE'S RETURN FROM HIS VOYAGE ABOUT THE WORLD, AND THE QUEEN'S MEETING HIM

Sir Francis, Sir Francis, Sir Francis is come;
Sir Robert, and eke Sir William his son,
And eke the good Earl of Huntington
Marched gallantly on the road.

Then came the Lord Chamberlain with his white staff,
And all the people began to laugh;
And then the Queen began to speak,
'You re welcome home, Sir Francis Drake.'

You gallants all o' the British blood,
Why don't you sail o' the ocean flood?
I protest you 're not all worth a filbert
If once compared to Sir Humphry Gilbert.

For he went out on a rainy day,
And to the new-found land found out his way,
With many a gallant both fresh and green,
And he ne'er came home again. God bless the Queen!
                                                        Anon.

Bodley MS. Ashm. 36–7. (Poem written c. 1584 ?)

WHO HATH HIS FANCY PLEASËD

Who hath his fancy pleasëd
    With fruits of happy sight,
Let here his eyes be raisëd
    On Nature's sweetest light;
A light which doth dissever
    And yet unite the eyes;
A light which, dying never,
    Is cause the looker dies.

She never dies, but lasteth
    In life of lover's heart;
He ever dies that wasteth
    In love his chiefest part:
Thus is her life still guarded
    In never-dying faith;
Thus is his death rewarded,
    Since she lives in his death.

Look, then, and die: the pleasure
    Doth answer well the pain:

Small loss of mortal treasure
   Who may immortal gain.
Immortal be her graces,
   Immortal is her mind:
They, fit for heavenly places;
   This, heaven in it doth bind.

But eyes these beauties see not,
   Nor sense that grace descries;
Yet eyes deprivëd be not
   From sight of her fair eyes—
Which as of inward glory
   They are the outward seal,
So may they live still sorry,
   Which die not in that weal.

But who hath fancies pleasëd
   With fruits of happy sight,
Let here his eyes be raisëd
   On Nature's sweetest light!   *Sidney.*

Certain sonnets never before printed. In *Arcadia,* 1598. (Written before 1585.)

THE NIGHTINGALE

The nightingale, as soon as April bringeth
Unto her rested sense a perfect waking,
While late bare earth, proud of new clothing, springeth,
Sings out her woes, a thorn her song-book making;
And, mournfully bewailing,
Her throat in tunes expresseth
What grief her breast oppresseth,
For Tereus' force on her chaste will prevailing.

O Philomela fair! oh, take some gladness
That here is juster cause of plaintful sadness:
Thine earth now springs, mine fadeth;
Thy thorn without, my thorn my heart invadeth.

Alas! she hath no other cause of anguish
But Tereus' love, on her by strong hand wroken;
Wherein she suffering, all her spirits languish,
Full womanlike complains her will was broken.
But I, who, daily craving,
Can not have to content me,
Have more cause to lament me,
Since wanting is more woe than too much having.
    O Philomela fair! oh, take some gladness
    That here is juster cause of plaintful sadness:
    Thine earth now springs, mine fadeth;
    Thy thorn without, my thorn my heart invadeth.

Ibid.   *Sidney.*

A FAREWELL

Oft have I mused, but now at length I find,
Why those that die, men say they do depart.
'Depart!'—a word so gentle, to my mind,
Weakly did seem to paint death's ugly dart.
But now the stars, with their strange course, do bind
Me one to leave, with whom I leave my heart;
I hear a cry of spirits, faint and blind,
That, parting thus, my chiefest part I part.
Part of my life, the loathèd part to me,
Lives to impart my weary clay some breath;
But that good part, wherein all comforts be,
Now dead, doth show departure is a death—

Yea, worse than death: death parts both woe and joy:
From joy I part, still living in annoy.   *Sidney.*

Certain sonnets never before printed. In *Arcadia*, 1598. (Written before
1585.)

RING OUT YOUR BELLS!

Ring out your bells! Let mourning shows be spread!
For Love is dead.
    All love is dead, infected
    With plague of deep disdain;
    Worth, as nought worth, rejected;
    And faith, fair scorn doth gain.
        From so ungrateful fancy,
        From such a female franzy,
        From them that use men thus,
        Good Lord, deliver us!

Weep! neighbours, weep! Do you not hear it said
That Love is dead?
    His deathbed, peacock's folly;
    His winding-sheet is shame;
    His will, false-seeming holy;
    His sole exec'tor, blame.
        From so ungrateful fancy,
        From such a female franzy,
        From them that use men thus,
        Good Lord, deliver us!

Let dirge be sung, and trentals rightly read!
For Love is dead.
    Sir Wrong his tomb ordaineth
    My mistress' marble heart;
    Which epitaph containeth—

'Her eyes were once his dart.'
> *From so ungrateful fancy,*
> *From such a female franzy,*
> *From them that use men thus,*
> *Good Lord, deliver us!*

Alas, I lie: rage hath this error bred;
Love is not dead.
> Love is not dead, but sleepeth
> In her unmatchëd mind,
> Where she his counsel keepeth,
> Till due desert she find.
>> *Therefore, from so vile fancy,*
>> *To call such wit a franzy,*
>> *Who love can temper thus,*
>> *Good Lord, deliver us!*   *Sidney.*

Ibid.

LEAVE ME, O LOVE!

Leave me, O Love, which reachest but to dust,
And thou, my mind, aspire to higher things;
Grow rich in that which never taketh rust:
Whatever fades, but fading pleasure brings.
Draw in thy beams, and humble all thy might
To that sweet yoke where lasting freedoms be,
Which breaks the clouds and opens forth the light
That doth both shine and give us sight to see.
Oh, take fast hold! Let that light be thy guide
In this small course which birth draws out to death,
And think how evil becometh him to slide
Who seeketh heaven, and comes of heavenly breath.
> Then, farewell, world! thy uttermost I see.
> Eternal Love, maintain thy life in me!   *Sidney.*

Ibid.

CUPID'S INDICTMENT

O yes, O yes! if any maid
Whom leering Cupid has betrayed
To frowns of spite, to eyes of scorn,
And would in madness now see torn
The boy in pieces,—let her come
Hither, and lay on him her doom.

O yes, O yes! has any lost
A heart which many a sigh hath cost?
Is any cozened of a tear
Which as a pearl disdain does wear?
Here stands the thief,—let her but come
Hither, and lay on him her doom.

Is any one undone by fire,
And turned to ashes through desire?
Did ever any lady weep,
Being cheated of her golden sleep
Stolen by sick thoughts?—the pirate 's found,
And in her tears he shall be drowned.

Read his indictment, let him hear
What he 's to trust to. Boy, give ear!   *Lyly (?)*

Galathea, 1592. (Written 1585–8 ? Text 1632.)

OF HIS CYNTHIA

Away with these self-loving lads,
Whom Cupid's arrow never glads!
Away, poor souls, that sigh and weep
In love of those that lie asleep!
    For Cupid is a meadow god,
    And forceth none to kiss the rod.

Sweet Cupid's shafts, like destiny,
Doth causeless good or ill decree.
Desert is born out of his bow,
Reward upon his wing doth go.
    What fools are they that have not known
    That Love likes no laws but his own!

My songs they be of Cynthia's praise,
I wear her rings on holidays;
In every tree I write her name,
And every day I read the same.
    Where honour Cupid's rival is,
    There miracles are seen of his.

If Cynthia crave her ring of me,
I blot her name out of the tree.
If doubt do darken things held dear,
Then well fare nothing once a year!
    For many run, but one must win;
    Fools, only, hedge the cuckoo in.

The worth that worthiness should move
Is love, that is the bow of Love.
And love as well the foster can
As can the mighty nobleman.
    Sweet saint, 'tis true you worthy be,
    Yet without love nought worth to me.   *Brooke.*

Caelica, in *Certain Learned and Elegant Works*, 1633. (Written before
1586.) *

MORE THAN MOST FAIR

More than most fair, full of that heavenly fire
    Kindled above to show the Maker's glory!
Beauty's first-born, in whom all powers conspire

To write the Graces' life, and Muses' story!—
If in my heart all saints else be defaced,
Honour the shrine where you alone are placed.

Thou window of the sky, and pride of spirits,
  True character of honour in perfection!
Thou heavenly creature, judge of earthly merits,
  And glorious prison of man's pure affection!—
If in my heart all nymphs else be defaced,
Honour the shrine where you alone are placed.

Brooke.

Caelica, 1633. (Written before 1586.)

YOU LITTLE STARS THAT LIVE IN SKIES

You little stars that live in skies,
  And glory in Apollo's glory,
In whose aspècts conjoinëd lies
  The heaven's will and nature's story,
Joy to be likened to those eyes,
  Which eyes make all eyes glad or sorry:
For when you force thoughts from above,
These overrule your force by love.

And thou, O Love, which in these eyes
  Hast married Reason with Affection,
And made them saints of Beauty's skies
  Where joys are shadows of perfection,
Lend me thy wings that I may rise
  Up not by worth but thy election:
For I have vowed, in strangest fashion,
To love and never seek compassion.   *Brooke.*

Ibid.

MYRA

I, with whose colours Myra dressed her head,
  I, that ware posies of her own hand-making,
I, that mine own name in the chimneys read
    By Myra finely wrought ere I was waking,—
      Must I look on, in hope time coming may
      With change bring back my turn again to play?

I, that on Sunday at the church-stile found
  A garland sweet, with true-love knots in flowers,
Which I to wear about mine arm was bound,
    That each of us might know that all was ours,—
      Must I now lead an idle life in wishes,
      And follow Cupid for his loaves and fishes?

I, that did wear the ring her mother left,
  I, for whose love she gloried to be blamed,
I, with whose eyes her eyes committed theft,
    I, who did make her blush when I was named,—
      Must I lose ring, flowers, blush, theft, and go naked,
      Watching with sighs till dead love be awakëd?

I, that, when drowsy Argus fell asleep,
  Like jealousy o'erwatchëd with desire,
Was even warnëd modesty to keep,
    While her breath, speaking, kindled Nature's fire,—
      Must I look on a-cold, while others warm them?
      Do Vulcan's brothers in such fine nets arm them?

Was it for this that I might Myra see
  Washing the water with her beauties white?
Yet would she never write her love to me.

Thinks wit of change, while thoughts are in delight?
　Mad girls must safely love as they may leave;
　No man can print a kiss: lines may deceive.

Caelica, 1633. (Written before 1586.)   *Brooke.*

A DOUBTFUL CHOICE

Were I a king I could command content.
　Were I obscure, unknown should be my cares.
And were I dead, no thoughts should me torment,
　　Nor words, nor wrongs, nor loves, nor hopes, nor fears.
A doubtful choice, of three things one to crave,
A kingdom, or a cottage, or a grave.   *Oxford.*

B.M. Add. MS. 22583. (Poem written before 1586.)*

TICHBORNE'S ELEGY, WRITTEN IN THE TOWER BEFORE HIS EXECUTION, 1586

My prime of youth is but a frost of cares;
　My feast of joy is but a dish of pain;
My crop of corn is but a field of tares;
　And all my good is but vain hope of gain:
The day is past, and yet I saw no sun;
And now I live, and now my life is done.

My tale was heard, and yet it was not told;
　My fruit is fall'n, and yet my leaves are green;
My youth is spent, and yet I am not old;
　I saw the world, and yet I was not seen:
My thread is cut, and yet it is not spun;
And now I live, and now my life is done.

I sought my death, and found it in my womb;
　I looked for life, and saw it was a shade;

I trod the earth, and knew it was my tomb;
   And now I die, and now I was but made:
My glass is full, and now my glass is run;
And now I live, and now my life is done.

Verses of Praise and Joy, 1586.   *Tichborne.*

CONTENT

In crystal towers and turrets richly set
   With glittering gems that shine against the sun,
In regal rooms of jasper and of jet,
   Content of mind not always likes to wone;
But oftentimes it pleaseth her to stay
In simple cotes closed in with walls of clay.   *Whitney.*

A Choice of Emblems, 1586.*

A MIND CONTENT

Sweet are the thoughts that savour of content;
   The quiet mind is richer than a crown;
Sweet are the nights in careless slumber spent;
   The poor estate scorns fortune's angry frown:
Such sweet content, such minds, such sleep, such bliss,
Beggars enjoy, when princes oft do miss.

The homely house that harbours quiet rest;
   The cottage that affords no pride nor care;
The mean that 'grees with country music best;
   The sweet consort of mirth and music's fare;
Obscurëd life sets down a type of bliss:
A mind content both crown and kingdom is.   *Greene.*

Greene's Farewell to Folly, 1591. (Registered 1587.)

wone] dwell.   music's fare] 1591; modest fare, W. J. Linton, 1882.

IN PRAISE OF HIS LADY

Like as the Bay, that bears on branches sweet
  The Laurel leaf that lasteth alway green,
To change his hue for weather, dry or weet,
  Or else to lose his leaf, is seldom seen;
So doth my dear for aye continue still,
  As faithful as the loving turtle-dove,
Rewarding me according to my will
  With faithful heart for my most trusty love.
And sith the time that we our love began,
  Most trusty she yet hath endurëd aye,
And changeth not for any other man;
  So constant she of faith in heart doth stay.
Wherefore unto that tree I her compare,
  That never loseth leaf, no more doth she
Lose triëd truth, however that she fare,
  But always one by love in heart to me.
Then boast I on this branch of Bays most pure,
  Sith that so sweet I find it at my heart,
And love while that my life shall aye endure,
  And till that death our bodies two shall part.

                                              Grove.

Pelops and Hippodamia, 1587.

O CUPID! MONARCH OVER KINGS

O Cupid! monarch over kings,
Wherefore hast thou feet and wings?
It is to show how swift thou art,
When thou wound'st a tender heart!
Thy wings being clipped, and feet held still,
Thy bow so many could not kill.

It is all one, in Venus' wanton school,
Who highest sits, the wise man or the fool.
  Fools in love's college
  Have far more knowledge
  To read a woman over,
  Than a neat prating lover:
    Nay, 'tis confessed
    That fools please women best.   *Lyly* (?)

Mother Bombie, 1594. (Acted 1587–90. Text 1632.)

MY MIND TO ME A KINGDOM IS

My mind to me a kingdom is,
 Such present joys therein I find,
That it excels all other bliss
 That earth affords or grows by kind.
Though much I want which most would have,
Yet still my mind forbids to crave.

No princely pomp, no wealthy store,
 No force to win the victory,
No wily wit to salve a sore,
 No shape to feed a loving eye;
To none of these I yield as thrall,
For why my mind doth serve for all.

I see how plenty suffers oft,
 And hasty climbers soon do fall;
I see that those which are aloft
 Mishap doth threaten most of all;
They get with toil, they keep with fear:
Such cares my mind could never bear.

earth] MS. correction; first written, world. For why] Because.

Content I live, this is my stay—
  I seek no more than may suffice;
I press to bear no haughty sway;
  Look, what I lack my mind supplies:
Lo! thus I triumph like a king,
Content with that my mind doth bring.

Some have too much, yet still do crave;
  I little have, and seek no more.
They are but poor, though much they have,
  And I am rich with little store:
They poor, I rich; they beg, I give;
They lack, I leave; they pine, I live.

I laugh not at another's loss;
  I grudge not at another's gain;
No worldly waves my mind can toss;
  My state at one doth still remain:
I fear no foe, I fawn no friend;
I loathe not life, nor dread my end.

Some weigh their pleasure by their lust,
  Their wisdom by their rage of will;
Their treasure is their only trust,
  A cloakèd craft their store of skill:
But all the pleasure that I find
Is to maintain a quiet mind.

My wealth is health and perfect ease,
  My conscience clear my choice defence;
I neither seek by bribes to please,
  Nor by deceit to breed offence:
Thus do I live; thus will I die;
Would all did so as well as I!   *Dyer.*

Bodley MS. Rawl. Poet. 85. (Variant in W. Byrd's *Psalms, Sonnets, and Songs*, 1588.)

FAIR IS MY LOVE

Fair is my Love, for April in her face;
  Her lovely breasts September claims his part;
And lordly Jùly in her eyes takes place;
  But cold December dwelleth in her heart:
Blest be the months that sets my thoughts on fire!
Accurst that month that hind'reth my desire!

Like Phoebus' fire, so sparkles both her eyes;
  As air perfumed with amber is her breath;
Like swelling waves her lovely teats do rise;
  As earth her heart, cold, dateth me to death:
Ay me, poor man, that on the earth do live,
When unkind earth death and despair doth give!

In pomp sits mercy seated in her face;
  Love 'twixt her breasts his trophies doth imprint;
Her eyes shines favour, courtesy, and grace;
  But touch her heart, ah, that is framed ·of flint!
That 'fore my harvest in the grass bears grain,
The rock will wear, washed with a winter's rain.

Greene.

Perimedes, the Blacksmith, 1588.

IF WOMEN COULD BE FAIR

If women could be fair, and yet not fond,
Or that their love were firm, not fickle still,
I would not marvel that they make men bond
By service long to purchase their good will;
But when I see how frail those creatures are,
I muse that men forget themselves so far.

To mark the choice they make, and how they change,
How oft from Phoebus they do flee to Pan;

Unsettled still, like haggards wild they range,
These gentle birds that fly from man to man,—
Who would not scorn and shake them from the fist,
And let them fly, fair fools, which way they list?

Yet for disport we fawn and flatter both,
To pass the time when nothing else can please,
And train them to our lure with subtle oath,
Till, weary of their wiles, ourselves we ease;
And then we say when we their fancy try,
To play with fools, oh, what a fool was I!   *Oxford.*

Bodley MS. Rawl. Poet. 85. (Variant in W. Byrd's *Psalms, Sonnets, and Songs,* 1588.)

A FAREWELL TO FALSE LOVE

Farewell, false Love, the oracle of lies,
    A mortal foe and enemy to rest,
An envious boy, from whom all cares arise,
    A bastard vile, a beast with rage possessed,
A way of error, a temple full of treason,
In all effects contrary unto reason.

A poisoned serpent covered all with flowers,
    Mother of sighs, and murderer of repose,
A sea of sorrows whence are drawn such showers
    As moisture lend to every grief that grows;
A school of guile, a net of deep deceit,
A gilded hook that holds a poisoned bait.

A fortress foiled, which reason did defend,
    A siren song, a fever of the mind,

whence] 1631; from whence, 1588.

A maze wherein affection finds no end,
   A raging cloud that runs before the wind,
A substance like the shadow of the sun,
A goal of grief for which the wisest run.

A quenchless fire, a nurse of trembling fear,
   A path that leads to peril and mishap,
A true retreat of sorrow and despair,
   An idle boy that sleeps in pleasure's lap,
A deep mistrust of that which certain seems,
A hope of that which reason doubtful deems.

Sith then thy trains my younger years betrayed,
   And for my faith ingratitude I find;
And sith repentance hath my wrongs bewrayed,
   Whose course was ever contrary to kind:
False love, desire, and beauty frail, adieu!
Dead is the root whence all these fancies grew.

Raleigh(?)

W. Byrd's *Psalms, Sonnets, and Songs,* 1588; also Bodley MS. Rawl. Poet. 85.*

THOUGH AMARYLLIS DANCE IN GREEN

Though Amaryllis dance in green
      Like Fairy Queen,
      And sing full clear;
Corinna can, with smiling, cheer.
Yet since their eyes make heart so sore,
Hey ho! chill love no more.

My sheep are lost for want of food,
      And I so wood
      That all the day
I sit and watch a herd-maid gay,

chill] I will.   wood] mad, distracted.

Who laughs to see me sigh so sore;
Hey ho! chill love no more.

Her loving looks, her beauty bright,
        Is such delight
        That all in vain
I love to like, and lose my gain
For her, that thanks me not therefore.
Hey ho! chill love no more.

Ah, wanton eyes! my friendly foes
        And cause of woes,
        Your sweet desire
Breeds flames of ice, and freezing fire.
Ye scorn to see me weep so sore:
Hey ho! chill love no more.

Love ye who list, I force him not:
        Sith God it wot,
        The more I wail,
The less my sighs and tears prevail:
What shall I do, but say therefore,
Hey ho! chill love no more.   *Anon.*

W. Byrd's *Psalms, Sonnets, and Songs,* 1588.

THE QUIET LIFE

What pleasure have great princes
        More dainty to their choice
Than herdmen wild, who careless
        In quiet life rejoice,
And fortune's fate not fearing
Sing sweet in summer morning?

---

freezing] Bullen 1891; freeze in, 1588.   sith] since.

Their dealings, plain and rightful,
   Are void of all deceit;
They never know how spiteful
   It is to kneel and wait
On favourite presumptuous
Whose pride is vain and sumptuous.

All day their flocks each tendeth;
   At night they take their rest;
More quiet than who sendeth
   His ship into the East,
Where gold and pearl are plenty,
But getting, very dainty.

For lawyers and their pleading,
   They esteem it not a straw;
They think that honest meaning
   Is of itself a law;
Where conscience judgeth plainly
They spend no money vainly.

Oh, happy who thus liveth,
   Not caring much for gold;
With clothing which sufficeth
   To keep him from the cold!
Though poor and plain his diet
Yet merry it is, and quiet.   *Anon.*

Ibid.

SAMELA

Like to Diana in her summer weed,
Girt with a crimson robe of brightest dye,
               Goes fair Samela;
Whiter than be the flocks that straggling feed,

When washed by Arethusa faint they lie,
                    Is fair Samela;
As fair Aurora in her morning-grey,
Decked with the ruddy glister of her love,
                    Is fair Samela;
Like lovely Thetis on a calmëd day,
Whenas her brightness Neptune's fancy move,
                    Shines fair Samela;
Her tresses gold, her eyes like glassy streams,
Her teeth are pearl, the breasts are ivory
                    Of fair Samela;
Her cheeks, like rose and lily, yield forth gleams,
Her brows, bright arches framed of ebony:
                    Thus fair Samela
Passeth fair Venus in her bravest hue,
And Juno in the show of majesty
                    (For she 's Samela),
Pallas in wit: all three, if you well view,
For beauty, wit, and matchless dignity,
                    Yield to Samela.   *Greene.*

Menaphon, 1589.

WEEP NOT, MY WANTON

Weep not, my wanton, smile upon my knee;
When thou art old there 's grief enough for thee.
          Mother's wag, pretty boy,
          Father's sorrow, father's joy;
          When thy father first did see
          Such a boy by him and me,
          He was glad, I was woe;
          Fortune changed made him so,
          When he left his pretty boy,
          Last his sorrow, first his joy.

Weep not, my wanton, smile upon my knee;
When thou art old there 's grief enough for thee.
> Streaming tears that never stint,
> Like pearl-drops from a flint,
> Fell by course from his eyes,
> That one another's place supplies;
> Thus he grieved in every part,
> Tears of blood fell from his heart,
> When he left his pretty boy,
> Father's sorrow, father's joy.

Weep not, my wanton, smile upon my knee;
When thou art old there 's grief enough for thee.
> The wanton smiled, father wept,
> Mother cried, baby leapt;
> More he crowed, more we cried,
> Nature could not sorrow hide:
> He must go, he must kiss
> Child and mother, baby bliss,
> For he left his pretty boy,
> Father's sorrow, father's joy.

Weep not, my wanton, smile upon my knee;
When thou art old there 's grief enough for thee.

Ibid.   *Greene.*

A JIG

> Through the shrubs as I can crack,
> > For my lambs' little ones,
> > 'Mongst many pretty ones—
> Nymphs, I mean,—whose hair was black
> > As the crow;
> > Like the snow
> Her face and brows shinëd, I ween;

I saw a little one,
A bonny pretty one,
As bright, buxom, and as sheen
As was she,
On her knee
That lulled the god, whose arrows warms
Such merry little ones,
Such fair-faced pretty ones,
As dally in love's chiefest harms.
Such was mine,
Whose gay eyne
Made me love. I gan to woo
This sweet little one,
This bonny pretty one.
I wooed hard, a day or two,
Till she bad
'Be not sad,
Woo no more, I am thine own,
Thy dearest little one,
Thy truest pretty one!'
Thus was faith and firm love shown,
As behoves
Shepherds' loves.   *Greene.*

Menaphon, 1589.

OF HIS MISTRESS

Tune on my pipe the praises of my Love,
And, midst thy oaten harmony, recount
How fair she is that makes thy music mount,
And every string of thy heart's harp to move.

Shall I compare her form unto the sphere
Whence sun-bright Venus vaunts her silver shine?

Ah, more than that, by just compare, is thine,
Whose crystal looks the cloudy heavens do clear.

How oft have I descending Titan seen
    His burning locks couch in the sea-queen's lap;
    And beauteous Thetis his red body wrap
In watery robes, as he her lord had been.

Whenas my nymph, impatient of the night,
    Bade bright Atreus with his train give place,
    Whiles she led forth the day with her fair face,
And lent each star a more than Delian light.

Not Jove, or Nature—should they both agree
    To make a woman of the firmament
    Of his mixed purity—could not invent
A sky-born form so beautiful as she.   *Greene.*

Ibid.

LOVE AND JEALOUSY

When gods had framed the sweet of women's face,
    And locked men's looks within their golden hair,
That Phoebus blushed to see their matchless grace,
    And heavenly gods on earth did make repair;
To quip fair Venus' overweening pride,
Love's happy thoughts to jealousy were tied.

Then grew a wrinkle on fair Venus' brow;
    The amber sweet of love was turned to gall;
Gloomy was heaven; bright Phoebus did avow
    He could be coy, and would not love at all,
Swearing, no greater mischief could be wrought
Than love united to a jealous thought.   *Greene.*

Ciceronis Amor, 1589.

THE EARTH, LATE CHOKED WITH SHOWERS

The earth, late choked with showers,
    Is now arrayed in green;
Her bosom springs with flowers,
    The air dissolves her teen:
The heavens laugh at her glory,
Yet bide I sad and sorry.

The woods are decked with leaves,
    And trees are clothëd gay;
And Flora, crowned with sheaves,
    With oaken boughs doth play:
Where I am clad in black,
The token of my wrack.

The birds upon the trees
    Do sing with pleasant voices,
And chant in their degrees
    Their loves and lucky choices:
When I, whilst they are singing,
With sighs mine arms am wringing.

The thrushes seek the shade,
    And I my fatal grave;
Their flight to heaven is made,
    My walk on earth I have:
They free, I thrall; they jolly,
I sad and pensive wholly.   *Lodge.*

Scylla's Metamorphosis, 1589.

THE PASSIONATE SHEPHERD TO HIS LOVE

Come live with me and be my Love,
And we will all the pleasures prove

That valleys, groves, hills, and fields,
Woods, or steepy mountains yields.

And we will sit upon the rocks
Seeing the shepherds feed their flocks,
By shallow rivers, to whose falls
Melodious birds sing madrigals.

And I will make thee beds of roses
And a thousand fragrant posies,
A cap of flowers, and a kirtle
Embroidered all with leaves of myrtle;

A gown made of the finest wool,
Which from our pretty lambs we pull;
Fair linëd slippers for the cold,
With buckles of the purest gold;

A belt of straw and ivy buds
With coral clasps and amber studs:
And if these pleasures may thee move,
Come live with me and be my Love.

The shepherd swains shall dance and sing
For thy delight each May morning:
If these delights thy mind may move,
Then live with me and be my Love.   *Marlowe.*

England's Helicon, 1600. (Poem written c. 1589.)* Quoted, *Merry Wives of Windsor*, III. i. 17–29.

THE NYMPH'S REPLY TO THE SHEPHERD

If all the world and love were young,
And truth in every shepherd's tongue,

These pretty pleasures might me move
To live with thee and be thy Love.

Time drives the flocks from field to fold,
When rivers rage and rocks grow cold;
And Philomel becometh dumb;
The rest complains of cares to come.

The flowers do fade, and wanton fields
To wayward winter reckoning yields:
A honey tongue, a heart of gall,
Is fancy's spring, but sorrow's fall.

Thy gowns, thy shoes, thy beds of roses,
Thy cap, thy kirtle, and thy posies
Soon break, soon wither, soon forgotten,
In folly ripe, in reason rotten.

Thy belt of straw and ivy buds,
Thy coral clasps and amber studs,
All these in me no means can move
To come to thee and be thy Love.

But could youth last, and love still breed,
Had joys no date, nor age no need,
Then these delights my mind might move
To live with thee and be thy Love.   *Raleigh* (?)

England's Helicon, 1600. (Poem written c. 1589?)*

CRUEL YOU BE

Cruel you be who can say nay,
    Since ye delight in other's woe:

Unwise am I, ye may well say,
　For that I have honoùred you so:
But blameless I, who could not choose,
　To be enchanted by your eye:
But ye to blame, thus to refuse
　My service, and to let me die.　　*Puttenham.*

The Art of English Poesie, 1589.

ADIEU LOVE, UNTRUE LOVE

While that the sun with his beams hot
　Scorchëd the fruits in vale and mountain,
Philon the shepherd, late forgot,
　Sitting besides a crystal fountain
In shadow of a green oak tree,
Upon his pipe this song played he:
　　　Adieu Love, adieu Love, untrue Love!
　　　Untrue Love, untrue Love, adieu Love!
　　　Your mind is light, soon lost for new love.

So long as I was in your sight
　I was your heart, your soul, your treasure;
And evermore you sobbed, you sighed,
　Burning in flames beyond all measure.
Three days endured your love to me,
And it was lost in other three.
　　　Adieu Love, adieu Love, untrue Love! &c.

Another shepherd you did see,
　To whom your heart was soon enchainëd;
Full soon your love was leapt from me,
　Full soon my place he had obtainëd:
Soon came a third your love to win,

And we were out, and he was in.
    Adieu Love, adieu Love, untrue Love! &c.

Sure you had made me passing glad
    That you your mind so soon removëd,
Before that I the leisure had
    To choose you for my best belovëd:
For all my love was past and done
Two days before it was begun.
    Adieu Love, adieu Love, untrue Love!
    Untrue Love, untrue Love, adieu Love!
    Your mind is light, soon lost for new love.   *Anon.*

W. Byrd's *Songs of Sundry Natures*, 1589.

SYRINX

Pan's Syrinx was a girl indeed,
Though now she 's turned into a reed;
From that dear reed Pan's pipe does come,
A pipe that strikes Apollo dumb;
Nor flute, nor lute, nor gittern can
So chant it as the pipe of Pan:
Cross-gartered swains and dairy girls,
With faces smug and round as pearls,
When Pan's shrill pipe begins to play,
With dancing wear out night and day:
The bagpipe's drone his hum lays by
When Pan sounds up his minstrelsy;
His minstrelsy! oh, base! this quill—
Which at my mouth with wind I fill—
Puts me in mind, though her I miss,
That still my Syrinx' lips I kiss.   *Lyly (?)*

Midas, 1592. (Acted 1589–90. Text 1632.)

DAPHNE

My Daphne's hair is twisted gold,
Bright stars a-piece her eyes do hold,
My Daphne's brow enthrones the graces,
My Daphne's beauty stains all faces;
On Daphne's cheek grow rose and cherry,
On Daphne's lip a sweeter berry;
Daphne's snowy hand but touched does melt,
And then no heavenlier warmth is felt;
My Daphne's voice tunes all the spheres,
My Daphne's music charms all ears.
Fond am I thus to sing her praise;
These glories now are turned to bays.   *Lyly (?)*

Ibid.

THE SHEPHERD'S WIFE'S SONG

Ah, what is love? It is a pretty thing,
As sweet unto a shepherd as a king;
             And sweeter too,
For kings have cares that wait upon a crown,
And cares can make the sweetest love to frown:
             Ah then, ah then,
If country loves such sweet desires do gain,
What lady would not love a shepherd swain?

His flocks once folded, he comes home at night
As merry as a king in his delight;
             And merrier too,
For kings bethink them what the state require,
Where shepherds careless carol by the fire:
             Ah then, ah then,
If country loves such sweet desires do gain,
What lady would not love a shepherd swain?

He kisseth first, then sits as blithe to eat
His cream and curds as doth the king his meat;
       And blither too,
For kings have often fears when they do sup,
Where shepherds dread no poison in their cup:
       Ah then, ah then,
If country loves such sweet desires do gain,
What lady would not love a shepherd swain?

To bed he goes, as wanton then, I ween,
As is a king in dalliance with a queen;
       More wanton too,
For kings have many griefs affects to move,
Where shepherds have no greater grief than love:
       Ah then, ah then,
If country loves such sweet desires do gain,
What lady would not love a shepherd swain?

Upon his couch of straw he sleeps as sound
As doth the king upon his beds of down;
       More sounder too,
For cares cause kings full oft their sleep to spill,
Where weary shepherds lie and snort their fill:
       Ah then, ah then,
If country loves such sweet desires do gain,
What lady would not love a shepherd swain?

Thus with his wife he spends the year, as blithe
As doth the king at every tide or sithe;
       And blither too,
For kings have wars and broils to take in hand,
Where shepherds laugh and love upon the land:
       Ah then, ah then,

sithe] occasion, time.

If country loves such sweet desires do gain,
What lady would not love a shepherd swain?   *Greene.*

Greene's Mourning Garment, 1590.*

HEXAMETRA ALEXIS IN LAUDEM ROSAMUNDI

Oft have I heard my lief Corydon report on a love-day,
When bonny maids do meet with the swains in the valley by
    Tempe,
How bright-eyed his Phyllis was, how lovely they glancëd
When fro th' arches ebon black flew looks as a lightning,
That set afire with piercing flames even hearts adamantine.
Face rose-hued, cherry-red, with a silver taint like a lily,
Venus' pride might abate, might abash with a blush to behold
    her.
Phoebus' wires, compared to her hairs, unworthy the praising;
Juno's state and Pallas' wit disgraced with the graces
That graced her, whom poor Corydon did choose for a
    love-mate.
Ah! but had Corydon now seen the star that Alexis
Likes and loves so dear that he melts to sighs when he sees
    her:
Did Corydon but see those eyes, those amorous eyelids,
From whence fly holy flames of death or life in a moment:
Ah! did he see that face, those hairs that Venus Apollo
'Bashed to behold, and both, disgraced, did grieve that a
    creature
Should exceed in hue, compare both a god and a goddess:
Ah! had he seen my sweet paramour, the saint of Alexis,
Then had he said 'Phyllis, sit down surpassëd in all points,
For there is one more fair than thou, beloved of Alexis.'
Ibid.   *Greene.*

lief] dear, beloved.   saint] N.A.; taint, 1590.*

ROSALIND'S MADRIGAL

Love in my bosom like a bee
   Doth suck his sweet;
Now with his wings he plays with me,
   Now with his feet.
Within mine eyes he makes his nest,
His bed amidst my tender breast;
My kisses are his daily feast,
And yet he robs me of my rest:
   Ah, wanton, will ye?

And if I sleep, then percheth he
   With pretty flight,
And makes his pillow of my knee
   The livelong night.
Strike I my lute, he tunes the string;
He music plays if so I sing;
He lends me every lovely thing;
Yet cruel he my heart doth sting:
   Whist, wanton, still ye!—

Else I with roses every day
   Will whip you hence,
And bind you, when you long to play,
   For your offence.
I 'll shut mine eyes to keep you in,
I 'll make you fast it for your sin,
I 'll count your power not worth a pin,—
Alas! what hereby shall I win
   If he gainsay me?

What if I beat the wanton boy
   With many a rod?

He will repay me with annoy,
    Because a god.
Then sit thou safely on my knee,
And let thy bower my bosom be;
Lurk in mine eyes, I like of thee.
O Cupid, so thou pity me,
    Spare not, but play thee!   *Lodge.*

Rosalind, 1590. (Text 1592.)*

A FANCY

First shall the heavens want starry light,
The seas be robbëd of their waves;
The day want sun, and sun want bright,
The night want shade, the dead men graves;
    The April, flowers and leaf and tree,
    Before I false my faith to thee.

First shall the tops of highest hills,
By humble plains be overpried;
And poets scorn the Muses' quills;
And fish forsake the water-glide;
    And Iris lose her coloured weed,
    Before I fail thee at thy need.

First direful hate shall turn to peace,
And love relent in deep disdain;
And death his fatal stroke shall cease,
And envy pity every pain;
    And pleasure mourn, and sorrow smile,
    Before I talk of any guile.

First time shall stay his stayless race,
And winter bless his brows with corn;

And snow bemoisten Jùly's face,
And winter spring, and summer mourn,
  Before my pen by help of fame
  Cease to recite thy sacred name.   *Lodge.*

Rosalind, 1590. (Text 1592.)

ROSALIND

Like to the clear in highest sphere
Where all imperial glory shines,
Of selfsame colour is her hair
Whether unfolded, or in twines:
  Heigh ho, fair Rosalind!
Her eyes are sapphires set in snow,
Resembling heaven by every wink;
The gods do fear whenas they glow,
And I do tremble when I think,
  Heigh ho, would she were mine!

Her cheeks are like the blushing cloud
That beautifies Aurora's face,
Or like the silver crimson shroud
That Phoebus' smiling looks doth grace;
  Heigh ho, fair Rosalind!
Her lips are like two budded roses
Whom ranks of lilies neighbour nigh,
Within which bounds she balm encloses
Apt to entice a deity:
  Heigh ho, would she were mine!

Her neck like to a stately tower
Where Love himself imprisoned lies,
To watch for glances every hour

From her divine and sacred eyes:
   Heigh ho, fair Rosalind!
Her paps are centres of delight,
Her breasts are orbs of heavenly frame,
Where Nature moulds the dew of light
To feed perfection with the same:
   Heigh ho, would she were mine!

With orient pearl, with ruby red,
With marble white, with sapphire blue,
Her body every way is fed,
Yet soft in touch and sweet in view:
   Heigh ho, fair Rosalind!
Nature herself her shape admires;
The gods are wounded in her sight;
And Love forsakes his heavenly fires
And at her eyes his brand doth light:
   Heigh ho, would she were mine!

Then muse not, Nymphs, though I bemoan
The absence of fair Rosalind,
Since for her fair there is fairer none,
Nor for her virtues so divine:
   Heigh ho, fair Rosalind;
Heigh ho, my heart! would God that she were mine!

Lodge.

Ibid.

HIS GOLDEN LOCKS TIME HATH TO SILVER TURNED

His golden locks time hath to silver turned;
   O time too swift, O swiftness never ceasing!
His youth 'gainst time and age hath ever spurned,
   But spurned in vain; youth waneth by increasing:

Beauty, strength, youth, are flowers but fading seen;
Duty, faith, love, are roots, and ever green.

His helmet now shall make a hive for bees;
    And, lovers' sonnets turned to holy psalms,
A man-at-arms must now serve on his knees,
    And feed on prayers, which are age his alms:
But though from court to cottage he depart,
His saint is sure of his unspotted heart.

And when he saddest sits in homely cell,
    He 'll teach his swains this carol for a song,—
'Blest be the hearts that wish my sovereign well,
    Curst be the souls that think her any wrong.'
Goddess, allow this agèd man his right,
To be your beadsman now that was your knight.

Peele.

Polyhymnia, 1590.

OF DEATH

Alas, with what tormenting fire
Us martyreth this blind desire
    To stay our life from flying!
How ceaselessly our minds doth rack,
How heavy lies upon our back,
    This dastard fear of dying!

Death rather healthful succour gives,
Death rather all mishaps relieves
    That life upon us throweth;
And ever to us doth unclose
The door whereby from cureless woes
    Our weary soul out goeth.

What goddess else more mild than she
To bury all our pains can be?
　　What remedy more pleasing?
Our painëd hearts when dolour stings
And nothing rest or respite brings,
　　What help have we more easing?

Hope, which to us doth comfort give
And doth our fainting hearts revive,
　　Hath not such force in anguish:
For, promising a vain relief,
She oft us fails in midst of grief,
　　And helpless lets us languish.

But Death, who call on her at need,
Doth never with vain semblant feed,
　　But, when them sorrow paineth,
So rids their souls of all distress,
Whose heavy weight did them oppress,
　　That not one grief remaineth.

Countess of Pembroke.

Antonius, 1592. (Written 1590.)*

BEHOLD, O MAN

Behold, O man, that toilsome pains dost take,
The flowers, the fields, and all that pleasant grows,
How they themselves do thine ensample make,
Whiles nothing-envious nature them forth throws
Out of her fruitful lap; how, no man knows,
They spring, they bud, they blossom fresh and fair,
And deck the world with their rich pompous shows;
　Yet no man for them taketh pains or care,
Yet no man to them can his careful pains compare.

The lily, lady of the flowering field,
The flower-de-luce, her lovely paramour,
Bid thee to them thy fruitless labours yield,
And soon leave off this toilsome weary stour:
Lo! lo, how brave she decks her bounteous bower,
With silken curtains and gold coverlets,
Therein to shroud her sumptuous belamour,
Yet neither spins nor cards, ne cares nor frets,
But to her mother nature all her care she lets.

Why then dost thou, O man, that of them all
Art lord, and eke of nature sovereign,
Wilfully make thyself a wretched thrall,
And waste thy joyous hours in needless pain,
Seeking for danger and adventures vain?
What boots it all to have, and nothing use?
Who shall him rue, that, swimming in the main,
Will die for thirst, and water doth refuse?
Refuse such fruitless toil, and present pleasures choose.

Spenser.

The Faerie Queen, 1590. (Bk. ii. Cant. vi.)

GATHER THE ROSE

The whiles some one did chant this lovely lay—
Ah, see, who so fair thing dost fain to see,
In springing flower the image of thy day;
Ah, see the virgin rose, how sweetly she
Doth first peep forth with bashful modesty,
That fairer seems, the less ye see her may;
Lo, see, soon after, how more bold and free
Her barèd bosom she doth broad display;
Lo, see, soon after, how she fades and falls away.

So passeth, in the passing of a day,
Of mortal life, the leaf, the bud, the flower,
Ne more doth flourish after first decay,
That erst was sought to deck both bed and bower
Of many a lady, and many a paramour:
Gather therefore the rose whilst yet is prime,
For soon comes age that will her pride deflower:
Gather the rose of love whilst yet is time,
Whilst loving thou may'st lovëd be with equal crime.

Spenser.

Ibid. (Bk. II. Cant. xii.)

PHYLLIDA AND CORYDON

In the merry month of May,
In a morn by break of day,
Forth I walked by the woodside,
Whenas May was in his pride.
There I spiëd all alone
Phyllida and Corydon.
Much ado there was, God wot,
He would love and she would not.
She said, never man was true;
He said, none was false to you.
He said, he had loved her long;
She said, love should have no wrong.
Corydon would kiss her then;
She said, maids must kiss no men
Till they did for good and all.
Then she made the shepherd call
All the heavens to witness truth,
Never loved a truer youth.
Thus with many a pretty oath,

Yea and nay, and faith and troth,
Such as silly shepherds use
When they will not love abuse;
Love, which had been long deluded,
Was with kisses sweet concluded.
And Phyllida with garlands gay
Was made the Lady of the May.   *Breton.*

*The Honourable Entertainment given to the Queen's Majesty in Progress
at Elvetham,* 1591.

A PASTORAL

Sweet birds! that sit and sing amid the shady valleys,
And see how sweetly Phyllis walks amid her garden alleys,
Go round about her bower, and sing as ye are bidden:
To her is only known his faith that from the world is hidden.
And she among you all that hath the sweetest voice,
Go chirp of him that never told, yet never changed, his
choice.

And not forget his faith that lived for ever loved
Yet never made his fancy known, nor ever favour moved;
And ever let your ground of all your grace be this—
'To you, to you, to you the due of love and honour is,
On you, on you, on you our music all attendeth,
For as on you our Muse begun, in you all music endeth!'

Breton(?)

Britton's Bower of Delights, 1597. (Registered and first printed, 1591.)*

HARK, ALL YOU LADIES

Hark, all you ladies that do sleep!
The fairy queen Proserpina

Bids you awake, and pity them that weep.
        You may do in the dark
            What the day doth forbid.
        Fear not the dogs that bark;
            Night will have all hid.

But if you let your lovers moan,
        The fairy queen Proserpina
Will send abroad her fairies everyone,
        That shall pinch black and blue
            Your white hands and fair arms,
        That did not kindly rue
            Your paramours' harms.

In myrtle arbours on the downs,
        The fairy queen Proserpina
This night by moonshine, leading merry rounds,
        Holds a watch with sweet Love,
            Down the dale, up the hill,
        No plaints nor griefs may move
            Their holy vigil.

All you that will hold watch with Love,
        The fairy queen Proserpina
Will make you fairer than Diana's dove.
        Roses red, lilies white,
            And the clear damask hue,
        Shall on your cheeks alight.
            Love will adorn you.

All you that love, or loved before,
        The fairy queen Proserpina
Bids you increase that loving humour more.
        They that have not yet fed

On delight amorous,
She vows that they shall lead
Apes in Avernus.   *Campion.*

Astrophel and Stella, 1591.

KISSES

My Love bound me with a kiss
　That I should no longer stay;
When I felt so sweet a bliss
　I had less power to part away:
Alas! that women doth not know
Kisses make men loth to go.

Yes, she knows it but too well,
　For I heard when Venus' dove
In her ear did softly tell
　That kisses were the seals of love:
Oh, muse not then though it be so,
Kisses make men loth to go.

Wherefore did she thus inflame
　My desires, heat my blood,
Instantly to quench the same
　And starve whom she had given food?
I the common sense can show,
Kisses make men loth to go.

Had she bid me go at first
　It would ne'er have grieved my heart,
Hope delayed had been the worst.
　But ah, to kiss and then to part!—
How deep it struck, speak, gods, you know
Kisses make men loth to go.   *Campion(?)*

R. Jones' *Songs and Airs*, ii, 1601. (First stanza in *Astrophel and Stella*, 1591.)

SONNET

The azured vault, the crystal circles bright,
The gleaming fiery torches powdered there;
The changing round, the shining beamy light,
The sad and bearded fires, the monsters fair;
The prodigies appearing in the air;
The rearding thunders and the blustering winds;
The fowls in hue and shape and nature rare,
The pretty notes that winged musicians finds;
In earth, the savoury flowers, the metalled minds,
The wholesome herbs, the hautie pleasant trees,
The silver streams, the beasts of sundry kinds,
The bounded roars and fishes of the seas,—
    All these, for teaching man, the Lord did frame
    To do his will whose glory shines in thame.

The Lepanto, 1591   *King James I.*

PLUCK THE FRUIT AND TASTE THE PLEASURE

Pluck the fruit and taste the pleasure,
    Youthful Lordings, of delight;
Whilst occasion gives you seizure,
    Feed your fancies and your sight:
      After death, when you are gone,
      Joy and pleasure is there none.

Here on earth nothing is stable,
    Fortune's changes well are known;
Whilst as youth doth then enable,
    Let your seeds of joy be sown:
      After death, when you are gone,
      Joy and pleasure is there none.

---

rearding] roaring.   minds] mines.   hautie] tall, high.

Feast it freely with your lovers,
  Blithe and wanton sweets do fade,
Whilst that lovely Cupid hovers
  Round about this lovely shade:
    Sport it freely one to one,
    After death is pleasure none.

Now the pleasant spring allureth,
  And both place and time invites:
But, alas, what heart endureth
  To disclaim his sweet delights?
    After death, when we are gone,
    Joy and pleasure is there none.   *Lodge.*

Robert, second Duke of Normandy, 1591.

WHAT THING IS LOVE?

What thing is love? for, well I wot, love is a thing.
It is a prick, it is a sting,
It is a pretty pretty thing;
It is a fire, it is a coal,
Whose flame creeps in at every hole;
And as my wit doth best devise,
Love's dwelling is in ladies' eyes:
From whence do glance love's piercing darts
That make such holes into our hearts;
And all the world herein accord
Love is a great and mighty lord,
And when he list to mount so high,
With Venus he in heaven doth lie,
And evermore hath been a god
Since Mars and she played even and odd.   *Peele.*

The Hunting of Cupid, [1591]. Drummond MSS. vol. vii.*
But, alas] Mod. eds.; Out alas, 1591.

WITH FRAGRANT FLOWERS WE STREW THE WAY

With fragrant flowers we strew the way,
And make this our chief holiday:
For though this clime were blessed of yore,
Yet was it never proud before.
    O beauteous Queen of second Troy,
    Accept of our unfeignëd joy!

Now th' air is sweeter than sweet balm,
And satyrs dance about the palm;
Now earth, with verdure newly dight,
Gives perfect sign of her delight.
    O beauteous Queen of second Troy,
    Accept of our unfeignëd joy!

Now birds record new harmony,
And trees do whistle melody;
Now every thing that nature breeds
Doth clad itself in pleasant weeds.
    O beauteous Queen of second Troy,
    Accept of our unfeignëd joy!   *Watson.*

*The Honourable Entertainment given to the Queen's Majesty in Progress
at Elvetham*, 1591.

SONNET

I saw the object of my pining thought
Within a garden of sweet Nature's placing;
Wherein an arbour, artificial wrought,
By workman's wondrous skill the garden gracing,
Did boast his glory, glory far renownëd,
For in his shady boughs my mistress slept:
And with a garland of his branches crownëd,
Her dainty forehead from the sun ykept.

Imperious Love upon her eyelids tending,
Playing his wanton sports at every beck,
And into every finest limb descending,
From eyes to lips, from lips to ivory neck;
   And every limb supplied, and t' every part
   Had free accèss, but durst not touch her heart.

The Tears of Fancy, 1593. (Written before 1592.)   *Watson.*

SONG

Whenas the rye reach to the chin,
And chopcherry, chopcherry ripe within,
Strawberries swimming in the cream,
And schoolboys playing in the stream;
Then oh, then oh, then oh, my true Love said,
Till that time come again
She could not live a maid.   *Peele.*

The Old Wife's Tale, 1595. (Written c. 1591–4.)

WHAT IF A DAY OR A MONTH OR A YEAR

What if a day, or a month, or a year
   Crown thy desire with a thousand sweet contentings;
Cannot the chance of a night or an hour
   Cross thy delight with as many sad tormentings?
      Fortune, honour, beauty, youth,
        Are but blossoms dying;
      Wanton pleasures, doting love,
        Are but shadows flying.
         All our joys
         Are but toys,
       Idle thoughts deceiving.
        None have power

supplied] filled.   month] MS. 112; night, MS. 148.   as many] MS. 112;
a thousand, MS. 148.

Of an hour
In their lives' bereaving.

Earth's but a point to the world; and a man
    Is but a point to the earth's comparèd centre.
Shall then a point in a point be so vain
    As to triumph in a silly point's adventure?
            All is hazard that we have,
                Here is no abiding;
            Days of pleasure are but streams
                Through fair meadows gliding.
                    Weal or woe,
                    Time doth go,
                In time 's no returning.
                    Secret fates
                    Guide our states
                Both in mirth and mourning.   *Campion(?)*

Bodley MS. Rawl. Poet. 148, [c. 1599].* (Also in MS. Rawl. Poet. 112,
c. 1592.)

AN ODE

Now each creature joys the other,
    Passing happy days and hours;
One bird reports unto another
    In the fall of silver showers;
Whilst the earth, our common mother,
    Hath her bosom decked with flowers.

Whilst the greatest torch of heaven
    With bright rays warms Flora's lap;
Making nights and days both even,
    Cheering plants with fresher sap;
My field of flowers, quite bereaven,
    Wants refresh of better hap.

are but] MS. 112; like to, MS. 148.   weal] MS. 112; wealth, MS. 148.

Echo, daughter of the air,
  Babbling guest of rocks and hills,
Knows the name of my fierce Fair,
  And sounds the accents of my ills:
Each thing pities my despair,
  Whilst that she her lover kills.

Whilst that she, O cruel maid!
  Doth me and my love despise,
My life's flourish is decayed
  That depended on her eyes:
But her will must be obeyed.
  And well he ends, for love who dies.   *Daniel.*

Delia, 1592. (Text 1602.)

SONNETS

Fair is my Love, and cruel as she 's fair;
Her brow-shades frowns, although her eyes are sunny;
Her smiles are lightning, though her pride despair,
And her disdains are gall, her favours honey.
A modest maid, decked with a blush of honour,
Whose feet do tread green paths of youth and love;
The wonder of all eyes that look upon her,
Sacred on earth, designed a saint above.
Chastity and beauty, which were deadly foes,
Live reconcilëd friends within her brow;
And had she pity to conjoin with those,
Then who had heard the plaints I utter now?
  For had she not been fair, and thus unkind,
  My Muse had slept, and none had known my mind.
                                              Daniel.
Ibid.

Look, Delia, how we esteem the half-blown rose,
The image of thy blush and summer's honour,
Whilst yet her tender bud doth undisclose
That full of beauty, Time bestows upon her;
No sooner spreads her glory in the air,
But straight her wide-blown pomp comes to decline;
She then is scorned, that late adorned the fair:
So fade the roses of those cheeks of thine.
No April can revive thy withered flowers,
Whose springing grace adorns thy glory now:
Swift speedy Time, feathered with flying hours,
Dissolves the beauty of the fairest brow.
  Then do not thou such treasure waste in vain,
  But love now whilst thou may'st be loved again.

Daniel.

Ibid.

But love whilst that thou may'st be loved again,
Now whilst thy May hath filled thy lap with flowers;
Now whilst thy beauty bears without a stain,
Now use the summer smiles, ere winter lours.
And whilst thou spread'st unto the rising sun
The fairest flower that ever saw the light,
Now joy thy time before thy sweet be done;
And, Delia, think thy morning must have night,
And that thy brightness sets at length to west,
When thou wilt close up that which now thou show'st;
And think the same becomes thy fading best,
Which then shall most inveil and shadow most.
  Men do not weigh the stalk for that it was,
  When once they find her flower, her glory, pass.

Daniel.

Ibid.

When men shall find thy flower, thy glory, pass,
And thou, with careful brow sitting alone,
Receivëd hast this message from thy glass,
That tells the truth and says that all is gone;
Fresh shalt thou see in me the wounds thou madest,
Though spent thy flame, in me the heat remaining:
I that have loved thee thus before thou fadest,
My faith shall wax, when thou art in thy waning.
The world shall find this miracle in me,
That fire can burn when all the matter 's spent:
Then what my faith hath been thyself shalt see,
And that thou wast unkind thou may'st repent.
   Thou may'st repent that thou hast scorned my tears,
   When winter snows upon thy sable hairs.

Daniel.

Delia, 1592. (Text 1602.)

Beauty, sweet Love, is like the morning dew,
Whose short refresh upon the tender green
Cheers for a time, but till the sun doth shew,
And straight 'tis gone as it had never been.
Soon doth it fade that makes the fairest flourish,
Short is the glory of the blushing rose,
The hue which thou so carefully dost nourish,
Yet which at length thou must be forced to lose.
When thou, surcharged with burthen of thy years,
Shalt bend thy wrinkles homeward to the earth,
And that, in beauty's lease expired, appears
The date of age, the Kalends of our death—
   But ah, no more! this must not be foretold,
   For women grieve to think they must be old.

Daniel.

Ibid.

I must not grieve my Love, whose eyes would read
Lines of delight, whereon her youth might smile:
Flowers have a time before they come to seed,
And she is young, and now must sport the while:
And sport, sweet maid, in season of these years,
And learn to gather flowers before they wither;
And where the sweetest blossoms first appears
Let love and youth conduct thy pleasures thither.
Lighten forth smiles to clear the clouded air,
And calm the tempest which my sighs do raise:
Pity and smiles do best become the fair,
Pity and smiles must only yield thee praise.
   Make me to say, when all my griefs are gone,
   'Happy the heart that sighed for such a one!'

Daniel.

Ibid.

Care-charmer Sleep, son of the sable night,
Brother to death, in silent darkness born,
Relieve my languish, and restore the light;
With dark forgetting of my care return.
And let the day be time enough to mourn
The shipwreck of my ill-adventured youth:
Let waking eyes suffice to wail their scorn,
Without the torment of the night's untruth.
Cease, dreams, the images of day-desires,
To model forth the passions of the morrow;
Never let rising sun approve you liars,
To add more grief to aggravate my sorrow:
   Still let me sleep, embracing clouds in vain,
   And never wake to feel the day's disdain.

Daniel.

Ibid.

Let others sing of knights and paladins
In agëd accents and untimely words,
Paint shadows in imaginary lines,
Which well the reach of their high wits records:
But I must sing of thee, and those fair eyes
Authentic shall my verse in time to come,
When yet the unborn shall say, 'Lo, where she lies,
Whose beauty made him speak that else was dumb.'
These are the arks, the trophies, I erect,
That fortify thy name against old age;
And these thy sacred virtues must protect
Against the dark and Time's consuming rage.
    Though the error of my youth in them appear,
    Suffice they show I lived, and loved thee dear.

Daniel.

Delia, 1592. (Text 1602.)

FIE, FIE ON BLIND FANCY!

Fie, fie on blind fancy!
It hinders youth's joy:
Fair virgins, learn by me
To count Love a toy.
When Love learned first the A B C of delight,
And knew no figures nor conceited phrase,
He simply gave to due desert her right,
He led not lovers in dark winding ways;
He plainly willed to love, or flatly answered no.
But now who lists to prove, shall find it nothing so.
Fie, fie, then, on fancy!
It hinders youth's joy:
Fair virgins, learn by me
To count Love a toy.

For since he learned to use the poet's pen,
He learned likewise with smoothing words to feign,
Witching chaste ears with trothless tongues of men,
And wrongëd faith with falsehood and disdain.
He gives a promise now, anon he sweareth no:
Who listeth for to prove, shall find his changings so.

>   *Fie, fie, then, on fancy!*
>   *It hinders youth's joy:*
>   *Fair virgins, learn by me*
>   *To count Love a toy.*   **Greene.**

Greene's Groatsworth of Wit, 1592.

BEAUTY, ALAS, WHERE WAST THOU BORN

Beauty, alas, where wast thou born,
Thus to hold thyself in scorn?
Whenas Beauty kissed to woo thee,
Thou by Beauty dost undo me:
        Heigh-ho! despise me not.

I and thou in sooth are one,
Fairer thou, I fairer none:
Wanton thou, and wilt thou, wanton,
Yield a cruel heart to plant on?
Do me right, and do me reason;
Cruelty is cursëd treason:
        Heigh-ho! I love, heigh-ho! I love,
        Heigh-ho! and yet he eyes me not.

                                        Lodge, or *Greene.*

A Looking Glass for London and England, 1594. (Mentioned in Henslowe's
Diary, March 1591/2.)

MY MISTRESS

My mistress is a paragon,
   The fairest fair alive:
Atrides and Aeacides
   For fair less fair did strive.
Her colour fresh as damask rose,
   Her breath as violet,
Her body white as ivory,
   As smooth as polished jet,
As soft as down: and were she down
   Jove might come down and kiss
A love so fresh, so sweet, so white,
   So smooth, so soft, as this.   *Warner.*

Albion's England, Bk. vii., 1592.

SPRING

Spring, the sweet spring, is the year's pleasant king;
Then blooms each thing, then maids dance in a ring,
Cold doth not sting, the pretty birds do sing:
   Cuckoo, jug-jug, pu-we, to-witta-woo!

The palm and may make country houses gay,
Lambs frisk and play, the shepherds pipe all day,
And we hear aye birds tune this merry lay:
   Cuckoo, jug-jug, pu-we, to-witta-woo!

The fields breathe sweet, the daisies kiss our feet,
Young lovers meet, old wives a-sunning sit,
In every street these tunes our ears do greet:
   Cuckoo, jug-jug, pu-we, to-witta-woo!
      Spring, the sweet spring!   *Nashe.*

Summer's Last Will and Testament, 1600. (Acted c. 1592–3.)

A-MAYING, A-PLAYING

Trip and go, heave and ho!
Up and down, to and fro!
From the town to the grove,
Two and two, let us rove
A-maying, a-playing:
Love hath no gainsaying,
So merrily trip and go!   *Nashe.*

Ibid.

FAIR SUMMER DROOPS

Fair summer droops, droop men and beasts therefore;
So fair a summer look for never more:
All good things vanish less than in a day,
Peace, plenty, pleasure, suddenly decay.
  Go not yet away, bright soul of the sad year,
  The earth is hell when thou leav'st to appear.

What, shall those flowers that decked thy garland erst,
Upon thy grave be wastefully dispersed?
O trees, consume your sap in sorrow's source;
Streams, turn to tears your tributary course.
  Go not yet hence, bright soul of the sad year,
  The earth is hell when thou leav'st to appear.

Ibid.   *Nashe.*

AUTUMN

Autumn hath all the summer's fruitful treasure;
Gone is our sport, fled is poor Croydon's pleasure.
Short days, sharp days, long nights come on apace:
Ah, who shall hide us from the winter's face?

Cold doth increase, the sickness will not cease,
And here we lie, God knows, with little ease.
   From winter, plague and pestilence, good Lord, deliver us!

London doth mourn, Lambeth is quite forlorn;
Trades cry, woe worth that ever they were born!
The want of term is town and city's harm;
Close chambers we do want to keep us warm.
Long banishèd must we live from our friends:
This low-built house will bring us to our ends.
   From winter, plague and pestilence, good Lord, deliver us!
                                                    Nashe.

Summer's Last Will and Testament, 1600. (Acted c. 1592–3.)

ADIEU! FAREWELL EARTH'S BLISS!

   Adieu! farewell earth's bliss!
   This world uncertain is:
   Fond are life's lustful joys,
   Death proves them all but toys.
   None from his darts can fly:
   I am sick, I must die.
            Lord, have mercy on us!

   Rich men, trust not in wealth!
   Gold cannot buy you health;
   Physic himself must fade;
   All things to end are made;
   The plague full swift goes by:
   I am sick, I must die.
            Lord, have mercy on us!

   Beauty is but a flower
   Which wrinkles will devour:
   Brightness falls from the air;

Queens have died young and fair;
Dust hath closed Helen's eye:
I am sick, I must die.
>   *Lord, have mercy on us!*

Strength stoops unto the grave:
Worms feed on Hector brave;
Swords may not fight with fate;
Earth still holds ope her gate;
Come! come! the bells do cry.
I am sick, I must die.
>   *Lord, have mercy on us!*

Wit with his wantonness
Tasteth death's bitterness:
Hell's executioner
Hath no ears for to hear
What vain art can reply:
I am sick, I must die.
>   *Lord, have mercy on us!*

Haste, therefore, each degree
To welcome destiny:
Heaven is our heritage,
Earth but a player's stage:
Mount we unto the sky.
I am sick, I must die.
>   *Lord, have mercy on us!*

Nashe.

Ibid.

SONNET

Ah, sweet Content! where is thy mild abode?
Is it with shepherds and light-hearted swains

Which sing upon the downs, and pipe abroad,
Tending their flocks and cattle on the plains?
Ah, sweet Content! where dost thou safely rest?
In heaven with angels which the praises sing
Of him that made, and rules at his behest,
The minds and hearts of every living thing?
Ah, sweet Content! where doth thine harbour hold?
Is it in churches, with religious men
Which please the gods with prayërs manifold,
And in their studies meditate it then?
    Whether thou dost in heaven or earth appear,
    Be where thou wilt, thou wilt not harbour here.

Barnes.

Parthenophil and Parthenophe, 1593.

AN ODE

Why doth heaven bear a sun
   To give the world an heat?
   Why, there, have stars a seat?
On earth, when all is done,
Parthenophe's bright sun
   Doth give a greater heat;

And in her heaven there be
   Such fair bright blazing stars,
   Which still make open wars
With those in heaven's degree:
These stars far brighter be
   Than brightest of heaven's stars.

Why doth earth bring forth roses,
   Violets, or lilies,
   Or bright daffodillies?

In her clear cheeks she closes
Sweet damask roses;
    In her neck, white lilies;

Violets in her veins.
    Why do men sacrifice
    Incense to deities?
Her breath more favour gains,
And please the heavenly veins
    More than rich sacrifice.   *Barnes.*

Ibid.

CORYDON TO HIS PHYLLIS

Alas, my heart! mine eye hath wrongëd thee,
    Presumptuous eye, to gaze on Phyllis' face,
Whose heavenly eye no mortal man may see
    But he must die, or purchase Phyllis' grace.
        Poor Corydon! the nymph, whose eye doth move thee,
        Doth love to draw, but is not drawn to love thee.

Her beauty, Nature's pride and shepherds' praise;
    Her eye, the heavenly planet of my life;
Her matchless wit and grace her fame displays,
    As if that Jove had made her for his wife:
        Only her eyes shoot fiery darts to kill,
        Yet is her heart as cold as Caucase hill.

My wings too weak to fly against the sun,
    Mine eyes unable to sustain her light,
My heart doth yield that I am quite undone—
    Thus hath fair Phyllis slain me with her sight:
        My bud is blasted, withered is my leaf,
        And all my corn is rotted in the sheaf.

Phyllis, the golden fetter of my mind!
   My fancy's idol and my vital power!
Goddess of nymphs and honour of thy kind!
   This age's phoenix, beauty's bravest bower!—
      Poor Corydon for love of thee must die,
      Thy beauty's thrall, and conquest of thine eye.

Leave, Corydon, to plough the barren field,
   Thy buds of hope are blasted with disgrace;
For Phyllis' looks no hearty love do yield,
   Nor can she love, for all her lovely face.
      Die, Corydon! the spoil of Phyllis' eye;
      She cannot love, and therefore thou must die!

Dyer.

The Phoenix Nest, 1593.

SONNET

Like Memnon's rock, touched with the rising sun,
Which yields a sound and echoes forth a voice;
But, when it 's drowned in western seas, is dumb,
And drowsy-like leaves off to make a noise:
So I, my Love, enlightened with your shine,
A poet's skill within my soul I shroud,
Not rude like that which finer wits decline,
But such as Muses to the best allowed:
But when your figure and your shape is gone,
I speechless am, like as I was before;
Or if I write, my verse is filled with moan,
And blurred with tears by falling in such store:
   Then muse not, Licia, if my Muse be slack;
   For when I wrote I did thy beauty lack.

G. Fletcher (the elder).

Licia, 1593.

OF FORTUNE

Fortune, in power imperious,
Used o'er the world and worldlings thus
        To tyrannize:
When she hath heaped her gifts on us,
        Away she flies.

Her feet, more swift than is the wind,
Are more inconstant in their kind
        Than autumn blasts;
A woman's shape, a woman's mind,
        That seldom lasts.

One while she bends her angry brow,
And of no labour will allow;
        Another while
She fleers again, I know not how,
        Still to beguile.

Fickle in our adversities,
And fickle when our fortunes rise,
        She scoffs at us,
That, blind herself, can blear our eyes
        To trust her thus.

The sun, that lends the earth his light,
Beheld her never over-night
        Lie calmly down,
But, in the morrow following, might
        Perceive her frown.

She hath not only power and will
To abuse the vulgar wanting skill,

But, when she list,
To kings and clowns doth equal ill
Without resist.

From chance is nothing franchisëd:
And till the time that they are dead
Is no man blessed:
He only that no death doth dread
Doth live at rest.   *Kyd.*

Cornelia, 1594.* (Written 1593.)

A FANCY

When I admire the rose
That Nature makes repose
In you the best of many,
More fair and blessed than any,
And see how curious art
Hath deckëd every part,
I think, with doubtful view,
Whether you be the rose, or the rose is you.   *Lodge.*

The Life and Death of William Longbeard, 1593.

LOVE GUARDS THE ROSES OF THY LIPS

Love guards the roses of thy lips
    And flies about them like a bee;
If I approach he forward skips,
    And if I kiss he stingeth me.

Love in thine eyes doth build his bower,
    And sleeps within their pretty shine;

guards] Bullen, 1891; guides, 1593.

And if I look the boy will lour,
   And from their orbs shoots shafts divine.

Love works thy heart within his fire,
   And in my tears doth firm the same;
And if I tempt it will retire,
   And of my plaints doth make a game.

Love, let me cull her choicest flowers;
   And pity me, and calm her eye;
Make soft her heart, dissolve her lours;
   Then will I praise thy deity.

But if thou do not, Love, I 'll truly serve her
In spite of thee, and by firm faith deserve her.   *Lodge.*

Phyllis: honoured with Pastoral Sonnets, 1593.

PHYLLIS

My Phyllis hath the morning sun
   At first to look upon her;
And Phyllis hath morn-waking birds
   Her risings for to honour.
My Phyllis hath prime-feathered flowers
   That smile when she treads on them;
And Phyllis hath a gallant flock
   That leaps since she doth own them.
But Phyllis hath so hard a heart—
   Alas that she should have it!—
As yields no mercy to desart,
   Nor grace to those that crave it.

Sweet sun, when thou lookest on,
   Pray her regard my moan;

doth firm] temper, as iron.

Sweet birds, when you sing to her,
To yield some pity, woo her;
Sweet flowers, whenas she treads on,
Tell her, her beauty deads one:
And if in life her love she nill agree me,
Pray her, before I die she will come see me.   *Lodge.*

Phyllis, 1593.

AN ODE

Now I find thy looks were feignéd,
Quickly lost and quickly gainéd.
Soft thy skin like wool of wethers;
Heart unstable, light as feathers;
Tongue untrusty, subtle sighted;
Wanton will with change delighted.
   Siren pleasant, foe to reason,
   Cupid plague thee for this treason!

Of thine eyes I made my mirror,
From thy beauty came mine error;
All thy words I counted witty,
All thy smiles I deeméd pity;
Thy false tears that me aggrievéd
First of all my trust deceivéd.
   Siren pleasant, foe to reason,
   Cupid plague thee for this treason!

Feigned acceptance when I askéd,
Lovely words with cunning maskéd,
Holy vows but heart unholy,
Wretched man! my trust was folly.
Lily-white and pretty winking,

nill] will not.

Solemn vows but sorry thinking.
  Siren pleasant, foe to reason,
  Cupid plague thee for this treason!

Now I see—oh, seemly cruel!—
Others warm them at my fuel.
Wit shall guide me in this durance
Since in love is no assurance.
Change thy pasture, take thy pleasure,
Beauty is a fading treasure.
  Siren pleasant, foe to reason,
  Cupid plague thee for this treason!

Prime youth lasts not, age will follow
And make white these tresses yellow;
Wrinkled face for looks delightful
Shall acquaint the dame despiteful;
And when time shall date thy glory
Then too late thou wilt be sorry.
  Siren pleasant, foe to reason,
  Cupid plague thee for thy treason!   Lodge.

Ibid. (Also in *The Phoenix Nest*, 1593.)

FOR PITY, PRETTY EYES, SURCEASE

For pity, pretty eyes, surcease
To give me war, and grant me peace!
Triumphant eyes, why bear you arms
Against a heart that thinks no harms,
A heart already quite appalled,
A heart that yields and is enthralled?
Kill rebels, proudly that resist;
Not those that in true faith persist

date] *The Phoenix Nest;* eat, *Phyllis.*

And, conquered, serve your deity.
Will you, alas, command me die?
Then die I yours, and death my cross;
But unto you pertains the loss.   *Lodge.*

The Phoenix Nest, 1593.

LOVE'S WITCHERY

My bonny lass, thine eye,
        So sly,
Hath made me sorrow so;
Thy crimson cheeks, my dear,
        So clear,
Have so much wrought my woe;

Thy pleasing smiles and grace,
        Thy face,
Have ravished so my sprites,
That life is grown to nought
            Through thought
Of love, which me affrights.

For fancy's flames of fire
        Aspire
Unto such furious power
As, but the tears I shed
        Make dead
The brands, would me devour;

I should consume to nought
            Through thought
Of thy fair shining eye,
Thy cheeks, thy pleasing smiles,
            The wiles
That forced my heart to die:

Thy grace, thy face, the part
                    Where art
Stands gazing still to see
The wondrous gifts and power,
                    Each hour,
That hath bewitchëd me.   *Lodge.*

Ibid.

WHAT CUNNING CAN EXPRESS

What cunning can express
The favour of her face,
To whom in this distress
    do appeal for grace?
    A thousand Cupids fly
    About her gentle eye.

From which each throws a dart
That kindleth soft sweet fire
Within my sighing heart,
Possessëd by desire;
    No sweeter life I try
    Than in her love to die.

The lily in the field,
That glories in his white,
For pureness now must yield,
And render up his right;
    Heaven pictured in her face
    Doth promise joy and grace.

Fair Cynthia's silver light,
That beats on running streams,
Compares not with her white,

Whose hairs are all sunbeams.
  Her virtues so do shine
  As day unto mine eyne.

With this there is a red
Exceeds the damask rose,
Which in her cheeks is spread,
Whence every favour grows.
  In sky there is no star
  That she surmounts not, far.

When Phoebus from the bed
Of Thetis doth arise,
The morning blushing red
In fair carnation-wise,
  He shows it in her face
  As queen of every grace.

This pleasant lily white,
This taint of roseate red,
This Cynthia's silver light,
This sweet fair Dea spread,
  These sunbeams in mine eye,
  These beauties make me die.   *Oxford.*

The Phoenix Nest, 1593.

A DESCRIPTION OF LOVE

Now what is love, I pray thee tell?
It is that fountain and that well
Where pleasure and repentance dwell.
It is perhaps that saucing bell
That tolls all into heaven or hell:
And this is love, as I hear tell.

---

taint] tint.

Yet what is love, I pray thee say?
It is a work on holy day.
It is December matched with May,
When lusty bloods in fresh array
Hear ten months after of the play:
And this is love, as I hear say.

Yet what is love, I pray thee sain?
It is a sunshine mixed with rain.
It is a tooth-ache, or like pain;
It is a game where none doth gain;
The lass saith No, and would full fain:
And this is love, as I hear sain.

Yet what is love, I pray thee say?
It is a yea, it is a nay,
A pretty kind of sporting fray;
It is a thing will soon away;
Then take the vantage while you may:
And this is love, as I hear say.

Yet what is love, I pray thee show?
A thing that creeps, it cannot go;
A prize that passeth to and fro;
A thing for one, a thing for mo;
And he that proves must find it so:
And this is love, sweet friend, I trow.   *Raleigh.*

Ibid.

ON SIR PHILIP SIDNEY

You knew,—who knew not Astrophil?
(That I should live to say I knew,
And have not in possession still!)

Things known permit me to renew;
  Of him you know his merit such,
  I cannot say, you hear, too much.

Within these woods of Arcady
He chief delight and pleasure took,
And on the mountain Partheny,
Upon the crystal liquid brook,
  The Muses met him every day
  That taught him sing, to write, and say.

When he descended down the mount,
His personage seemed most divine;
A thousand graces one might count
Upon his lovely cheerful eyne;
  To hear him speak and sweetly smile,
  You were in Paradise the while.

A sweet attractive kind of grace,
A full assurance given by looks,
Continual comfort in a face,
The lineaments of Gospel books;
  I trow that countenance cannot lie
  Whose thoughts are legible in the eye.

Was never eye did see that face,
Was never ear did hear that tongue,
Was never mind did mind his grace,
That ever thought the travel long;
  But eyes, and ears, and every thought,
  Were with his sweet perfections caught.

Above all others this is he,
Which erst approvëd in his song

That love and honour might agree,
And that pure love will do no wrong.
  Sweet saints! it is no sin nor blame
  To love a man of virtuous name.

Did never love so sweetly breathe
In any mortal breast before;
Did never Muse inspire beneath
A poet's brain with finer store:
  He wrote of love with high conceit,
  And beauty reared above her height.   *Royden.*

The Phoenix Nest, 1593. (An excerpt from *An Elegy, or friend's passion for
his Astrophil.*)*

TO NIGHT

O Night! O jealous Night, repugnant to my pleasures!
O Night so long desired, yet cross to my content!
There's none but only thou that can perform my pleasures,
Yet none but only thou that hindereth my intent.

Thy beams, thy spiteful beams, thy lamps that burn too
    brightly,
Discover all my trains and naked lay my drifts:
That night by night I hope, yet fail my purpose nightly,
Thy envious glaring gleam defeateth so my shifts.

Sweet Night! withhold thy beams, withhold them till
    to-morrow,
Whose joys in lack so long a hell of torments breeds;
Sweet Night, sweet gentle Night! do not prolong my
    sorrow:
Desire is guide to me, and love no loadstar needs.

L.1, pleasures] 1593; W. J. Linton, 1882, suggests 'measures.'

Let sailors gaze on stars and moon so freshly shining;
Let them that miss the way be guided by the light:
I know my lady's bower, there needs no more divining,
Affection sees in dark, and love hath eyes by night.

Dame Cynthia! couch awhile, hold in thy horns from
    shining,
And glad not louring Night with thy too glorious rays;
But be she dim and dark, tempestuous and repining,
That in her spite my sport may work thy endless praise.

And when my will is wrought, then, Cynthia, shine—good
    lady!—
All other nights and days, in honour of that night,
That happy heavenly night, that night so dark and shady,
Wherein my Love had eyes that lighted my delight.

Anon.

The Phoenix Nest, 1593. Cf. *A Midsummer Night's Dream*, v. i. 171–4.

SONNET

Like to an hermit poor, in place obscure,
I mean to spend my days in endless doubt,
To wail such woes as time cannot recure,
Where none but Love shall ever find me out.
My food shall be of care and sorrow made,
My drink nought else but tears fall'n from mine eyes;
And for my light, in such obscurëd shade,
The flames shall serve that from my heart arise.
A gown of grief my body shall attire;
And broken hope the staff of all my stay;
Of late repentance, linked with long desire,
The couch is made wherein my limbs I 'll lay;

from shining] W. J. Linton, 1882; for shining, 1593.   limbs I'll lay] 1593;
bones do lay, MS.

And at my gate despair shall linger still,
To let in death when Love and fortune will.   *Anon.*

Bodley MS. Rawl. Poet. 85. (Slight variant in *The Phoenix Nest*, 1593.)

SWEET VIOLETS, LOVE'S PARADISE

Sweet violets, Love's paradise, that spread
  Your gracious odours, which you couchèd bear
      Within your paly faces,
Upon the gentle wing of some calm breathing wind
  That plays amidst the plain,
  If by the favour of propitious stars you gain
Such grace as in my lady's bosom place to find,
      Be proud to touch those places;
  And when her warmth your moisture forth doth wear,
Whereby her dainty parts are sweetly fed,
  Your honours of the flowery meads, I pray,
    You pretty daughters of the earth and sun,
  With mild and seemly breathing straight display
    My bitter sighs, that have my heart undone.

Vermilion roses, that with new day's rise
  Display your crimson folds, fresh-looking, fair,
      Whose radiant bright disgraces
The rich adornèd rays of roseate rising morn;
  Ah! if her virgin's hand
  Do pluck your pure, ere Phoebus view the land
And veil your gracious pomp in lovely Nature's scorn;
      If chance my mistress traces
  Fast by your flowers to take the summer's air,
Then, woeful blushing, tempt her glorious eyes
  To spread their tears, Adonis' death reporting,
    And tell Love's torments, sorrowing for her friend,
  Whose drops of blood within your leaves consorting,
    Report fair Venus moans withouten end.

Then may remorse, in pitying of my smart,
Dry up my tears, and dwell within her heart.   *Anon.*

The Phoenix Nest, 1593.

CANZONET

See, see, mine own sweet jewel,
See what I have here for my darling:
A robin-redbreast and a starling.
These I give both, in hope to move thee—
And yet thou say'st I do not love thee.   *Anon.*

T. Morley's *Canzonets,* 1593.*

DAPHNIS TO GANYMEDE

If thou wilt come and dwell with me at home,
My sheep-cote shall be strowed with new green rushes;
We 'll haunt the trembling prickets as they roam
About the fields, along the hawthorn bushes:
  I have a piebald cur to hunt the hare:
  So we will live with dainty forest fare.

Nay, more than this, I have a garden plot,
Wherein there wants nor herbs, nor roots, nor flowers,—
Flowers to smell, roots to eat, herbs for the pot,—
And dainty shelters when the welkin lours:
  Sweet smelling beds of lilies and of roses,
  Which rosemary banks and lavender encloses.

There grows the gillyflower, the mint, the daisy
Both red and white, the blue-veined violet,
The purple hyacinth, the spike to please thee,

The scarlet-dyed carnation bleeding yet,
  The sage, the savory, and sweet marjoram,
  Hyssop, thyme, and eye-bright, good for the blind and
    dumb;

The pink, the primrose, cowslip, and daffadilly,
The harebell blue, the crimson columbine,
Sage, lettuce, parsley, and the milk-white lily,
The rose, and speckled flower called sops-in-wine,
  Fine pretty kingcups, and the yellow boots
  That grows by rivers, and by shallow brooks;

And many thousand moe, I cannot name,
Of herbs and flowers that in gardens grow,
I have for thee; and conies that be tame,
Young rabbits, white as swan, and black as crow,
  Some speckled here and there with dainty spots;
  And more, I have two milch and milk-white goats.

All these, and more, I'll give thee for thy love,
If these, and more, may tice thy love away:
I have a pigeon-house, in it a dove,
Which I love more than mortal tongue can say;
  And, last of all, I'll give thee a little lamb
  To play withal, new-weanèd from her dam.   *Barnfield.*

The Affectionate Shepherd, 1594. (An excerpt.)

A PASTORAL

On a hill there grows a flower,
  Fair befall the dainty sweet!
By that flower there is a bower
  Where the heavenly Muses meet.

In that bower there is a chair,
   Fringëd all about with gold,
Where doth sit the fairest fair
   That did ever eye behold.

It is Phyllis fair and bright,
   She that is the shepherds' joy;
She that Venus did despite,
   And did blind her little boy.

This is she, the wise, the rich,
   That the world desires to see;
This is *ipsa quae* the which
   There is none but only she.

Who would not this face admire?
   Who would not this saint adore?
Who would not this sight desire,
   Though he thought to see no more?

O fair eyes! yet let me see
   One good look, and I am gone;
Look on me, for I am he,
   Thy poor silly Corydon.

Thou that art the shepherds' queen,
   Look upon thy silly swain;
By thy comfort have been seen
   Dead men brought to life again.

Make him live that, dying long,
   Never durst for comfort seek:

That the world] 1597; And the world, MS.

Thou shalt hear so sweet a song
    Never shepherd sung the like.   *Breton.*

B.M. Add. MS. 34064, [c. 1596]. (Variant in *The Arbor of Amorous Devices*, 1597. Registered 1594.)*

A SWEET LULLABY

Come, little babe, come, silly soul,
Thy father's shame, thy mother's grief,
Born as I doubt to all our dole,
And to thyself unhappy chief:
    Sing lullaby and lap it warm,
    Poor soul that thinks no creature harm.

Thou little think'st and less dost know
The cause of this thy mother's moan;
Thou want'st the wit to wail her woe,
And I myself am all alone;
    Why dost thou weep? why dost thou wail,
    And knowest not yet what thou dost ail?

Come, little wretch!—Ah, silly heart!
Mine only joy, what can I more?
If there be any wrong thy smart,
That may the destinies implore,
    'Twas I, I say, against my will:
    I wail the time, but be thou still.

And dost thou smile? Oh, thy sweet face!
Would God himself he might thee see!
No doubt thou wouldst soon purchase grace,
I know right well, for thee and me:
    But come to mother, babe, and play,
    For father false is fled away.

Sweet boy, if it by fortune chance
Thy father home again to send,
If death do strike me with his lance,
Yet may'st thou me to him commend:
    If any ask thy mother's name,
      Tell how by love she purchased blame.

Then will his gentle heart soon yield:
I know him of a noble mind:
Although a lion in the field,
A lamb in town thou shalt him find:
    Ask blessing, babe, be not afraid!
      His sugared words hath me betrayed.

Then may'st thou joy and be right glad,
Although in woe I seem to moan:
Thy father is no rascal lad,
A noble youth of blood and bone,
    His glancing looks, if he once smile,
      Right honest women may beguile.

Come, little boy, and rock asleep!
Sing lullaby, and be thou still!
I, that can do nought else but weep,
Will sit by thee and wail my fill:
    God bless my babe, and lullaby,
      From this thy father's quality.   *Breton(?)*

The Arbor of Amorous Devices, 1597. (Registered 1594.)

SONNETS

Dear to my soul! then leave me not forsaken!
Fly not! my heart within thy bosom sleepeth:
Even from myself and sense I have betaken

Me unto thee, for whom my spirit weepeth;
And on the shore of that salt teary sea,
Couched in a bed of unseen seeming pleasure
Where, in imaginary thoughts, thy fair self lay;
But being waked, robbed of my life's best treasure,
I call the heavens, air, earth, and seas to hear
My love, my truth, and black disdained estate,
Beating the rocks with bellowings of despair,
Which still with plaints my words reverberate:
  Sighing, 'Alas, what shall become of me?'
  Whilst Echo cries, 'What shall become of me?'

Diana, 1594.   *Constable.*

If ever Sorrow spoke from soul that loves,
As speaks a spirit in a man possessed,
In me her spirit speaks, my soul it moves,
Whose sigh-swoln words breed whirlwinds in my breast:
Or like the echo of a passing bell
Which, sounding on the water, seems to howl,
So rings my heart a fearful heavy knell,
And keeps all night in consort with the owl:
My cheeks with a thin ice of tears is clad,
Mine eyes, like morning stars, are bleared and red,
What resteth then but I be raging mad,
To see that she, my care's chief conduit-head,
  When all streams else help quench my burning heart,
  Shuts up her springs, and will no grace impart.

Ibid.   *Constable.*

My lady's presence makes the roses red,
Because to see her lips they blush for shame.
The lily's leaves, for envy, pale became,
And her white hands in them this envy bred.

The marigold the leaves abroad doth spread,
Because the sun's and her power is the same.
The violet of purple colour came,
Dyed in the blood she made my heart to shed.
In brief: all flowers from her their virtue take;
From her sweet breath their sweet smells do proceed;
The living heat which her eyebeams doth make
Warmeth the ground, and quickeneth the seed.
   The rain, wherewith she watereth the flowers,
   Falls from mine eyes, which she dissolves in showers.

Constable.

Diana, 1594.

THE DANCE OF LOVE

This is true Love, by that true Cupid got,
Which danceth galliards in your amorous eyes,
But to your frozen heart approacheth not;
Only your heart he dares not enterprize;
And yet through every other part he flies,
    And everywhere he nimbly danceth now,
    That in yourself, yourself perceive not how.

For your sweet beauty, daintily transfused
With due proportion throughout every part,
What is it but a dance where Love hath used
His finer cunning and more curious art;
Where all the elements themselves impart,
    And turn, and wind, and mingle with such measure,
    That th' eye that sees it, surfeits with the pleasure?

Love in the twinkling of your eyelids danceth;
Love danceth in your pulses, and your veins;
Love, when you sew, your needle's point advanceth,
And makes it dance a thousand curious strains

Of winding rounds, whereof the form remains,
 To show that your fair hands can dance the *Hay*,
 Which your fine feet would learn as well as they.

And when your ivory fingers touch the strings
Of any silver-sounding instrument,
Love makes them dance to those sweet murmurings,
With busy skill and cunning excellent.
Oh, that your feet those tunes would represent
 With artificial motions to and fro,
 That Love, this art in every part might show.

Sir J. Davies.

Orchestra, or a Poem of Dancing, 1596. (An excerpt. Poem registered 1594.)

TITYRUS TO HIS FAIR PHYLLIS

The silly swain whose love breeds discontent,
Thinks death a trifle, life a loathsome thing,
 Sad he looks, sad he lies;
But when his fortune's malice doth relent,
Then of love's sweetness he will sweetly sing;
 Thus he lives, thus he dies.
Then Tityrus, whom love hath happy made,
Will rest thrice happy in this myrtle shade;
 For though love at first did grieve him,
 Yet did love at last relieve him. *Dickenson.*

The Shepherd's Complaint, [c. 1594].

BETHSABE BATHING

Hot sun, cool fire, tempered with sweet air,
Black shade, fair nurse, shadow my white hair:
Shine, sun; burn, fire; breathe, air, and ease me;
Shine, sun; burn, fire; breathe, air, and ease me;

Shadow, my sweet nurse, keep me from burning,
Make not my glad cause cause of mourning.
>   Let not my beauty's fire
>   Inflame unstaid desire,
>   Nor pierce any bright eye
>   That wand'reth lightly.   *Peele.*

David and Bethsabe, 1599. (Registered 1594.)

SONNET

It shall be said I died for Coelia!
Then quick, thou grisly man of Erebus,
Transport me hence unto Proserpina,
To be adjudged as 'wilful amorous':
To be hung up within the liquid air,
For all the sighs which I in vain have wasted:
To be through Lethe's waters cleansëd fair,
For those dark clouds which have my looks o'ercasted:
To be condemned to everlasting fire,
Because at Cupid's fire I wilful brent me;
And to be clad, for deadly dumps, in mire.
Among so many plagues which shall torment me
>   One solace I shall find, when I am over:
>   It will be known I died a constant lover!   *Percy.*

Sonnets to the fairest Coelia, 1594.

TO AVISA

>   Nay then, farewell, if this be so:
>   If you be of the purer stamp,
>   'Gainst wind and tide I cannot row,
>   I have no oil to feed that lamp:

brent] burnt.

        Be not too rash, deny not flat,
        For you refuse you know not what.

But rather take a farther day
For farther trial of my faith,
And rather make some wise delay
To see, and take some farther breath:
        He may too rashly be denied
        Whose faithful heart was never tried.

And though I be by jury cast,
Yet let me live a while in hope:
And though I be condemned at last,
Yet let my fancy have some scope:
        And though the body fly away,
        Yet let me with the shadow play.   *Willoby* (?)

Willobie his Avisa, 1594.*

SONNET

When, from the tower whence I derive love's heaven,
Mine eyes, quick pursuivants, the sight attached
Of thee, all splendent, I, as out of sweven,
Myself gan rouse, like one from sleep awaked.
Coveting eyes controlled my slowly gait,
And wooed desire to wing my feet for flight;
Yet unresolved, fear did with eyes debate,
And said 'twas but tralucence of the light!
But when approached where thou thy stand didst take,
At gaze I stood, like deer, when 'ghast he spies
Some white in thick. Ah, then the arrow strake
Thorough mine heart, sent from thy tiller eyes.

sweven] dream.   tralucence] translucence.   thick] thicket.   tiller] part
of cross-bow which controls direction of arrow.

Dead in thine aim, thou seized what 'longed to thee:
Mine heart, Zepheria, then became thy fee.   *Anon.*

Zepheria, 1594.

THE BLACKBIRD

In midst of woods or pleasant grove
    Where all sweet birds do sing,
Methought I heard so rare a sound,
    Which made the heavens to ring.
The charm was good, the noise full sweet,
    Each bird did play his part;
And I admired to hear the same;
    Joy sprung into my heart.

The blackbird made the sweetest sound,
    Whose tunes did far excel,
Full pleasantly and most profound
    Was all things placëd well.
Thy pretty tunes, mine own sweet bird,
    Done with so good a grace,
Extols thy name, prefers the same
    Abroad in every place.

Thy music grave, bedeckëd well
    With sundry points of skill,
Bewrays thy knowledge excellent,
    Engrafted in thy will.
My tongue shall speak, my pen shall write,
    In praise of thee to tell.
The sweetest bird that ever was,
    In friendly sort, farewell.   *Anon.*

J. Mundy's *Songs and Psalms,* 1594.

TIMES GO BY TURNS

The loppëd tree in time may grow again,
Most naked plants renew both fruit and flower;
The sorriest wight may find release of pain,
The driest soil suck in some moistening shower;
Times go by turns, and chances change by course,
From foul to fair, from better hap to worse.

The sea of fortune doth not ever flow,
She draws her favours to the lowest ebb;
Her tides hath equal times to come and go,
Her loom doth weave the fine and coarsest web;
No joy so great but runneth to an end,
No hap so hard but may in fine amend.

Not always fall of leaf, nor ever spring,
No endless night, yet not eternal day;
The saddest birds a season find to sing,
The roughest storm a calm may soon allay:
Thus, with succeeding turns, God tempereth all,
That man may hope to rise, yet fear to fall.

A chance may win that by mischance was lost;
The net that holds no great, takes little fish;
In some things all, in all things none are crossed;
Few all they need, but none have all they wish.
Unmeddled joys here to no man befall;
Who least, hath some; who most, hath never all.

Saint Peter's Complaint, 1595. (Written before 1595.)   *Southwell.*

UPON THE IMAGE OF DEATH

Before my face the picture hangs,
   That daily should put me in mind

Unmeddled] Unmixed.

Of those cold qualms and bitter pangs
    That shortly I am like to find:
But yet, alas, full little I
Do think hereon that I must die.

I often look upon a face
    Most ugly, grisly, bare, and thin;
I often view the hollow place
    Where eyes and nose had sometimes bin;
I see the bones across that lie,
Yet little think that I must die.

I read the label underneath,
    That telleth me whereto I must;
I see the sentence eke that saith
    'Remember, man, that thou art dust!'
But yet, alas, but seldom I
Do think indeed that I must die.

Continually at my bed's head
    A hearse doth hang, which doth me tell
That I ere morning may be dead,
    Though now I feel myself full well:
But yet, alas, for all this, I
Have little mind that I must die.

The gown which I do use to wear,
    The knife wherewith I cut my meat,
And eke that old and ancient chair
    Which is my only usual seat,—
All these do tell me I must die,
And yet my life amend not I.

qualms] S. Wastell, 1629; names, 1595.

My ancestors are turned to clay,
   And many of my mates are gone;
My youngers daily drop away,
   And can I think to 'scape alone?
No, no, I know that I must die,
And yet my life amend not I.

Not Solomon, for all his wit,
   Nor Samson, though he were so strong,
No king nor person ever yet
   Could 'scape, but death laid him along:
Wherefore I know that I must die,
And yet my life amend not I.

Though all the East did quake to hear
   Of Alexander's dreadful name,
And all the West did likewise fear
   To hear of Julius Caesar's fame,
Yet both by death in dust now lie:
Who then can 'scape, but he must die?

If none can 'scape death's dreadful dart,
   If rich and poor his beck obey,
If strong, if wise, if all do smart,
   Then I to 'scape shall have no way.
Oh! grant me grace, O God, that I
My life may mend, sith I must die.   *Southwell.*

Maeoniae, 1595. (Written before 1595.)

THE BURNING BABE

As I in hoary winter's night stood shivering in the snow,
Surprised I was with sudden heat which made my heart to
    glow;

And lifting up a fearful eye to view what fire was near,
A pretty Babe all burning bright did in the air appear,
Who scorchëd with excessive heat such floods of tears did
    shed,
As though his floods should quench his flames which with
    his tears were bred;
'Alas!' quoth he, 'but newly born, in fiery heats I fry,
Yet none approach to warm their hearts or feel my fire
    but I.
My faultless breast the furnace is, the fuel wounding thorns;
Love is the fire and sighs the smoke, the ashes shames and
    scorns;
The fuel Justice layeth on, and Mercy blows the coals,
The metal in this furnace wrought are men's defilëd souls,
For which, as now on fire I am, to work them to their good,
So will I melt into a bath, to wash them in my blood.'
With this he vanished out of sight, and swiftly shrunk away,
And straight I callëd unto mind that it was Christmas day.

Saint Peter's Complaint, 1602. (Written before 1595.)   *Southwell.*

SPRING

When daisies pied, and violets blue,
    And lady-smocks all silver-white,
And cuckoo-buds of yellow hue
    Do paint the meadows with delight,
The cuckoo then, on every tree,
Mocks married men, for thus sings he,
        Cuckoo, cuckoo!
        O word of fear,
Unpleasing to a married ear!

Spring, lines 2 and 3] Theobald's transposition, 1733; reverse order, 1598
and 1623.   Cuckoo, cuckoo!] See Note.

When shepherds pipe on oaten straws,
   And merry larks are ploughmen's clocks,
When turtles tread, and rooks, and daws,
   And maidens bleach their summer smocks,
The cuckoo then, on every tree,
Mocks married men, for thus sings he,
       Cuckoo, cuckoo!
       O word of fear,
Unpleasing to a married ear!   *Shakespeare.*

Love's Labour's Lost, 1598. (Written 1594–5 ?)*

WINTER

When icicles hang by the wall,
   And Dick the shepherd blows his nail,
And Tom bears logs into the hall,
   And milk comes frozen home in pail,
When blood is nipped, and ways be foul,
Then nightly sings the staring owl,
       Th-wit to-who!
       A merry note,
While greasy Joan doth keel the pot.

When all around the wind doth blow,
   And coughing drowns the parson's saw,
And birds sit brooding in the snow,
   And Marian's nose looks red and raw,
When roasted crabs hiss in the bowl,
Then nightly sings the staring owl,
       Th-wit to-who!
       A merry note,
While greasy Joan doth keel the pot.   *Shakespeare.*

Ibid.

foul] 1623; full, 1598.

ON A DAY—ALACK THE DAY!

On a day—alack the day!—
Love, whose month is ever May,
Spied a blossom, passing fair,
Playing in the wanton air:
Through the velvet leaves the wind,
All unseen, gan passage find;
That the lover, sick to death,
Wished himself the heaven's breath.
Air, quoth he, thy cheeks may blow;
Air, would I might triumph so!
But, alack, my hand is sworn
Ne'er to pluck thee from thy thorn:
Vow, alack, for youth unmeet,
Youth so apt to pluck a sweet.
Do not call it sin in me
That I am forsworn for thee:
Thou for whom Jove would swear
Juno but an Ethiope were,
And deny himself for Jove,
Turning mortal for thy love.   *Shakespeare.*

Love's Labour's Lost, 1598. (Written 1594–5 ?)

SO SWEET A KISS

So sweet a kiss the golden sun gives not
    To those fresh morning drops upon the rose,
As thy eye-beams, when their fresh rays have smote
    The night of dew that on my cheeks down flows:
Nor shines the silver moon one half so bright

---

gan] *Passionate Pilgrim*, 1599; can, 1598 and 1623.   wished] 1632, and
Passionate Pilgrim, 1599; wish, 1598 and 1623.

Through the transparent bosom of the deep,
As doth thy face through tears of mine give light:
   Thou shinest in every tear that I do weep;
No drop but as a coach doth carry thee,
   So ridest thou triumphing in my woe:
Do but behold the tears that swell in me,
   And they thy glory through my grief will show:
But do not love thyself; then thou wilt keep
My tears for glasses, and still make me weep.
O Queen of queens! how far dost thou excel,
No thought can think, nor tongue of mortal tell.

Shakespeare.

Ibid.

WHO IS SILVIA

Who is Silvia? what is she,
   That all our swains commend her?
Holy, fair, and wise is she;
   The heaven such grace did lend her,
That she might admirèd be.

Is she kind as she is fair?
   For beauty lives with kindness.
Love doth to her eyes repair,
   To help him of his blindness;
And, being helped, inhabits there.

Then to Silvia let us sing,
   That Silvia is excelling;
She excels each mortal thing,
   Upon the dull earth dwelling:
To her let us garlands bring.   *Shakespeare.*

The Two Gentlemen of Verona, 1623. (Written 1594–5?)

SONNET

The world's bright comforter, whose beamsome light
Poor creatures cheereth, mounting from the deep
His course doth in prefixëd compass keep;
And, as courageous giant, takes delight
To run his race and exercise his might,
Till him, down galloping the mountain's steep,
Clear Hesperus, smooth messenger of sleep,
Views; and the silver ornament of night
Forth brings, with stars past number in her train,
All which with sun's long borrowed splendour shine.
The seas, with full tide swelling, ebb again;
All years to their old quarters new resign;
    The winds forsake their mountain-chambers wild,
    And all in all things with God's virtue filled.   *Barnes.*

A Divine Century of Spiritual Sonnets, 1595.

SONNET

Muses, that sing love's sensual emperie,
And lovers kindling your enragëd fires
At Cupid's bonfires burning in the eye,
Blown with the empty breath of vain desires;
You, that prefer the painted cabinet
Before the wealthy jewels it doth store ye,
That all your joys in dying figures set,
And stain the living substance of your glory—
Abjure those joys, abhor their memory;
And let my Love the honoured subject be
Of love, and honour's còmplete history!
Your eyes were never yet let in to see
    The majesty and riches of the mind,
    But dwell in darkness; for your god is blind.

Ovid's Banquet of Sense, 1595.   *Chapman*

OF CUPID

Trust not his wanton tears,
  Lest they beguile ye;
Trust not his childish sigh,
  He breatheth slily.
Trust not his touch,
  His feeling may defile ye;
Trust nothing that he doth,
  The wag is wily.
If you suffer him to prate,
You will rue it over-late;
  Beware of him, for he is witty:
Quickly strive the boy to bind,
Fear him not, for he is blind:
  If he get loose, he shows no pity.   *Chettle.*

Piers Plainness' Seven Years' Prenticeship, 1595.

TO SIR PHILIP SIDNEY'S SOUL

Give pardon, blessèd soul, to my bold cries,
If they, importune, interrupt thy song,
Which now with joyful notes thou sing'st among
The angel-quiristers of heavenly skies.
Give pardon eke, sweet soul, to my slow eyes,
That since I saw thee now it is so long,
And yet the tears that unto thee belong
To thee as yet they did not sacrifice.
I did not know that thou wert dead before;
I did not feel the grief I did sustain;
The greater stroke astonisheth the more;
Astonishment takes from us sense of pain;
  I stood amazed when others' tears begun,
  And now begin to weep when they have done.
                                                          Constable.

An Apology for Poetry, 1595.

slow eyes] J. Gray, 1897; slow cries, 1595.

SONNETS

Rudely thou wrongest my dear heart's desire,
In finding fault with her too portly pride:
The thing which I do most in her admire
Is of the world unworthy most envìed;
For in those lofty looks is close implied
Scorn of base things and 'sdain of foul dishonour,
Threat'ning rash eyes which gaze on her so wide,
That loosely they ne dare to look upon her.
Such pride is praise, such portliness is honour,
That boldened innocence bears in her eyes;
And her fair countenance, like a goodly banner,
Spreads in defiance of all enemies.
    Was never in this world ought worthy tried,
    Without some spark of such self-pleasing pride.

Amoretti and Epithalamion, 1595.   *Spenser.*

Sweet is the rose, but grows upon a brere;
Sweet is the juniper, but sharp his bough;
Sweet is the eglantine, but pricketh near;
Sweet is the fir-bloom, but his branches rough;
Sweet is the cypress, but his rind is tough;
Sweet is the nut, but bitter is his pill;
Sweet is the broom-flower, but yet sour enough;
And sweet is moly, but his root is ill.
So every sweet with sour is tempered still,
That maketh it be coveted the more,
For easy things, that may be got at will,
Most sorts of men do set but little store.
    Why then should I account of little pain,
    That endless pleasure shall unto me gain?   *Spenser.*

Ibid.

brere] briar.   pill] peel.   account] take account.

Fresh Spring, the herald of love's mighty king,
In whose coat-armour richly are displayed
All sorts of flowers, the which on earth do spring,
In goodly colours gloriously arrayed,
Go to my Love, where she is careless laid
Yet in her winter's bower not well awake;
Tell her the joyous time will not be stayed
Unless she do him by the forelock take.
Bid her, therefore, herself soon ready make,
To wait on Love amongst his lovely crew;
Where every one that misseth then her make,
Shall be by him amerced with penance due.
   Make haste therefore, sweet Love, whilst it is prime,
   For none can call again the passëd time.   *Spenser.*

Ibid.

One day I wrote her name upon the strand,
But came the waves and washëd it away:
Again I wrote it with a second hand,
But came the tide and made my pains his prey.
'Vain man,' said she, 'that dost in vain essay
A mortal thing so to immortalize;
For I myself shall like to this decay,
And eke my name be wipëd out likewise.'
'Not so,' quod I, 'let baser things devise
To die in dust, but you shall live by fame;
My verse your virtues rare shall èternize,
And in the heavens write your glorious name:
   Where, whenas Death shall all the world subdue,
   Our love shall live, and later life renew.'   *Spenser.*

Ibid.

her make] her mate.

Lacking my Love, I go from place to place,
Like a young fawn that late hath lost the hind,
And seek each where, where last I saw her face,
Whose image yet I carry fresh in mind.
I seek the fields with her late footing signed;
I seek her bower with her late presence decked;
Yet nor in field nor bower I her can find;
Yet field and bower are full of her aspèct:
But when mine eyes I thereunto direct,
They idly back return to me again:
And when I hope to see their true objèct,
I find my self but fed with fancies vain.
   Cease then, mine eyes, to seek her self to see;
   And let my thoughts behold her self in me.   *Spenser.*

Amoretti and Epithalamion, 1595.

Fair is my Love, when her fair golden heares
With the loose wind ye waving chance to mark;
Fair, when the rose in her red cheeks appears;
Or in her eyes the fire of love does spark.
Fair, when her breast, like a rich-laden bark,
With precious merchandize she forth doth lay;
Fair, when that cloud of pride, which oft doth dark
Her goodly light, with smiles she drives away.
But fairest she, when so she doth display
The gate with pearls and rubies richly dight,
Through which her words so wise do make their way
To bear the message of her gentle sprite.
   The rest be works of nature's wonderment:
   But this the work of heart's astonishment.   *Spenser.*

Ibid.

heares] hairs.

Most glorious Lord of life! that, on this day,
Didst make thy triumph over death and sin;
And, having harrowed hell, didst bring away
Captivity thence captive, us to win:
This joyous day, dear Lord, with joy begin;
And grant that we, for whom thou didest die,
Being with thy dear blood clean washed from sin,
May live for ever in felicity!
And that thy love we weighing worthily,
May likewise love thee for the same again;
And for thy sake, that all like dear didst buy,
With love may one another entertain:
  So let us love, dear Love, like as we ought;
  Love is the lesson which the Lord us taught.

Ibid.   *Spenser.*

EPITHALAMION

Ye learnëd sisters, which have oftentimes
Been to me aiding, others to adorn,
Whom ye thought worthy of your graceful rimes,
That even the greatest did not greatly scorn
To hear their names sung in your simple lays,
But joyëd in their praise;
And when ye list your own mishaps to mourn,
Which death, or love, or fortune's wreck did raise,
Your string could soon to sadder tenor turn,
And teach the woods and waters to lament
Your doleful dreriment:
Now lay those sorrowful complaints aside;
And, having all your heads with garland crowned,
Help me mine own Love's praises to resound;

dreriment] dreariness, grief.

Ne let the same of any be envìed:
So Orpheus did for his own bride,
So I unto myself alone will sing,
The woods shall to me answer, and my echo ring.

Early, before the world's light-giving lamp
His golden beam upon the hills doth spread,
Having dispersed the night's uncheerful damp,
Do ye awake, and, with fresh lusty-head,
Go to the bower of my belovèd Love,
My truest turtle dove;
Bid her awake; for Hymen is awake,
And long since ready forth his mask to move,
With his bright tead that flames with many a flake,
And many a bachelor to wait on him,
In their fresh garments trim.
Bid her awake therefore, and soon her dight,
For lo! the wishèd day is come at last,
That shall, for all the pains and sorrows past,
Pay to her usury of long delight:
And, whilst she doth her dight,
Do ye to her of joy and solace sing,
That all the woods may answer, and your echo ring.

Bring with you all the Nymphs that you can hear,
Both of the rivers and the forests green,
And of the sea that neighbours to her near,
All with gay garlands goodly well-beseen.
And let them also with them bring in hand
Another gay garland,
For my fair Love, of lilies and of roses,
Bound true-love wise with a blue silk riband;
And let them make great store of bridal posies,
And let them eke bring store of other flowers,

tead] torch.

To deck the bridal bowers.
And let the ground whereas her foot shall tread,
For fear the stones her tender foot should wrong,
Be strewed with fragrant flowers all along,
And diapered like the discoloured mead;
Which done, do at her chamber door await,
For she will waken straight;
The whiles do ye this song unto her sing,
The woods shall to you answer, and your echo ring.

Ye Nymphs of Mulla, which with careful heed
The silver scaly trouts do tend full well,
And greedy pikes which use therein to feed,
(Those trouts and pikes all others do excel);
And ye likewise, which keep the rushy lake
Where none do fishes take;
Bind up the locks the which hang scattered light,
And in his waters, which your mirror make,
Behold your faces as the crystal bright,
That when you come whereas my Love doth lie,
No blemish she may spy.
And eke, ye lightfoot maids, which keep the deer,
That on the hoary mountain used to tower,
And the wild wolves, which seek them to devour,
With your steel darts do chase from coming near,
Be also present here,
To help to deck her, and to help to sing,
That all the woods may answer, and your echo ring.

Wake now, my Love, awake! for it is time;
The rosy morn long since left Tithone's bed,
All ready to her silver coach to climb;
And Phoebus gins to show his glorious head.
Hark, how the cheerful birds do chant their lays

---

discoloured] variegated.   deer] Mod. eds.; dore, 1595 and 1611.

And carol of love's praise!
The merry lark her matins sings aloft,
The thrush replies, the mavis descant plays,
The ouzel shrills, the ruddock warbles soft,
So goodly all agree, with sweet consent,
To this day's merriment.
Ah! my dear Love, why do ye sleep thus long,
When meeter were that ye should now awake,
To await the coming of your joyous make,
And hearken to the birds' love-learnèd song,
The dewy leaves among:
For they of joy and pleasance to you sing,
That all the woods them answer, and their echo ring.

My Love is now awake out of her dreams,
And her fair eyes, like stars that dimmèd were
With darksome cloud, now show their goodly beams
More bright than Hesperus his head doth rear.
Come now, ye damsels, daughters of delight,
Help quickly her to dight:
But first come ye fair Hours, which were begot
In Jove's sweet paradise of Day and Night;
Which do the seasons of the year allot,
And all that ever in this world is fair
Do make and still repair:
And ye three handmaids of the Cyprian queen,
The which do still adorn her beauty's pride,
Help to adorn my beautifulest bride;
And as ye her array, still throw between
Some graces to be seen,
And, as ye use to Venus, to her sing,
The whiles the woods shall answer, and your echo ring.

make] mate.   dreams] Mod. eds.; dreame, 1595 and 1611.

Now is my Love all ready forth to come:
Let all the virgins therefore well await;
And ye fresh boys that tend upon her groom
Prepare yourselves; for he is coming straight.
Set all your things in seemly good array,
Fit for so joyful day,
The joyful'st day that ever sun did see.
Fair Sun, show forth thy favourable ray,
And let thy life-full heat not fervent be,
For fear of burning her sunshiny face,
Her beauty to disgrace.
O fairest Phoebus! father of the Muse,
If ever I did honour thee aright,
Or sing the thing that mote thy mind delight,
Do not thy servant's simple boon refuse;
But let this day, let this one day be mine;
Let all the rest be thine;
Then I thy sovereign praises loud will sing,
That all the woods shall answer, and their echo ring.

Hark how the minstrels gin to shrill aloud
Their merry music that resounds from far,
The pipe, the tabor, and the trembling crowd,
That well agree withouten breach or jar!
But, most of all, the damsels do delight
When they their timbrels smite,
And thereunto do dance and carol sweet,
That all the senses they do ravish quite;
The whiles the boys run up and down the street
Crying aloud with strong confusèd noyce,
As if it were one voice,
'Hymen, io Hymen, Hymen!' they do shout;
That even to the heavens their shouting shrill

mote] might.   crowd] a kind of violin.   noyce] noise.

Doth reach, and all the firmament doth fill;
To which the people standing all about,
As in approvance do thereto applaud,
And loud advance her laud;
And evermore they 'Hymen, Hymen!' sing,
That all the woods them answer, and their echo ring.

Lo! where she comes along with portly pace,
Like Phoebe from her chamber of the east
Arising forth to run her mighty race,
Clad all in white, that seems a virgin best.
So well it her beseems, that ye would ween
Some angel she had been.
Her long loose yellow locks like golden wire,
Sprinkled with pearl, and pearling flowers atween,
Do like a golden mantle her attire:
And, being crownèd with a garland green,
Seem like some maiden queen.
Her modest eyes, abashèd to behold
So many gazers as on her do stare,
Upon the lowly ground affixèd are;
Ne dare lift up her countenance too bold,
But blush to hear her praises sung so loud,
So far from being proud.
Nathless do ye still loud her praises sing,
That all the woods may answer, and your echo ring.

Tell me, ye merchants' daughters, did ye see
So fair a creature in your town before;
So sweet, so lovely, and so mild as she,
Adorned with beauty's grace and virtue's store?
Her goodly eyes like sapphires shining bright,
Her forehead ivory white,
Her cheeks like apples which the sun hath rudded,

Her lips like cherries charming men to bite,
Her breast like to a bowl of cream uncrudded,
Her paps like lilies budded,
Her snowy neck like to a marble tower;
And all her body like a palace fair,
Ascending up, with many a stately stair,
To honour's seat and chastity's sweet bower.
Why stand ye still, ye virgins, in amaze
Upon her so to gaze,
Whiles ye forget your former lay to sing,
To which the woods did answer, and your echo ring?

But if ye saw that which no eyes can see,
The inward beauty of her lively sprite,
Garnished with heavenly gifts of high degree,
Much more then would ye wonder at that sight,
And stand astonished like to those which read
Medusa's mazeful head.
There dwells sweet love and constant chastity,
Unspotted faith and comely womanhood,
Regard of honour and mild modesty;
There virtue reigns as queen in royal throne,
And giveth laws alone,
The which the base affections do obey,
And yield their services unto her will;
Ne thought of thing uncomely ever may
Thereto approach to tempt her mind to ill.
Had ye once seen these her celestial treasures,
And unrevealèd pleasures,
Then would ye wonder, and her praises sing,
That all the woods should answer, and your echo ring.

Open the temple gates unto my Love,
Open them wide that she may enter in,

And all the posts adorn as doth behove,
And all the pillars deck with garlands trim,
For to receive this saint with honour due,
That cometh in to you:
With trembling steps, and humble reverence
She cometh in, before the Almighty's view.
Of her ye virgins learn obedience,
When so ye come into those holy places
To humble your proud faces.
Bring her up to th' high altar, that she may
The sacred ceremonies there partake,
The which do endless matrimony make;
And let the roaring organs loudly play
The praises of the Lord in lively notes;
The whiles, with hollow throats,
The choristers the joyous anthem sing,
That all the woods may answer, and their echo ring.

Behold, whiles she before the altar stands,
Hearing the holy priest that to her speaks
And blesseth her with his two happy hands,
How the red roses flush up in her cheeks,
And the pure snow with goodly vermill stain,
Like crimson dyed in grain;
That even the angels, which continually
About the sacred altar do remain,
Forget their service and about her fly,
Oft peeping in her face, that seems more fair
The more they on it stare.
But her sad eyes, still fastened on the ground,
Are governèd with goodly modesty,
That suffers not one look to glance awry,
Which may let in a little thought unsound.
Why blush ye, Love, to give to me your hand,

The pledge of all our band?
Sing, ye sweet angels, Alleluia sing,
That all the woods may answer, and your echo ring.

Now all is done: bring home the bride again,
Bring home the triumph of our victory;
Bring home with you the glory of her gain,
With joyance bring her and with jollity.
Never had man more joyful day than this,
Whom heaven would heap with bliss.
Make feast therefore now all this live-long day;
This day for ever to me holy is.
Pour out the wine without restraint or stay,
Pour not by cups, but by the bellyful,
Pour out to all that wull;
And sprinkle all the posts and walls with wine,
That they may sweat, and drunken be withal.
Crown ye god Bacchus with a coronal,
And Hymen also crown with wreaths of vine;
And let the Graces dance unto the rest,
For they can do it best:
The whiles the maidens do their carol sing,
To which the woods shall answer, and their echo ring.

Ring ye the bells, ye young men of the town,
And leave your wonted labours for this day:
This day is holy; do ye write it down,
That ye for ever it remember may.
This day the sun is in his chiefest height,
With Barnaby the bright,
From whence declining daily by degrees,
He somewhat loseth of his heat and light,
When once the Crab behind his back he sees.
But for this time it ill ordainèd was,

To choose the longest day in all the year,
And shortest night, when longest fitter were:
Yet never day so long but late would pass.
Ring ye the bells, to make it wear away,
And bonfires make all day,
And dance about them, and about them sing,
That all the woods may answer, and your echo ring.

Ah! when will this long weary day have end,
And lend me leave to come unto my Love?
How slowly do the hours their numbers spend!
How slowly does sad Time his feathers move!
Haste thee, O fairest planet, to thy home
Within the western foam:
Thy tirèd steeds long since have need of rest.
Long though it be, at last I see it gloom,
And the bright evening star with golden crest
Appear out of the east.
Fair child of beauty! glorious lamp of love!
That all the host of heaven in ranks dost lead,
And guidest lovers through the night's sad dread,
How cheerfully thou lookest from above,
And seem'st to laugh atween thy twinkling light,
As joying in the sight
Of these glad many, which for joy do sing,
That all the woods them answer, and their echo ring!

Now cease, ye damsels, your delights forepast;
Enough it is that all the day was yours:
Now day is done, and night is nighing fast,
Now bring the bride into the bridal bowers.
The night is come, now soon her disarray,
And in her bed her lay;

---

night's sad dread] 1611; night's dread, 1595.

Lay her in lilies and in violets,
And silken curtains over her display,
And odoured sheets, and Arras coverlets.
Behold how goodly my fair Love does lie
In proud humility!
Like unto Maia, whenas Jove her took
In Tempe, lying on the flowery grass
Twixt sleep and wake, after she weary was
With bathing in the Acidalian brook.
Now it is night, ye damsels may be gone,
And leave my Love alone,
And leave likewise your former lay to sing:
The woods no more shall answer, nor your echo ring.

Now welcome, night! thou night so long expected,
That long day's labour dost at last defray,
And all my cares, which cruel love collected,
Hast summed in one, and cancellèd for aye:
Spread thy broad wing over my Love and me,
That no man may us see;
And in thy sable mantle us enwrap,
From fear of peril and foul horror free.
Let no false treason seek us to entrap,
Nor any dread disquiet once annoy
The safety of our joy;
But let the night be calm and quietsome,
Without tempestuous storms or sad affray:
Like as when Jove with fair Alcmena lay,
When he begot the great Tirynthian groom:
Or like as when he with thyself did lie
And begot Majesty.
And let the maids and young men cease to sing;
Ne let the woods them answer, nor their echo ring.

Let no lamenting cries, nor doleful tears
Be heard all night within, nor yet without:
Ne let false whispers, breeding hidden fears,
Break gentle sleep with misconceivëd doubt.
Let no deluding dreams, nor dreadful sights,
Make sudden sad affrights;
Ne let house-fires, nor lightning's helpless harms,
Ne let the Pouke, nor other evil sprights,
Ne let mischievous witches with their charms,
Ne let hob-goblins, names whose sense we see not,
Fray us with things that be not:
Let not the screech owl nor the stork be heard,
Nor the night raven that still deadly yells;
Nor damnëd ghosts, called up with mighty spells,
Nor grisly vultures, make us once affeared:
Ne let the unpleasant choir of frogs still croaking
Make us to wish their choking.
Let none of these their dreary accents sing;
Ne let the woods them answer, nor their echo ring.

But let still Silence true night-watches keep,
That sacred peace may in assurance reign,
And timely sleep, when it is time to sleep,
May pour his limbs forth on the pleasant plain;
The whiles an hundred little wingëd loves,
Like diverse-feathered doves,
Shall fly and flutter round about the bed,
And in the secret dark, that none reproves,
Their pretty stealths shall work, and snares shall spread,
To filch away sweet snatches of delight,
Concealed through covert night.
Ye sons of Venus, play your sports at will!
For greedy pleasure, careless of your toys,

Pouke] Puck.

Thinks more upon her paradise of joys,
Than what ye do, albeit good or ill.
All night therefore attend your merry play,
For it will soon be day:
Now none doth hinder you, that say or sing;
Ne will the woods now answer, nor your echo ring.

Who is the same, which at my window peeps?
Or whose is that fair face that shines so bright?
Is it not Cynthia, she that never sleeps,
But walks about high heaven all the night?
O fairest goddess! do thou not envy
My Love with me to spy:
For thou likewise didst love, though now unthought,
And for a fleece of wool, which privily
The Latmian shepherd once unto thee brought,
His pleasures with thee wrought.
Therefore to us be favourable now;
And sith of women's labours thou hast charge,
And generation goodly dost enlarge,
Incline thy will to effect our wishful vow,
And the chaste womb inform with timely seed,
That may our comfort breed:
Till which we cease our hopeful hap to sing;
Ne let the woods us answer, nor our echo ring.

And thou, great Juno! which with awful might
The laws of wedlock still dost patronize,
And the religion of the faith first plight
With sacred rites hast taught to solemnize;
And eke for comfort often callèd art
Of women in their smart,—
Eternally bind thou this lovely band,
And all thy blessings unto us impart.

And thou, glad Genius! in whose gentle hand
The bridal bower and genial bed remain
Without blemish or stain,
And the sweet pleasures of their love's delight
With secret aid dost succour and supply,
Till they bring forth the fruitful progeny,—
Send us the timely fruit of this same night.
And thou, fair Hebe! and thou, Hymen free!
Grant that it may so be.
Till which we cease your further praise to sing;
Ne any woods shall answer, nor your echo ring.

And ye high heavens, the temple of the gods,
In which a thousand torches flaming bright
Do burn, that to us wretched earthly clods
In dreadful darkness lend desirèd light;
And all ye powers which in the same remain,
More than we men can feign,
Pour out your blessing on us plenteously,
And happy influence upon us rain,
That we may raise a large posterity,
Which from the earth, which they may long possess
With lasting happiness,
Up to your haughty palaces may mount;
And, for the guerdon of their glorious merit,
May heavenly tabernacles there inherit,
Of blessed saints for to increase the count.
So let us rest, sweet Love, in hope of this,
And cease till then our timely joys to sing:
The woods no more us answer, nor our echo ring!

Song made in lieu of many ornaments,
With which my Love should duly have been decked,
Which cutting off through hasty accidents,

> *Ye would not stay your due time to expect,*
> *But promised both to recompense;*
> *Be unto her a goodly ornament,*
> *And for short time an endless monument.*   Spenser.

Amoretti and Epithalamion, 1595.

EMARICDULFE

Within her hair Venus and Cupid sport them:
Sometime they twist it amberlike in gold,
To which the whistling winds do oft resort them
As if they strove to have the knots unrolled:
Sometime they let her golden tresses dangle,
And therewith nets and amorous gins they make,
Wherewith the hearts of lovers to entangle,
Which once enthralled, no ransom they will take:
But as two tyrants, sitting in their thrones,
Look on their slaves with tyrannizing eyes,
So they, no whit regarding lovers' moans,
Doom worlds of hearts to endless slaveries,
    Unless they, subject-like, swear to adore
    And serve Emaricdulfe for evermore.   E. C.

Emaricdulfe, 1595.

THE FRAILTY OF BEAUTY

The time will come when, looking in a glass,
    Thy rivelled face with sorrow thou shalt see,
And, sighing, say, 'It is not as it was:
    These cheeks were wont more fresh and fair to be;
But now, what once made me so much admired
Is least regarded, and of none desired.'

her golden] N.A.; their golden, 1595.

Though thou be fair, think beauty but a blast,
    A morning's dew, a shadow quickly gone,
A painted flower whose colour will not last:
    Time steals away when least we think thereon,
Most precious time, too wastefully expended,
Of which alone the sparing is commended.

Thy large smooth forehead wrinkled shall appear;
    Vermilion hue to pale and wan shall turn;
Time shall deface what youth hath held most dear;
    Yea, those clear eyes, which once my heart did burn,
Shall in their hollow circles lodge the night,
And yield more cause of terror than delight.   *J. C.*

Alcilia, 1595. (An excerpt.)*

LIKE FLOWERS WE SPRING

Like flowers we spring up fair but soon decaying;
Our days and years are in their prime declining;
Man's life on such uncertainties is founded:
The wheel of fickle fate is never staying;
Time every hour our thread of life untwining:
He that ere now with store of wealth abounded,
Anon through want is wounded.
Wayfaring men we are, pilgrims and strangers,
On earth we have no certain habitation,
Nor keep one constant station;
But, through a multitude of fears and dangers,
We travel up and down towards our ending,
Unto our silent graves mournfully wending.   *Anon.*

Christ Church MS. 740-2. (Poem written before 1596.)*

OVER HILL, OVER DALE

Over hill, over dale,
　　Thorough bush, thorough brier,
Over park, over pale,
　　Thorough flood, thorough fire,
I do wander everywhere,
Swifter than the moon's sphere;
And I serve the fairy queen,
To dew her orbs upon the green.
The cowslips tall her pensioners be;
In their gold coats spots you see,
Those be rubies, fairy favours,
In those freckles live their savours:
I must go seek some dewdrops here,
And hang a pearl in every cowslip's ear.

Shakespeare.

A Midsummer Night's Dream, 1600. (Written 1595–6?)

THE FAIRIES' LULLABY

You spotted snakes with double tongue,
　　Thorny hedgehogs, be not seen;
Newts and blind-worms do no wrong,
　　Come not near our fairy queen.
　　　Philomel, with melody,
　　　Sing in our sweet lullaby:
Lulla, lulla, lullaby; lulla, lulla, lullaby!
　　　Never harm, nor spell, nor charm,
　　　Come our lovely lady nigh;
　　　So, good night, with lullaby.

Weaving spiders, come not here:
　　Hence, you long-legged spinners, hence!

Beetles black, approach not near;
   Worm, nor snail, do no offence.
   Philomel, with melody,
   Sing in our sweet lullaby:
Lulla, lulla, lullaby; lulla, lulla, lullaby!
   Never harm, nor spell, nor charm,
   Come our lovely lady nigh;
   So, good night, with lullaby.   *Shakespeare.*

A Midsummer Night's Dream, 1600. (Written 1595–6?)

NOW THE HUNGRY LION ROARS

Now the hungry lion roars,
   And the wolf behowls the moon;
Whilst the heavy ploughman snores,
   All with weary task fordone.
Now the wasted brands do glow,
   Whilst the screech-owl, screeching loud,
Puts the wretch that lies in woe
   In remembrance of a shroud.
Now it is the time of night
   That the graves, all gaping wide,
Every one lets forth his sprite,
   In the churchway paths to glide:
And we fairies, that do run
   By the triple Hecate's team,
From the presence of the sun,
   Following darkness like a dream,
Now are frolic; not a mouse
Shall disturb this hallowed house:
I am sent with broom before,
To sweep the dust behind the door.   *Shakespeare.*

Ibid.

behowls] Warburton, 1733; beholds, 1600 and 1623.

THE UNKNOWN SHEPHERD'S COMPLAINT

My flock feeds not, my ewes breeds not,
My rams speeds not in their bliss:
Love is dying, faith defying,
Her denying, causer of this.
All my merry jigs are clean forgot,
All my lays of love are lost, God wot:
Where my joys were firmly linked by love
There annoys are placed without remove.
   One silly cross wrought all my loss;
   O frowning Fortune, cursèd fickle dame!
   For now I see inconstancy
   More in women than in men remain.

In black mourn I, all fear scorn I,
Lo, how forlorn I live in thrall!
Heart is bleeding, all help needing,
O cruel speeding fraught with gall!
My shepherd's pipe will sound no deal;
My wether's bell rings doleful knell;
My curtailed dog, which would have played,
Plays not at all but seems dismayed;
   My sighs so deep doth cause him to weep
   With howling noise to wail my woeful plight;
   My shrieks resounds through Arcadia grounds
   Like a thousand vanquished men in deadly fight.

Clear wells spring not, sweet birds sing not,
Green plants bring not forth; they die;
Herds stand weeping, flocks all sleeping,
Nymphs back creeping fearfully.
All the pleasures known to us poor swains,
All our merry meetings on the plains,

All our evening sports from greens are fled,
All our loves are lost, for Love is dead.
  Farewell, sweet lass, thy like ne'er was
  For a sweet content, the cause of all my woe:
  Poor Corydon must live alone,
  Other help for him there's none, there's none I know.

Barnfield (?)

B.M. Harl. MS. 6910, [c. 1596].* T. Weelkes' *Madrigals*, 1597. *The Passion-ate Pilgrim*, 1599. *England's Helicon*, 1600.

A GULLING SONNET

The lover under burthen of his love—
Which like to Etna did his heart oppress—
Did give such piteous groans, that he did move
The heavens at length to pity his distress:
But for the fates in their high court above
Forbade to make the grievous burthen less,
The gracious powers did all conspire to prove
If miracle this mischief might redress.
Therefore, regarding that the load was such
As no man might with one man's might sustain,
And that mild patïence imported much
To him that should endure an endless pain,
  By their decree he soon transformëd was
  Into a patient burden-bearing Ass.   *Sir J. Davies.*

Chetham MS. 8012. (Poem written c. 1596?)*

OF MAN AND WIFE

No love, to love of man and wife;
No hope, to hope of constant heart;
No joy, to joy in wedded life;
No faith, to faith in either part:

---

of his love] N.A.; of his M^{ris} love, MS.

Flesh is of flesh, and bone of bone
When deeds and words and thoughts are one.

No hate, to hate of man and wife;
No fear, to fear of double heart;
No death, to discontented life;
No grief, to grief when friends depart:
    They tear the flesh and break the bone
    That are in word or thought alone.

Thy friend an other friend may be,
But other self is not the same:
Thy wife the self-same is with thee,
In body, mind, in goods and name:
    No thine, no mine, may other call,
    Now all is one, and one is all.   *Eedes.*

Bodley MS. Rawl. Poet. 148. (Poem written in MS. c. 1596.)

THE BEE

Look how the industrious bee in fragrant May,
  When Flora gilds the earth with golden flowers,
Enveloped in her sweet perfumed array,
  Doth leave his honey-limed delicious bowers,
  More richly wrought than princes' stately towers,
Waving his silken wings amid the air,
And to the verdant gardens makes repair.

First falls he on a branch of sugared thyme,
  Then from the marigold he sucks the sweet,
And then the mint and then the rose doth climb,
  Then on the budding rosemary doth light,
  Till with sweet treasure having charged his feet,

Late in the evening home he turns again,
Thus profit is the guerdon of his pain.   *Fitzgeffry.*

Sir Francis Drake, 1596. (An excerpt.)

SONNETS

Fair is my Love that feeds among the lilies,
The lilies growing in that pleasant garden
Where Cupid's Mount that well belovëd hill is,
And where that little god himself is warden.
See where my Love sits in the beds of spices,
Beset all round with camphor, myrrh, and roses,
And interlaced with curious devices
Which her apart from all the world incloses!
There doth she tune her lute for her delight,
And with sweet music makes the ground to move,
Whilst I, poor I, do sit in heavy plight,
Wailing alone my unrespected love;
    Not daring rush into so rare a place,
    That gives to her, and she to it, a grace.   *Griffin.*

Fidessa, more chaste than kind, 1596.

I have not spent the April of my time,
The sweet of youth, in plotting in the air;
But do, at first adventure, seek to climb
Whilst flowers of blooming years are green and fair.
I am no leaving of all-withering age;
I have not suffered many winter lours;
I feel no storm unless my Love do rage,
And then in grief I spend both days and hours.
This yet doth comfort, that my flower lasted
Until it did approach my sun too near:

And then, alas, untimely was it blasted,
So soon as once thy beauty did appear.
  But, after all, my comfort rests in this,
  That for thy sake my youth decayëd is.   *Griffin.*
Ibid.

SONNET

O shady vales, O fair enrichëd meads,
O sacred woods, sweet fields, and rising mountains,
O painted flowers, green herbs, where Flora treads
Refreshed by wanton winds and watery fountains;
O all you wingëd quiristers of wood
That, perched aloft, your former pains report,
And straight again recount with pleasant mood
Your present joys in sweet and seemly sort;
O all you creatures whosoever thrive
On mother earth, in seas, by air or fire,
More blessed are you than I here under sun:
Love dies in me whenas he doth revive
In you; I perish under Beauty's ire
Where after storms, winds, frosts, your life is won.

A Margarite of America, 1596.   *Lodge.*

LOVE'S DESPAIR

I know, within my mouth, for bashful fear
  And dread of your disdain, my words will die;
I know I shall be stricken dumb, my dear,
  With doubt of your unpitiful reply.
I know, whenas I shall before you lie
  Prostrate and humble, craving help of you,
Misty aspects will cloud your sun-bright eye,
  And scornful looks o'ershade your beauty's hue.

I know, when I shall plead my love so true,
   So stainless, constant, loyal, and upright,
My truthful pleadings will not cause you rue
   The ne'er-heard state of my distressëd plight.
I know, when I shall come with face bedight
   With streaming tears, fall'n from my fountain eyes,
Breathing forth sighs of most heart-breaking might,
   My tears, my sighs, and me, you will despise.
I know, when with the power that in me lies,
   And all the prayers and vows that women move,
I shall in humblest mercy-moving wise
   Intreat, beseech, desire, and beg your love,
I know, sweet maiden, all will not remove
   Flint-hearted rigour from your rocky breast;
But all my means, my suit, and what I prove
   Proves bad, and I must live in all unrest—
Dying in life, and living still in death,
And yet nor die, nor draw a life-like breath.   *Lynch.*

Diella, 1596.

SONNET

My Love, I cannot thy rare beauties place
Under those forms which many writers use:
Some like to stones compare their mistress' face;
Some in the name of flowers do love abuse;
Some makes their love a goldsmith's shop to be,
Where orient pearls and precious stones abound:
In my conceit these far do disagree
The perfect praise of beauty forth to sound.
O Chloris, thou dost imitate thyself!
Self's imitating passeth precious stones,
Or all the Eastern-Indian golden pelf:

Thy red and white with purest fair atones.
   Matchless for beauty Nature hath thee framed,
   Only unkind and cruel thou art named.

Smith.

Chloris, 1596.

PRAYER TO VENUS

Great Venus, Queen of beauty and of grace,
The joy of gods and men, that under sky
Dost fairest shine and most adorn thy place,
That with thy smiling look dost pacify
The raging seas and mak'st the storms to fly;
Thee, goddess, thee the winds, the clouds do fear,
And when thou spread'st thy mantle forth on high,
The waters play and pleasant lands appear,
And heavens laugh, and all the world shows joyous cheer.

Then doth the daedal earth throw forth to thee
Out of her fruitful lap abundant flowers,
And then all living wights, soon as they see
The spring break forth out of his lusty bowers,
They all do learn to play the paramours;
First do the merry birds, thy pretty pages
Privily prickèd with thy lustful powers,
Chirp loud to thee out of their leavy cages,
And thee, their mother, call to cool their kindly rages.

Then do the savage beasts begin to play
Their pleasant frisks, and loathe their wonted food;
The lions roar, the tigers loudly bray,
The raging bulls rebellow through the wood,
And, breaking forth, dare tempt the deepest flood

atones] is at one, agrees.

To come where thou dost draw them with desire:
So all things else that nourish vital blood,
Soon as with fury thou dost them inspire,
In generation seek to quench their inward fire.

So all the world by thee at first was made,
And daily yet thou dost the same repair:
Ne ought on earth that merry is and glad,
Ne ought on earth that lovely is and fair,
But thou the same for pleasure didst prepare.
Thou art the root of all that joyous is,
Great god of men and women, queen of the air,
Mother of laughter, and well-spring of bliss,
Oh, grant that of my love at last I may not miss!   *Spenser.*

The Second Part of the Faerie Queen, 1596. (Bk. IV. Cant. x.)

PROTHALAMION

Calm was the day, and through the trembling air
Sweet-breathing Zephyrus did softly play
A gentle spirit, that lightly did delay
Hot Titan's beams, which then did glister fair;
When I, (whom sullen care,
Through discontent of my long fruitless stay
In princes' court, and expectation vain
Of idle hopes, which still do fly away
Like empty shadows, did afflict my brain,)
Walked forth to ease my pain
Along the shore of silver-streaming Thames;
Whose rutty bank, the which his river hems,
Was painted all with variable flowers,
And all the meads adorned with dainty gems
Fit to deck maidens' bowers,

And crown their paramours
Against the bridal day, which is not long:
   Sweet Thames! run softly, till I end my song.

There in a meadow by the river's side
A flock of nymphs I chancëd to espy,
All lovely daughters of the flood thereby,
With goodly greenish locks all loose untied
As each had been a bride;
And each one had a little wicker basket
Made of fine twigs entrailëd curiously,
In which they gathered flowers to fill their flasket,
And with fine fingers cropped full feateously
The tender stalks on high.
Of every sort which in that meadow grew
They gathered some; the violet, pallid blue,
The little daisy that at evening çloses,
The virgin lily and the primrose true,
With store of vermeil roses,
To deck their bridegrooms' posies
Against the bridal day, which was not long:
   Sweet Thames! run softly, till I end my song.

With that I saw two swans of goodly hue
Come softly swimming down along the Lee;
Two fairer birds I yet did never see;
The snow which doth the top of Pindus strew
Did never whiter shew,
Nor Jove himself, when he a swan would be
For love of Leda, whiter did appear;
Yet Leda was, they say, as white as he,
Yet not so white as these, nor nothing near;
So purely white they were
That even the gentle stream, the which them bare,

Seemed foul to them, and bade his billows spare
To wet their silken feathers, lest they might
Soil their fair plumes with water not so fair,
And mar their beauties bright,
That shone as heaven's light,
Against their bridal day, which was not long;
   Sweet Thames! run softly, till I end my song.

Eftsoons the nymphs, which now had flowers their fill,
Ran all in haste to see that silver brood
As they came floating on the crystal flood;
Whom when they saw, they stood amazèd still
Their wondering eyes to fill;
Them seemed they never saw a sight so fair,
Of fowls so lovely that they sure did deem
Them heavenly born, or to be that same pair
Which through the sky draw Venus' silver team;
For sure they did not seem
To be begot of any earthly seed,
But rather angels, or of angels' breed;
Yet were they bred of Somers-heat, they say,
In sweetest season, when each flower and weed
The earth did fresh array;
So fresh they seemed as day,
Even as their bridal day, which was not long:
   Sweet Thames! run softly, till I end my song.

Then forth they all out of their baskets drew
Great store of flowers, the honour of the field,
That to the sense did fragrant odours yield,
All which upon those goodly birds they threw,
And all the waves did strew,
That like old Peneus' waters they did seem

Somers-heat] Summer's heat, a pun on Somerset, their name.

When down along by pleasant Tempe's shore,
Scattered with flowers, through Thessaly they stream,
That they appear, through lilies' plenteous store,
Like a bride's chamber-floor.
Two of those nymphs meanwhile two garlands bound
Of freshest flowers which in that mead they found,
The which presenting all in trim array,
Their snowy foreheads therewithal they crowned,
Whilst one did sing this lay
Prepared against that day,
Against their bridal day, which was not long:
   Sweet Thames! run softly, till I end my song.

'Ye gentle birds! the world's fair ornament,
And heaven's glory, whom this happy hour
Doth lead unto your lovers' blissful bower,
Joy may you have, and gentle heart's content
Of your love's couplement;
And let fair Venus, that is queen of love,
With her heart-quelling son upon you smile,
Whose smile, they say, hath virtue to remove
All love's dislike, and friendship's faulty guile
For ever to assoil.
Let endless peace your steadfast hearts accord,
And blessèd plenty wait upon your board;
And let your bed with pleasures chaste abound,
That fruitful issue may to you afford,
Which may your foes confound,
And make your joys redound
Upon your bridal day, which is not long:
   Sweet Thames! run softly, till I end my song.'

So ended she; and all the rest around
To her redoubled that her undersong,

Which said their bridal day should not be long:
And gentle Echo from the neighbour ground
Their accents did resound.
So forth those joyous birds did pass along,
Adown the Lee that to them murmured low,
As he would speak but that he lacked a tongue,
Yet did by signs his glad affection show,
Making his stream run slow.
And all the fowl which in his flood did dwell
Gan flock about these twain, that did excel
The rest, so far as Cynthia doth shend
The lesser stars. So they, enrangëd well,
Did on those two attend,
And their best service lend
Against their wedding day, which was not long:
   Sweet Thames! run softly, till I end my song.

At length they all to merry London came,
To merry London, my most kindly nurse,
That to me gave this life's first native source,
Though from another place I take my name,
An house of ancient fame:
There when they came whereas those bricky towers
The which on Thames' broad agëd back do ride,
Where now the studious lawyers have their bowers,
There whilom wont the Templar knights to bide,
Till they decayed through pride:
Next whereunto there stands a stately place,
Where oft I gainëd gifts and goodly grace
Of that great lord, which therein wont to dwell,
Whose want too well now feels my friendless case;
But ah! here fits not well
Old woes, but joys to tell

shend] surpass.

Against the bridal day, which is not long:
  Sweet Thames! run softly, till I end my song.

Yet therein now doth lodge a noble peer,
Great England's glory and the world's wide wonder,
Whose dreadful name late through all Spain did thunder,
And Hercules' two pillars standing near
Did make to quake and fear:
Fair branch of honour, flower of chivalry!
That fillest England with thy triumphs' fame,
Joy have thou of thy noble victory,
And endless happiness of thine own name
That promiseth the same;
That through thy prowess and victorious arms
Thy country may be freed from foreign harms,
And great Eliza's glorious name may ring
Through all the world, filled with thy wide alarms,
Which some brave Muse may sing
To ages following,
Upon the bridal day, which is not long:
  Sweet Thames! run softly, till I end my song.

From those high towers this noble lord issùing,
Like radiant Hesper when his golden hair
In the ocean billows he hath bathèd fair,
Descended to the river's open viewing,
With a great train ensuing.
Above the rest were goodly to be seen
Two gentle knights of lovely face and feature,
Beseeming well the bower of any queen,
With gifts of wit and ornaments of nature
Fit for so goodly stature,
That like the twins of Jove they seemed in sight
Which deck the baldric of the heavens bright;

They two, forth pacing to the river's side,
Received those two fair brides, their love's delight;
Which, at the appointed tide,
Each one did make his bride
Against their bridal day, which is not long:
 Sweet Thames! run softly, till I end my song. *Spenser.*

Prothalamion, 1596.

TELL ME WHERE IS FANCY BRED

Tell me where is fancy bred,
Or in the heart, or in the head?
How begot, how nourishëd?
   Reply, reply.
It is engendered in the eyes,
With gazing fed; and fancy dies
In the cradle where it lies:
Let us all ring fancy's knell;
I 'll begin it,—Ding, dong bell.
   Ding, dong bell.   *Shakespeare.*

The Merchant of Venice, 1600. (Written 1596–7 ?)

MY THOUGHTS ARE WINGED WITH HOPES

My thoughts are winged with hopes, my hopes with love.
 Mount, love, unto the moon in clearest night,
And say, as she doth in the heavens move,
 In earth so wanes and waxeth my delight.
And whisper this but softly in her ears:
Hope oft doth hang the head, and Trust shed tears.

And you, my thoughts, that some mistrust do carry,
 If for mistrust my mistress do you blame,

in the eyes] 1623; in the eye, 1600.

Say, though you alter, yet you do not vary,
  As she doth change and yet remain the same.
Distrust doth enter hearts but not infect,
And love is sweetest seasoned with suspect.

If she for this with clouds do mask her eyes,
  And make the heavens dark with her disdain,
With windy sighs disperse them in the skies,
  Or with thy tears dissolve them into rain,
Thoughts, hopes, and love return to me no more
Till Cynthia shine as she hath done before.

Cumberland.*

J. Dowland's *Songs or Airs*, i., 1597.

WOULD GOD THAT IT WERE HOLIDAY!

Would God that it were holiday!
  Hey derry down, down derry,
That with my Love I might go play;
  With woe my heart is weary;
My whole delight is in her sight,
  Would God I had her company,
              Her company,
  Hey derry down, down adown.

My Love is fine, my Love is fair,
  Hey derry down, down derry,
No maid with her may well compare,
  In Kent or Canterbury;
From me my Love shall never move,
  Would God I had her company,
              Her company,
  Hey derry down, down adown.

To see her laugh, to see her smile,
   Hey derry down, down derry,
Doth all my sorrows clean beguile,
   And makes my heart full merry;
No grief doth grow where she doth go,
   Would God I had her company,
             Her company,
   Hey derry down, down adown.

When I do meet her on the green,
   Hey derry down, down derry,
Methinks she looks like beauty's queen,
   Which makes my heart full merry;
Then I her greet with kisses sweet;
   Would God I had her company,
             Her company,
   Hey derry down, down adown.

My Love comes not of churlish kind,
   Hey derry down, down derry,
But bears a gentle courteous mind,
   Which makes my heart full merry;
She is not coy, she is my joy,
   Would God I had her company,
             Her company,
   Hey derry down, down adown.

Till Sunday come, farewell, my dear!
   Hey derry down, down derry,
When we do meet we'll have good cheer,
   And then I will be merry:
If thou love me, I will love thee,

delight in thy] [c. 1675 ?]; delight thy, 1637.

And still delight in thy company,
                    Thy company,
Hey derry down, down adown.   *Deloney.*

The Gentle Craft, 1637. (Registered 1597.)

BUEN MATINA

Sweet, at this morn I chancëd
To peep into the chamber; lo! I glancëd,
And saw white sheets thy whiter skin disclosing,
And soft-sweet cheek on pillow soft reposing;
        Then said, 'Were I that pillow,
Dear, for thy love I would not wear the willow.'

R. Parry's *Sinetes Passions,* 1597.   *Salusbury.*

LAURA

Rich damask roses in fair cheeks do bide
    Of my sweet girl, like April in his prime;
But her hard heart, cold chilly snow doth hide,
    Of bitter Januar the perfect sign:
Her hair of gold shows yellow like the corn
    In July when the sun doth scorch the ground;
And her fair breast, ripe fruit, which doth adorn
    September rich: so as in her is found
Both Harvest, Summer, Winter, Spring, to be,
Which you in breast, hair, heart, and face, may see.

Laura, 1597.   *Tofte.*

A SHADOW

I heard a noise and wishëd for a sight,
I looked for life and did a shadow see
Whose substance was the sum of my delight,

Which came unseen, and so did go from me.
    Yet hath conceit persuaded my content
    There was a substance where the shadow went.

I did not play Narcissus in conceit,
I did not see my shadow in a spring:
I know mine eyes were dimmed with no deceit,
I saw the shadow of some worthy thing:
    For, as I saw the shadow glancing by,
    I had a glimpse of something in mine eye.

But what it was, alas, I cannot tell,
Because of it I had no perfect view:
But as it was, by guess, I wish it well
And will until I see the same anew.
    Shadow, or she, or both, or choose you whither:
    Blest be the thing that brought the shadow hither!

Anon.

Bodley MS. Rawl. Poet. 148. (Poem written in MS. c. 1597.)

TO HIS LOVE

Come away! come, sweet Love!
    The golden morning breaks;
All the earth, all the air,
    Of love and pleasure speaks.
Teach thine arms then to embrace,
    And sweet rosy lips to kiss,
    And mix our souls in mutual bliss:
Eyes were made for beauty's grace,
    Viewing, rueing, love's long pain,
    Procured by beauty's rude disdain.

Come away! come, sweet Love!
    The golden morning wastes,

whither] which.

While the sun, from his sphere,
  His fiery arrows casts,
Making all the shadows fly,
  Playing, staying, in the grove
  To entertain the stealth of love.
Thither, sweet Love, let us hie,
  Flying, dying, in desire,
  Winged with sweet hopes and heavenly fire.

Come away! come, sweet Love!
  Do not in vain adorn
Beauty's grace, that should rise
  Like to the naked morn.
Lilies on the river's side,
  And fair Cyprian flowers new-blown,
  Desire no beauties but their own:
Ornament is nurse of pride.
  Pleasure measure love's delight:
  Haste then, sweet Love, our wishèd flight!   *Anon.*

J. Dowland's *Songs or Airs,* i., 1597.

DEAR, IF YOU CHANGE

Dear, if you change, I 'll never choose again;
  Sweet, if you shrink, I 'll never think of love;
Fair, if you fail, I 'll judge all beauty vain;
  Wise, if too weak, moe wits I 'll never prove.
Dear, sweet, fair, wise, change, shrink, nor be not weak;
And, on my faith, my faith shall never break!

Earth with her flowers shall sooner heaven adorn;
  Heaven her bright stars through earth's dim globe shall
      move;
Fire heat shall lose, and frosts of flames be born;

Line 5] *i.e.* nor change, shrink, nor be weak.

Air, made to shine, as black as hell shall prove.
Earth, heaven, fire, air, the world transformed shall view,
Ere I prove false to faith, or strange to you.   *Anon.*

J. Dowland's *Songs or Airs*, i., 1597.

BROWN IS MY LOVE

Brown is my Love, but graceful:
    And each renownëd whiteness
Matched with thy lovely brown loseth its brightness.

Fair is my Love, but scornful:
    Yet have I seen despisëd
Dainty white lilies, and sad flowers well prizëd.   *Anon.*

Musica Transalpina, 1597.

O GRIEF!

O grief! even on the bud that fairly flowered
    The sun hath loured.
And ah! that breast which Love durst never venture,
    Bold Death did enter.
Pity, O heavens, that have my love in keeping,
    My cries and weeping.   *Anon.*

T. Morley's *Canzonets,* 1597.

SONG

Go and catch a falling star;
    Get with child a mandrake root;
Tell me where all past years are,
    Or who cleft the Devil's foot;
Teach me to hear mermaids singing,
Or to keep off envy's stinging,

And find
What wind
Serves to advance an honest mind.

If thou be'st born to strange sights,
    Things invisible to see,
Ride ten thousand days and nights
    Till age snow white hairs on thee;
Thou, when thou return'st, wilt tell me
All strange wonders that befell thee,
            And swear
            No where
Lives a woman true and fair.

If thou find'st one, let me know;
    Such a pilgrimage were sweet.
Yet do not; I would not go,
    Though at next door we might meet.
Though she were true when you met her,
And last till you write your letter,
            Yet she
            Will be
False, ere I come, to two or three.   *Donne.*

Poems, 1633. (Poem written before 1598.)*

THE MESSAGE

Send home my long-strayed eyes to me,
Which, oh! too long have dwelt on thee;
Yet since there they have learned such ill,
        Such forced fashions
        And false passions,
            That they be

Made by thee
Fit for no good sight, keep them still.

Send home my harmless heart again,
Which no unworthy thought could stain;
But if it be taught by thine
To make jestings
Of protestings,
And break both
Word and oath,
Keep it, for then 'tis none of mine.

Yet send me back my heart and eyes,
That I may know and see thy lies,
And may laugh and joy, when thou
Art in anguish
And dost languish
For some one
That will none,
Or prove as false as thou art now.   *Donne.*

Poems, 1633. (Poem written before 1598.)

LOVE'S DEITY

I long to talk with some old lover's ghost,
    Who died before the god of love was born:
I cannot think that he, who then loved most,
    Sunk so low as to love one which did scorn.
But since this god produced a destiny,
And that vice-nature, custom, lets it be,
    I must love her that loves not me.

Sure, they which made him god, meant not so much,
    Nor he in his young godhead practised it;

But when an even flame two hearts did touch,
   His office was indulgently to fit
Actives to passives. Correspondency
Only his subject was; it cannot be
   Love, till I love her that loves me.

But every modern god will now extend
   His vast prerogative as far as Jove.
To rage, to lust, to write to, to commend,
   All is the purlieu of the god of love.
Oh! were we wakened by this tyranny
To ungod this child again, it could not be
   I should love her, who loves not me.

Rebel and atheist too, why murmur I,
   As though I felt the worst that love could do?
Love may make me leave loving, or might try
   A deeper plague, to make her love me too;
Which, since she loves before, I am loath to see.
Falsehood is worse than hate; and that must be,
   If she, whom I love, should love me.   *Donne.*

Ibid.

THE LIFE OF MAN

The world 's a bubble, and the life of man
       Less than a span:
In his conception wretched, from the womb
       So to the tomb;
Curst from his cradle, and brought up to years
       With cares and fears.
Who then to frail mortality shall trust,
But limns the water, or but writes in dust.

Yet since with sorrow here we live oppressed,
      What life is best?
Courts are but only superficial schools
      To dandle fools:
The rural parts are turned into a den
      Of savage men:
And where 's a city from all vice so free,
But may be termed the worst of all the three?

Domestic cares afflict the husband's bed,
      Or pains his head:
Those that live single, take it for a curse,
      Or do things worse:
Some would have children; those that have them, moan
      Or wish them gone:
What is it, then, to have, or have no wife,
But single thraldom, or a double strife?

Our own affections still at home to please
      Is a disease:
To cross the seas to any foreign soil,
      Perils and toil:
Wars with their noise affright us; when they cease,
      We 're worse in peace;—
What then remains, but that we still should cry
Not to be born, or, being born, to die?   *Bacon.*

T. Farnaby's *Florilegium Epigrammatum Graecorum,* 1629. (Poem written
1597–8.)*

AN ODE

    As it fell upon a day
    In the merry month of May,
    Sitting in a pleasant shade
    Which a grove of myrtles made,

Beasts did leap and birds did sing,
Trees did grow and plants did spring;
Every thing did banish moan
Save the nightingale alone.
She, poor bird, as all forlorn,
Leaned her breast against a thorn,
And there sung the dolefull'st ditty
That to hear it was great pity.
Fie, fie, fie, now would she cry;
Teru, teru, by and by:
That to hear her so complain
Scarce I could from tears refrain;
For her griefs so lively shown
Made me think upon mine own.
Ah, thought I, thou mourn'st in vain,
None takes pity on thy pain:
Senseless trees, they cannot hear thee,
Ruthless beasts, they will not cheer thee;
King Pandion, he is dead,
All thy friends are lapped in lead:
All thy fellow birds do sing
Careless of thy sorrowing:
Even so, poor bird, like thee
None alive will pity me.   *Barnfield.*

Poems: in divers humours, 1598. (Text from *England's Helicon,* 1600.)*

TO HIS FRIEND MASTER R. L., IN PRAISE OF
MUSIC AND POETRY

If music and sweet poetry agree,
As they must needs, the sister and the brother,
Then must the love be great 'twixt thee and me,

---

against a thorn] 1600; up-till a thorn, 1598.   Ruthless beasts] 1600; Ruth-
less bears, 1598.

Because thou lov'st the one, and I the other.
Dowland to thee is dear, whose heavenly touch
Upon the lute doth ravish human sense;
Spenser, to me, whose deep conceit is such
As, passing all conceit, needs no defence.
Thou lov'st to hear the sweet melodious sound
That Phoebus' lute, the queen of music, makes;
And I in deep delight am chiefly drowned
Whenas himself to singing he betakes:
     One god is god of both, as poets feign;
     One knight loves both, and both in thee remain.

Poems: in divers humours, 1598.   *Barnfield.*

METHINKS 'TIS PRETTY SPORT

Methinks 'tis pretty sport to hear a child
Rocking a word in mouth yet undefiled;
The tender racquet rudely plays the sound
Which, weakly bandied, cannot back rebound;
And the soft air the softer roof doth kiss
With a sweet dying and a pretty miss,
Which hears no answer yet from the white rank
Of teeth not risen from their coral bank.
The alphabet is searched for letters soft
To try a word before it can be wrought;
And when it slideth forth, it goes as nice
As when a man doth walk upon the ice.   *Bastard.*

Chrestoleros, 1598.

EPITHALAMION TERATOS

Come, come, dear Night! Love's mart of kisses,
     Sweet close of his ambitious line,

The fruitful summer of his blisses,
　　Love's glory doth in darkness shine.

O come, soft rest of cares! come, Night!
　　Come naked virtue's only tire,
The reapëd harvest of the light
　　Bound up in sheaves of sacred fire.
　　　　Love calls to war;
　　　　　Sighs his alarms,
　　　　Lips his swords are,
　　　　　The field his arms.

Come, Night, and lay thy velvet hand
　　On glorious Day's outfacing face;
And all thy crownëd flames command
　　For torches to our nuptial grace.
　　　　Love calls to war;
　　　　　Sighs his alarms,
　　　　Lips his swords are,
　　　　　The field his arms.

No need have we of factious Day,
　　To cast, in envy of thy peace,
Her balls of discord in thy way;
　　Here beauty's day doth never cease.
　　　Day is abstracted here,
　　　And varied in a triple sphere,
Hero, Alcmane, Mya, so outshine thee,
Ere thou come here, let Thetis thrice refine thee.
　　　　Love calls to war;
　　　　　Sighs his alarms,
　　　　Lips his swords are,
　　　　　The field his arms.   *Chapman.*

Hero and Leander, 1598.

SONG

Weep, weep, ye woodmen! wail;
    Your hands with sorrow wring!
Your master Robin Hood lies dead,
    Therefore sigh as you sing.

Here lie his primer and his beads,
    His bent bow and his arrows keen,
His good sword and his holy cross:
    Now cast on flowers fresh and green.

And, as they fall, shed tears and say
    Well-a, well-a-day! well-a, well-a-day!
Thus cast ye flowers, and sing,
    And on to Wakefield take your way.   *Munday* (?)

The Death of Robert, Earl of Huntingdon, 1601. By Munday and Chettle.
(Mentioned in Henslowe's Diary, 1598.)

SONG

Fond affection, hence, and leave me!
    Try no more for to deceive me!
    Long ago thou didst perplex me,
    Now again seek not to vex me!
For since thou left'st off to assail me
Power nor passion could not quail me.

    As the lamb the wolf, I fly thee;
    As my foe, Love, I defy thee!
    Wend away, I care not for thee;
    Childish tyrant, I abhor thee;
For I know thou wilt deceive me:
Hence away, therefore, and leave me!   *Parry* (?)

The Mirror of Knighthood, iii., 1598.

THE SPIRIT OF NIGHT

On the death of a virtuous Lady

Attired in black, spangled with flames of fire,
Embroiderëd with stars in silent night,
While Phoebus doth the lower world inspire
With his bright beams and comfort-breathing sprite,
I come in clouds of grief, with pensive soul,
Sending forth vapours of black discontent
To fill the concave circle of the Pole,
And with my tears bedew each continent:
Because that she that made my night seem day
By her pure virtues' ever-shining lamps,
Now makes my night more black by her decay,
Wandering with ghosts in the Elysian camps:
    Wherefore I still will wear a mourning veil,
    For she is dead, and human flesh is frail.   *Rogers.*

Celestial Elegies, 1598.

LOVE'S LABOUR LOST

Love's Labour Lost, I once did see a play
Yclepëd so, so callëd to my pain,
Which I to hear to my small joy did stay,
Giving attendance on my froward dame;
    My misgiving mind presaging to me ill,
    Yet was I drawn to see it 'gainst my will.

This play, no play but plague was unto me,
For there I lost the Love I likëd most:
And what to others seemed a jest to be,
I, that, in earnest, found unto my cost:

To every one save me 'twas comical,
Whilst tragic-like to me it did befall.

Each actor played in cunning-wise his part,
But chiefly those entrapped in Cupid's snare:
Yet all was feignëd, 'twas not from the heart,
They seemed to grieve, but yet they felt no care;
   'Twas I that grief indeed did bear in breast,
   The others did but make a show in jest.

Yet neither feigning theirs, nor my mere truth,
Could make her once so much as for to smile:
Whilst she, despite of pity mild and ruth,
Did sit as scorning of my woes the while.
   Thus did she sit to see Love lose his Love,
   Like hardened rock that force nor power can move.

Tofte.

Alba, 1598.

WHAT NEEDETH ALL THIS TRAVAIL

What needeth all this travail and turmoiling,
   Shortening the life's sweet pleasure
   To seek this far-fetched treasure
In those hot climates under Phoebus broiling?
O fools, can you not see a traffic nearer
In my sweet lady's face, where Nature showeth
Whatever treasure eye sees or heart knoweth?—
   Rubies and diamonds dainty,
   And orient pearls such plenty,
Coral and ambergris sweeter and dearer
Than which the South Seas or Moluccas lend us,
Or either Indies, East or West, do send us.   *Anon.*

J. Wilbye's *English Madrigals,* 1598.

PHYLLIDA'S LOVE-CALL TO HER CORYDON,
AND HIS REPLYING

Phyl. Corydon, arise, my Corydon!
      Titan shineth clear.
Cor. Who is it that calleth Corydon?
      Who is it that I hear?
Phyl. Phyllida, thy true Love, calleth thee,
      Arise then, arise then,
         Arise and keep thy flock with me!
Cor. Phyllida, my true Love, is it she?
      I come then, I come then,
         I come and keep my flock with thee.

Phyl. Here are cherries ripe, my Corydon;
      Eat them for my sake.
Cor. Here's my oaten pipe, my lovely one,
      Sport for thee to make.
Phyl. Here are threads, my true Love, fine as silk,
      To knit thee, to knit thee
         A pair of stockings white as milk.
Cor. Here are reeds, my true Love, fine and neat,
      To make thee, to make thee
         A bonnet to withstand the heat.

Phyl. I will gather flowers, my Corydon,
      To set in thy cap.
Cor. I will gather pears, my lovely one,
      To put in thy lap.
Phyl. I will buy my true Love garters gay
      For Sundays, for Sundays,
         To wear about his legs so tall.
Cor. I will buy my true Love yellow say
      For Sundays, for Sundays,
         To wear about her middle small.

say] fine cloth, like serge.

Phyl. When my Corydon sits on a hill
    Making melody—
Cor. When my lovely one goes to her wheel
    Singing cheerily—
Phyl. Sure methinks my true Love doth excel
    For sweetness, for sweetness,
      Our Pan that old Arcadian knight.
Cor. And methinks my true Love bears the bell
    For clearness, for clearness,
      Beyond the nymphs that be so bright.

Phyl. Had my Corydon, my Corydon,
    Been, alack! her swain—
Cor. Had my lovely one, my lovely one,
    Been in Ida plain—
Phyl. Cynthia Endymion had refused,
    Preferring, preferring,
      My Corydon to play withal.
Cor. The queen of love had been excused,
    Bequeathing, bequeathing,
      My Phyllida the golden ball.

Phyl. Yonder comes my mother, Corydon,
    Whither shall I fly?
Cor. Under yonder beech, my lovely one,
    While she passeth by.
Phyl. Say to her thy true Love was not here;
    Remember, remember,
      To-morrow is another day.
Cor. Doubt me not, my true Love, do not fear;
    Farewell then, farewell then,
      Heaven keep our loves alway. *Anon.*

England's Helicon, 1600. (Set to music, c. 1598, in Bodley MS. Rawl. Poet. 148.)

Our Pan] 1600; Sir Pan, 1598. her swain] Bullen, 1887; my swain, 1600 and 1598.

SONNETS

When I do count the clock that tells the time,
And see the brave day sunk in hideous night;
When I behold the violet past prime,
And sable curls all silvered o'er with white;
When lofty trees I see barren of leaves,
Which erst from heat did canopy the herd,
And summer's green all girded up in sheaves,
Borne on the bier with white and bristly beard—
Then of thy beauty do I question make,
That thou among the wastes of time must go,
Since sweets and beauties do themselves forsake
And die as fast as they see others grow;
   And nothing 'gainst Time's scythe can make defence
   Save breed, to brave him when he takes thee hence.

Sonnets, 1609. (Written before 1599.)*
                                 Shakespeare.

Shall I compare thee to a summer's day?
Thou art more lovely and more temperate:
Rough winds do shake the darling buds of May,
And summer's lease hath all too short a date:
Sometime too hot the eye of heaven shines,
And often is his gold complexion dimmed:
And every fair from fair sometime declines,
By chance, or nature's changing course, untrimmed.
But thy eternal summer shall not fade,
Nor lose possession of that fair thou ow'st,
Nor shall death brag thou wander'st in his shade,
When in eternal lines to time thou grow'st;
   So long as men can breathe, or eyes can see,
   So long lives this, and this gives life to thee.

Ibid.
                                   Shakespeare.

all silvered] Malone, 1780; or silvered, 1609.   ow'st] own'st.

When, in disgrace with fortune and men's eyes,
I all alone beweep my outcast state,
And trouble deaf heaven with my bootless cries,
And look upon myself, and curse my fate,
Wishing me like to one more rich in hope,
Featured like him, like him with friends possessed,
Desiring this man's art, and that man's scope,
With what I most enjoy contented least;
Yet in these thoughts myself almost despising,
Haply I think on thee, and then my state,
Like to the lark at break of day arising
From sullen earth, sings hymns at heaven's gate;
   For thy sweet love remembered such wealth brings
   That then I scorn to change my state with kings.

Shakespeare.

Sonnets, 1609. (Written before 1599.)

When to the sessions of sweet silent thought
I summon up remembrance of things past,
I sigh the lack of many a thing I sought,
And with old woes new wail my dear time's waste;
Then can I drown an eye, unused to flow,
For precious friends hid in death's dateless night,
And weep afresh love's long since cancelled woe,
And moan the expense of many a vanished sight.
Then can I grieve at grievances foregone,
And heavily from woe to woe tell o'er
The sad account of fore-bemoanèd moan,
Which I new pay as if not paid before:
   But if the while I think on thee, dear friend,
   All losses are restored, and sorrows end.

Shakespeare.

Ibid.

If thou survive my well-contented day
When that churl death my bones with dust shall cover,
And shalt by fortune once more re-survey
These poor rude lines of thy deceasèd lover;
Compare them with the bettering of the time,
And though they be outstripped by every pen,
Reserve them for my love, not for their rhyme
Exceeded by the height of happier men.
Oh, then vouchsafe me but this loving thought—
'Had my friend's Muse grown with this growing age,
A dearer birth than this his love had brought,
To march in ranks of better equipage:
   But since he died, and poets better prove,
   Theirs for their style I 'll read, his for his love.'

Shakespeare.

Ibid.

Full many a glorious morning have I seen
Flatter the mountain-tops with sovereign eye,
Kissing with golden face the meadows green,
Gilding pale streams with heavenly alchemy;
Anon permit the basest clouds to ride
With ugly rack on his celestial face,
And from the forlorn world his visage hide,
Stealing unseen to west with this disgrace:
Even so my sun one early morn did shine
With all-triumphant splendour on my brow;
But out, alack! he was but one hour mine;
The region cloud hath masked him from me now.
   Yet him for this my love no whit disdaineth;
   Suns of the world may stain when heaven's sun staineth.

Shakespeare.

Ibid.

What is your substance, whereof are you made,
That millions of strange shadows on you tend?
Since every one hath, every one, one shade,
And you, but one, can every shadow lend.
Describe Adonis, and the counterfeit
Is poorly imitated after you;
On Helen's cheek all art of beauty set,
And you in Grecian tires are painted new:
Speak of the spring and foison of the year,
The one doth shadow of your beauty show,
The other as your bounty doth appear;
And you in every blessëd shape we know.
   In all external grace you have some part,
   But you like none, none you, for constant heart.

Shakespeare.

Sonnets, 1609. (Written before 1599.)

Oh, how much more doth beauty beauteous seem
By that sweet ornament which truth doth give!
The rose looks fair, but fairer we it deem
For that sweet odour which doth in it live.
The canker-blooms have full as deep a dye
As the perfumëd tincture of the roses,
Hang on such thorns, and play as wantonly
When summer's breath their maskëd buds discloses:
But, for their virtue only is their show,
They live unwooed and unrespected fade;
Die to themselves.   Sweet roses do not so:
Of their sweet deaths are sweetest odours made:
   And so of you, beauteous and lovely youth,
   When that shall vade, by verse distils your truth.

Shakespeare.

Ibid.

Like as the waves make towards the pebbled shore,
So do our minutes hasten to their end;
Each changing place with that which goes before,
In sequent toil all forwards do contend.
Nativity, once in the main of light,
Crawls to maturity, wherewith being crowned,
Crooked eclipses 'gainst his glory fight,
And Time that gave doth now his gift confound.
Time doth transfix the flourish set on youth
And delves the parallels in beauty's brow,
Feeds on the rarities of nature's truth,
And nothing stands but for his scythe to mow:
  And yet to times in hope my verse shall stand,
  Praising thy worth, despite his cruel hand.

Shakespeare.

Ibid.

When I have seen by Time's fell hand defaced
The rich proud cost of outworn buried age;
When sometime lofty towers I see down-razed,
And brass eternal slave to mortal rage;
When I have seen the hungry ocean gain
Advantage on the kingdom of the shore,
And the firm soil win of the watery main,
Increasing store with loss and loss with store;
When I have seen such interchange of state,
Or state itself confounded to decay;
Ruin hath taught me thus to ruminate,
That Time will come and take my love away.
  This thought is as a death, which cannot choose
  But weep to have that which it fears to lose.

Shakespeare.

Ibid.

No longer mourn for me, when I am dead,
Than you shall hear the surly sullen bell
Give warning to the world that I am fled
From this vile world, with vilest worms to dwell;
Nay, if you read this line, remember not
The hand that writ it, for I love you so
That I in your sweet thoughts would be forgot,
If thinking on me then should make you woe.
Oh, if, I say, you look upon this verse
When I perhaps compounded am with clay,
Do not so much as my poor name rehearse,
But let your love even with my life decay;
   Lest the wise world should look into your moan,
   And mock you with me after I am gone.   *Shakespeare.*

Sonnets, 1609. (Written before 1599.)

That time of year thou may'st in me behold
When yellow leaves, or none, or few, do hang
Upon those boughs which shake against the cold,
Bare ruined choirs, where late the sweet birds sang.
In me thou see'st the twilight of such day
As after sunset fadeth in the west;
Which by and by black night doth take away,
Death's second self, that seals up all the rest.
In me thou see'st the glowing of such fire,
That on the ashes of his youth doth lie,
As the death-bed whereon it must expire,
Consumed with that which it was nourished by.
   This thou perceiv'st, which makes thy love more strong,
   To love that well which thou must leave ere long.
                                   Shakespeare.

Ibid.
ruined] 1640; rn'wd, 1609.

Farewell! thou art too dear for my possessing,
And like enough thou know'st thy estimate:
The charter of thy worth gives thee releasing;
My bonds in thee are all determinate.
For how do I hold thee but by thy granting?
And for that riches where is my deserving?
The cause of this fair gift in me is wanting,
And so my patent back again is swerving.
Thyself thou gav'st, thy own worth then not knowing,
Or me, to whom thou gav'st it, else mistaking;
So thy great gift, upon misprision growing,
Comes home again, on better judgement making.
    Thus have I had thee as a dream doth flatter,
    In sleep, a king; but waking, no such matter.

Shakespeare.

Ibid.

Then hate me when thou wilt; if ever, now;
Now, while the world is bent my deeds to cross,
Join with the spite of fortune, make me bow,
And do not drop in for an after-loss:
Ah! do not, when my heart hath 'scaped this sorrow,
Come in the rearward of a conquered woe;
Give not a windy night a rainy morrow,
To linger out a purposed overthrow.
If thou wilt leave me, do not leave me last,
When other petty griefs have done their spite,
But in the onset come; so shall I taste
At first the very worst of fortune's might;
    And other strains of woe, which now seem woe,
    Compared with loss of thee will not seem so.

Shakespeare.

Ibid.

They that have power to hurt and will do none,
That do not do the thing they most do show,
Who, moving others, are themselves as stone,
Unmovëd, cold, and to temptation slow;
They rightly do inherit heaven's graces,
And husband nature's riches from expense;
They are the lords and owners of their faces,
Others but stewards of their excellence.
The summer's flower is to the summer sweet,
Though to itself it only live and die,
But if that flower with base infection meet,
The basest weed outbraves his dignity:
　　For sweetest things turn sourest by their deeds;
　　Lilies that fester smell far worse than weeds.

Shakespeare.

Sonnets, 1609. (Written before 1599.)

How like a winter hath my absence been
From thee, the pleasure of the fleeting year!
What freezings have I felt, what dark days seen,
What old December's bareness everywhere!
And yet this time removed was summer's time;
The teeming autumn, big with rich increase,
Bearing the wanton burthen of the prime
Like widowed wombs after their lords' decease:
Yet this abundant issue seemed to me
But hope of orphans, and unfathered fruit;
For summer and his pleasures wait on thee,
And, thou away, the very birds are mute;
　　Or if they sing, 'tis with so dull a cheer,
　　That leaves look pale, dreading the winter 's near.

Shakespeare.

Ibid.

From you I have been absent in the spring,
When proud-pied April, dressed in all his trim,
Hath put a spirit of youth in every thing,
That heavy Saturn laughed and leaped with him.
Yet nor the lays of birds, nor the sweet smell
Of different flowers in odour and in hue,
Could make me any summer's story tell,
Or from their proud lap pluck them where they grew:
Nor did I wonder at the lily's white,
Nor praise the deep vermilion in the rose;
They were but sweet, but figures of delight,
Drawn after you, you pattern of all those.
   Yet seemed it winter still, and, you away,
   As with your shadow I with these did play.

Shakespeare.

Ibid.

My love is strengthened, though more weak in seeming;
I love not less, though less the show appear:
That love is merchandised whose rich esteeming
The owner's tongue doth publish every where.
Our love was new, and then but in the spring,
When I was wont to greet it with my lays;
As Philomel in summer's front doth sing,
And stops her pipe in growth of riper days:
Not that the summer is less pleasant now
Than when her mournful hymns did hush the night,
But that wild music burthens every bough,
And sweets grown common lose their dear delight.
   Therefore, like her, I sometime hold my tongue,
   Because I would not dull you with my song.

Shakespeare.

Ibid.

To me, fair friend, you never can be old,
For as you were when first your eye I eyed,
Such seems your beauty still. Three winters cold
Have from the forests shook three summers' pride;
Three beauteous springs to yellow autumn turned
In process of the seasons have I seen;
Three April perfumes in three hot Junes burned,
Since first I saw you fresh, which yet are green.
Ah! yet doth beauty, like a dial-hand,
Steal from his figure, and no pace perceived;
So your sweet hue, which methinks still doth stand,
Hath motion, and mine eye may be deceived:
   For fear of which, hear this, thou age unbred,
   Ere you were born was beauty's summer dead.

Shakespeare.

Sonnets, 1609. (Written before 1599.)

When in the chronicle of wasted time
I see descriptions of the fairest wights,
And beauty making beautiful old rhyme
In praise of ladies dead and lovely knights,
Then, in the blazon of sweet beauty's best,
Of hand, of foot, of lip, of eye, of brow,
I see their antique pen would have expressed
Even such a beauty as you master now.
So all their praises are but prophecies
Of this our time, all you prefiguring;
And, for they looked but with divining eyes,
They had not skill enough your worth to sing:
   For we, which now behold these present days,
   Have eyes to wonder, but lack tongues to praise.

Shakespeare.

Ibid.

skill] Tyrwhitt, 1780; still, 1609.

Oh, never say that I was false of heart,
Though absence seemed my flame to qualify.
As easy might I from myself depart
As from my soul, which in thy breast doth lie:
That is my home of love: if I have ranged,
Like him that travels, I return again,
Just to the time, not with the time exchanged,
So that myself bring water for my stain.
Never believe, though in my nature reigned
All frailties that besiege all kinds of blood,
That it could so preposterously be stained,
To leave for nothing all thy sum of good;
    For nothing this wide universe I call,
    Save thou, my rose; in it thou art my all.

Shakespeare.

Ibid.

Let me not to the marriage of true minds
Admit impediments: love is not love
Which alters when it alteration finds,
Or bends with the remover to remove.
Oh, no! it is an ever-fixèd mark
That looks on tempests, and is never shaken;
It is the star to every wandering bark,
Whose worth 's unknown, although his height be taken.
Love 's not Time's fool, though rosy lips and cheeks
Within his bending sickle's compass come;
Love alters not with his brief hours and weeks,
But bears it out even to the edge of doom:
    If this be error, and upon me proved,
    I never writ, nor no man ever loved.

Shakespeare.

Ibid.

How oft, when thou, my music, music play'st
Upon that blessëd wood whose motion sounds
With thy sweet fingers, when thou gently sway'st
The wiry concord that mine ear confounds,
Do I envy those jacks that nimble leap
To kiss the tender inward of thy hand,
Whilst my poor lips, which should that harvest reap,
At the wood's boldness by thee blushing stand.
To be so tickled, they would change their state
And situation with those dancing chips,
O'er whom thy fingers walk with gentle gait,
Making dead wood more blessed than living lips.
   Since saucy jacks so happy are in this,
   Give them thy fingers, me thy lips to kiss.

Sonnets, 1609. (Written before 1599.)   *Shakespeare.*

Poor soul, the centre of my sinful earth,
Foiled by these rebel powers that thee array,
Why dost thou pine within and suffer dearth,
Painting thy outward walls so costly gay?
Why so large cost, having so short a lease,
Dost thou upon thy fading mansion spend?
Shall worms, inheritors of this excess,
Eat up thy charge? Is this thy body's end?
Then, soul, live thou upon thy servant's loss,
And let that pine to aggravate thy store;
Buy terms divine in selling hours of dross;
Within be fed, without be rich no more:
   So shalt thou feed on death, that feeds on men,
   And death once dead, there 's no more dying then.

Ibid.   *Shakespeare.*

thy fingers] lines 11 and 14, Gildon, 1710; their fingers, 1609.   Foiled by]
Palgrave, 1896; My sinful earth, 1609.

WIT, WHITHER WILT THOU?

Wit, whither wilt thou? Woe is me!
  Always musing, fie for shame!
Sorry I am the same to see,
    That love hath brought thee out of frame—
        Out of frame and temper too;
        This can love and fancy do!

Once I knew thee well advised;
  But now, I am sure, 'tis nothing so.
Love thy senses hath disguised,
    And her beauty bred thy woe—
        Thy woe, thy time, thy downfall too;
        This can love and fancy do!

Pale, and wan, and worn with care,
  And all to melancholy bent:
Thus doth madmen use to fare
    When their wits with love are spent—
        Content with discontentments too;
        This can love and fancy do!

Those humours purge that stops thy breath!
  Purge those fancies from thy head!
Such conceits will breed thy death:
    She will laugh when thou art dead—
        Laugh she will, and lie down too;
        These conceits will women do!

A bird in hand 's worth two in brier;
  Why then should I say 'Woe 's me!'

Because the things that I desire
  Are true and constant unto me?
      Therefore, I say, cast care from thee,
      And never more say 'Woe is me!'   *Anon.*

Shirburn Ballads MS.* (Poem written before 1599.) Quoted, *As you like
it,* IV. i. 168.

OH, WHO REGARDS

Oh, who regards a wounded soul's lamenting,
Grieving to hear him grievously complaining?
Oh, who affects a sinner's sad repenting,
Or lends an ear to Music's mournful straining?
  Alas! there 's now no sorrowful relation—
                    No sad relation
  Can melt our frozen hearts into compassion,
                    Into compassion.   *Anon.*

Christ Church MS. 1074–7. (Poem written before 1599.)*

SIGH NO MORE, LADIES

Sigh no more, ladies, sigh no more;
  Men were deceivers ever;
One foot in sea, and one on shore,
  To one thing constant never:
Then sigh not so, but let them go,
  And be you blithe and bonny,
Converting all your sounds of woe
  Into Hey nonny, nonny!

Sing no more ditties, sing no moe
  Of dumps so dull and heavy;

The fraud of men was ever so,
    Since summer first was leavy:
Then sigh not so, but let them go,
    And be you blithe and bonny,
Converting all your sounds of woe
    Into Hey nonny, nonny!   *Shakespeare.*

Much Ado about Nothing, 1600. (Written 1598–9?)

TO THE SPRING

Earth now is green, and heaven is blue,
Lively spring which makes all new,
Jolly spring, doth enter:
Sweet young sunbeams do subdue
Angry, agèd winter.

Blasts are mild, and seas are calm,
Every meadow flows with balm,
The earth wears all her riches;
Harmonious birds sing such a psalm
As ear and heart bewitches.

Reserve, sweet spring, this nymph of ours
Eternal garlands of thy flowers,
Green garlands never wasting;
In her ,shall last our State's fair spring,
Now and for ever flourishing,
As long as heaven is lasting.   *Sir J. Davies.*

Hymns of Astraea, in Acrostic Verse, 1599.

To the Spring] Note: Initial letters of lines form ELISABETHA REGINA.

MAN

I know my body 's of so frail a kind,
   As force without, fevers within, can kill;
I know the heavenly nature of my mind,
   But 'tis corrupted both in wit and will.

I know my soul hath power to know all things,
   Yet is she blind and ignorant in all;
I know I am one of nature's little kings,
   Yet to the least and vilest things am thrall.

I know my life 's a pain, and but a span;
   I know my sense is mocked with everything;
And, to conclude, I know myself a man,
   Which is a proud, and yet a wretched thing.

Sir J. Davies.

Nosce Teipsum, 1599. (An excerpt.)

SONG

Virtue's branches wither, virtue pines,
   O pity, pity, and alack the time!
Vice doth flourish, vice in glory shines,
   Her gilded boughs above the cedar climb.

Vice hath golden cheeks, O pity, pity!
   She in every land doth monarchize:
Virtue is exiled from every city,
   Virtue is a fool, vice only wise.

O pity, pity! virtue weeping dies,
   Vice laughs to see her faint, alack the time!
This sinks; with painted wings the other flies:
   Alack, that best should fall, and bad should climb!

O pity, pity, pity! mourn, not sing!
Vice is a saint, virtue an underling.
Vice doth flourish, vice in glory shines,
Virtue's branches wither, virtue pines.   *Dekker.*

Old Fortunatus, 1600. (Acted 1599.)

OH, THE MONTH OF MAY!

Oh, the month of May, the merry month of May,
So frolic, so gay, and so green, so green, so green!
Oh, and then did I unto my true Love say,
Sweet Peg, thou shalt be my Summer's Queen.

Now the nightingale, the pretty nightingale,
The sweetest singer in all the forest's quire,
Entreats thee, sweet Peggy, to hear thy true Love's tale:
Lo, yonder she sitteth, her breast against a brier.

But oh, I spy the cuckoo, the cuckoo, the cuckoo;
See where she sitteth; come away, my joy:
Come away, I prithee, I do not like the cuckoo
Should sing where my Peggy and I kiss and toy.

Oh, the month of May, the merry month of May,
So frolic, so gay, and so green, so green, so green;
And then did I unto my true Love say,
Sweet Peg, thou shalt be my Summer's Queen.   *Dekker.*

The Shoemaker's Holiday, 1600. (Mentioned in Henslowe's Diary, 1599.)

TROLL THE BOWL!

Cold 's the wind, and wet 's the rain,
Saint Hugh be our good speed!

Ill is the weather that bringeth no gain,
   Nor helps good hearts in need.

Troll the bowl, the jolly nut-brown bowl,
   And here, kind mate, to thee!
Let 's sing a dirge for Saint Hugh's soul,
   And down it merrily.

Down-a-down, hey, down-a-down,
   Hey derry derry down-a-down!
Ho! well done, to me let come,
   Ring compass, gentle joy!

Troll the bowl, the nut-brown bowl,
   And here, kind, &c. (*as often as there be men
      to drink*).

(*At last, when all have drunk, this verse:*)

Cold 's the wind, and wet 's the rain,
   Saint Hugh be our good speed!
Ill is the weather that bringeth no gain,
   Nor helps good hearts in need.   *Dekker.*

The Shoemaker's Holiday, 1600.

SONNETS

To nothing fitter can I thee compare
Than to the son of some rich pennyfather,
Who, having now brought on his end with care,
Leaves to his son all he had heaped together;
This new rich novice, lavish of his chest,
To one man gives, doth on another spend,
Then here he riots, yet among the rest

Haps to lend some to one true honest friend.
Thy gifts thou in obscurity dost waste,
False friends thy kindness, born but to deceive thee,
Thy love that is on the unworthy placed,
Time hath thy beauty, which with age will leave thee;
  Only that little which to me was lent
  I give thee back, when all the rest is spent.   *Drayton.*

Idea, 1599. (Text 1619.)

An evil spirit, your beauty haunts me still,
Wherewith, alas, I have been long possessed,
Which ceaseth not to tempt me to each ill,
Nor gives me once but one poor minute's rest;
In me it speaks, whether I sleep or wake,
And when by means to drive it out I try,
With greater torments then it me doth take,
And tortures me in most extremity;
Before my face it lays down my despairs,
And hastes me on unto a sudden death,
Now tempting me to drown myself in tears,
And then in sighing to give up my breath.
  Thus am I still provoked to every evil
  By this good wicked spirit, sweet angel-devil.

Ibid.   *Drayton.*

THE LOWEST TREES HAVE TOPS

The lowest trees have tops; the ant her gall;
  The fly her spleen; the little sparks their heat:
The slender hairs cast shadows, though but small;
  And bees have stings, although they be not great.
Seas have their source, and so have shallow springs;
And love is love, in beggars as in kings.

Where rivers smoothest run, deep are the fords;
   The dial stirs, yet none perceives it move;
The firmest faith is in the fewest words;
   The turtles cannot sing, and yet they love.
True hearts have eyes and ears, no tongues to speak;
They hear and see, and sigh; and then they break.   *Dyer.*

A Poetical Rhapsody, 1602. (Variant, 1599, in Bodley MS. Rawl. Poet. 148.)

HAPPY WERE HE

Happy were he could finish forth his fate
   In some unhaunted desert, most obscure
From all societies, from love and hate
   Of worldly folk; then might he sleep secure;
Then wake again, and give God ever praise,
   Content with hips and haws and bramble-berry;
In contemplation spending all his days,
   And change of holy thoughts to make him merry;
Where, when he dies, his tomb may be a bush,
Where harmless robin dwells with gentle thrush.   *Essex.*

Bodley MS. Ashm. 781. (Variant in Chetham MS. 8012. Poem written
1599?)*

SONG

When love on time and measure makes his ground—
Time that must end, though love can never die,—
'Tis love betwixt a shadow and a sound,
A love not in the heart but in the eye;
     A love that ebbs and flows, now up, now down;
     A morning's favour and an evening's frown.

Sweet looks show love, yet they are but as beams;
Fair words seem true, yet they are but as wind;

God ever praise] Chet. MS.; God praise, Ashm. MS.

Eyes shed their tears, yet are but outward streams;
Sighs paint a sadness in the falsest mind:
> Looks, words, tears, sighs, show love when love they
> leave:
> False hearts can weep, sigh, swear, and yet deceive.
>
> *Lilliat(?)*

R. Jones' *Songs and Airs*, i., 1600. (First stanza in Bodley MS. Rawl. Poet.
148; c. 1599.)

THE NUT-BROWN ALE

The nut-brown ale, the nut-brown ale,
Puts down all drink when it is stale!
The toast, the nutmeg, and the ginger
Will make a sighing man a singer.
Ale gives a buffet in the head,
  But ginger under-props the brain;
When ale would strike a strong man dead
  Then nutmeg tempers it again.
The nut-brown ale, the nut-brown ale,
Puts down all drink when it is stale!   *Marston(?)*

Histriomastix, 1610.* (Acted c. 1599.)

AGE AND YOUTH

> Crabbëd Age and Youth
> Cannot live together:
> Youth is full of pleasance,
> Age is full of care;
> Youth like summer morn,
> Age like winter weather,
> Youth like summer brave,
> Age like winter bare:
> Youth is full of sport,
> Age's breath is short,

Youth is nimble, Age is lame:
Youth is hot and bold,
Age is weak and cold,
Youth is wild, and Age is tame.
Age, I do abhor thee,
Youth, I do adore thee;
Oh, my Love, my Love is young!
Age, I do defy thee—
O sweet shepherd, hie thee,
For methinks thou stays too long.

Shakespeare (?) *

The Passionate Pilgrim, 1599.

FAIR IS MY LOVE

Fair is my Love, but not so fair as fickle;
Mild as a dove, but neither true nor trusty;
Brighter than glass, and yet, as glass is, brittle;
Softer than wax, and yet, as iron, rusty:
   A lily pale, with damask dye to grace her,
   None fairer, nor none falser to deface her.

Her lips to mine how often hath she joinëd,
Between each kiss her oaths of true love swearing!
How many tales to please me hath she coinëd,
Dreading my love, the loss whereof still fearing!
   Yet in the midst of all her pure protestings,
   Her faith, her oaths, her tears, and all were jestings.

She burned with love, as straw with fire flameth;
She burned out love, as soon as straw outburneth;
She framed the love, and yet she foiled the framing;
She bade love last, and yet she fell a-turning.

---

midst] 1612; mids, 1599.

Was this a lover, or a lecher whether?
Bad in the best, though excellent in neither.

Ibid.   *Shakespeare(?)* *

IT WAS A LORDING'S DAUGHTER

It was a lording's daughter, the fairest one of three,
That likëd of her master as well as well might be,
Till looking on an Englishman, the fairest that eye could see,
  Her fancy fell a-turning.

Long was the combat doubtful that love with love did fight,
To leave the master loveless, or kill the gallant knight:
To put in practice either, alas, it was a spite
  Unto the silly damsel.

But one must be refusëd; more mickle was the pain
That nothing could be usëd to turn them both to gain,
For of the two the trusty knight was wounded with disdain:
  Alas, she could not help it!

Thus art with arms contending was victor of the day,
Which by a gift of learning did bear the maid away:
Then, lullaby, the learnëd man hath got the lady gay;
  For now my song is ended.   *Shakespeare(?)* *

Ibid.

SWEET ROSE, FAIR FLOWER

Sweet rose, fair flower, untimely plucked, soon vaded,
Plucked in the bud, and vaded in the spring!
Bright orient pearl, alack, too timely shaded!

---

whether] which.

Fair creature, killed too soon by death's sharp sting,
   Like a green plum that hangs upon a tree,
   And falls, through wind, before the fall should be!—

I weep for thee, and yet no cause I have,
For why thou lefts me nothing in thy will:
And yet thou lefts me more than I did crave,
For why I cravèd nothing of thee still:
   O yes, dear friend, I pardon crave of thee,
   Thy discontent thou didst bequeath to me.

Shakespeare (?) *

The Passionate Pilgrim, 1599.

RIVERS

Fair Danubie is praised for being wide;
   Nilus commended for the sevenfold head;
Euphrates for the swiftness of the tide,
   And for the garden whence his course is led;
   The banks of Rhine with vines are overspread:
Take Loire and Po, yet all may not compare
With English Thamesis for buildings rare.   *Storer.*

The Life and Death of Thomas Wolsey, Cardinal, 1599.*

OH, SLEEP, FOND FANCY

Oh, sleep, fond Fancy, my head, alas, thou tirest
With false delight of that which thou desirest.
Sleep, sleep, I say, and leave my thoughts molesting,
Thy master's head hath need of sleep and resting.

Anon.

J. Bennet's *Madrigals,* 1599.

For why] Because.

A LITTLE PRETTY BONNY LASS

A little pretty bonny lass was walking
    In midst of May before the sun gan rise.
I took her by the hand and fell to talking
    Of this and that, as best I could devise.
I swore I would, yet still she said I should not
Do what I would, and yet for all I could not.

J. Farmer's *English Madrigals*, 1599.

Anon.

YOU BLESSËD BOWERS

You blessëd bowers, whose green leaves now are spreading,
    Shadow the sunshine from my mistress' face.
And you, sweet roses, only for her bedding
    When weary she doth take her resting-place,
You fair white lilies, and pretty flowers all,
Give your attendance at my mistress' call.

Anon.

Ibid.

CHANGE THY MIND SINCE SHE DOTH CHANGE

Change thy mind since she doth change,
    Let not fancy still abuse thee.
Thy untruths cannot seem strange
    When her falsehood doth accuse thee.
Love is dead, and thou art free,
She doth live, but dead to thee.

Whilst she loved thee best awhile,
    See how still she did delay thee,
Using shows for to beguile
    Those vain hopes which have betrayed thee.

Now thou see'st, but all too late,
Love loves truth, which women hate.

Love, farewell, more dear to me
    Than my life which thou preserved'st.
Life, thy joy is gone from thee,
    Others have what thou deserved'st,
They envỳ what 's not their own:
Happier life to live alone.

Yet thus much to ease my mind:
    Let her know what she hath gotten,
She, who time hath proved unkind,
    Having changed, is quite forgotten.
Fortune now hath done her worst;
Would she had done so at first.

Love no more since she is gone;
    She is gone and loves another.
Having been deceived by one,
    Leave to love, and love no other.
She was false, bid her adieu.
She was best, but yet untrue.   *Essex.*

Bodley MS. Rawl. Poet. 85. (Poem written before 1600.)*

AS YOU CAME FROM THE HOLY LAND

As you came from the holy land
    Of Walsingham,
Met you not with my true Love
    By the way as you came?

'How shall I know your true Love,
    That have met many one,

As I went to the holy land,
    That have come, that have gone?'

She is neither white, nor brown,
    But as the heavens fair;
There is none hath a form so divine
    In the earth, or the air.

'Such a one did I meet, good sir!
    Such an angelic face,
Who like a queen, like a nymph, did appear
    By her gait, by her grace.'

She hath left me here all alone,
    All alone, as unknown,
Who sometimes did me lead with herself,
    And me loved as her own.

'What 's the cause that she leaves you alone,
    And a new way doth take,
Who loved you once as her own,
    And her joy did you make?'

I have loved her all my youth;
    But now old, as you see,
Love likes not the falling fruit
    From the withered tree.

Know that Love is a careless child,
    And forgets promise past;
He is blind, he is deaf when he list,
    And in faith never fast.

His desire is a dureless content,
    And a trustless joy:

He is won with a world of despair,
    And is lost with a toy.

Of womenkind such indeed is the love,
    Or the word love abused,
Under which many childish desires
    And conceits are excused.

But true love is a durable fire,
    In the mind ever burning,
Never sick, never old, never dead,
    From itself never turning.   *Raleigh* (?)

Bodley MS. Rawl. Poet. 85. (Poem written before 1600.)* Quoted, *Hamlet*,
IV. V. 23–4.

THE SILENT LOVER

I

Our passions are most like to floods and streams,
    The shallow murmur, but the deep are dumb;
So, when affection yields discourse, it seems
    The bottom is but shallow whence they come.
They that are rich in words, must needs discover
That they are poor in that which makes a lover.

II

Wrong not, sweet empress of my heart,
    The merit of true passion,
With thinking that he feels no smart,
    That sues for no compassion;
Since, if my plaints serve not to prove
    The conquest of your beauty,
They come not from defect of love,
    But from excess of duty.

excess] MS. Ashm.; access, MS. Rawl. Poet.

For knowing that I sue to serve
   A saint of such perfection
As all desire—yet none deserve—
   A place in her affection,
I rather choose to want relief
   Than venture the revealing;
When glory recommends the grief,
   Despair distrusts the healing.

Thus those desires that aim too high
   For any mortal lover,
When reason cannot make them die,
   Discretion doth them cover.
Yet, when discretion doth bereave
   The plaints that they should utter,
Then your discretion may perceive
   That silence is a suitor.

Silence in love bewrays more woe
   Than words though ne'er so witty;
A beggar that is dumb, you know,
   Deserveth double pity.
Then misconceive not, dearest heart,
   My true, though secret passion;
He smarteth most that hides his smart,
   And sues for no compassion.   *Raleigh.*

Bodley MS. Rawl. Poet. 160. (Variant of II. in Bodl. MS. Ashm. 781. Poems
written before 1600 ?) *

AWAY TO TWIVER, AWAY, AWAY!

And did you not hear of a mirth that befell
   The morrow after a wedding day,
At carrying a bride at home to dwell?
   And away to Twiver, away, away!

The quintain was set and the garlands were made,
   'Tis pity old custom should ever decay;
And woe be to him that was horsed on a jade,
   For he carried no credit away, away!

We met a consort of fiddle-de-dees,
   We set them a-cock-horse, and made them to play
The *Winning of Bullen* and *Upsie-frees;*
   And away to Twiver, away, away!

There was ne'er a lad in all the parish
   That would go to the plough that day
But on his fore-horse his wench he carries;
   And away to Twiver, away, away!

The butler was quick and the ale he did tap,
   The maidens did make the chamber full gay;
The serving-men gave me a fuddling-cap,
   And I did carry it away, away!

The smith of the town his liquor so took
   That he was persuaded the ground looked blue;
And I dare boldly to swear on a book
   Such smiths as he there are but a few.

A posset was made and the women did sip
   And simpering said they could eat no more;
Full many a maid was laid on the lip:
   I 'll say no more but so give o'er.   *Anon.*

The Famous History of Friar Bacon, 1627. (Earliest extant edition. First
printed 16th Cent.)*

SONG

And can the physician make sick men well?
And can the magician a fortune divine?
Without lily, germander, and sops-in-wine,
> With sweet-briar
> And bon-fire
> And strawberry wire
> And columbine.

Within and out, in and out, round as a ball,
With hither and thither, as straight as a line,
With lily, germander, and sops-in wine.
> With sweet-briar
> And bon-fire
> And strawberry wire
> And columbine.

When Saturn did live, there lived no poor,
The king and the beggar with roots did dine,
With lily, germander, and sops-in wine.
> With sweet-briar
> And bon-fire
> And strawberry wire
> And columbine.   *Anon.*

Robin Good-fellow, Part ii. 1628. (Written before 1600?)*

ROBIN GOOD-FELLOW'S SONG

Round about, little ones, quick, quick and nimble;
In and out, wheel about, run, hop, or amble.
Join your hands lovingly; well done, musician!

---

quick, quick] 1639; quick, 1628.

Mirth keepeth man in health, like a physician.
Elves, urchins, goblins all, and little fairies
That do filch, black and pinch maids of the dairies—
  Make a ring on this grass with your quick measures:
  Tom shall play, and I 'll sing, for all your pleasures.

Pinch and Patch, Gull and Grim, go you together,
For you can change your shapes like to the weather;
Sib and Tib, Lick and Lull, you all have tricks too,
Little Tom Thumb that pipes shall go betwixt you.
Tom, tickle up thy pipes, till they be weary,
I will laugh, ho, ho, ho! and make me merry.
  Make a ring on this grass with your quick measures:
  Tom shall play, I will sing, for all your pleasures.

The moon shines fair and bright, and the owl hollos;
Mortals now take their rests upon their pillows:
The bat 's abroad likewise, and the night raven
Which doth use for to call men to death's haven.
Now the mice peep abroad, and the cats take them:
Now do young wenches sleep till their dreams wake them.
  Make a ring on the grass with your quick measures:
  Tom shall play, I will sing, for all your pleasures.

Robin Good-fellow, Part ii. 1628. (Written before 1600?)   *Anon.*

LOVE CANNOT LIVE

Mine eye bewrays
My heart's desires:
Ill luck delays
That love requires.
Love cannot live
Where hope decays:

Love cannot give,
That time delays.
Love cannot live
Where favour dies:
Hope cannot give
That hap denies.   *Anon.*

Bodley MS. Rawl. Poet. 85. (Poem written before 1600.)*

UNDER THE GREENWOOD TREE

Under the greenwood tree,
Who loves to lie with me,
And turn his merry note
Unto the sweet bird's throat,
Come hither, come hither, come hither;
Here shall he see
No enemy
But winter and rough weather.

Who doth ambition shun,
And loves to live i' the sun,
Seeking the food he eats,
And pleased with what he gets,
Come hither, come hither, come hither;
Here shall he see
No enemy
But winter and rough weather.   *Shakespeare.*

As you like it, 1623. (Written 1599–1600 ?)

BLOW, BLOW, THOU WINTER WIND

Blow, blow, thou winter wind,
Thou are not so unkind

As man's ingratitude;
   Thy tooth is not so keen,
   Because thou art not seen,
      Although thy breath be rude.
Heigh ho! sing, heigh ho! unto the green holly:
Most friendship is feigning, most loving mere folly:
      Then, heigh ho, the holly!
      This life is most jolly.

   Freeze, freeze, thou bitter sky,
   That dost not bite so nigh
      As benefits forgot:
   Though thou the waters warp,
   Thy sting is not so sharp
      As friend remembered not.
Heigh ho! sing, heigh ho! unto the green holly:
Most friendship is feigning, most loving mere folly:
      Then, heigh ho, the holly!
      This life is most jolly.   *Shakespeare.*

As you like it, 1623. (Written 1599–1600 ?)

IT WAS A LOVER AND HIS LASS

It was a lover and his lass,
   With a hey, and a ho, and a hey nonny no,
That o'er the green corn fields did pass
   In spring time, the only pretty ring time,
   When birds do sing, hey ding a ding a ding:
   Sweet lovers love the spring.

Between the acres of the rye,
   With a hey, and a ho, and a hey nonny no,
These pretty country fools would lie,
   In spring time, the only pretty ring time,

When birds do sing, hey ding a ding a ding:
Sweet lovers love the spring.

This carol they began that hour,
With a hey, and a ho, and a hey nonny no,
How that a life was but a flower
In spring time, the only pretty ring time,
When birds do sing, hey ding a ding a ding:
Sweet lovers love the spring.

Then pretty lovers take the time
With a hey, and a ho, and a hey nonny no,
For love is crownëd with the prime
In spring time, the only pretty ring time,
When birds do sing, hey ding a ding a ding:
Sweet lovers love the spring.   *Shakespeare.*

Ibid. Text from T. Morley's *First Book of Airs,* 1600.*

O MISTRESS MINE, WHERE ARE YOU ROAMING?

O mistress mine, where are you roaming?
Oh, stay and hear! your true Love 's coming,
That can sing both high and low:
Trip no further, pretty sweeting;
Journeys end in lovers' meeting,
Every wise man's son doth know.

What is love? 'tis not hereafter;
Present mirth hath present laughter;
What 's to come is still unsure:
In delay there lies no plenty:
Then come kiss me, sweet-and-twenty,
Youth 's a stuff will not endure.   *Shakespeare.*

Twelfth Night, 1623. (Written 1599–1600 ?)*

COME AWAY, COME AWAY, DEATH

Come away, come away, death,
And in sad cypress let me be laid;
    Fly away, fly away, breath;
I am slain by a fair cruel maid.
My shroud of white, stuck all with yew,
            Oh, prepare it!
My part of death, no one so true
            Did share it.

Not a flower, not a flower sweet,
On my black coffin let there be strown;
    Not a friend, not a friend greet
My poor corpse, where my bones shall be thrown:
A thousand thousand sighs to save,
            Lay me, oh, where
Sad true lover never find my grave,
            To weep there!   *Shakespeare.*

Twelfth Night, 1623. (Written 1599–1600?)

WHEN THAT I WAS AND A LITTLE TINY BOY

When that I was and a little tiny boy,
    With hey, ho, the wind and the rain,
A foolish thing was but a toy,
    For the rain it raineth every day.

But when I came to man's estate,
    With hey, ho, the wind and the rain,
'Gainst knaves and thieves men shut their gate,
    For the rain it raineth every day.

But when I came, alas, to wive,
    With hey, ho, the wind and the rain,

Fly away, fly] Rowe, 1709; Fye away, fie, 1623.

By swaggering could I never thrive,
  For the rain it raineth every day.

But when I came unto my beds,
  With hey, ho, the wind and the rain,
With toss-pots still had drunken heads,
  For the rain it raineth every day.

A great while ago the world begun,
  With hey, ho, the wind and the rain,
But that 's all one, our play is done,
  And we 'll strive to please you every day.

*Ibid.**   *Shakespeare.*

A PALINODE

As withereth the primrose by the river,
As fadeth summer's sun from gliding fountains,
As vanisheth the light-blown bubble ever,
As melteth snow upon the mossy mountains:
So melts, so vanisheth, so fades, so withers
The rose, the shine, the bubble, and the snow
Of praise, pomp, glory, joy—which short life gathers—
Fair praise, vain pomp, sweet glory, brittle joy.
The withered primrose by the mourning river,
The faded summer's sun from weeping fountains,
The light-blown bubble vanishëd for ever,
The molten snow upon the naked mountains,
  Are emblems that the treasures we up-lay
  Soon wither, vanish, fade, and melt away.

For as the snow, whose lawn did overspread
The ambitious hills, which giant-like did threat
To pierce the heaven with their aspiring head,

___

begun] Rowe, 1709; begon, 1623.

Naked and bare doth leave their craggy seat;
Whenas the bubble, which did empty fly
The dalliance of the undiscernëd wind,
On whose calm rolling waves it did rely,
Hath shipwreck made, where it did dalliance find;
And when the sunshine which dissolved the snow,
Coloured the bubble with a pleasant vary,
And made the rathe and timely primrose grow,
Swarth clouds withdrawn (which longer time do tarry)—
   Oh, what is praise, pomp, glory, joy, but so
   As shine by fountains, bubbles, flowers, or snow?

England's Helicon, 1600.   *Bolton.*

I WOULD THOU WERT NOT FAIR

I would thou wert not fair, or I were wise;
I would thou hadst no face, or I no eyes;
I would thou wert not wise, or I not fond;
Or thou not free, or I not so in bond.

But thou art fair, and I can not be wise:
Thy sun-like face hath blinded both mine eyes;
Thou canst not but be wise, nor I but fond;
Nor thou but free, nor I but still in bond.

Yet am I wise to think that thou art fair;
Mine eyes their pureness in thy face repair;
Nor am I fond, that do thy wisdom see;
Nor yet in bond, because that thou art free.

Then in thy beauty only make me wise;
And in thy face the Graces guide mine eyes;

---

fond] foolish.

And in thy wisdom only see me fond;
And in thy freedom keep me still in bond.

So shalt thou still be fair, and I be wise;
Thy face shine still upon my clearèd eyes;
Thy wisdom only see how I am fond;
Thy freedom only keep me still in bond.

So would I thou wert fair, and I were wise;
So would thou hadst thy face, and I mine eyes;
So would I thou wert wise, and I were fond,
And thou wert free and I were still in bond.

Breton.

The Strange Fortunes of Two Excellent Princes, 1600.

AN ODD CONCEIT

Lovely kind, and kindly loving,
Such a mind were worth the moving;
Truly fair, and fairly true—
Where are all these, but in you?

Wisely kind, and kindly wise;
Blessèd life, where such love lies!
Wise, and kind, and fair, and true—
Lovely live all these in you.

Sweetly dear, and dearly sweet;
Blessèd, where these blessings meet!
Sweet, fair, wise, kind, blessèd, true—
Blessèd be all these in you!

Breton.

Melancholic Humours, 1600.

SAY THAT I SHOULD SAY I LOVE YE

Say that I should say I love ye,
  Would you say 'tis but a saying?
But if love in prayërs move ye,
  Will you not be moved with praying?

Think I think that love should know ye,
  Will you think 'tis but a thinking?
But if love the thought do show ye,
  Will ye lose your eyes with winking?

Write that I do write you blessëd,
  Will you write 'tis but a writing?
But if truth and love confess it,
  Will ye doubt the true inditing?

No, I say, and think, and write it,
  Write, and think, and say your pleasure;
Love, and truth, and I indite it,
  You are blessëd out of measure.   *Breton.*

England's Helicon, 1600.

DIAPHENIA

Diaphenia, like the daffadowndilly,
  White as the sun, fair as the lily,
Heigh ho, how I do love thee!
  I do love thee as my lambs
  Are belovëd of their dams;
How blest were I if thou wouldst prove me!

Diaphenia, like the spreading roses,
  That in thy sweets all sweets encloses,

Fair sweet, how I do love thee!
  I do love thee as each flower
  Loves the sun's life-giving power,
For, dead, thy breath to life might move me.

  Diaphenia, like to all things blessëd,
  When all thy praises are expressëd,
Dear joy, how I do love thee!
  As the birds do love the spring,
  Or the bees their careful king:
Then in requite, sweet virgin, love me!

Ibid.   *Constable.*

SWEET CONTENT

Art thou poor, yet hast thou golden slumbers?
     O sweet content!
Art thou rich, yet is thy mind perplexed?
     O punishment!
Dost thou laugh to see how fools are vexed
To add to golden numbers, golden numbers?
O sweet content! O sweet, O sweet content!
    Work apace, apace, apace, apace;
    Honest labour bears a lovely face;
   Then hey nonny nonny, hey nonny nonny!

Canst drink the waters of the crispëd spring?
     O sweet content!
Swimm'st thou in wealth, yet sink'st in thine own tears?
     O punishment!
Then he that patiently want's burden bears
No burden bears, but is a king, a king!
O sweet content! O sweet, O sweet content!

Work apace, apace, apace, apace;
Honest labour bears a lovely face;
Then hey nonny nonny, hey nonny nonny!

Dekker(?)

Patient Grissill, 1603. By Chettle, Haughton, and Dekker. (Acted 1600.)

BEAUTY, ARISE!

Beauty, arise, show forth thy glorious shining!
Thine eyes feed love, for them he standeth pining;
Honour and youth attend to do their duty
To thee, their only sovereign, Beauty.
Beauty, arise, whilst we, thy servants, sing
Io to Hymen, wedlock's jocund king.
  Io to Hymen, Io, Io, sing,
    Of wedlock, love, and youth, is Hymen king.

Beauty, arise, thy glorious lights display,
Whilst we sing Io, glad to see this day.
  Io to Hymen, Io, Io, sing,
    Of wedlock, love, and youth, is Hymen king.

*Ibid.**   *Dekker*(?)

LULLABY

Golden slumbers kiss your eyes,
Smiles awake you when you rise.
Sleep, pretty wantons, do not cry,
And I will sing a lullaby:
Rock them, rock them, lullaby.

Care is heavy, therefore sleep you;
You are care, and care must keep you.
Sleep, pretty wantons, do not cry,

And I will sing a lullaby:
Rock them, rock them, lullaby.   *Dekker*(?)

Ibid.

THE SHEPHERD'S DAFFODIL

Gorbo, as thou cam'st this way
   By yonder little hill,
Or as thou through the fields didst stray,
   Saw'st thou my Daffodil?

She's in a frock of Lincoln green,
   Which colour likes her sight,
And never hath her beauty seen
   But through a veil of white;

Than roses, richer to behold,
   That trim up lovers' bowers,
The pansy and the marigold,
   Though Phoebus' paramours.

'Thou well describ'st the daffodil;
   It is not full an hour
Since by the spring near yonder hill
   I saw that lovely flower.'

Yet my fair flower thou didst not meet,
   Nor news of her didst bring,
And yet my Daffodil's more sweet
   Than that by yonder spring.

'I saw a shepherd that doth keep
   In yonder field of lilies,

Was making, as he fed his sheep,
   A wreath of daffodillies.'

Yet, Gorbo, thou delud'st me still,
   My flower thou didst not see;
For, know, my pretty Daffodil
   Is worn of none but me:

To show itself but near her seat
   No lily is so bold,
Except to shade her from the heat,
   Or keep her from the cold.

'Through yonder vale as I did pass,
   Descending from the hill,
I met a smirking bonny lass,
   They call her Daffodil;

'Whose presence, as along she went,
   The pretty flowers did greet
As though their heads they downward bent
   With homage to her feet;

'And all the shepherds that were nigh,
   From top of every hill
Unto the valleys, loud did cry,
   "There goes sweet Daffodil!"'

Ay, gentle shepherd, now with joy
   Thou all my flocks dost fill,
That's she alone, kind shepherd's boy,
   Let us to Daffodil.   *Drayton.*

From *The Ninth Eclogue*, in *Poems*, 1619. (Also as a separate poem, in
England's Helicon, 1600.)

A ROUNDELAY

Tell me, thou skilful shepherd's swain,
  Who 's yonder in the valley set?
Oh, it is she whose sweets do stain
  The lily, rose, the violet!

Why doth the sun against his kind
  Stay his bright chariot in the skies?
He pauseth, almost stricken blind
  With gazing on her heavenly eyes.

Why do thy flocks forbear their food,
  Which sometime was their chief delight?
Because they need no other good,
  That live in presence of her sight.

How come those flowers to flourish still,
  Not withering with sharp winter's breath?
She hath robbed Nature of her skill,
  And comforts all things with her breath.

Why slide these brooks so slow away,
  As swift as the wild roe that were?
Oh, muse not, shepherd, that they stay
  When they her heavenly voice do hear!

From whence come all those goodly swains,
  And lovely girls attired in green?
From gathering garlands on the plains
  To crown thy Syl, our shepherds' queen:

The sun, that lights this world below,
  Flocks, brooks, and flowers can witness bear,

---

stain] shame.   stricken] 1600; strooken, 1619.

These shepherds and these nymphs do know—
　　Thy Sylvia is as chaste as fair.　　　　　*Drayton.*

From *The Ninth Eclogue*, in *Poems*, 1619. (Variant, as a separate poem, in *England's Helicon*, 1600.)

SLOW, SLOW, FRESH FOUNT

Slow, slow, fresh fount, keep time with my salt tears:
　　Yet slower, yet; oh, faintly, gentle springs,
List to the heavy part the music bears,
　　Woe weeps out her division when she sings.
　　　　　Droop herbs and flowers;
　　　　　Fall grief in showers;
　　　　　Our beauties are not ours;
　　　　　　Oh, I could still,
Like melting snow upon some craggy hill,
　　　　　Drop, drop, drop, drop,
Since nature's pride is now a withered daffodil.　　　*Jonson.*

Cynthia's Revels, 1601. (Acted 1600.)*

HYMN TO DIANA

Queen and huntress, chaste and fair,
　　Now the sun is laid to sleep,
Seated in thy silver chair,
　　State in wonted manner keep:
　　　Hesperus entreats thy light,
　　　Goddess excellently bright.

Earth, let not thy envious shade
　　Dare itself to interpose;
Cynthia's shining orb was made
　　Heaven to clear when day did close:

Bless us then with wishëd sight,
Goddess excellently bright.

Lay thy bow of pearl apart,
  And thy crystal shining quiver;
Give unto the flying hart
  Space to breathe, how short soever:
    Thou that mak'st a day of night,
    Goddess excellently bright.   *Jonson.*

Ibid.

THE GLOVE

Thou more than most sweet glove,
Unto my more sweet love,
Suffer me to store with kisses
This empty lodging that now misses
  The pure rosy hand that ware thee,
  Whiter than the kid that bare thee.
      Thou art soft, but that was softer;
      Cupid's self hath kissed it ofter
      Than e'er he did his mother's doves,
      Supposing her the queen of loves
      That was thy mistress, best of gloves.

Ibid.   *Jonson.*

SONG

Delicious beauty, that doth lie
Wrapped in a skin of ivory,
Lie still, lie still upon thy back,
And, Fancy, let no sweet dreams lack
To tickle her, to tickle her with pleasing thoughts.

But if thy eyes are open full,
Then deign to view an honest gull
That stands, that stands expecting still
When that thy casement open will;
And bless his eyes, and bless his eyes with one kind glance.

Jack Drum's Entertainment, 1601. (Registered 1600.)   *Marston* (?)

BEAUTY SAT BATHING BY A SPRING

Beauty sat bathing by a spring
   Where fairest shades did hide her;
The winds blew calm, the birds did sing,
   The cool streams ran beside her.
My wanton thoughts enticed mine eye
   To see what was forbidden:
But better memory said, fie!
   So vain desire was chidden.
       Hey nonny, nonny, &c.

Into a slumber then I fell,
   When fond imagination
Seemëd to see, but could not tell
   Her feature or her fashion.
But even as babes in dreams do smile,
   And sometime fall a-weeping,
So I awaked, as wise this while
   As when I fell a-sleeping.
       Hey nonny, nonny, &c.   *Munday.*

England's Helicon, 1600.

OF DISDAINFUL DAPHNE

Shall I say that I love you,
   Daphne disdainful?

Sore it costs as I prove you,
   Loving is painful.

Shall I say what doth grieve me?
   Lovers lament it.
Daphne will not relieve me;
   Late I repent it.

Shall I die, shall I perish,
   Through her unkindness?
Love, untaught love to cherish,
   Showeth his blindness.

Shall the hills, shall the valleys,
   The fields, the city,
With the sound of my outcries,
   Move her to pity?·

The deep falls of fair rivers
   And the winds turning
Are the true music-givers
   Unto my mourning;

Where my flocks daily feeding,
   Pining for sorrow
At their master's heart-bleeding,
   Shot with Love's arrow.

From her eyes to my heart-string
   Was the shaft lancèd;
It made all the woods to ring,
   By which it glancèd.

When this nymph had used me so,
  Then did she hide her;
Hapless I did Daphne know,
  Hapless I spied her.

Thus turtle-like I wailed me,
  For my love's losing;
Daphne's trust thus did fail me:
  Woe worth such choosing!   *Nowell.*

England's Helicon, 1600.

IN PRAISE OF HIS DAPHNIS

Tune on my pipe the praises of my Love,
      Love fair and bright;
Fill earth with sound, and airy heavens above,
      Heavens Jove's delight,
      With Daphnis' praise.

To pleasant Tempe groves and plains about,
      Plains shepherd's pride,
Resounding echoes of her praise ring out,
      Ring far and wide
      My Daphnis' praise.

When I begin to sing, begin to sound,
      Sounds loud and shrill,
Do make each note unto the sky rebound,
      Skies calm and still,
      With Daphnis' praise.

Her tresses are like wires of beaten gold,
      Gold bright and sheen,

Nowell] M. H. Nowell, 1600; M. N. Howell, 1614.

Like Nisus' golden hair that Scylla polled,
        Scylla o'erseen
        Through Minos' love.

Her eyes like shining lamps in midst of night,
        Night dark and dead,
Or as the stars that give the seamen light,
        Light for to lead
        Their wandering ships.

Amidst her cheeks the rose and lily strive,
        Lily snow-white,
When their contend doth make their colour thrive,
        Colour too bright
        For shepherds' eyes.

Her lips like scarlet of the finest dye,
        Scarlet blood-red;
Teeth white as snow which on the hills doth lie,
        Hills overspread
        By winter's force.

Her skin as soft as is the finest silk,
        Silk soft and fine,
Of colour like unto the whitest milk,
        Milk of the kine
        Of Daphnis' herd.

As swift of foot as is the pretty roe,
        Roe swift of pace,
When yelping hounds pursue her to and fro,
        Hounds fierce in chase,
        To reave her life.

Scylla o'erseen] N.A.; Scyll o'erseen, 1600.

Cease tongue to tell of any more compares,
        Compares too rude,
Daphnis' deserts and beauty are too rare:
        Then here conclude
        Fair Daphnis' praise.   *Sir J. Wotton.*

England's Helicon, 1600.

IN PRAISE OF HIS LOVE

Jolly shepherd, shepherd on a hill,
        On a hill so merrily,
        On a hill so cheerily,
Fear not, shepherd, there to pipe thy fill,
Fill every dale, fill every plain:
        Both sing and say, 'Love feels no pain.'

Jolly shepherd, shepherd on a green,
        On a green so merrily,
        On a green so cheerily,
Be thy voice shrill, be thy mirth seen,
Heard to each swain, seen to each trull:
        Both sing and say, 'Love's joy is full.'

Jolly shepherd, shepherd in the sun,
        In the sun so merrily,
        In the sun so cheerily,
Sing forth thy songs, and let thy rhymes run
Down to the dales, to the hills above:
        Both sing and say, 'No life to love.'

Jolly shepherd, shepherd in the shade,
        In the shade so merrily,
        In the shade so cheerily,

Joy in thy life, life of the shepherd's trade,
Joy in thy love, love full of glee:
  Both sing and say, 'Sweet love for me.'

Jolly shepherd, shepherd here or there,
    Here or there so merrily,
    Here or there so cheerily,
Or in thy chat, either at thy cheer,
In every jig, in every lay
  Both sing and say, 'Love lasts for aye.'

Jolly shepherd, shepherd Daphnis' love,
    Daphnis' love so merrily,
    Daphnis' love so cheerily,
Let thy fancy never more remove,
Fancy be fixed, fixed not to fleet:
  Still sing and say, 'Love's yoke is sweet.'

Ibid.   *Sir J. Wotton.*

A NYMPH'S DISDAIN OF LOVE

'Hey, down a down!' did Dian sing,
  Amongst her virgins sitting,
'Than love there is no vainer thing,
  For maidens most unfitting.'
And so think I, with a down, down, derry!

When women knew no woe,
  But lived themselves to please,
Men's feigning guiles they did not know,
  The ground of their disease.

disease] dis-ease.

Unborn was false suspect,
   No thought of jealousy;
From wanton toys and fond affect
   The virgin's life was free.
     'Hey, down a down!' did Dian sing, &c.

At length, men usèd charms,
   To which what maids gave ear,
Embracing gladly endless harms,
   Anon enthrallèd were.
Thus women welcomed woe
   Disguised in name of love,
A jealous hell, a painted show:
   So shall they find, that prove.
     'Hey, down a down!' did Dian sing,
       Amongst her virgins sitting,
     'Than love there is no vainer thing,
       For maidens most unfitting.'
     And so think I, with a down, down, derry!

Anon.

England's Helicon, 1600.

CLEAR OR CLOUDY, SWEET AS APRIL SHOWERING

Clear or cloudy, sweet as April showering,
   Smooth or frowning, so is her face to me;
Pleased or smiling, like mild May all flowering,
   When skies blue silk, and meadows carpets be;
Her speeches, notes of that night bird that singeth,
Who thought all sweet, yet jarring notes out-ringeth.

Her grace, like June when earth and trees be trimmed
   In best attire of còmplete beauty's height;
Her love, again like summer's days, be dimmed

With little clouds of doubtful constant faith:
Her trust, her doubt, like rain and heat in skies
Gently thund'ring, she lightning to mine eyes.

Sweet summer-spring that breatheth life and growing
　　In weeds as much as into herbs and flowers,
And sees of service divers sorts in sowing,
　　Some haply seeming, and some being, yours;
Rain on your herbs and flowers that truly serve,
And let your weeds lack dew, and duly sterve.　　*Anon.*

J. Dowland's *Songs or Airs*, ii., 1600.

I SAW MY LADY WEEP

　　I saw my lady weep,
And Sorrow proud to be advancëd so
In those fair eyes where all perfections keep.
　　Her face was full of woe;
But such a woe, believe me, as wins more hearts
Than Mirth can do with her enticing parts.

　　Sorrow was there made fair,
And Passion wise; tears a delightful thing;
Silence beyond all speech a wisdom rare.
　　She made her sighs to sing,
And all things with so sweet a sadness move,
As made my heart at once both grieve and love.

　　O fairer than aught else
The world can show! leave off in time to grieve.
Enough, enough: your joyful looks excels:
　　Tears kills the heart, believe.
Oh, strive not to be excellent in woe,
Which only breeds your beauty's overthrow.　　*Anon.*

Ibid.

as much as into] N.A.; as into, 1600.　　sterve] starve.

FINE KNACKS FOR LADIES

Fine knacks for ladies, cheap, choice, brave and new!
　　Good pennyworths,—but money cannot move:
I keep a fair but for the Fair to view,—
　　A beggar may be liberal of love.
Though all my wares be trash, the heart is true,
　　　　　　　　　　The heart is true.

Great gifts are guiles and look for gifts again;
　　My trifles come as treasures from my mind:
It is a precious jewel to be plain;
　　Sometimes in shell the orient'st pearls we find.
Of others take a sheaf, of me a grain!
　　　　　　　　　Of me a grain!

Within this pack pins, points, laces, and gloves,
　　And divers toys fitting a country fair;
But in my heart, where duty serves and loves,
　　Turtles and twins, court's brood, a heavenly pair—
Happy the heart that thinks of no removes!
　　　　　　　　Of no removes!　　　　*Anon.*

J. Dowland's *Songs or Airs*, ii., 1600.

FAIRY DANCES

I

By the moon we sport and play,
With the night begins our day:
As we dance the dew doth fall;
Trip it, little urchins all,
Lightly as the little bee,
Two by two, and three by three,
And about go we, and about go we.

But in my] N.A.; But my, 1600.*　　court's] courtship's, love's (?).

II
Round about, round about,
   In a fair ring a,
Thus we dance, thus we dance,
   And thus we sing a,
Trip and go, to and fro,
   Over this green a,
All about, in and out,
   For our brave queen a.   *Anon.*

The Maid's Metamorphosis, 1600.

FAREWELL, DEAR LOVE! SINCE THOU WILT NEEDS BE GONE

Farewell, dear Love! since thou wilt needs be gone:
Mine eyes do show my life is almost done.
         Nay, I never will die
         So long as I can spy;
         There be many moe
         Though that she do go.
      There be many moe, I fear not.
      Why then, let her go, I care not.

Farewell, farewell! since this I find is true,
I will not spend more time in wooing you.
         But I will seek elsewhere
         If I may find her there.
         Shall I bid her go?
         What and if I do?
      Shall I bid her go, and spare not?
      Oh, no, no, no, no, I dare not.

Ten thousand times farewell!   Yet stay awhile,
Sweet, kiss me once; sweet kisses time beguile.

I have no power to move:
How now, am I in love?
Wilt thou needs be gone?
Go then, all is one.
Wilt thou needs be gone?   Oh, hie thee!
Nay; stay, and do no more deny me.

Once more farewell! I see 'loth to depart'
Bids oft adieu to her that holds my heart.
But, seeing I must lose
Thy love which I did choose.
Go thy ways for me,
Since it may not be.
Go thy ways for me.   But whither?
Go, oh, but where I may come thither.

What shall I do?   My love is now departed.
She is as fair as she is cruel-hearted:
She would not be entreated
With prayërs oft repeated.
If she come no more,
Shall I die therefore?
If she come no more, what care I?
Faith, let her go, or come, or tarry!   *Anon.*

R. Jones' *Songs and Airs*, i, 1600. Quoted, *Twelfth Night*, ii. iii. 109–21.

IF FATHERS KNEW BUT HOW TO LEAVE

If fathers knew but how to leave
   Their children wit as they do wealth,
And could constrain them to receive
   That physic which brings perfect health,
The world would not admiring stand
A woman's face and woman's hand.

Women confess they must obey,
  We men will needs be servants still;
We kiss their hands, and what they say
  We must commend, be 't never so ill:
Thus we, like fools, admiring stand
Her pretty foot and pretty hand.

We blame their pride, which we increase
  By making mountains of a mouse;
We praise because we know we please;
  Poor women are too credulous
To think that we admiring stand
Or foot, or face, or foolish hand.   *Anon.*

Ibid.

WONDERS

Thulë, the period of cosmography,
  Doth vaunt of Hecla, whose sulphureous fire
Doth melt the frozen clime and thaw the sky;
  Trinacrian Etna's flames ascend not higher:
These things seem wondrous, yet more wondrous I,
Whose heart with fear doth freeze, with love doth fry.

The Andalusian merchant, that returns
  Laden with cochineal and china dishes,
Reports in Spain how strangely Fogo burns
  Amidst an ocean full of flying fishes:
These things seem wondrous, yet more wondrous I,
Whose heart with fear doth freeze, with love doth fry.
                                   Anon.

T. Weelkes' *Madrigals of 6 parts*, 1600.

ART THOU GONE IN HASTE?

Art thou gone in haste?
　　I 'll not forsake thee!
Runn'st thou ne'er so fast,
　　I 'll o'ertake thee!
O'er the dales or the downs,
　　Through the green meadows,
From the fields, through the towns,
　　To the dim shadows!

All along the plain,
　　To the low fountains;
Up and down again,
　　From the high mountains:
Echo, then, shall again
　　Tell her I follow,
And the floods to the woods
　　Carry my holla.
　　　　　　Holla!
Ce! la! ho! ho! hu!   *Anon.*

The Thracian Wonder, 1661. (Written c. 1600.)

LOVE IS A LAW

Love is a law, a discord of such force,
That 'twixt our sense and reason makes divorce;
Love 's a desire, that to obtain betime,
We lose an age of years plucked from our prime;
Love is a thing to which we soon consent,
As soon refuse, but sooner far repent.

Then what must women be that are the cause
That love hath life? that lovers feel such laws?
They 're like the winds upon Lepanthae's shore

That still are changing. Oh, then love no more!
A woman's love is like that Syrian flower,
That buds, and spreads, and withers in an hour.   *Anon.*

Ibid.

FOLLOW THY FAIR SUN

Follow thy fair sun, unhappy shadow!
    Though thou be black as night,
    And she made all of light,
Yet follow thy fair sun, unhappy shadow!

Follow her, whose light thy light depriveth!
    Though here thou liv'st disgraced,
    And she in heaven is placed,
Yet follow her whose light the world reviveth!

Follow those pure beams, whose beauty burneth!
    That so have scorchëd thee
    As thou still black must be
Till her kind beams thy black to brightness turneth.

Follow her, while yet her glory shineth!
    There comes a luckless night
    That will dim all her light;
And this the black unhappy shade divineth.

Follow still, since so thy fates ordainëd!
    The sun must have his shade,
    Till both at once do fade,
The sun still proud, the shadow still disdainëd.

                                           Campion.

P. Rosseter's *A Book of Airs,* 1601.

proud] P. Vivian, 1909; prou'd, 1601; proved, Bullen, 1888.

THOU ART NOT FAIR

Thou art not fair, for all thy red and white,
   For all those rosy ornaments in thee.
Thou art not sweet, though made of mere delight,
   Nor fair nor sweet unless thou pity me.
I will not sooth thy fancies. Thou shalt prove
That beauty is no beauty without love.

Yet love not me, nor seek thou to allure
   My thoughts with beauty, were it more divine.
Thy smiles and kisses I can not endure,
   I 'll not be wrapped up in those arms of thine.
Now show it, if thou be a woman right,
Embrace, and kiss, and love me in despite.   *Campion.*

P. Rosseter's *A Book of Airs*, 1601.

FOLLOW YOUR SAINT

Follow your saint, follow with accents sweet!
Haste you, sad notes, fall at her flying feet!
There, wrapped in cloud of sorrow, pity move,
And tell the ravisher of my soul I perish for her love:
But, if she scorns my never-ceasing pain,
Then burst with sighing in her sight and ne'er return again.

All that I sung still to her praise did tend,
Still she was first, still she my songs did end;
Yet she my love and music both doth fly,
The music that her echo is and beauty's sympathy.
Then let my notes pursue her scornful flight:
It shall suffice that they were breathed and died for her
    delight.

Ibid.   *Campion.*

MY SWEETEST LESBIA, LET US LIVE AND LOVE

My sweetest Lesbia, let us live and love,
And though the sager sort our deeds reprove,
Let us not weigh them. Heaven's great lamps do dive
Into their west, and straight again revive;
But, soon as once set is our little light,
Then must we sleep one ever-during night.

If all would lead their lives in love like me,
Then bloody swords and armour should not be;
No drum nor trumpet peaceful sleeps should move,
Unless alarm came from the camp of love.
But fools do live and waste their little light,
And seek with pain their ever-during night.

When timely death my life and fortune ends,
Let not my hearse be vexed with mourning friends;
But let all lovers, rich in triumph, come
And with sweet pastimes grace my happy tomb:
And, Lesbia, close up thou my little light,
And crown with love my ever-during night.   *Campion.*

Ibid.

AMARYLLIS

I care not for these ladies that must be wooed and prayed;
Give me kind Amaryllis, the wanton country maid.
Nature Art disdaineth; her beauty is her own.
Her when we court and kiss, she cries: forsooth, let go!
But when we come where comfort is, she never will say no.

If I love Amaryllis, she gives me fruit and flowers;
But if we love these ladies, we must give golden showers.

Give them gold that sell love, give me the nut-brown lass,
Who when we court and kiss, she cries: forsooth, let go!
But when we come where comfort is, she never will say no.

These ladies must have pillows and beds by strangers wrought.
Give me a bower of willows, of moss and leaves unbought,
And fresh Amaryllis with milk and honey fed,
Who when we court and kiss, she cries: forsooth, let go!
But when we come where comfort is, she never will say no.

Campion.

P. Rosseter's *A Book of Airs*, 1601.

CORINNA

When to her lute Corinna sings,
Her voice revives the leaden strings,
And doth in highest notes appear
As any challenged echo clear.
But when she doth of mourning speak,
Even with her sighs the strings do break.

And as her lute doth live or die;
Led by her passion, so must I.
For when of pleasure she doth sing,
My thoughts enjoy a sudden spring;
But if she doth of sorrow speak,
Even from my heart the strings do break.   *Campion.*

Ibid.

WHEN THOU MUST HOME TO SHADES OF UNDERGROUND

When thou must home to shades of underground,
    And there arrived, a new admirèd guest,
The beauteous spirits do ingirt thee round,

White Iope, blithe Helen and the rest,
To hear the stories of thy finished love
From that smooth tongue whose music hell can move;

Then wilt thou speak of banqueting delights,
    Of masks and revels which sweet youth did make,
Of tourneys and great challenges of knights,
    And all these triumphs for thy beauty's sake.
When thou hast told these honours done to thee,
Then tell, oh, tell how thou didst murder me!   *Campion.*
bid.

THE MAN OF LIFE UPRIGHT

The man of life upright,
    Whose guiltless heart is free
From all dishonest deeds
    And thought of vanity:

The man whose silent days
    In harmless joys are spent,
Whom hopes cannot delude
    Nor sorrow discontent:

That man needs neither towers
    Nor armour for defence,
Nor secret vaults to fly
    From thunder's violence.

He only can behold
    With unaffrighted eyes
The horrors of the deep
    And terrors of the skies.

Thus scorning all the cares
  That fate or fortune brings,
He makes the heaven his book,
  His wisdom heavenly things,

Good thoughts his only friends,
  His wealth a well-spent age,
The earth his sober inn
  And quiet pilgrimage.   *Campion.*

P. Rosseter's *A Book of Airs*, 1601.

DITTY

O holy Love, religious saint!
Man's only honey-tasting pleasure!
Thy glory, learning cannot paint,
For thou art all our worldly treasure:
Thou art the treasure, treasure of the soul,
That great celestial powers dost control.

What greater bliss than to embrace
The perfect pattern of delight.
Whose heart-enchanting eye doth chase
All storms of sorrow from man's sight?
Pleasure, delight, wealth, and earth-joys do lie
In Venus' bosom, bosom of pure beauty.

That mind that tasteth perfect love
Is far remoted from annoy:
Cupid, that god, doth sit above,
That tips his arrows all with joy:
And this makes poets in their verse to sing—
Love is a holy, holy, holy thing.   *Chester.*

Love's Martyr, 1601.

HER HAIR

When the least whistling wind begins to sing,
And gently blows her hair about her neck,
Like to a chime of bells it soft doth ring,
And with the pretty noise the wind doth check,
  Able to lull asleep a pensive heart
  That of the round world's sorrows bears a part.

Ibid. (An excerpt.)   *Chester.*

SONG

If I freely may discover
What would please me in my lover,
I would have her fair and witty,
Savouring more of court than city;
A little proud, but full of pity;
Light and humorous in her toying;
Oft building hopes, and soon destroying;
Long, but sweet in the enjoying;
Neither too easy nor too hard:
All extremes I would have barred.

She should be allowed her passions,
So they were but used as fashions;
Sometimes froward, and then frowning,
Sometimes sickish, and then swowning,
Every fit with change still crowning.
Purely jealous I would have her,
Then only constant when I crave her;
'Tis a virtue should not save her.
Thus, nor her delicates would cloy me,
Neither her peevishness annoy me.   *Jonson.*

The Poetaster, 1602. (Acted 1601.)

LULLABY

Upon my lap my sovereign sits
 And sucks upon my breast.
Meanwhile his love sustains my life,
 And gives my body rest.
  Sing lullaby, my little boy,
  Sing lullaby, my only joy.

When thou hast taken thy repast,
 Repose, my babe, on me;
So may thy mother and thy nurse
 Thy cradle also be.
  Sing lullaby, my little boy,
  Sing lullaby, my only joy.

I grieve that duty doth not work
 All what my wishing would,
Because I would not be to thee
 But in the best I should.
  Sing lullaby, my little boy,
  Sing lullaby, my only joy.

Yet as I am, and as I may,
 I must and will be thine,
Though all too little for thyself.
 Vouchsafing to be mine.
  Sing lullaby, my little boy,
  Sing lullaby, my only joy.   *Verstegan.*

Odes, 1601. (And in M. Peerson's *Private Music*, 1620.)*

my only joy] 1620; my lives joy, 1601.

A VISION OF THE WORLD'S INSTABILITY

I saw a Holly sprig brought from a hurst,
And in a princely garden set it was,
Where of all trees it strove to be the first
In stately height, whereto it grew apace:
Tall cedar trees it overtoppëd far,
And, all with coral berries overspread,
It seemed the roses' beauty for to mar
And to deface it with a scarlet red:
Whereat the Gard'ner when he it suspected,
Or might perhaps mis-ween, this tree's intent,
For all first favour now grew ill-affected,
And all the boughs away did race and rent:
   Thus stood disgraced the stock so brave before,
   Which now of grief grew dead, and sprung no more.

Verstegan.

Ibid.

JERUSALEM, MY HAPPY HOME

Jerusalem, my happy home,
   When shall I come to thee?
When shall my sorrows have an end?
   Thy joys when shall I see?

O happy city of the Saints!
   O sweet and pleasant soil!
In thee no sorrow may be found,
   No grief, no care, no toil.

There is no damp nor foggy mist,
   No cloud nor darksome night:

---

roses'] roses, 1601; possibly rose's.   race] cut.

There every Saint shines like the sun,
  There God himself gives light.

In thee no sickness may be found,
  No hurt, no ache, no sore:
In thee there is no dread of death:
  There 's life for evermore.

There is no rain, no sleet, no snow,
  No filth may there be found:
There is no sorrow, nor no care,
  All joy doth there abound.

Jerusalem, my happy home,
  When shall I come to thee?
When shall my sorrows have an end?
  Thy joys when shall I see?

Thy walls are all of precious stones,
  Thy streets pavëd with gold;
Thy gates are eke of precious pearl
  Most glorious to behold.

Thy turrets and thy pinnacles
  With diamonds do shine:
Thy houses covered are with gold,
  Most perfect, pure, and fine.

Thy gardens and thy pleasant walks
  Continually are green;
There grows the sweet and fairest flowers
  That ever erst was seen.

Thy turrets . . . pinnacles] MS.; Thy pinnacles and carbuncles, 1601.

There cinnamon, there civet sweet,
   There balm springs from the ground:
No tongue can tell, no heart conceive
   The joys that there abound.

Thy happy Saints, Jerusalem,
   Do bathe in endless bliss:
None but those blessèd souls can tell
   How great thy glory is.

Throughout thy streets, with silver streams
   The flood of life doth flow;
Upon whose banks on every side
   The wood of life doth grow.

Those trees do evermore bear fruit,
   And evermore do spring;
There evermore the Saints do sit,
   And evermore do sing.

There David stands with harp in hand
   As Master of the Quire:
Ten thousand times that man were blessed
   That might his music hear.

Our Lady sings *Magnificat*
   With tune surpassing sweet;
And all the virgins bear their parts,
   Sitting about her feet.

Te Deum doth Saint Ambrose sing,
   Saint Augustine the like:

Old Simeon and good Zachary
   Have not their songs to seek.

There Magdalen hath lost her moan,
   And she likewise doth sing
With happy Saints, whose harmony
   In every street doth ring.

There all do live in such delight,
   Such pleasure and such play,
That thousand thousand years ago
   Doth seem but yesterday.

Jerusalem, my happy home,
   When shall I come to thee?
When shall my sorrows have an end?
   Thy joys when shall I see?

                              F. B., P[resbyter].*

The Song of Mary, 1601. (Longer version in B.M. Add. MS. 15225.)

LOVE WINGED MY HOPES

Love winged my hopes and taught me how to fly
Far from base earth, but not to mount too high:
      For true pleasure
      Lives in measure,
    Which, if men forsake,
Blinded they into folly run, and grief for pleasure take.

But my vain hopes, proud of their new-taught flight,
Enamoured sought to woo the sun's fair light,
      Whose rich brightness
      Moved their lightness

> To aspire so high,
That, all scorched and consumed with fire, now drowned in
  woe they lie.

 And none but Love their woeful hap did rue;
 For Love did know that their desires were true.
        Though Fate frownèd,
        And now drownèd
     They in sorrow dwell,
It was the purest light of heaven for whose fair love they fell.

Anon.

R. Jones' *Songs and Airs*, ii., 1601.

CUPID

> Love's god is a boy,
> None but cowherds regard him;
> His dart is a toy,
> Great opinion hath marred him;
> The fear of the wag
> Hath made him so brag;
> Chide him, he 'll fly thee
> And not come nigh thee.
Little boy, pretty knave, shoot not at random,
For if you hit me, slave, I 'll tell your grandam.

> Fond Love is a child
> And his compass is narrow;
> Young fools are beguiled
> With the fame of his arrow;
> He dareth not strike
> If his stroke do mislike:
> Cupid, do you hear me?
> Come not too near me.

---

cowherds] cowards.

Little boy, pretty knave, hence I beseech you,
For if you hit me, slave, in faith I 'll breech you.

    The ape loves to meddle
    When he finds a man idle;
    Else is he a-flirting
    Where his mark is a-courting;
    When women grow true
    Come teach me to sue;
    Then I 'll come to thee,
    Pray thee and woo thee.
Little boy, pretty knave, make me not stagger,
For if you hit me, slave, I 'll call thee, beggar.

Anon.

R. Jones' *Songs and Airs*, ii., 1601.

CONTENT THYSELF WITH THY ESTATE

Content thyself with thy estate,
    Seek not to climb above the skies;
For often love is mixed with hate,
    And 'twixt the flowers the serpent lies:
Where fortune sends her greatest joys,
There once possessed they are but toys.

What thing can earthly pleasure give
    That breeds delight when it is past?
Or who so quietly doth live
    But storms of cares do drown at last?
This is the law of worldly hire,
The more we have, the more desire.

Wherefore I hold him best at ease
    That lives content with his estate,

---

slave, stzs. 2 and 3] E. H. Fellowes, 1920; knave, 1601.

And doth not sail in worldly seas
    Where *mine* and *thine* do breed debate:
This noble mind, even in a clown,
Is more than to possess a crown.   *Anon.*

R. Carlton's *Madrigals*, 1601.*

THE GOOD-MORROW

I wonder, by my troth, what thou and I
Did, till we loved: were we not weaned till then?
But sucked on country pleasures, childishly?
Or snorted we in the Seven Sleepers' den?
'Twas so; but this, all pleasures fancies be;
If ever any beauty I did see,
Which I desired, and got, 'twas but a dream of thee.

And now good-morrow to our waking souls,
Which watch not one another out of fear;
For love all love of other sights controls,
And makes one little room an everywhere.
Let sea-discoverers to new worlds have gone;
Let maps to other, worlds on worlds have shown,
Let us possess one world; each hath one, and is one.

My face in thine eye, thine in mine appears,
And true plain hearts do in the faces rest;
Where can we find two better hemispheres
Without sharp north, without declining west?
What ever dies, was not mixed equally;
If our two loves be one, or thou and I
Love so alike that none do slacken, none can die.

Poems, 1633. (Poem written before 1602.)   *Donne.*

but this] except this.   maps to other] *i.e.* to others.   none] neither one.

THE PROHIBITION

Take heed of loving me;
At least remember I forbade it thee;
Not that I shall repair my unthrifty waste
Of breath and blood, upon thy sighs and tears,
By being to thee then what to me thou wast;
But so great joy our life at once outwears.
Then, lest thy love by my death frustrate be,
If thou love me, take heed of loving me.

Take heed of hating me,
Or too much triumph in the victory;
Not that I shall be mine own officer,
And hate with hate again retaliate;
But thou wilt lose the style of conqueror,
If I, thy conquest, perish by thy hate.
Then, lest my being nothing lessen thee,
If thou hate me, take heed of hating me.

Yet, love and hate me too,
So these extremes shall ne'er their office do;
Love me, that I may die the gentler way;
Hate me, because thy love is too great for me;
Or let these two, themselves, not me, decay;
So shall I live thy stage, not triumph be.
Lest thou thy love and hate and me undo,
To let me live, oh, love and hate me too!   *Donne.*

Poems, 1633. (Poem written before 1602.)

LOVERS' INFINITENESS

If yet I have not all thy love,
Dear, I shall never have it all;

---

thee then what to me] 1635; me then that which, 1633.   So shall I live]
i.e. So shall I, alive.   stage] 1635; stay, 1633.

I cannot breathe one other sigh, to move,
Nor can intreat one other tear to fall;
And all my treasure, which should purchase thee,
Sighs, tears, and oaths, and letters, I have spent;
Yet no more can be due to me,
Than at the bargain made was meant:
If then thy gift of love were partïal,
That some to me, some should to others fall,
    Dear, I shall never have thee all.

Or if then thou gavest me all,
All was but all which thou hadst then;
But if in thy heart since, there be, or shall
New love created be by other men,
Which have their stocks entire, and can in tears,
In sighs, in oaths, and letters, outbid me,
This new love may beget new fears,
For this love was not vowed by thee.
And yet it was, thy gift being general;
The ground, thy heart, is mine; what ever shall
    Grow there, dear, I should have it all.

Yet I would not have all yet;
He that hath all can have no more;
And since my love doth every day admit
New growth, thou shouldst have new rewards in store;
Thou canst not every day give me thy heart,
If thou canst give it, then thou never gavest it:
Love's riddles are, that though thy heart depart,
It stays at home, and thou with losing savest it:
But we will have a way more liberal
Than changing hearts, to join them; so we shall
    Be one, and one another's all.   *Donne.*

Ibid.

THE CANONIZATION

For God's sake hold your tongue, and let me love;
 Or chide my palsy, or my gout;
 My five grey hairs, or ruined fortune flout;
With wealth your state, your mind with arts improve;
  Take you a course, get you a place,
  Observe his Honour, or his Grace;
Or the King's real, or his stampèd face
 Contemplate; what you will, approve,
 So you will let me love.

Alas! alas! who 's injured by my love?
 What merchant's ships have my sighs drowned?
 Who says my tears have overflowed his ground?
When did my colds a forward spring remove?
  When did the heats which my veins fill
  Add one more to the plaguy bill?
Soldiers find wars, and lawyers find out still
 Litigious men, which quarrels move,
 Though she and I do love.

Call us what you will, we are made such by love;
 Call her one, me another fly,
 We are tapers too, and at our own cost die,
And we in us find the eagle and the dove.
  The phoenix riddle hath more wit
  By us; we two being one, are it;
So, to one neutral thing both sexes fit,
 We die and rise the same, and prove
 Mysterious by this love.

We can die by it, if not live by love,
 And if unfit for tombs and hearse

---

real] a distinct disyllable, reäl. plaguy bill] weekly bill of mortality
during the plague.

Our legends be, it will be fit for verse;
And if no piece of chronicle we prove,
      We 'll build in sonnets pretty rooms;
      As well a well-wrought urn becomes
The greatest ashes, as half-acre tombs,
      And by these hymns all shall approve
      Us canonized for love;

And thus invoke us, 'You, whom reverend love
      Made one another's hermitage;
      You, to whom love was peace, that now is rage;
Who did the whole world's soul contract, and drove
      Into the glasses of your eyes,
      So made such mirrors, and such spies,
That they did all to you epitomize—
      Countries, towns, courts beg from above
      A pattern of your love.'   *Donne.*

Poems, 1633. (Poem written before 1602.)

THE DREAM

Dear Love, for nothing less than thee
Would I have broke this happy dream;
            It was a theme
For reason, much too strong for fantasy;
Therefore thou wak'dst me wisely; yet
My dream thou brok'st not, but continued'st it;
Thou art so truth that thoughts of thee suffice
To make dreams truths, and fables histories;
Enter these arms, for since thou thought'st it best
Not to dream all my dream, let 's act the rest.

As lightning, or a taper's light,
Thine eyes, and not thy noise, waked me;

your love] 1669; our love, 1633.

             Yet I thought thee
(For thou lovest truth) an angel, at first sight;
But when I saw thou sawest my heart,
And knew'st my thoughts, beyond an angel's art,
When thou knew'st what I dreamt, when thou knew'st when
Excess of joy would wake me, and cam'st then,
I must confess, it could not choose but be
Profane, to think thee any thing but thee.

Coming and staying showed thee, thee,
But rising makes me doubt that now
             Thou art not thou.
That love is weak where fear 's as strong as he;
'Tis not all spirit, pure and brave,
If mixture it of fear, shame, honour, have.
Perchance as torches, which must ready be,
Men light and put out, so thou deal'st with me;
Thou cam'st to kindle, go'st to come; then I
Will dream that hope again, but else would die.   *Donne.*

Poems, 1633. (Poem written before 1602.)

THE EXPIRATION

So, so, break off this last lamenting kiss,
    Which sucks two souls, and vapours both away;
Turn, thou ghost, that way, and let me turn this,
    And let ourselves benight our happiest day.
We asked none leave to love; nor will we owe
Any so cheap a death as saying, 'Go.'

Go; and if that word have not quite killed thee,
    Ease me with death, by bidding me go too.
Or, if it have, let my word work on me,

And a just office on a murderer do.
Except it be too late, to kill me so,
Being double dead, going, and bidding, 'Go.'   *Donne.*

Ibid. (Also in A. Ferrabosco's *Airs*, 1609.) *

THE RELIC

When my grave is broke up again
Some second guest to entertain
(For graves have learned that woman-head,
To be to more than one a bed),
        And he that digs it, spies
A bracelet of bright hair about the bone,
        Will he not let us alone,
And think that there a loving couple lies,
Who thought that this device might be some way
To make their souls at the last busy day
Meet at this grave, and make a little stay?

If this fall in a time, or land,
Where misdevotion doth command,
Then he that digs us up will bring
Us to the bishop and the king
        To make us relics; then
Thou shalt be a Mary Magdalen, and I
        A something else thereby;
All women shall adore us, and some men.
And, since at such time miracles are sought,
I would have that age by this paper taught
What miracles we harmless lovers wrought.

First we loved well and faithfully,
Yet knew not what we loved, nor why;

Difference of sex no more we knew,
Than our guardian angels do;
Coming and going we
Perchance might kiss, but not between those meals;
Our hands ne'er touched the seals,
Which nature, injured by late law, sets free:
These miracles we did; but now, alas!
All measure, and all language, I should pass,
Should I tell what a miracle she was.   *Donne.*

Poems, 1633. (Poem written before 1602.)

SONG

Love for such a cherry lip
Would be glad to pawn his arrows;
Venus here to take a sip
Would sell her doves and team of sparrows.
But they shall not so;
Hey nonny, nonny no!
None but I this lip must owe,
Hey nonny, nonny no!

Did Jove see this wanton eye,
Ganymede must wait no longer;
Phoebe here one night did lie,
Would change her face and look much younger.
But they shall not so;
Hey nonny, nonny no!
None but I this lip must owe;
Hey nonny, nonny no!   *Middleton.*

Blurt, Master-Constable, 1602. (Acted 1601–1602.)

owe] own.   did lie] *i.e.* did she lie here one night.

A TRUE LOVE DITTY

Pity, pity, pity,
Pity, pity, pity,
That word begins that ends a true love ditty.
Your blessëd eyes, like a pair of suns,
Shine in the sphere of smiling;
Your pretty lips, like a pair of doves,
Are kisses still compiling.
Mercy hangs upon your brow, like a precious jewel;
Oh, let not then,
Most lovely maid, best to be loved of men,
Marble lie upon your heart, that will make you cruel.
Pity, pity, pity,
Pity, pity, pity,
That word begins that ends a true love ditty.

Middleton.

Ibid.

MIDNIGHT

Midnight's bell goes ting, ting, ting, ting, ting,
Then dogs do howl, and not a bird does sing
But the nightingale, and she cries twit, twit, twit:
Owls then on every bough do sit;
Ravens croak on chimneys' tops;
The cricket in the chamber hops,
And the cats cry mew, mew, mew.
The nibbling mouse is not asleep,
But he goes peep, peep, peep, peep, peep,
And the cats cry mew, mew, mew,
And still the cats cry mew, mew, mew.   *Middleton.*

Ibid.

twit] repeated four times, 1602.

OF THE MOON

Look how the pale queen of the silent night
Doth cause the ocean to attend upon her,
And he, as long as she is in his sight,
With his full tide is ready her to honour:
But when the silver wagon of the moon
Is mounted up so high he cannot follow,
The sea calls home his crystal waves to moan,
And with low ebb doth manifest his sorrow.
So you, that are the sovereign of my heart,
Have all my joys attending on your will:
My joys low ebbing when you do depart,
When you return, their tide my heart doth fill.
   So as you come, and as you do depart,
   Joys ebb and flow within my tender heart.   *Best.*

A Poetical Rhapsody, 1602. (Text 1611.)*

LAURA

Rose-cheeked Laura, come;
Sing thou smoothly with thy beauty's
Silent music, either other
    Sweetly gracing.

Lovely forms do flow
From concent divinely framèd;
Heaven is music, and thy beauty's
    Birth is heavenly.

These dull notes we sing
Discords need for helps to grace them;
Only beauty purely loving
    Knows no discord;

---

moan] mone, 1602; moue, 1611 and 1621.   concent] concord.

> But still moves delight,
> Like clear springs renewed by flowing,
> Ever perfect, ever in them-
>   Selves eternal.   *Campion.*

Observations in the Art of English Poesy, 1602.

SONG

Lady, you are with beauties so enrichëd,
        Of body and of mind,
        As I can hardly find
Which of them all hath most my heart bewitchëd:

Whether your skin so white, so smooth, so tender,
        Or face so lovely fair,
        Or heart-ensnaring hair,
Or dainty hand, or leg and foot so slender;

Or whether your sharp wit and lively spirit,
        Where pride can find no place,
        Or your most pleasing grace,
Or speech, which doth true eloquence inherit.

Most lovely all, and each of them do move me
        More than words can express;
        But yet I must confess
I love you most because you please to love me.

A Poetical Rhapsody, 1602.   *F. Davison.*

MY ONLY STAR

My only star,
Why, why are your dear eyes,
Where all my life's peace lies,

---

heart-ensnaring] 1608 and 1611; long heart-binding, 1602.

With me at war?
Why, to my ruin tending,
Do they still lighten woe
On him that loves you so,
That all his thoughts in you have birth and ending?

Hope of my heart,
Oh, wherefore do the words,
Which your sweet tongue affords,
No hope impart?
But, cruel without measure,
To my eternal pain
Still thunder forth disdain
On him whose life depends upon your pleasure?

Sunshine of joy,
Why do your gestures, which
All eyes and hearts bewitch,
My bliss destroy?
And pity's sky o'erclouding,
Of hate an endless shower
On that poor heart still pour,
Which in your bosom seeks his only shrouding?

F. Davison.

A Poetical Rhapsody, 1602.*

HIS FAREWELL TO HIS UNKIND AND UNCONSTANT MISTRESS

Sweet, if you like and love me still,
And yield me love for my good-will,
And do not from your promise start,
When your fair hand gave me your heart;
If dear to you I be

As you are dear to me,
Then yours I am and will be ever;
No time nor place my love shall sever,
But faithful still I will persèver,
Like constant marble stone,
Loving but you alone.

But if you favour moe than me,
Who love thee still and none but thee,
If others do the harvest gain
That 's due to me for all my pain,
If that you love to range
And oft to chop and change;
Then get you some new-fangled mate;
My doting love shall turn to hate,
Esteeming you—though too too late—
Not worth a pebble stone,
Loving not me alone.   *F. Davison.*

Ibid.

MADRIGAL

The sound of thy sweet name, my dearest treasure,
Delights me more than sight of other faces:
A glimpse of thy sweet face breeds me more pleasure
Than any other's kindest words and graces.

One gracious word that from thy lips proceedeth,
I value more than others' dove-like kisses:
And thy chaste kiss in my conceit exceedeth
Others' embraces, and love's chiefest blisses.
F. Davison.

Ibid. (Text 1611.)*

MADRIGAL

Some there are as fair to see to,
But by art and not by nature:
Some as tall and goodly be too,
But want beauty to their stature:
Some have gracious kind behaviour,
But are foul or simple creatures:
Some have wit, but want sweet favour,
Or are proud of their good features.
    Only you in court or city
    Are both fair, tall, kind, and witty.   *F. Davison.*

A Poetical Rhapsody, 1602.

AT HER FAIR HANDS

At her fair hands how have I grace entreated
      With prayërs oft repeated!
      Yet still my love is thwarted.
Heart, let her go, for she 'll not be convarted.
         Say, shall she go?
         Oh no, no, no, no, no!
She is most fair, though she be marble-hearted.

How often have my sighs declared my anguish
      Wherein I daily languish;
      Yet doth she still procure it.
Heart, let her go, for I cannot endure it.
         Say, shall she go?
         Oh no, no, no, no, no!
She gave the wound, and she alone must cure it.

The trickling tears that down my cheeks have flowëd
      My love have often showëd;

Yet still unkind I prove her.
Heart, let her go, for nought I do can move her.
Say, shall she go?
Oh no, no, no, no, no!
Though she me hate, I cannot choose but love her.

But shall I still a true affection owe her,
Which prayers, sighs, tears do show her?
And shall she still disdain me?
Heart, let her go, if they no grace can gain me.
Say, shall she go?
Oh no, no, no, no, no!
She made me hers, and hers she will retain me.

But if the love that hath, and still doth burn me,
No love at length return me,
Out of my thoughts I 'll set her.
Heart, let her go; oh heart, I pray thee, let her!
Say, shall she go?
Oh no, no, no, no, no!
Fixed in the heart, how can the heart forget her?

But if I weep and sigh and often wail me,
Till tears, sighs, prayërs fail me,
Shall yet my love persèver?
Heart, let her go, if she will right thee never.
Say, shall she go?
Oh no, no, no, no, no!
Tears, sighs, prayers fail, but true love lasteth ever.

W. Davison.
Ibid.

ODE

Absence, hear thou my protestation
Against thy strength,

Distance and length:
Do what thou canst for alteration,
        For hearts of truest mettle
        Absence doth join, and time doth settle.

Who loves a mistress of such quality,
        He soon hath found
        Affection's ground
Beyond time, place, and all mortality.
        To hearts that cannot vary
        Absence is present, time doth tarry.

My senses want their outward motions
        Which now within
        Reason doth win,
Redoubled in her secret notions:
        Like rich men that take pleasure
        In hiding more than handling treasure.

By absence this good means I gain,
        That I can catch her,
        Where none can watch her,
In some close corner of my brain:
        There I embrace and kiss her,
        And so I both enjoy and miss her.

A Poetical Rhapsody, 1602.   *Donne* (?) or *Hoskins* (?)*

SONNET

Dear, why should you command me to my rest
When now the night doth summon all to sleep?
Methinks this time becometh lovers best,
Night was ordained together friends to keep.
How happy are all other living things

Which, though the day disjoin by several flight,
The quiet evening yet together brings,
And each returns unto his love at night!
O thou that are so courteous else to all,
Why shouldst thou, Night, abuse me only thus,
That every creature to his kind dost call,
And yet 'tis thou dost only sever us?
     Well could I wish it would be ever day,
     If when night comes you bid me go away.

Idea, 1602. (Text 1619.)   *Drayton.*

YE LITTLE BIRDS THAT SIT AND SING

Ye little birds that sit and sing
     Amidst the shady valleys,
And see how Phyllis sweetly walks
     Within her garden-alleys;
Go, pretty birds, about her bower;
Sing, pretty birds, she may not lour;
Ah, me! methinks I see her frown;
     Ye pretty wantons, warble!

Go, tell her through your chirping bills,
     As you by me are bidden,
To her is only known my love,
     Which from the world is hidden.
Go, pretty birds, and tell her so;
See that your notes strain not too low,
For still, methinks, I see her frown;
     Ye pretty wantons, warble!

Go, tune your voices' harmony,
     And sing, I am her lover;
Strain loud and sweet, that every note

With sweet content may move her:
And she that hath the sweetest voice,
Tell her I will not change my choice;
Yet still, methinks, I see her frown;
    Ye pretty wantons, warble!

Oh, fly! make haste! see, see, she falls
    Into a pretty slumber!
Sing round about her rosy bed
    That, waking, she may wonder:
Say to her, 'tis her lover true
That sendeth love to you, to you!
And when you hear her kind reply,
    Return with pleasant warblings.   *T. Heywood*(?)

The Fair Maid of the Exchange, 1607. (Written c. 1602.)*

EPITAPH ON S. P.

A child of Queen Elizabeth's Chapel

Weep with me, all you that read
    This little story;
And know, for whom a tear you shed
    Death's self is sorry.
'Twas a child that so did thrive
    In grace and feature,
As Heaven and Nature seemed to strive
    Which owned the creature.

Years he numbered scarce thirteen,
    When Fates turned cruel;
Yet three filled zodiacs had he been
    The stage's jewel;
And did act, what now we moan,
    Old men so duly,

S. P.] Solomon Pavy.

As sooth the Parcae thought him one,
    He played so truly.

So, by error, to his fate
    They all consented;
But, viewing him since—alas, too late!—
    They have repented;
And have sought, to give new birth,
    In baths to steep him;
But, being so much too good for earth,
    Heaven vows to keep him.   *Jonson.*

Epigrams, 1616. (Poem written c. 1602.)

SONNET

Were I as base as is the lowly plain,
And you, my Love, as high as heaven above,
Yet should the thoughts of me, your humble swain,
Ascend to heaven in honour of my love.
Were I as high as heaven above the plain,
And you, my Love, as humble and as low
As are the deepest bottoms of the main,
Wheresoe'er you were, with you my love should go.
Were you the earth, dear Love, and I the skies,
My love should shine on you like to the sun,
And look upon you with ten thousand eyes
Till heaven waxed blind, and till the world were dun.
    Wheresoe'er I am, below, or else above you,
    Wheresoe'er you are, my heart shall truly love you.
                                  Sylvester(?)

A Poetical Rhapsody, 1602.

IN PRAISE OF A BEGGAR'S LIFE

Bright shines the sun; play, beggars, play!
Here 's scraps enough to serve to-day.

dun] dark. See Note. 1602 ascribes poem to 'I. S.'

What noise of viols is so sweet
   As when our merry clappers ring?
What mirth doth want where beggars meet?
   A beggar's life is for a king.
Eat, drink, and play; sleep when we list;
Go where we will, so stocks be missed.
     Bright shines the sun; play, beggars, play!
     Here 's scraps enough to serve to-day.

The world is ours, and ours alone;
   For we alone have worlds at will;
We purchase not, all is our own;
   Both fields and streets we beggars fill.
Nor care to get, nor fear to keep,
Did ever break a beggar's sleep.
     Bright shines the sun; play, beggars, play!
     Here 's scraps enough to serve to-day.   A. W.

A Poetical Rhapsody, 1602.*

DISPRAISE OF LOVE, AND LOVERS' FOLLIES

If love be life, I long to die,
   Live they that list for me;
And he that gains the most thereby
   A fool at least shall be;
But he that feels the sorest fits
'Scapes with no less than loss of wits.
    Unhappy life they gain
    Which love do entertain.

In day by feignëd looks they live,
   By lying dreams in night;
Each frown a deadly wound doth give,

Unhappy life] 1611 and 1621; An happy life, 1602 and 1608.

Each smile a false delight.
If 't hap their lady pleasant seem,
It is for other's love they deem;
       If void she seem of joy,
       Disdain doth make her coy.

Such is the peace that lovers find,
    Such is the life they lead,
Blown here and there with every wind,
    Like flowers in the mead;
Now war, now peace, then war again,
Desire, despair, delight, disdain;
       Though dead, in midst of life;
       In peace, and yet at strife.   *A. W.*

Ibid.

WHERE HIS LADY KEEPS HIS HEART

Sweet Love, mine only treasure,
       For service long unfeignëd,
       Wherein I nought have gainëd,
Vouchsafe this little pleasure,
       To tell me in what part
       My lady keeps my heart.

If in her hair so slender,
       Like golden nets untwinëd,
       Which fire and art have finëd;
Her thrall my heart I render,
       For ever to abide
       With locks so dainty tied.

If in her eyes she bind it;
       Wherein that fire was framëd,

By which it is inflaměd,
I dare not look to find it:
I only wish it sight,
To see that pleasant light.

But if her breast have deignëd
With kindness to receive it,
I am content to leave it,
Though death thereby were gainëd:
Then, lady, take your own,
That lives for you alone.

A. W.

A Poetical Rhapsody, 1602.

DESIRE'S GOVERNMENT

Where wit is over-ruled by will,
    And will is led by fond Desire,
There Reason were as good be still,
    As speaking, kindle greater fire;
For where Desire doth bear the sway,
The heart must rule, the head obey.

What boots the cunning pilot's skill,
    To tell which way to shape their course,
When he that steers will have his will,
    And drive them where he list, perforce?
So Reason shows the truth in vain,
Where fond Desire as king doth reign.

A. W.

Ibid.

TO TIME

Eternal Time, that wastest without waste,
    That art and art not, diest, and livest still;

Most slow of all, and yet of greatest haste;
　　Both ill and good, and neither good nor ill:
　　　　How can I justly praise thee, or dispraise?
　　　　Dark are thy nights, but bright and clear thy days.

Both free and scarce, thou giv'st and tak'st again;
　　Thy womb that all doth breed, is tomb to all;
What so by thee hath life, by thee is slain;
　　From thee do all things rise, by thee they fall:
　　　　Constant, inconstant, moving, standing still;
　　　　Was, Is, Shall be, do thee both breed and kill.

I lose thee, while I seek to find thee out;
　　The farther off, the more I follow thee;
The faster hold, the greater cause of doubt;
　　Was, Is, I know; but *Shall,* I cannot see.
　　　　All things by thee are measured; thou, by none:
　　　　All are in thee; thou, in thyself alone.　　　　*A. W.*

Ibid.

FOR HER HEART ONLY

Only, sweet Love, afford me but thy heart,
Then close thine eyes within their ivory covers,
That they to me no beam of light impart,
Although they shine on all thy other lovers.
As for thy lip of ruby, cheek of rose,
Though I have kissed them oft with sweet content,
I am content that sweet content to lose;
If thy sweet will will bar me, I assent.
Let me not touch thy hand, but through thy glove,
Nor let it be the pledge of kindness more;
Keep all thy beauties to thyself, sweet Love,

cheek] 1608, and later eds.; cheeks, 1602.

I ask not such bold favours as before.
   I beg but this, afford me but thy heart,
    For then, I know, thou wilt the rest impart.   *Anon.*

A Poetical Rhapsody, 1602.

MADRIGAL

My Love in her attire doth show her wit,
   It doth so well become her;
For every season she hath dressings fit,
   For winter, spring, and summer.
   No beauty she doth miss
   When all her robes are on;
   But Beauty's self she is
   When all her robes are gone.   *Anon.*

Ibid.

PHYLLIDA FLOUTS ME

Oh, what a plague is love! How shall I bear it?
She will unconstant prove, I greatly fear it.
She so molests my mind, that my wit faileth.
She wavers with the wind, as the ship saileth.
    Please her the best I may,
    She looks another way.
    Alack and well-a-day!
      Phyllida flouts me.

At the fair, yesterday, she would not see me,
But turned another way, when she came nigh me.
Dick had her in to dine; he might intreat her.
Will had her to the wine; I could not get her.
    With Daniel did she dance;
    At me she looked askance.

O thrice unhappy chance!
Phyllida flouts me.

I cannot work and sleep, both at all season:
Love wounds my heart so deep, without all reason.
I do consume, alas! with care and sorrow,
Even like a sort of beasts pinde in a meadow.
I shall be dead, I fear,
Within this thousand year;
And all for very care:
Phyllida flouts me.

She hath a clout of mine, wrought with good coventry,
Which she keeps for a sign of my fidelity;
But, in faith, if she flinch, she shall not wear it;
To Tib, my t'other wench, I mean to bear it.
Yet it will kill my heart
So quickly to depart.
Death, kill me with thy dart!
Phyllida flouts me.

Yesternight, very late, as I was walking,
I saw one in the gate, with my Love talking.
Every word that she spoke, he gave her kissing,
Which she as kindly took as mother's blessing.
But when I come to kiss,
She very dainty is.
Oh, what a hell is this!
Phyllida flouts me.

Fair maid, be not so coy, never disdain me!
I am my mother's boy; Sweet, entertain me!
She 'll give me, when she dies, all things befitting:

---

pinde] two readings possible: pinned, *i.e.* enclosed; and pined.

Her poultry and her bees, with her goose sitting,
    A pair of mattress beds,
    A barrel full of shreds,—
    And yet, for all my goods,
        Phyllida flouts me.

I saw my face, of late, in a fair fountain;
I know there 's none so feat, in all the mountain.
Lasses do leave their sheep and flock above me,
And for my love do weep, and fain would have me.
    Maidens in every place
    Strives to behold my face;
    And yet—O heavy case!—
        Phyllida flouts me.

Maiden, look what you do, and in time take me!
I can have other two, if you forsake me:
For Doll, the dairy-maid, laughed on me lately,
And wanton Winifred favours me greatly.
    One threw milk on my clothes;
    T'other plays with my nose:
    What loving signs be those!
        Phyllida flouts me.

Come to me, pretty peat, let me embrace thee!
Though thou be fair and feat, do not disgrace me;
For I will constant prove (make no denial!)
And be thy dearest Love—proof maketh trial.
    If ought do breed thy pain,
    I can procure thy gain;
    Yet, bootless, I complain—
        Phyllida flouts me.

Thou shalt eat curds and cream, all the year lasting;
And drink the crystal stream, pleasant in tasting;
Whig and whey whilst thou burst, and bramble-berries,
Pie-lids and pasty-crust, pears, plums, and cherries.
> Thy garments shall be thin,
> Made of a wether's skin—
> Yet all not worth a pin!
> *Phyllida flouts me.*

I found a stock-dove's nest, and thou shalt have it.
The cheese-cake, in my chest, for thee I save it.
I will give thee rush-rings, key-nobs, and cushnets,
Pence, purse, and other things, bells, beads, and bracelets.
> My sheep-hook, and my dog,
> My bottle, and my bag—
> Yet all not worth a rag!
> *Phyllida flouts me.*

Thy glorious beauty's gleam dazzles my eyesight,
Like the sun's brightest beam shining at midnight.
O my heart! O my heels! Fie on all wenches!
Pluck up thy courage, Giles; bang him that flinches!
> Back to thy sheep again,
> Thou silly shepherd's swain;
> Thy labour is in vain!
> *Phyllida flouts me.*   *Anon.*

Shirburn Ballads MS. (Variant in Roxburghe Collection III. See Note for
emendations. Poem written before 1603.)

FLOW, O MY TEARS!

Flow, O my tears, to mitigate my sorrow!
> Alas, a flood will not suffice me:

---

cushnets] cushionets, pin-cushions.

My store of tears is spent, and who a tear can borrow?
When human pity flies me,
   Then, O my soul, betake thee
      To God by prayer,
      Whose love did ne'er
        Forsake thee.

                                         Anon.

Christ Church MS. 740–2. (Song written before 1603.)*

YOLP, YOLP, YOLP, YOLP

Hark! They cry! I hear by that
The dogs have put the hare from quat:
Then woe be unto little Wat!
    Yolp, yolp, yolp, yolp.

Hollo in the hind dogs, hollo!
So come on then—solla! solla!—
And let us so blithely follow.
    Yolp, yolp, yolp, yolp.

Oh, the dogs are out of sight,
But the cry is my delight:
Hark how Jumball hits it right!
    Yolp, yolp, yolp, yolp.

Over briars, over bushes!
Who 's affeard of pricks and pushes
He 's no hunter worth two rushes.
    Yolp, yolp, yolp, yolp.

But how long thus shall we wander?
Oh, the hare 's a lusty stander!

---

quat] squat, sitting.   Wat] name often given to the hare.

Follow apace! The dogs are yonder!
Yolp, yolp, yolp, yolp. *Anon.*

A Twelfe night Merriment, 1602–3. Bodley MS. Rawl. Poet. 212.

THE GORDIAN KNOT

The Gordian knot, which Alexander great
   Did whilom cut with his all-conquering sword,
Was nothing like thy busk-point, pretty peat,
   Nor could so fair an augury afford;
Which if I chance to cut or else untie,
Thy little world I 'll conquer presently.   *Tomkis(?)*

Lingua, 1607. (Written 1602–7.)

MAB THE MISTRESS-FAIRY

This is Mab the mistress-fairy
That doth nightly rob the dairy,
And can hurt or help the churning
As she please, without discerning:

She that pinches country wenches
If they rub not clean their benches,
And with sharper nails remembers
When they rake not up their embers;
But if so they chance to feast her,
In a shoe she drops a tester.

This is she that empties cradles,
Takes out children, puts in ladles;
Trains forth midwives in their slumber
With a sieve the holes to number;

---

busk-point] stay-lace.   peat] pet.

And then leads them from her burrows
Home through ponds and water-furrows.

She can start our franklin's daughters
In their sleep with shrieks and laughters,
And on sweet Saint Anne's night
Feed them with a promised sight,
Some of husbands, some of lovers,
Which an empty dream discovers.

Jonson.

A Particular Entertainment of the Queen and Prince their Highness to Althrope, 1603.*

ON MY FIRST SON

Farewell, thou child of my right hand, and joy!
My sin was too much hope of thee, loved boy;
Seven years thou wert lent to me, and I thee pay,
Exacted by thy fate, on the just day.
Oh, could I lose all father now! For why
Will man lament the state he should envy—
To have so soon 'scaped world's and flesh's rage,
And, if no other misery, yet age?
Rest in soft peace, and, asked, say here doth lie
Ben Jonson his best piece of poetry:
For whose sake, henceforth, all his vows be such
As what he loves may never like too much.

Jonson.

Epigrams, 1616. (Poem written 1603.)

THE PASSIONATE MAN'S PILGRIMAGE

Give me my scallop-shell of Quiet;
My staff of Faith to walk upon;
My scrip of Joy, immortal diet;
My bottle of Salvation;

My gown of Glory, hope's true gage;
And thus I 'll take my pilgrimage.
Blood must be my body's balmer—
No other balm will there be given—
Whilst my soul, like a white palmer,
Travels to the land of Heaven;
Over the silver mountains,
Where spring the nectar fountains—
And there I 'll kiss
The bowl of Bliss,
And drink my eternal fill
On every milken hill:
My soul will be a-dry before,
But after it will ne'er thirst more.
And by the happy blissful way,
More peaceful pilgrims I shall see,
That have shook off their gowns of clay,
And go apparelled fresh like me:
I 'll bring them first
To slake their thirst,
And then to taste those nectar suckets,
At the clear wells
Where sweetness dwells,
Drawn up by saints in crystal buckets.
And when our bottles and all we
Are filled with immortality,
Then the holy paths we 'll travel,
Strewed with rubies thick as gravel.
Ceilings of diamonds, sapphire floors,
High walls of coral, and pearl bowers.
From thence to Heaven's bribeless hall,
Where no corrupted voices brawl;
No conscience molten into gold;
Nor forged accusers bought and sold;

No cause deferred; nor vain-spent journey;
For there Christ is the King's Attorney,
Who pleads for all without degrees,
And he hath angels, but no fees.
When the grand twelve million jury
Of our sins and sinful fury,
'Gainst our souls black verdicts give,
Christ pleads his death, and then we live.
Be thou my speaker, taintless Pleader,
Unblotted Lawyer, true Proceeder!
Thou movest salvation even for alms,
Not with a bribèd lawyer's palms.
And this is my eternal plea
To him that made heaven, earth, and sea,
Seeing my flesh must die so soon,
And want a head to dine next noon,—
Just at the stroke, when my veins start and spread,
Set on my soul an everlasting head:
Then am I ready, like a palmer fit,
To tread those blest paths which before I writ.

Diaphantus, 1604. (Poem written c. 1603.)*   *Raleigh.*

WEEP YOU NO MORE

Weep you no more, sad fountains;
    What need you flow so fast?
Look how the snowy mountains
    Heaven's sun doth gently waste.
        But my sun's heavenly eyes
            View not your weeping,
            That now lies sleeping
        Softly, now softly lies
            Sleeping.

angels] also gold coins of the period.

Sleep is a reconciling,
   A rest that peace begets:
Doth not the sun rise smiling
    When fair at even he sets?
     Rest you then, rest, sad eyes,
      Melt not in weeping,
       While she lies sleeping
     Softly, now softly lies
       Sleeping.   *Anon.*

J. Dowland's *Songs or Airs*, iii., 1603.

SONG

O Love, how strangely sweet
   Are thy weak passions,
That love and joy should meet
   In self-same fashions!
Oh, who can tell
   The cause why this should move?
But only this,
   No reason ask of Love.   *Marston.*

The Dutch Courtesan, 1605. (Written 1603–4.)

PACK, CLOUDS, AWAY

Pack, clouds, away, and welcome day,
   With night we banish sorrow;
Sweet air, blow soft; mount, lark, aloft
   To give my Love good-morrow!
Wings from the wind, to please her mind,
   Notes from the lark I 'll borrow;
Bird, prune thy wing, nightingale, sing,
   To give my Love good-morrow!
    To give my Love good-morrow
    Notes from them all I 'll borrow,

Wake from the nest, robin-redbreast,
  Sing, birds, in every furrow;
And from each bill, let music shrill
  Give my fair Love good-morrow!
Blackbird and thrush in every bush,
  Stare, linnet, and cock-sparrow,
You pretty elves, amongst yourselves
  Sing my fair Love good-morrow!
    To give my Love good-morrow
    Sing, birds, in every furrow!   *T. Heywood.*

The Rape of Lucrece, 1608. (Written 1603–8. Song omitted 1608; printed 1630.)*

PRETTY TWINKLING STARRY EYES

Pretty twinkling starry eyes!
How did Nature first devise
Such a sparkling in your sight
As to give Love such delight
As to make him, like a fly,
Play with looks until he die?

Sure ye were not made at first
For such mischief to be cursed,
As to kill affection's care
That doth only truth declare.
Where worth's wonders never wither
Love and beauty live together.

Blessëd eyes! then give your blessing,
That, in passion's best expressing,
Love, that only lives to grace ye,
May not suffer pride deface ye;

stare] starling.

But, in gentle thought's directions,
Show the praise of your perfections.   *Breton.*

The Passionate Shepherd, 1604.

THE MERRY COUNTRY LAD

Who can live in heart so glad
As the merry country lad?
Who upon a fair green balk
May at pleasure sit and walk,
And amid the azure skies
See the morning sun arise,
While he hears in every spring
How the birds do chirp and sing:
Or before the hounds in cry
See the hare go stealing by:
Or along the shallow brook,
Angling with a baited hook,
See the fishes leap and play
In a blessèd sunny day:
Or to hear the partridge call
Till she have her covey all:
Or to see the subtle fox,
How the villain plies the box;
After feeding on his prey,
How he closely sneaks away,
Through the hedge and down the furrow
Till he gets into his burrow:
Then the bee to gather honey;
And the little black-haired coney,
On a bank for sunny place,
With her forefeet wash her face,—
Are not these, with thousands moe

Than the courts of kings do know,
The true pleasing spirit's sights
That may breed true love's delights?   *Breton.*

The Passionate Shepherd, 1604.*

MY WOE MUST EVER LAST

She is gone, she is lost, she is found, she is ever fair:
    Sorrow draws weakly where love draws not too:
Woe's cries sound nothing, but only in love's ear:
    Do then by dying what life cannot do. . . .
Unfold thy flocks and leave them to the fields,
    To feed on hills or dales where likes them best
Of what the summer or the spring-time yields,
    For love and time hath given thee leave to rest.
Thy heart which was their fold, now in decay
    By often storms and winter's many blasts,
All torn and rent becomes misfortune's prey;
    False hope, my shepherd's staff, now age hath brast.
My pipe, which love's own hand gave my desire
    To sing her praises and my woe upon,
Despair hath often threatened to the fire
    As vain to keep now all the rest are gone.
Thus home I draw, as death's long night draws on,
    Yet, every foot, old thoughts turn back mine eyes;
Constraint me guides, as old age draws a stone
    Against the hill, which over-weighty lies
For feeble arms or wasted strength to move:
    My steps are backward, gazing on my loss—
My mind's affection and my soul's sole love,
    Not mixed with fancy's chaff or fortune's dross.
To God I leave it, who first gave it me,
    And I her gave, and she returned again

Line 4] The four dots appear in Raleigh's autograph.   brast] broken.

As it was hers; so let his mercies be
   Of my last comforts the essential mean.

But be it so or not, the effects are past:
   Her love hath end; my woe must ever last. *Raleigh.*

Hatfield MSS., vol. cxliv. The close of *The 21st and last Book of the Ocean, to Cynthia*. [Written c. 1604 ?]. (This is in Raleigh's writing, and is the only surviving 'Book' of the Continuation of his lost poem, *Cynthia*.)*

HER PRAISES

She, like the morning, is still fresh and fair.
   The elements, of her they all do borrow,—
The earth, the fire, the waters, and the air,
   Their strength, heat, moisture, liveliness. No sorrow
Can virtue change. Beauty hath but one place.
The heart 's still perfect, though impaled the face.

O eyes! no eyes, but stars still clearly shining!
   O face! no face, but shape of angels' fashion!
O lips! no lips, but bliss by kiss refining!
   O heart! no heart, but of true love right passion!
O eyes, face, lips, and heart, if not too cruel,
To see, feel, taste, and love earth's rarest jewel.

Diaphantus, 1604. (An excerpt.)   *Scoloker.*

MADRIGAL

When in her face mine eyes I fix,
A fearful boldness takes my mind,
Sweet honey Love with gall doth mix,
   And is unkindly kind:
     It seems to breed,

---

impaled] defended as with a palisade.

                    And is indeed
              A special pleasure to be pined.
                 No danger then I dread:
           For though I went a thousand times to Styx,
           I know she can revive me with her eye,
             As many looks, as many lives to me:
                 And yet had I a thousand hearts,
                 As many looks, as many darts,
                    Might make them all to die.   *Stirling.*

Aurora, 1604.

SONNETS

I envy not Endymion now no more,
Nor all the happiness his sleep did yield
While as Diana, straying through the field,
Sucked from his sleep-sealed lips balm for her sore:
Whilst I embraced the shadow of my death,
I, dreaming, did far greater pleasure prove,
And quaffed with Cupid sugared draughts of love,
Then, Jove-like, feeding on a nectared breath.
Now judge which of us two might be most proud:
He got a kiss, yet not enjoyed it right;
And I got none, yet tasted that delight
Which Venus on Adonis once bestowed:
    He only got the body of a kiss,
    And I the soul of it, which he did miss.   *Stirling.*

Ibid.

Oh, if thou knew'st how thou thyself dost harm,
And dost prejudge thy bliss, and spoil my rest;
Then thou wouldst melt the ice out of thy breast
And thy relenting heart would kindly warm.

Oh, if thy pride did not our joys control,
What world of loving wonders shouldst thou see!
For if I saw thee once transformed in me,
Then in thy bosom I would pour my soul;
Then all thy thoughts should in my visage shine,
And if that ought mischanced thou shouldst not moan
Nor bear the burthen of thy griefs alone;
No, I would have my share in what were thine:
    And whilst we thus should make our sorrows one,
    This happy harmony would make them none.

Ibid.   *Stirling.*

Let others of the world's decaying tell,
I envy not those of the golden age
That did their careless thoughts for nought engage,
But, cloyed with all delights, lived long and well.
And as for me, I mind to applaud my fate:
Though I was long in coming to the light
Yet may I mount to fortune's highest height,
So great a good could never come too late.
I 'm glad that it was not my chance to live
Till as that heavenly creature first was born,
Who as an angel doth the earth adorn
And buried virtue in the tomb revive:
    For vice overflows the world with such a flood,
    That in it all, save she, there is no good.   *Stirling.*

Ibid.

SISTER, AWAKE!

Sister, awake! close not your eyes,
    The day her light discloses;
And the bright morning doth arise
    Out of her bed of roses.

See the clear sun, the world's bright eye,
   In at our window peeping;
Lo, how he blusheth to espy
   Us idle wenches sleeping!
Therefore awake, make haste I say,
   And let us without staying
All in our gowns of green so gay
   Into the park a maying.   *Anon.*

T. Bateson's *English Madrigals*, i., 1604.

TAKE, OH, TAKE THOSE LIPS AWAY

Take, oh, take those lips away,
   That so sweetly were forsworn;
And those eyes, the break of day,
   Lights that do mislead the morn:
But my kisses bring again,
          Bring again;
Seals of love, but sealed in vain,
          Sealed in vain.   *Shakespeare.*

Measure for Measure, 1623. (Written 1604–5 ?)

ULYSSES AND THE SIREN

Siren

Come, worthy Greek! Ulysses, come,
   Possess these shores with me:
The winds and seas are troublesome,
   And here we may be free.
Here we may sit and view their toil
   That travail in the deep,
And joy the day in mirth the while,
   And spend the night in sleep.

Ulysses

Fair Nymph, if fame or honour were
    To be attained with ease,
Then would I come and rest with thee,
    And leave such toils as these.
But here it dwells, and here must I
    With danger seek it forth:
To spend the time luxuriously
    Becomes not men of worth.

Siren

Ulysses, oh, be not deceived
    With that unreal name!
This honour is a thing conceived,
    And rests on others' fame;
Begotten only to molest
    Our peace, and to beguile
The best thing of our life—our rest,
    And give us up to toil.

Ulysses

Delicious Nymph, suppose there were
    Nor honour nor report,
Yet manliness would scorn to wear
    The time in idle sport:
For toil doth give a better touch
    To make us feel our joy,
And ease finds tediousness as much
    As labour yields annoy.

Siren

Then pleasure likewise seems the shore,
    Whereto tends all your toil,

Which you forego, to make it more,
   And perish oft the while.
Who may disport them diversely
   Find never tedious day,
And ease may have variety
   As well as action may.

Ulysses

But natures of the noblest frame
   These toils and dangers please;
And they take comfort in the same
   As much as you in ease;
And with the thought of actions past
   Are recreated still;
When pleasure leaves a touch, at last,
   To show that it was ill.

Siren

That doth opinion only cause
   That 's out of custom bred,
Which makes us many other laws
   Than ever nature did.
No widows wail for our delights,
   Our sports are without blood;
The world, we see, by warlike wights
   Receives more hurt than good.

Ulysses

But yet the state of things require
   These motions of unrest;
And these great spirits of high desire
   Seem born to turn them best;
To purge the mischiefs that increase

And all good order mar;
For oft we see a wicked peace,
    To be well changed for war.

Siren

Well, well, Ulysses, then I see
    I shall not have thee here;
And therefore I will come to thee,
    And take my fortune there.
I must be won, that cannot win,
    Yet lost were I not won;
For beauty hath created bin
    To undo, or be undone.   *Daniel.*

Certain small Poems, 1605.

SONNETS

So shoots a star as doth my mistress glide
At midnight through my chamber, which she makes
Bright as the sky when moon and stars are spied,
Wherewith my sleeping eyes amazëd wake:
Which ope no sooner than herself she shuts
Out of my sight, away so fast she flies:
Which me in mind of my slack service puts;
For which all night I wake, to plague mine eyes.
Shoot, star, once more! and if I be thy mark
Thou shalt hit me, for thee I 'll meet withal.
Let mine eyes once more see thee in the dark,
Else they, with ceaseless waking, out will fall:
    And if again such time and place I lose
    To close with thee, let mine eyes never close.
                                            Davies of Hereford.

Wit's Pilgrimage, [c. 1605].*

It is as true as strange, else trial feigns,
That whosoever in the moonshine sleeps
Are hardly waked, the moon so rules the brains;
For she is sovereign of the brains and deeps:
So thou, fair Cynthia, with thy borrowed beams—
Borrowed of glory's Sun, great lord of light,—
Mak'st me still sleep in love, whose golden dreams
Give love right current—sith well-coined—delight.
I cannot wake while thou on me dost shine,
Thy shining so makes me so sweetly dream:
For still methinks I kiss those lips of thine,
And—nothing else, for I will not blaspheme:
    But thought is free, and dreams are dreams, and so
    I dream, and dream, and dream; but let that go.

Wit's Pilgrimage, [c. 1605].   *Davies of Hereford.*

COME, MY CELIA, LET US PROVE

Come, my Celia, let us prove,
While we can, the sports of love;
Time will not be ours for ever,
He, at length, our good will sever.
Spend not then his gifts in vain:
Suns that set may rise again;
But if once we lose this light,
'Tis with us perpetual night.
Why should we defer our joys?
Fame and rumour are but toys.
Cannot we delude the eyes
Of a few poor household spies?
Or his easier ears beguile,
Thus removèd by our wile?
'Tis no sin love's fruits to steal,

> But the sweet thefts to reveal;
> To be taken, to be seen.
> These have crimes accounted been.   *Jonson.*

Volpone, 1616. (First printed 1607. Acted 1605.)

FOOLS

Fools, they are the only nation
Worth men's envy or admiration;
Free from care or sorrow-taking,
Selves and others merry making:
All they speak or do is sterling.
Your fool he is your great man's dearling,
And your lady's sport and pleasure;
Tongue and bable are his treasure.
E'en his face begetteth laughter,
And he speaks truth free from slaughter;
He 's the grace of every feast,
And sometimes the chiefest guest;
Hath his trencher and his stool,
When wit waits upon the fool.
        Oh, who would not be
        He, he, he?   *Jonson.*

Ibid.

FAIN WOULD I CHANGE THAT NOTE

Fain would I change that note
    To which fond love hath charmed me.
Long, long to sing by rote,
    Fancying that that harmed me.
Yet when this thought doth come,
'Love is the perfect sum
    Of all delight,'

---

buble] bauble.

I have no other choice
Either for pen or voice
    To sing or write.

O Love, they wrong thee much
    That say thy sweet is bitter,
When thy ripe fruit is such
    As nothing can be sweeter.
Fair house of joy and bliss,
Where truest pleasure is,
    I do adore thee.
I know thee what thou art,
I serve thee with my heart
    And fall before thee.   *Anon.*

T. Hume's *Musical Humours*, 1605.

WHITHER SO FAST?

Whither so fast? See how the kindly flowers
    Perfumes the air, and all to make thee stay.
The climbing woodbind, clipping all these bowers,
    Clips thee likewise for fear thou pass away.
    Fortune our friend, our foe will not gainsay.
Stay but awhile, Phoebe no tell-tale is;
She her Endymion, I 'll my Phoebe kiss.

Fear not, the ground seeks but to kiss thy feet.
    Hark, hark how Philomela sweetly sings,
Whilst water-wanton fishes, as they meet,
    Strike crotchet time amidst these crystal springs,
    And Zephyrus 'mongst the leaves sweet murmur rings.
Stay but awhile, Phoebe no tell-tale is;
She her Endymion, I 'll my Phoebe kiss.

See how the heliotrope, herb of the sun,
  Though he himself long since be gone to bed,
Is not of force thine eyes' bright beams to shun,
  But with their warmth his goldy leaves unspread,
  And on my knee invites thee rest thy head.
Stay but awhile, Phoebe no tell-tale is;
She her Endymion, I 'll my Phoebe kiss.   *Anon.*

F. Pilkington's *Songs or Airs*, i., 1605.

THE CHARM

1 *Witch.* Thrice the brinded cat hath mewed.
2 *Witch.* Thrice and once the hedge-pig whined.
3 *Witch.* Harpier cries 'Tis time, 'tis time.
1 *Witch.* Round about the cauldron go:
       In the poisoned entrails throw.
       Toad, that under cold stone
       Days and nights has thirty-one,
       Sweltered venom sleeping got,
       Boil thou first i' the charmèd pot!
  All. Double, double toil and trouble;
       Fire burn, and cauldron bubble.

2 *Witch.* Fillet of a fenny snake,
       In the cauldron boil and bake;
       Eye of newt and toe of frog,
       Wool of bat and tongue of dog,
       Adder's fork and blind-worm's sting,
       Lizard's leg and owlet's wing,
       For a charm of powerful trouble,
       Like a hell-broth boil and bubble.
  All. Double, double toil and trouble;
       Fire burn, and cauldron bubble.

3 *Witch*. Scale of dragon, tooth of wolf,
              Witch's mummy, maw and gulf
              Of the ravined salt-sea shark,
              Root of hemlock digged i' the dark,
              Liver of blaspheming Jew,
              Gall of goat, and slips of yew
              Slivered in the moon's eclipse,
              Nose of Turk and Tartar's lips,
              Finger of birth-strangled babe
              Ditch-delivered by a drab,
              Make the gruel thick and slab:
              Add thereto a tiger's chaudron,
              For the ingredients of our cau'dron.
All.   Double, double toil and trouble;
              Fire burn, and cauldron bubble.

2 *Witch*. Cool it with a baboon's blood,
              Then the charm is firm and good.

Macbeth, 1623. (Written 1605–6?)   *Shakespeare*.

COME, SLEEP

Come, Sleep, and with thy sweet deceiving
        Lock me in delight awhile!
        Let some pleasing dreams beguile
        All my fancies; that from thence
        I may feel an influence,
All my powers of care bereaving!

Though but a shadow, but a sliding,
        Let me know some little joy!
        We that suffer long annoy
        Are contented with a thought

witch's] N.A.; witches, 1623.   cau'dron] cawdron, 1623, in this line only;
elsewhere either caldron or cauldron.

Through an idle fancy wrought:
Oh, let my joys have some abiding!   *Beaumont.*

The Woman-Hater, 1607. By Beaumont and Fletcher. (Acted c. 1606.)

SONNET

Go you, O winds that blow from north to south,
Convey my secret sighs unto my sweet;
Deliver them from mine unto her mouth,
And make my commendations till we meet.
But if perhaps her proud aspiring sp'rit
Will not accept nor yet receive the same,
The breast and bulwark of her bosom beat,
Knock at her heart, and tell from whence you came;
Importune her, nor cease nor shrink for shame:
Sport with her curls of amber-coloured hair,
And when she sighs, immix yourselves with thame,
Give her her own, and thus beguile the fair.
   Blow winds, fly sighs, where as my heart doth hant,
   And secretly commend me to my sanct.   *Craig.*

The Amorous Songs, Sonnets, and Elegies, 1606.

TO CUPID

Maidens, why spare ye?
Or whether not dare ye
   Correct the blind shooter?
Because wanton Venus,
So oft that doth pain us,
   Is her son's tutor.

Now in the spring
He proveth his wing;

---

thame] them.   hant] haunt.   sanct] saint.

The field is his bower,
And as the small bee
About flyeth he
    From flower to flower;

And wantonly roves
Abroad in the groves,
    And in the air hovers,
Which when it him deweth,
His feathers he meweth
    In sighs of true lovers.

And since doomed by fate
(That well knew his hate)
    That he should be blind;
For very despite
Our eyes be his white,
    So wayward his kind.

If his shafts losing
(Ill his mark choosing),
    Or his bow broken,
The moan Venus maketh,
And care that she taketh,
    Cannot be spoken.

To Vulcan commending
Her love, and straight sending
    Her doves and her sparrows,
With kisses, unto him,
And all but to woo him
    To make her son arrows.

Telling what he hath done,
Saith she, 'Right, mine own son!'

In her arms she him closes,
Sweets on him fans,
Laid in down of her swans,
    His sheets leaves of roses.

And feeds him with kisses;
Which, oft, when he misses,
    He ever is froward:
The mother's o'erjoying
Makes by much coying
    The child so untoward.

Yet in a fine net
That a spider set,
    The maidens had caught him,
Had she not been near him
And chancëd to hear him,
    More good they had taught him.   *Drayton.*

Poems, lyric and pastoral, [1606]. (Text 1619.)

AGINCOURT

Fair stood the wind for France
When we our sails advance,
Nor now to prove our chance
    Longer will tarry;
But putting to the main,
At Caux, the mouth of Seine,
With all his martial train
    Landed King Harry.

And taking many a fort,
Furnished in warlike sort,
Marcheth towards Agincourt

In happy hour;
Skirmishing day by day
With those that stopped his way,
Where the French general lay
    With all his power;

Which, in his height of pride,
King Henry to deride,
His ransom to provide
    To the king sending;
Which he neglects the while
As from a nation vile,
Yet with an angry smile
    Their fall portending.

And turning to his men,
Quoth our brave Henry then,
'Though they to one be ten,
    Be not amazèd;
Yet have we well begun,
Battles so bravely won
Have ever to the sun
    By fame been raisèd.

'And for myself,' quoth he,
'This my full rest shall be:
England ne'er mourn for me,
    Nor more esteem me;
Victor I will remain
Or on this earth lie slain,
Never shall she sustain
    Loss to redeem me.

'Poitiers and Cressy tell,
When most their pride did swell,

Under our swords they fell;
    No less our skill is
Than when our grandsire great,
Claiming the regal seat,
By many a warlike feat
    Lopped the French lilies.'

The Duke of York so dread
The eager vaward led;
With the main Henry sped,
    Amongst his henchmen.
Exeter had the rear,
A braver man not there;
O Lord, how hot they were
    On the false Frenchmen!

They now to fight are gone,
Armour on armour shone,
Drum now to drum did groan,
    To hear was wonder:
That with the cries they make
The very earth did shake;
Trumpet to trumpet spake,
    Thunder to thunder.

Well it thine age became,
O noble Erpingham,
Which didst the signal aim
    To our hid forces!
When, from a meadow by,
Like a storm suddenly

---

vaward] vanguard.   with the cries] 1606; with cries, 1619.

The English archery
        Struck the French horses:

With Spanish yew so strong,
Arrows a cloth-yard long,
That like to serpents stung,
        Piercing the weather;
None from his fellow starts,
But, playing manly parts,
And like true English hearts,
        Stuck close together.

When down their bows they threw,
And forth their bilbos drew,
And on the French they flew,
        Not one was tardy;
Arms were from shoulders sent,
Scalps to the teeth were rent,
Down the French peasants went:
        Our men were hardy.

This while our noble King,
His broad sword brandishing,
Down the French host did ding
        As to o'erwhelm it;
And many a deep wound lent,
His arms with blood besprent,
And many a cruel dent
        Bruisèd his helmet.

Gloucester, that duke so good,
Next of the royal blood,

bilbos] swords, originally from Bilboa, Spain.

For famous England stood
    With his brave brother:
Clarence, in steel so bright,
Though but a maiden knight,
Yet in that furious fight
    Scarce such another.

Warwick in blood did wade,
Oxford the foe invade,
And cruel slaughter made
    Still as they ran up;
Suffolk his axe did ply,
Beaumont and Willoughby
Bare them right doughtily,
    Ferrers and Fanhope.

Upon Saint Crispin's day
Fought was this noble fray,
Which fame did not delay
    To England to carry;
Oh, when shall English men
With such acts fill a pen?
Or England breed again
    Such a King Harry?   *Drayton.*

Poems, lyric and pastoral, [1606]. (Text 1619.)

IF I COULD SHUT THE GATE

If I could shut the gate against my thoughts
   And keep out sorrow from this room within,
Or memory could cancel all the notes
   Of my misdeeds, and I unthink my sin:
How free, how clear, how clean my soul should lie,
Discharged of such a loathsome company!

Or were there other rooms without my heart
   That did not to my conscience join so near,
Where I might lodge the thoughts of sin apart
   That I might not their clam'rous crying hear;
What peace, what joy, what ease should I possess,
Freed from their horrors that my soul oppress!

But, O my Saviour, who my refuge art,
   Let thy dear mercies stand 'twixt them and me,
And be the wall to separate my heart
   So that I may at length repose me free;
That peace, and joy, and rest may be within,
And I remain divided from my sin.   *Anon.*

J. Danyel's *Songs for the Lute*, 1606.

NOW THE EARTH, THE SKIES, THE AIR

Now the earth, the skies, the air,
     All things fair,
Seems new-born thoughts t' infuse;
Whilst the returning spring
     Joys each thing,
And blasted hopes renews.

When I, when only I alone
     Left to moan,
Find no times born for me:
No flowers, no meadow springs,
     No bird sings
But notes of misery.   *Anon.*

Ibid.

WHY CANST THOU NOT

Why canst thou not, as others do,
  Look on me with unwounding eyes,
And yet look sweet, but yet not so,
  Smile, but not in killing wise?
Arm not thy graces to confound;
Only look, but do not wound.

Why should mine eyes see more in you
  Than they can see in all the rest?
For I can others' beauties view
  And not find my heart oppressed.
Oh, be as others are to me,
Or let me be more to thee!   *Anon.*

Ibid.

THE QUEEN OF PAPHOS, ERYCINE

The Queen of Paphos, Erycine,
  In heart did rose-cheeked Adon love;
He mortal was, but she divine,
  And oft with kisses did him move;
With great gifts still she did him woo,
But he would never yield thereto.

Then since the Queen of Love by Love
  To love was once a subject made,
And could thereof no pleasure prove
  By day, by night, by light or shade,
Why, being mortal, should I grieve,
Since she herself could not relieve?

She was a goddess heavenly
   And loved a fair-faced earthly boy,
Who did contemn her deity
   And would not grant her hope of joy;
For Love doth govern by a fate
That here plants will and there leaves hate.

But I, a hapless mortal wight,
   To an immortal beauty sue;
No marvel then she loathes my sight
   Since Adon Venus would not woo.
Hence, groaning sighs!   mirth be my friend!
Before my life, my love shall end.   *Anon.*

J. Bartlet's *A Book of Airs*, 1606.

THE FAIREST OF HER DAYS

Who doth behold my mistress' face
   And seeth not, good hap hath he.
Who hears her speak and marks her grace,
   Shall think none ever spake but she.
In short for to resound her praise,
She is the fairest of her days.

Who knows her wit, and not admires,
   Shall show himself devoid of skill.
Her virtues kindle strange desires
   In those that think upon her still.
In short for to resound her praise,
She is the fairest of her days.

Her red is like unto the rose
   When from a bud unto the sun
Her tender leaves she doth disclose,

The first degree of ripeness won.
In short for to resound her praise,
She is the fairest of her days.

And with her red mixed is a white
   Like to that same of fair moonshine
That doth upon the water light
   And makes the colour seem divine.
In short for to resound her praise,
She is the fairest of her days.   *Anon.*

Ibid.

MIRTH

'Tis mirth that fills the veins with blood,
More than wine, or sleep, or food;
Let each man keep his heart at ease;
No man dies of that disease.
He that would his body keep
From diseases, must not weep;
But whoever laughs and sings,
Never he his body brings
Into fevers, gouts, or rheums,
Or lingeringly his lungs consumes;
Or meets with achës in the bone,
Or catarrhs, or griping stone:
But contented lives for aye;
The more he laughs, the more he may.

                         Beaumont (?)

The Knight of the Burning Pestle, 1613. By Beaumont and Fletcher.
(Written 1607?)

JILLIAN OF BERRY

For Jillian of Berry she dwells on a hill,
And she hath good beer and ale to sell,

And of good fellows she thinks no ill,
And thither will we go now, now now,
   And thither will we go now.
And when you have made a little stay,
You need not ask what is to pay,
But kiss your hostess, and go your way;
And thither will we go now, now, now,
   And thither will we go now.   *Beaumont* (?)

The Knight of the Burning Pestle, 1613. By Beaumont and Fletcher.
(Written 1607 ?)

COME, YOU WHOSE LOVES ARE DEAD

Come, you whose loves are dead,
   And, whiles I sing,
   Weep, and wring
Every hand, and every head
Bind with cypress and sad yew;
Ribbons black and candles blue
For him that was of men most true!

Come with heavy mourning,
   And on his grave
   Let him have
Sacrifice of sighs and groaning;
Let him have fair flowers enow,
White and purple, green and yellow,
For him that was of men most true!
                       J. Fletcher (?)

Ibid.

now, now, now] 1635; now, now, now, now, 1613.   mourning] 1613 and
1635; moaning, Seward 1750.

THERE IS A LADY SWEET AND KIND

There is a lady sweet and kind,
Was never face so pleased my mind;
I did but see her passing by,
And yet I love her till I die.

Her gesture, motion, and her smiles,
Her wit, her voice, my heart beguiles,
Beguiles my heart, I know not why,
And yet I love her till I die.

Her free behaviour, winning looks,
Will make a lawyer burn his books;
I touched her not, alas! not I,
And yet I love her till I die.

Had I her fast betwixt mine arms,
Judge you that think such sports were harms,
Were 't any harm? no, no, fie, fie,
For I will love her till I die.

Should I remain confinëd there
So long as Phoebus in his sphere,
I to request, she to deny,
Yet would I love her till I die.

Cupid is wingëd and doth range,
Her country so my love doth change:
But change she earth, or change she sky,
Yet will I love her till I die.   *Anon.*

T. Ford's *Music of Sundry Kinds*, 1607.

A DITTY

Peace, peace, peace, make no noise,
  Pleasure and fear lie sleeping;
End, end, end your idle toys,
  Jealous eyes will be peeping:
Kiss, kiss and part, though not for hate, for pity;
Ha' done, ha' done, ha' done, for I ha' done my ditty.

Humour out of breath, 1608. (Acted 1607–8?)   *Day.*

EPITAPH ON A SOLDIER

His body lies interred within this mould,
Who died a young man yet departed old;
And in all strength of youth that man can have
Was ready still to drop into his grave:
For aged in virtue, with a youthful eye
He welcomed it, being still prepared to die,
And living so, though young deprived of breath,
He did not suffer an untimely death;
But we may say of his brave blest decease—
He died in war, and yet he died in peace.   *Tourneur.*

The Atheist's Tragedy, 1611. (Written 1607–11.)

MADRIGAL

Dear, when I did from you remove,
I left my joy, but not my love;
  That never can depart.
It neither higher can ascend,
  Nor lower bend.
Fixed in the centre of my heart,
  As in his place,

And lodgëd so, how can it change,
    Or you grow strange?
Those are earth's properties and base.
Each where, as the bodies divine,
Heaven's lights and you to me will shine.

Herbert of Cherbury.

Occasional Verses, 1665. (Written c. 1608.)*

A DITTY IN IMITATION OF THE SPANISH

Now that the April of your youth adorns
    The garden of your face,
Now that for you each knowing lover mourns,
    And all seek to your grace—
Do not repay affectïon with scorns.

What though you may a matchless beauty vaunt,
    And that all hearts can move
By such a power as seemeth to enchant?
    Yet, without help of love,
Beauty no pleasure to itself can grant.

Then think each minute that you lose, a day;
    The longest youth is short,
The shortest age is long; Time flies away
    And makes us but his sport,
And that which is not Youth's, is Age's prey.

See but the bravest horse that prideth most,
    Though he escaped the war,
Either from master to the man is lost,
    Or turned into the car;
Or else must die with being ridden post.

Then lose not beauty, lovers, time, and all;
    Too late your fault you see
When that in vain you would these days recall.
    Nor can you virtuous be
When, without these, you have not wherewithal.

Occasional Verses, 1665. (Written c. 1608.)   *Herbert of Cherbury.*

SONG

Four arms, two necks, one wreathing;
Two pairs of lips, one breathing;
Two hearts that multiply
Sighs interchangeably:

The thought of this confounds me,
And as I speak it wounds me.
It cannot be expressed.
Good help me, whilst I rest.

Bad stomachs have their loathing,
And oh, this all is no thing:
This 'no' with griefs both prove
Report oft turns to love.   *Anon.*

T. Weelkes' *Airs or Fantastic Spirits*, 1608. (Also in Christ Church MS. 439.)

FARA DIDDLE DYNO

Ha ha! ha ha! This world doth pass
    Most merrily I 'll be sworn,
For many an honest Indian ass
    Goes for a unicorn.
            Fara diddle dyno,
            This is idle fyno.

turns to love] MS.; turns in love, 1608.

Tie hie! tie hie! O sweet delight!
   He tickles this age that can
Call Tullia's ape a marmasyte
   And Leda's goose a swan.
                 Fara diddle dyno,
                 This is idle fyno.

So so! so so! Fine English days!
   For false play is no reproach,
For he that doth the coachman praise
   May safely use the coach.
                 Fara diddle dyno,
                 This is idle fyno.

Ibid.   *Anon.*

COME, LOVE, LET 'S WALK

Come, Love, let 's walk into the spring,
Where we may hear the blackbird sing,
The robin-redbreast and the thrush,
The nightingale in thorny bush,
The mavis sweetly carolling,
These to my Love content will bring.

In yonder dale there are fine flowers,
And many pleasant shady bowers,
A purling brook whose silver streams
Are beautified by Phoebus' beams,
Which stealing through the trees for fear,
Because Diana bathes her there.

See where this nymph with all her train
Comes tripping o'er the park amain,

---

marmasyte] marmoset.

And in this grove here will she stay,
At barley-break to sport and play;
Where we may sit us down and see
Fair beauty mixed with chastity.   *Anon.*

H. Youll's *Canzonets*, 1608.

ONCE I THOUGHT TO DIE FOR LOVE

Once I thought to die for love,
Till I found that women prove
    Traitors in their smiling.
They say men unconstant be,
But themselves love change we see,
Till new grows old, and old grows stale, and all is but
    beguiling.   *Anon.*

Ibid.

— Is this wisdom or mere spite?
This thought, on the end — or long past end —
of a relationship is in my mind. — — —
Women, 'Ya can't live with them, ~~can't~~ w/o them!
02 July 92

HAPPY HE

Happy he
Who, to sweet home retired,
Shuns glory so admired,
    And to himself lives free.
Whilst he who strives with pride to climb the skies
Falls down with foul disgrace before he rise.

Let who will
The active life commend,
And all his travels bend
    Earth with his fame to fill:
Such fame, so forced, at last dies with his death,
Which life maintained by others' idle breath.

My delights,
To dearest home confined,
Shall there make good my mind,
Not awed with Fortune's spites:
High trees heaven blasts, winds shake and honours fell,
When lowly plants long time in safety dwell.

All I can
My worldly strife shall be
They one day say of me:
'He died a good old man.'
On his sad soul a heavy burden lies
Who, known to all, unknown to himself dies.   *Anon.*

R. Jones' *Ultimum Vale*, 1608.

DO NOT, OH, DO NOT PRIZE

Do not, oh, do not prize thy beauty at too high a rate;
Love to be loved while thou art lovely, lest thou love too late:
Frowns print wrinkles in thy brows
At which spiteful age doth smile,
Women in their froward vows
Glorying to beguile.

Wert thou the only world's admirèd, thou canst love but one;
And many have before been loved, thou art not loved alone:
Couldst thou speak with heavenly grace,
Sappho might with thee compare;
Blush the roses in thy face,
Rosamund was as fair.

Pride is the canker that consumeth beauty in her prime;
They that delight in long debating feel the curse of time:

All things with the time do change
   That will not the time obey;
Some even to themselves seem strange
   Thorough their own delay.   *Anon.*

R. Jones' *Ultimum Vale*, 1608.

WHAT REMAINS BUT ONLY DYING?

Shall I look to ease my grief?
   No, my sight is lost with eyeing:
Shall I speak and beg relief?
   No, my voice is hoarse with crying:
   What remains but only dying?

Love and I of late did part,
   But the boy, my peace envying,
Like a Parthian threw his dart
   Backward, and did wound me flying:
   What remains but only dying?

She whom then I lookèd on,
   My remembrance beautifying,
Stays with me though I am gone,
   Gone and at her mercy lying:
   What remains but only dying?

Shall I try her thoughts and write?
   No, I have no means of trying:
If I should, yet at first sight
   She would answer with denying:
   What remains but only dying?

Thus my vital breath doth waste,
   And, my blood with sorrow drying,

Sighs and tears make life to last
  For a while, their place supplying:
  What remains but only dying?   *Anon.*

Ibid.

UPON A DIAMOND CUT IN FORM OF A HEART, SET WITH A CROWN ABOVE AND A BLOODY DART PIERCING IT, SENT IN A NEW YEAR'S GIFT

Thou sent to me a heart was crowned,
  I thought it had been thine;
But when I saw it had a wound
  I knew the heart was mine.

A bounty of a strange conceit,
  To give mine own to me,
And give it in a worse estate
  Than it was given to thee.

The heart I sent, it had no pain,
  It was entire and sound;
But thou didst send it back again
  Sick of a deadly wound.

O heavens! how would you use a heart
  That should rebellious be,
When you undo it with a dart,
  That yields itself to thee?

Yet wish I it had no more pain
  Than from the wound proceeds:
More for the sending back again,
  Than for the wound, it bleeds.

Envy will say some mis-desert
   Hath caused thee turn 't away,
And where it was thy fault, thy art
   The blame on it will lay.

Yet thou dost know that no defect
   In it thou couldst reprove,
Thou only feared it should infect
   Thy loveless heart with love:

A crime which if it could commit
   Would so endear 't to thee
That thou would rather harbour it
   Than send it back to me.

Yet keep it still, or if, poor heart!
   It hath been thine too long,
Send me it back as free from smart
   As it was free from wrong.   *Ayton.*

B.M. Add. MS. 10308. (Poem written before 1609?)*

WHEN THOU DIDST THINK I DID NOT LOVE

When thou didst think I did not love,
   Then thou didst dote on me;
Now, when thou find'st that I do prove
   As kind as kind can be,
      Love dies in thee.

What way to fire the mercury
   Of thy inconstant mind?
Methinks it were good policy
   For me to turn unkind,
      To make thee kind.

Yet will I not good nature strain
 To buy, at so great cost,
That which, before I do obtain,
 I make account almost
                    That it is lost.

And though I might myself excuse
 By imitating thee,
Yet will I no examples use
 That may bewray in me
                    Lightness to be.

But since I gave thee once my heart,
 My constancy shall show
That though thou play the woman's part
 And from a friend turn foe,
                    Men do not so.   *Ayton.*

Ibid.

ON A WOMAN'S INCONSTANCY

I loved thee once, I 'll love no more,
 Thine be the grief as is the blame!
Thou are not what thou was before,
 What reason I should be the same?
          He that can love, unloved again,
           Hath better store of love than brain.
               God send me love, my debts to pay,
                While unthrifts fool their love away!

Nothing could have my love o'erthrown
 If thou had still continued mine:
Nay, if thou had remained thine own,
 I might perchance have yet been thine.

But thou thy freedom did recall,
That it thou might elsewhere enthral.
And then how could I but disdain
A captive's captive to remain?

When new desires had conquered thee,
And changed the object of thy will,
It had been lethargy in me,
No constancy, to love thee still:
Yea, it had been a sin to go
And prostitute affection so,
Since we are taught no prayers to say
To such as must to others pray.

Yet do thou glory in thy choice;
Thy choice, of his good fortune boast:
I 'll neither grieve, nor yet rejoice,
To see him gain what I have lost:
The height of my disdain shall be
To laugh at him, to blush for thee,
To love thee still, but go no more
A begging at a beggar's door.   *Ayton.*

B.M. Add. MS. 10308. (Poem written before 1609?)

TO HIS FORSAKEN MISTRESS

I do confess thou 'rt smooth and fair,
And I might have gone near to love thee,
Had I not found the slightest prayer
That lips could move, had power to move thee;
But I can let thee now alone,
As worthy to be loved by none.

I do confess thou 'rt sweet, yet find
Thee such an unthrift of thy sweets,

Thy favours are but like the wind
  Which kisseth everything it meets;
      And since thou canst with more than one,
      Thou 'rt worthy to be kissed by none.

The morning rose, that untouched stands
  Armed with her briars, how sweet she smells!
But plucked and strained through ruder hands,
  Her sweets no longer with her dwells,
      But scent and beauty both are gone,
      And leaves fall from her, one by one.

Such fate, ere long, will thee betide
  When thou hast handled been a while,
With sere flowers to be thrown aside;
  And I shall sigh, when some will smile,
      To see thy love to every one
      Hath brought thee to be loved by none.   *Ayton*(?)

J. Playford's *Select Airs*, 1659. (Poem written before 1609?)*

SONNET

Death, be not proud, though some have callèd thee
Mighty and dreadful, for thou art not so:
For those, whom thou think'st thou dost overthrow,
Die not, poor Death; nor yet canst thou kill me.
From rest and sleep, which but thy pictures be,
Much pleasure, then from thee much more must flow;
And soonest our best men with thee do go,
Rest of their bones, and souls' delivery.
Thou art slave to fate, chance, kings, and desperate men,
And doth with poison, war, and sickness dwell;
And poppy or charms can make us sleep as well
And better than thy stroke; why swell'st thou then?

One short sleep past, we wake eternally,
And Death shall be no more: Death, thou shalt die.

Poems, 1633. (Poem written before 1609?)*   *Donne.*

COME, SHEPHERDS, COME!

Come, shepherds, come!
            Come away
            Without delay,
Whilst the gentle time doth stay.
      Green woods are dumb,
And will never tell to any
Those dear kisses, and those many
Sweet embraces that are given;
Dainty pleasures, that would even
Raise in coldest age a fire,
And give virgin-blood desire.
            Then, if ever,
            Now or never,
            Come and have it:
            Think not I
            Dare deny,
            If you crave it.   *J. Fletcher.*

The Faithful Shepherdess, [1609–10]. (Acted c. 1608–9.)

SONG

Do not fear to put thy feet
Naked in the river sweet;
Think not leech, or newt, or toad,
Will bite thy foot, when thou hast trod:
Nor let the water rising high,
As thou wad'st in, make thee cry

And sob; but ever live with me,
And not a wave shall trouble thee!   *J. Fletcher.*

Ibid.

THE GOD OF SHEEP

All ye woods, and trees, and bowers,
All ye virtues and ye powers
That inhabit in the lakes,
In the pleasant springs or brakes,
    Move your feet
      To our sound,
    Whilst we greet
      All this ground
With his honour and his name
That defends our flocks from blame.

He is great, and he is just,
He is ever good, and must
Thus be honoured. Daffadillies,
Roses, pinks, and lovèd lilies
      Let us fling,
      Whilst we sing,
      Ever holy,
      Ever holy,
Ever honoured, ever young!
Thus great Pan is ever sung.   *J. Fletcher.*

Ibid.

THE EVENING KNELL

Shepherds all, and maidens fair,
Fold your flocks up, for the air

Gins to thicken, and the sun
Already his great course hath run.
See the dewdrops how they kiss
Every little flower that is,
Hanging on their velvet heads
Like a rope of crystal beads:
See the heavy clouds low falling,
And bright Hesperus down calling
The dead Night from under ground;
At whose rising, mists unsound,
Damps and vapours fly apace,
Hovering o'er the wanton face
Of these pastures, where they come,
Striking dead both blood and bloom:
Therefore, from such danger lock
Every one his lovëd flock;
And let your dogs lie loose without,
Lest the wolf come as a scout
From the mountain, and, ere day,
Bear a lamb or kid away;
Or the crafty thievish fox
Break upon your simple flocks.
To secure yourselves from these,
Be not too secure in ease;
Let one eye his watches keep,
Whilst the t'other eye doth sleep;
So you shall good shepherds prove,
And for ever hold the love
Of our great god. Sweetest slumbers,
And soft silence, fall in numbers
On your eye-lids! So, farewell!
Thus I end my evening's knell.   *J. Fletcher.*

The Faithful Shepherdess, [1609–10].* (Acted c. 1608–9.)

SONG

Shine out, fair Sun, with all your heat,
   Show all your thousand-coloured light!
Black Winter freezes to his seat;
   The grey wolf howls, he does so bite;
Crookt Age on three knees creeps the street;
   The boneless fish close quaking lies
And eats for cold his aching feet;
   The stars in icicles arise:
Shine out, and make this winter night
Our beauty's Spring, our Prince of Light!   *Anon.*

The Masque of the Twelve Months. (J. P. Collier's MS., *temp.* James I.
Written 1608–12 ?)*

STILL TO BE NEAT

Still to be neat, still to be dressed,
As you were going to a feast;
Still to be powdered, still perfumed:
Lady, it is to be presumed,
Though art's hid causes are not found,
All is not sweet, all is not sound.

Give me a book, give me a face,
That makes simplicity a grace;
Robes loosely flowing, hair as free:
Such sweet neglect more taketh me
Than all the adulteries of art;
They strike mine eyes, but not my heart.   *Jonson.*

Epicoene, or the Silent Woman, 1616. (Acted 1609.)

Sun] N.A., Suns, 1848.

THE WITCHES' CHARMS

1 *Charm.* Dame, dame! the watch is set:
Quickly come, we all are met.
From the lakes and from the fens,
From the rocks and from the dens,
From the woods and from the caves,
From the churchyards, from the graves,
From the dungeon, from the tree
That they die on, here are we!

                    Comes she not yet?
                    Strike another heat!

2 *Charm.* The weather is fair, the wind is good:
Up, dame, o' your horse of wood!
Or else tuck up your gray frock,
And saddle your goat or your green cock,
And make his bridle a bottom of thrid
To roll up how many miles you have rid.
Quickly come away,
For we all stay.

                    Not yet? nay then
                    We 'll try her again.

3 *Charm.* The owl is abroad, the bat and the toad,
    And so is the cat-a-mountain;
The ant and the mole sit both in a hole,
    And frog peeps out o' the fountain.
The dogs they do bay, and the timbrels play,
    The spindle is now a-turning;
The moon it is red, and the stars are fled,
    But all the sky is a-burning:
The ditch is made, and our nails the spade:

---

bottom of thrid] ball of thread.   cat-a-mountain] wild cat.

With pictures full, of wax and of wool,
Their livers I stick with needles quick;
There lacks but the blood to make up the flood.
Quickly, dame, then bring your part in!
Spur, spur, upon little Martin!
Merrily, merrily, make him sail,
A worm in his mouth and a thorn in 's tail,
Fire above, and fire below,
With a whip i' your hand to make him go!

       O now she 's come!
       Let all be dumb.   *Jonson.*

The Masque of Queens, 1609. (Text 1616.)

WHEN STARS ARE SHROUDED

When stars are shrouded
    With dusky night,
    They yield no light,
Being so clouded.

When the wind moveth
    And waves doth rear,
    The sea, late clear,
Foul and dark proveth.

And rivers creeping
    Down a high hill,
    Stand often still,
Rocks them back keeping.

If thou wouldst brightly
    See truth's clear rays,
    Or walk those ways
Which lead most rightly,

All joy forsaking,
 Fear thou must fly,
 And hopes defy,
No sorrow taking.

For where these terrors
 Reign in the mind,
 They it do bind
In cloudy errors.

I. T.

Five Books of Philosophical Comfort, 1609.

LOVE NOT ME

Love not me for comely grace,
For my pleasing eye or face;
Nor for any outward part,
No, nor for my constant heart:
 For those may fail or turn to ill,
 So thou and I shall sever.
Keep therefore a true woman's eye,
And love me still, but know not why;
 So hast thou the same reason still
 To doat upon me ever.

Anon.

J. Wilbye's *Madrigals*, ii., 1609.

FAIN I WOULD

Fain I would, but oh, I dare not
 Speak my thoughts at full to praise her:
'Speak the best,' cries Love, 'and spare not;
 Thy speech can no higher raise her:
Thy speech than thy thought is lower,
Yet thy thoughts doth not half know her.'

Anon.

A. Ferrabosco's *Airs*, 1609. (Also in Christ Church MS. 439.)*
thought is] MS.; thoughts are, 1609.

AND IS IT NIGHT?

And is it night? are they thine eyes that shine?
    Are we alone, and here? and here, alone?
May I come near, may I but touch thy shrine?
    Is jealousy asleep, and is he gone?
O Gods, no more! silence my lips with thine!
Lips, kisses, joys, hap,—blessings most divine!

Oh, come, my dear! our griefs are turned to night,
    And night to joys; night blinds pale envy's eyes;
Silence and sleep prepare us our delight;
    Oh, cease we then our woes, our griefs, our cries:
Oh, vanish words! words do but passions move;
O dearest life! joy's sweet! O sweetest love!   *Anon.*

R. Jones' *A Musical Dream*, 1609.

AN INSCRIPTION

Grass of levity,
Span in brevity,
Flowers' felicity,
Fire of misery,
Winds' stability,
Is mortality.   *Anon.*

St. Mary Magdalene, Milk Street, London. Dated 1609. (Stowe's *Survey of London*, 1618.)

LINES WRITTEN AT CAMBRIDGE, TO
W. R., ESQUIRE

Ah! might I in some humble Kentish dale
For ever eas'ly spend my slow-paced hours,
Much should I scorn fair Eton's pleasant vale,

Or Windsor, Tempe's self, and proudest towers:
There would I sit safe from the stormy showers,
And laugh the troublous winds and angry sky—
Piping (ah) might I live, and piping might I die!

And would my lucky fortune so much grace me,
As in low Cranebrook, or high Brenchly's hill,
Or in some cabin near thy dwelling, place me,
There would I gladly sport and sing my fill,
And teach my tender Muse to raise her quill;
And that high Mantuan shepherd' self to dare,
If ought with that high Mantuan shepherd mought compare.

There would I chant either thy Gemma's praise,
Or else my Fusca (fairest shepherdess),
Or, when me list my slender pipe to raise,
Sing of Eliza's fixéd mournfulness,
And much bewail such woeful heaviness,
Whilst she a dear-loved hart (ah, luckless!) slew:
Whose fall she all too late, too soon, too much, did rue.

But seeing now I am not as I would,
But here among the unhonoured willows' shade
The muddy Chame doth me enforcéd hold,
Here I forswear my merry piping trade:
My little pipe of seven reeds ymade
(Ah, pleasing pipe!) I 'll hang upon this bough—
Thou Chame, and Chamish nymphs, bear witness of my vow!

P. Fletcher.

Poetical Miscellanies, in *The Purple Island*, 1633. (Poem written before 1610 ?)*

Cranebrook] Cranbrook, Fletcher's birthplace.   Mantuan shepherd] Virgil.
mought] might.   Stz. 3, ll. 4–7] allusion to Queen Elizabeth and Essex.
Chame] Cam.

HYMN

Drop, drop, slow tears,
    And bathe those beauteous feet,
Which brought from heaven
    The news and Prince of peace:
Cease not, wet eyes,
    His mercies to intreat;
To cry for vengeance
    Sin doth never cease:
In your deep floods
    Drown all my faults and fears;
Nor let his eye
    See sin, but through my tears.   *P. Fletcher.*
Ibid.

SONG

Fond men! whose wretched care the life soon ending,
By striving to increase your joy, do spend it;
And spending joy, yet find no joy in spending;
You hurt your life by striving to amend it,
And seeking to prolong it, soonest end it:
    Then, while fit time affords thee time and leisure,
    Enjoy while yet thou may'st thy life's sweet pleasure:
Too foolish is the man that starves to feed his treasure.

Love is life's end (an end, but never ending),
All joys, all sweets, all happiness, awarding;
Love is life's wealth (ne'er spent, but ever spending),
More rich by giving, taking by discarding;
Love 's life's reward, rewarded in rewarding:
    Then, from thy wretched heart fond care remove.
    Ah! shouldst thou live but once love's sweets to prove,
Thou wilt not love to live, unless thou live to love.

P. Fletcher(?)
Brittain's Ida, 1628.* (Written before 1610 ?)

IF WHEN I DIE

If, when I die, to hell's eternal shade
As an idolater condemned I be,
Because a mortal beauty that doth fade
I have too long adored in cruel thee,
　　Think not to 'scape, for—for thy tyranny—
　　Thou there shall be condemned as well as I;
And for thy greater plague two hells shalt prove:
The one the true, wherein thy self shalt be;
My hated looks the other, pale with love,
Shall seem each day and hour new hell to thee.
　　But I, beholding thy bright shining eyes,
　　Shall heaven enjoy amidst hell's miseries.　　*Fowler*(?)

Hawthornden MSS., vol. xiii. (Poem written before 1610?)*

SONG

Hark! hark! the lark at heaven's gate sings
　　And Phoebus gins arise,
His steeds to water at those springs
　　On chaliced flowers that lies;
And winking Mary-buds begin to ope their golden eyes:
With every thing that pretty is, my lady sweet, arise;
　　　　　　　　　　　　Arise, arise.

Cymbeline, 1623. (Written 1609–10?)　　　　　*Shakespeare.*

FEAR NO MORE

Fear no more the heat o' the sun,
　　Nor the furious winter's rages;
Thou thy worldly task hast done,
　　Home art gone, and ta'en thy wages:
Golden lads and girls all must,
As chimney-sweepers, come to dust.

Fear no more the frown o' the great;
   Thou art past the tyrant's stroke:
Care no more to clothe and eat;
   To thee the reed is as the oak:
The sceptre, learning, physic, must
All follow this, and come to dust.

Fear no more the lightning-flash,
   Nor the all-dreaded thunder-stone;
Fear not slander, censure rash;
   Thou hast finished joy and moan:
All lovers young, all lovers must
Consign to thee, and come to dust.

No exorciser harm thee!
Nor no witchcraft charm thee!
Ghost unlaid forbear thee!
Nothing ill come near thee!
Quiet consummation have;
And renownëd be thy grave!   *Shakespeare.*

Ibid.

AWAY, DELIGHTS!

Away, delights! go seek some other dwelling,
    For I must die.
Farewell, false Love! thy tongue is ever telling
    Lie after lie.
For ever let me rest now from thy smarts;
    Alas, for pity, go,
    And fire their hearts
That have been hard to thee! mine was not so.

Never again deluding love shall know me,
    For I will die;
And all those griefs that think to overgrow me,
    Shall be as I:
For ever will I sleep, while poor maids cry—
     'Alas, for pity, stay,
     And let us die
With thee! men cannot mock us in the clay.'

The Captain, 1647. (Written c. 1609–12.)
                   J. Fletcher.

TELL ME, DEAREST, WHAT IS LOVE?

Tell me, dearest, what is love?
'Tis a lightning from above;
   'Tis an arrow, 'tis a fire,
   'Tis a boy they call Desire;
     'Tis a grave,
     Gapes to have
Those poor fools that long to prove.

Tell me more, are women true?
Yes, some are, and some as you.
   Some are willing, some are strange
   Since you men first taught to change.
     And till troth
     Be in both,
All shall love, to love anew.

Tell me more yet, can they grieve?
Yes, and sicken sore, but live,

clay] Seward, 1750; day, 1647 and 1679.

And be wise, and delay,
When you men are as wise as they.
Then I see,
Faith will be,
Never till they both believe.   *J. Fletcher.*

Ibid.*

A DIRGE

Call for the robin-redbreast and the wren,
Since o'er shady groves they hover
And with leaves and flowers do cover
The friendless bodies of unburied men.
Call unto his funeral dole
The ant, the field-mouse, and the mole,
To rear him hillocks that shall keep him warm
And, when gay tombs are robbed, sustain no harm;
But keep the wolf far thence, that 's foe to men,
For with his nails he 'll dig them up again.   *Webster.*

The White Devil, 1612. (Written 1609–12.)

THINK'ST THOU TO SEDUCE ME THEN

Think'st thou to seduce me then with words that have no
meaning?
Parrots so can learn to prate, our speech by pieces gleaning;
Nurses teach their children so about the time of weaning.

Learn to speak first, then to woo: to wooing much pertaineth:
He that courts us, wanting art, soon falters when he feigneth,
Looks asquint on his discourse and smiles when he com-
plaineth.

Skilful anglers hide their hooks, fit baits for every season,
But with crooked pins fish thou, as babes do that want reason:
Gudgeons only can be caught with such poor tricks of treason.

Ruth, forgive me, if I erred from human heart's compassion,
When I laughed sometimes too much to see thy foolish
    fashion:
But, alas, who less could do, that found so good occasion?

Campion.

The Fourth Book of Airs, [c. 1617]. (Variant in W. Corkine's *Airs,* i., 1610.)

ARE THEY SHADOWS THAT WE SEE?

Are they shadows that we see?
And can shadows pleasure give?
Pleasures only shadows be,
Cast by bodies we conceive,
And are made the things we deem
In those figures which they seem.

But these pleasures vanish fast
Which by shadows are expressed,
Pleasures are not, if they last;
In their passing is their best:
Glory is most bright and gay
In a flash, and so away.

Feed apace then, greedy eyes,
On the wonder you behold:
Take it sudden as it flies,
Though you take it not to hold:
When your eyes have done their part,
Thought must length it in the heart.   *Daniel.*

Tethys' Festival, 1610.

THE AUTHOR LOVING THESE HOMELY MEATS SPECIALLY, VIZ.: CREAM, PANCAKES, BUTTERED PIPPIN-PIES (LAUGH, GOOD PEOPLE) AND TOBACCO; WRIT TO THAT WORTHY AND VIRTUOUS GENTLEWOMAN, WHOM HE CALLETH MISTRESS, AS FOLLOWETH

If there were, oh! an Hellespont of cream
Between us, milk-white mistress, I would swim
To you, to show to both my love's extreme,
Leander-like,—yea! dive from brim to brim.
But met I with a buttered pippin-pie
Floating upon 't, that would I make my boat
To waft me to you without jeopardy,
Though sea-sick I might be while it did float.
Yet if a storm should rise, by night or day,
Of sugar-snows and hail of caraways,
Then, if I found a pancake in my way,
It like a plank should bring me to your kays;
   Which having found, if they tobacco kept,
   The smoke should dry me well before I slept.
                           Davies of Hereford.

The Scourge of Folly, [n.d.]. (Registered 1610.)

WOOING SONG

Love is the blossom where there blows
Every thing that lives or grows:
Love doth make the heavens to move
And the sun doth burn in love:
Love the strong and weak doth yoke,
And makes ivy climb the oak,
Under whose shadows lions wild,

---

kays] quays.

Softened by love, grow tame and mild:
Love no med'cine can appease,
He burns the fishes in the seas:
Not all the skill his wounds can stench,
Not all the sea his fire can quench:
Love did make the bloody spear
Once a leavy coat to wear,
While in his leaves there shrouded lay
Sweet birds, for love that sing and play:
And of all love's joyful flame
I the bud and blossom am.
        Only bend thy knee to me,
        Thy wooing shall thy winning be.

See, see the flowers that below
Now as fresh as morning blow;
And of all, the virgin rose
That as bright Aurora shows;
How they all unleavèd die,
Losing their virginity!
Like unto a summer shade,
But now born, and now they fade.
Every thing doth pass away;
There is danger in delay:
Come, come gather then the rose,
Gather it, or it you lose!
All the sand of Tagus' shore
Into my bosom casts his ore:
All the valleys' swimming corn
To my house is yearly borne:
Every grape of every vine
Is gladly bruised to make me wine;
While ten thousand kings, as proud,

stench] staunch.

To carry up my train have bowed,
And a world of ladies send me
In my chambers to attend me:
All the stars in heaven that shine,
And ten thousand more, are mine:
  Only bend thy knee to me,
  Thy wooing shall thy winning be.
        G. Fletcher (the younger).

Christ's Victory and Triumph, 1610.

EASTER MORN

Say, earth, why hast thou got thee new attire,
And stick'st thy habit full of daisies red?
Seems that thou dost to some high thought aspire,
And some new-found-out bridegroom mean'st to wed:
Tell me, ye trees, so fresh apparellèd,—
  So never let the spiteful canker waste you,
  So never let the heavens with lightning blast you,—
Why go you now so trimly dressed, or whither haste you?

Answer me, Jordan, why thy crooked tide
So often wanders from his nearest way,
As though some other way thy stream would slide,
And fain salute the place where something lay.
And you, sweet birds, that, shaded from the ray,
  Sit carolling and piping grief away,
  The while the lambs, to hear you, dance and play,
Tell me, sweet birds, what is it you so fain would say?

And thou, fair spouse of earth, that every year
Gett'st such a numerous issue of thy bride,
How chance thou hotter shin'st, and draw'st more near?
Sure thou somewhere some worthy sight hast spied,
That in one place for joy thou canst not bide:

And you, dead swallows, that so lively now
   Through the flit air your wingèd passage row,
How could new life into your frozen ashes, flow?

Ye primroses and purple violets,
Tell me, why blaze ye from your leavy bed,
And woo men's hands to rent you from your sets,
As though you would somewhere be carrièd,
With fresh perfumes, and velvets garnishèd?
     But ah! I need not ask, 'tis surely so,
    You all would to your Saviour's triumphs go,
There would ye all await, and humble homage do.

                         G. Fletcher (the younger).

Christ's Victory and Triumph, 1610. (An excerpt.)

HOW MANY NEW YEARS HAVE GROWN OLD

How many new years have grown old
Since first your servant old was new!
How many long hours have I told
Since first my love was vowed to you!
And yet, alas! she doth not know
Whether her servant love or no.

How many walls as white as snow,
And windows clear as any glass,
Have I conjùred to tell you so,
Which faithfully performèd was!
And yet you 'll swear you do not know
Whether your servant love or no.

How often hath my pale lean face,
With true charàcters of my love,

---

dead swallows] the old idea of hibernation.

Petitionëd to you for grace,
Whom neither sighs nor tears can move!
O cruel, yet do you not know
Whether your servant love or no?

And wanting oft a better token,
I have been fain to send my heart,
Which now your cold disdain hath broken.
Nor can you heal 't by any art:
Oh, look upon 't, and you shall know
Whether your servant love or no.   *Anon.*

R. Jones' *The Muses' Garden for Delights*, 1610.

THE SEA HATH MANY THOUSANDS SANDS

The sea hath many thousands sands,
    The sun hath motes as many,
The sky is full of stars, and love
    As full of woes as any.
Believe me, that do know the elf,
And make no trial by thyself.

It is in truth a pretty toy
    For babes to play withal.
But, oh, the honeys of our youth
    Art oft our age's gall!
Self-proof in time will make thee know
He was a prophet told thee so:

A prophet that Cassandra-like
    Tells truth without belief,
For headstrong youth will run his race
    Although his goal be grief.

Love's martyr, when his heat is past,
Proves Care's confessor at the last. *Anon.*

R. Jones' *The Muses' Garden for Delights*, 1610.

POOR IS THE LIFE THAT MISSES

Poor is the life that misses
The lover's greatest treasure,
Innumerable kisses,
Which end in endless pleasure.
Oh, then, if this be so,
Shall I a virgin die? Fie no! *Anon.*

M. East's *The Third Set of Books*, 1610.

SHALL A FROWN OR ANGRY EYE

Shall a frown or angry eye,
Shall a word unfitly placëd,
Shall a shadow make me fly
As if I were with tigers chasëd?
Love must not be so disgracëd.

Shall I woo her in despite?
Shall I turn her from her flying?
Shall I tempt her with delight?
Shall I laugh out her denying?
No: beware of lovers' crying.

Shall I then with patient mind,
Still attend her wayward pleasure?
Time will make her prove more kind,
Let her coyness then take leisure:
Pains are worthy such a treasure. *Anon.*

W. Corkine's *Airs*, i., 1610.

SWEET, LET ME GO!

Sweet, let me go! Sweet, let me go!
What do you mean to vex me so?
Cease, cease, cease your pleading force!
Do you think thus to extort remorse?
Now, now! no more! alas, you overbear me;
And I would cry, but some would hear, I fear me.

Ibid.   *Anon.*

WHEN DAFFODILS BEGIN TO PEER

When daffodils begin to peer,
    With heigh! the doxy over the dale,
Why, then comes in the sweet o' the year;
    For the red blood reigns in the winter's pale.

The white sheet bleaching on the hedge,
    With heigh! the sweet birds, oh, how they sing!
Doth set my pugging tooth on edge;
    For a quart of ale is a dish for a king.

The lark, that tirra-lirra chaunts,
    With heigh! with heigh! the thrush and the jay,
Are summer songs for me and my aunts
    While we lie tumbling in the hay.   *Shakespeare.*

The Winter's Tale, 1623. (Written 1610–11 ?)

A MERRY HEART

Jog on, jog on, the footpath way,
    And merrily hent the stile-a:
A merry heart goes all the day,
    Your sad tires in a mile-a.   *Shakespeare.*

Ibid.
pugging] thievish.   With heigh! with heigh] 1632; With heigh! 1623.

COME BUY! COME BUY!

Lawn as white as driven snow;
Cypress black as e'er was crow;
Gloves as sweet as damask roses;
Masks for faces, and for noses;
Bugle-bracelet, necklace-amber,
Perfume for a lady's chamber:
Golden quoifs and stomachers,
For my lads to give their dears;
Pins and poking-sticks of steel,
What maids lack from head to heel:
    Come buy of me, come; come buy, come buy;
    Buy, lads, or else your lasses cry:
    Come buy.   *Shakespeare.*

The Winter's Tale, 1623. (Written 1610–11?)

LOVE'S EMBLEMS

Now the lusty spring is seen;
   Golden yellow, gaudy blue,
   Daintily invite the view;
Everywhere on every green
Roses blushing as they blow,
   And enticing men to pull,
Lilies whiter than the snow,
   Woodbines of sweet honey full:
      All love's emblems, and all cry,
      'Ladies, if not plucked, we die.'

Yet the lusty spring hath stayed;
   Blushing red and purest white
   Daintily to love invite
Every woman, every maid:
Cherries kissing as they grow,

And inviting men to taste,
  Apples even ripe below,
    Winding gently to the waste:
      All love's emblems, and all cry,
        'Ladies, if not plucked, we die.'   *J. Fletcher.*

The Tragedy of Valentinian, 1647. (Written 1610–14.)

HEAR, YE LADIES THAT DESPISE

Hear, ye ladies that despise,
  What the mighty Love has done;
Fear examples, and be wise:
  Fair Calisto was a nun;
Leda, sailing on the stream
  To deceive the hopes of man,
Love accounting but a dream,
    Doted on a silver swan;
      Danaë, in a brazen tower,
      Where no love was, loved a shower.

Hear, ye ladies that are coy,
  What the mighty Love can do;
Fear the fierceness of the boy:
  The chaste moon he makes to woo;
Vesta, kindling holy fires,
  Circled round about with spies,
Never dreaming loose desires,
    Doting at the altar dies;
      Ilion, in a short hour, higher
      He can build, and once more fire.   *J. Fletcher.*

Ibid.

waste] *i.e.* decay, 1647; waist, Mod. eds.   shower] 1679; flower, 1647.
hour] 1679; tower, 1647.

BRIDAL SONG

Hold back thy hours, old Night, till we have done;
  The day will come too soon;
Young maids will curse thee, if thou steal'st away
And leav'st their losses open to the day:
    Stay, stay, and hide
  The blushes of the bride.

Stay, gentle Night, and with thy darkness cover
  The kisses of her lover;
Stay, and confound her tears and her loud cryings,
Her weak denials, vows, and often-dyings;
    Stay, and hide all:
  But help not, though she call.   *Beaumont*(?)

The Maid's Tragedy, 1619. By Beaumont and Fletcher. (Written 1611?)

LAY A GARLAND ON MY HEARSE

Lay a garland on my hearse
  Of the dismal yew;
Maidens, willow branches bear,
  Say I diëd true.

My Love was false, but I was firm
  From my hour of birth.
Upon my buried body lay
  Lightly, gently, earth.   *J. Fletcher*(?)

Ibid. (Text 1622.)*

SONG

Sweetest Love, I do not go
  For weariness of thee,

---

though] 1622; if, 1619.

Nor in hope the world can show
   A fitter love for me;
     But since that I
Must die at last, 'tis best
To use myself in jest
   Thus by feigned deaths to die.

Yesternight the sun went hence,
   And yet is here to-day;
He hath no desire nor sense,
   Nor half so short a way:
     Then fear not me,
But believe that I shall make
Speedier journeys, since I take
   More wings and spurs than he.

Oh, how feeble is man's power,
   That, if good fortune fall,
Cannot add another hour,
   Nor a lost hour recall!
     But come bad chance,
And we join to it our strength,
And we teach it art and length,
   Itself o'er us to advance.

When thou sigh'st, thou sigh'st not wind,
   But sigh'st my soul away;
When thou weep'st, unkindly kind,
   My life's blood doth decay.
     It cannot be
That thou lov'st me as thou say'st,
If in thine my life thou waste,
   Thou art the best of me.

Let not thy divining heart
   Forethink me any ill;
Destiny may take thy part,
   And may thy fears fulfil.
     But think that we
Are but turned aside to sleep:
They who one another keep
    Alive, ne'er parted be.   *Donne.*

Poems, 1633. (Poem written 1611?)

HYMN TO DIANA

Hail, beauteous Dian, queen of shades,
That dwells beneath these shadowy glades,
Mistress of all those beauteous maids
   That are by her allowëd.
Virginity we all profess,
Abjure the worldly vain excess,
And will to Dian yield no less
   Than we to her have vowëd.
The shepherds, satyrs, nymphs, and fauns
For thee will trip it o'er the lawns.

Come, to the forest let us go,
And trip it like the barren doe;
The fauns and satyrs still do so,
   And freely thus they may do.
The fairies dance and satyrs sing,
And on the grass tread many a ring,
And to their caves their ven'son bring;
   And we will do as they do.
The shepherds, satyrs, nymphs, and fauns
For thee will trip it o'er the lawns.

Our food is honey from the bees,
And mellow fruits that drop from trees;
In chase we climb the high degrees
    Of every steepy mountain.
And when the weary day is past,
We at the evening hie us fast,
And after this, our field repast,
    We drink the pleasant fountain.
The shepherds, satyrs, nymphs, and fauns
For thee will trip it o'er the lawns.   T. *Heywood.*

The Golden Age, 1611.

A CATCH

Buzz! quoth the Blue-Fly,
Hum! quoth the Bee;
Buzz and hum! they cry,
    And so do we.
In his ear! in his nose!
Thus,—do you see?
He eat the Dormouse—
    Else it was he.   *Jonson.*

Oberon, the Fairy Prince, a Masque, 1616. (Acted 1611.)

PARTING

Weep eyes, break heart!
My Love and I must part.
Cruel fates true love do soonest sever;
Oh, I shall see thee never, never, never!
Oh, happy is the maid whose life takes end
Ere it knows parent's frown or loss of friend!
Weep eyes, break heart!
My love and I must part.   *Middleton.*

A Chaste Maid in Cheapside, 1630. (Written 1611?)

SONNET

Ponder thy cares, and sum them all in one,
Get the account of all thy heart's disease;
Reckon the torments do thy mind displease,
Write up each sigh, each plaint, each tear, each groan;
Remember on thy grief conceived by day,
And call to mind thy night's disturbëd rest;
Think on those visions did thy soul molest
While as thy wearied corpse a-sleeping lay;
And when all those thou hast enrolled aright
Into the count-book of thy daily care,
Extract them truly; then present the sight
With them of flinty Caelia, the fair,
    That she may see if yet moe ills remains
    For to be paid to her unjust disdains.   *Murray.*

Caelia, 1611.

THE BELLMAN'S SONG

Maids to bed and cover coal;
Let the mouse out of her hole;
Crickets in the chimney sing
Whilst the little bell doth ring:
If fast asleep, who can tell
When the clapper hits the bell?   *Anon.*

T. Ravenscroft's *Melismata*, 1611.

THE COURTIER'S GOOD-MORROW TO HIS MISTRESS

Canst thou love and lie alone?
Love is so disgraced.

Pleasure is best wherein is rest
    In a heart embraced.
        Rise, rise, rise!
    Daylight do not burn out!
Bells do ring and birds do sing;
    Only I that mourn out.

Morning star doth now appear,
Wind is hushed and sky is clear:
Come, come away! come, come away!
Canst thou love and burn out day?
        Rise, rise, rise!
    Daylight do not burn out!
Bells do ring and birds do sing;
    Only I that mourn out.   *Anon.*

*Ibid.**

AWAKE, MINE EYES!

Awake, mine eyes! see Phoebus bright arising,
    And lesser lights to shades obscure descending.
Glad Philomel sits, tunes of joy devising,
        Whilst in sweet notes
        From warbling throats
        The sylvan choir
        With like desire
    To her are echoes sending.   *Anon.*

W. Byrd's *Psalms, Songs and Sonnets*, 1611.

sky is] N.A.; skies, 1611.   Philomel] E. H. Fellowes, 1920; Philomela, 1611.

RISE, LADY MISTRESS, RISE!

Rise, lady mistress, rise!
  The night hath tedious been;
No sleep hath fallen into my eyes,
  Nor slumbers made me sin.
Is not she a saint, then, say,
Thought of whom keeps sin away?

Rise, madam, rise and give me light,
  Whom darkness still will cover,
And ignorance darker than night,
  Till thou smile on thy lover.
All want day till thy beauty rise,
For the grey morn breaks from thine eyes.   *Field.*

Amends for Ladies, 1618. (Written before 1612.)

FAIR, RICH, AND YOUNG

Fair, rich, and young: how rare is her perfection,
Were it not mingled with one foul infection!
I mean, so proud a heart, so curst a tongue,
As makes her seem nor fair, nor rich, nor young.

Epigrams, 1618. (Written before 1612.)*   *Sir J. Harington.*

COME UNTO THESE YELLOW SANDS

Come unto these yellow sands,
  And then take hands:
Curtsied when you have and kissed
  The wild waves whist,
Foot it featly here and there;

And, sweet sprites, the burthen bear.
>   Hark, hark!
>   *Bow-wow.*
>   The watch-dogs bark:
>   *Bow-wow.*
>   Hark, hark! I hear
>   The strain of strutting chanticleer
>   Cry, Cock-a-didle-dow.   *Shakespeare.*

The Tempest, 1623. (Written 1611–2 ?)

FULL FATHOM FIVE

Full fathom five thy father lies;
>   Of his bones are coral made;
Those are pearls that were his eyes:
>   Nothing of him that doth fade
But doth suffer a sea-change
Into something rich and strange.
Sea-nymphs hourly ring his knell:
>   *Ding-dong.*
Hark! now I hear them,—Ding-dong, bell.

Ibid.   *Shakespeare.*

WHERE THE BEE SUCKS

Where the bee sucks, there suck I;
In a cowslip's bell I lie;
There I couch when owls do cry;
On the bat's back I do fly
After summer merrily:
Merrily, merrily, shall I live now
Under the blossom that hangs on the bough.

Ibid.   *Shakespeare.*

the burthen bear] Dryden, 1670; bear the burthen, 1623.

LOVERS, REJOICE!

Lovers, rejoice! your pains shall be rewarded;
The god of love himself grieves at your crying;
No more shall frozen honour be regarded,
Nor the coy faces of a maid denying.
No more shall virgins sigh, and say 'We dare not,
For men are false, and what they do they care not.'
All shall be well again;   then do not grieve;
Men shall be true, and women shall believe.

Lovers, rejoice! what you shall say henceforth,
When you have caught your sweethearts in your arms,
It shall be accounted oracle and worth;
No more faint-hearted girls shall dream of harms,
And cry they are too young; the god hath said,
Fifteen shall make a mother of a maid:
Then, wise men, pull your roses yet unblown:
Love hates the too-ripe fruit that falls alone.

Beaumont, or *Fletcher*.

Cupid's Revenge, 1615. (Acted 1612.)

BREAK OF DAY

Stay, O sweet, and do not rise!
The light that shines comes from thine eyes;
The day breaks not, it is my heart,
Because that you and I must part.
    Stay, or else my joys will die
    And perish in their infancy.

Donne (?)

First included in Donne's *Poems*, 7th Ed., 1669. (Anon. variants in
O. Gibbons' *Madrigals*, 1612; and in J. Dowland's *A Pilgrim's Solace*, 1612.)

regarded] 1630; rewarded, 1615.

EPITAPH ON ELIZABETH, L. H.

Wouldst thou hear what man can say
In a little?   Reader, stay.
Underneath this stone doth lie
As much beauty as could die;
Which in life did harbour give
To more virtue than doth live.
If at all she had a fault,
Leave it buried in this vault.
One name was *Elizabeth*,
Th' other, let it sleep with death:
Fitter, where it died, to tell
Than that it lived at all.   Farewell.   *Jonson.*

Epigrams, 1616. (Registered 1612.)

DISDAIN ME STILL

Disdain me still, that I may ever love,
For who his Love enjoys, can love no more;
The war once past, with peace men cowards prove,
And ships returned do rot upon the shore:
    Then though thou frown, I 'll say thou art most fair,
    And still I 'll love, though still I must despair.

As heat 's to life, so is desire to love,
For these once quenched, both life and love are done:
Let not my sighs, nor tears, thy virtue move;
Like basest metals, do not melt too soon.
    Laugh at my woes, although I ever mourn,
    Love surfeits with rewards, his nurse is scorn.   *Pembroke.*

Poems, 1660.* (Also in J. Dowland's *A Pilgrim's Solace*, 1612.)

A PARADOX

Why should thy look requite so ill
                All other eyes,
Making them prisoners to thy will
Where alone thy beauty lies?
When men's eyes first looked upon thee
They bestowed thy beauty on thee.

When thy colours first were seen
                By judging sight,
Had men's eyes praised black or green,
Then thy face had not been bright:
He that loved thee, then would find
Thee as little fair as kind.

If all others had been blind,
                Fair had not been;
None thy red and white could find
Fleeting, if thou wert unseen:
To touch white skins is not divine,
Ethiopes' lips are soft as thine.   *Pembroke.*

Poems, 1660. (Poem written c. 1612?)

WHY DO WE LOVE

Why do we love these things which we call women,
    Which are like feathers blown with every wind,
Regarding least those which do most esteem them,
    And most deceitful when they seem most kind;
        And all the virtue that their beauty graces,
        It is but painted like unto their faces?

Their greatest glory is in rich attire,
    Which is extracted from some hopeful livers
Whose wits and wealth are bent to their desire,

When they regard the gift more than the givers;
  And to increase their hopes of future bliss,
  They 'll sometimes stretch their conscience for a kiss.

Some love the winds that bring in golden flowers,
  And some are merely won with commendation;
Some love and hate, and all within two hours,
  And that 's a fault amongst them most in fashion;
    But put them all within a scale together,
    Their worth in weight will scarce pull down a feather.

And yet I would not discommend them all,
  If I did know some worth to be in any;
'Tis strange, that since the time of Adam's fall,
  That God did make none good, and made so many;
    And if he did, for those I truly mourn,
    Because they died before that I was born.   *Rudyerd.*

Ibid.*

HEAR ME YET

Dear, though your mind stand so averse
That no assaulting words can pierce,
Your swift and angry flight forbear.
What need you doubt? what need you fear?
In vain I strive your thoughts to move,
But stay and hear me yet, sweet Love.

Words may entreat you, not enforce,
Speak though I might till I were hoarse.
Already you resolve, I know,
No gentle look or grace to show.
My passions all must hapless rove;
But stay and hear me yet, sweet Love.

Sith here no help nor hope remains
To ease my grief or end my pains,
I 'll seek in lowest shades to find
Rest for my heart, peace for my mind.
Go thou, more cruel far than fair,
And now leave me to my despair.

Anon.

W. Corkine's *Airs*, ii., 1612.

TO ASK FOR ALL THY LOVE

To ask for all thy love and thy whole heart,
  'Twere madness.
 I do not sue, nor can admit,
 Fairest, from you to have all yet:
Who giveth all hath nothing to impart
  But sadness.

He that receiveth all, can have no more
  Than seeing.
 My love by length of every hour
 Gathers new strength, new growth, new flower;
You must have daily new rewards in store,
  Still being.

You cannot every day give me your heart
  For merit:
 Yet, if you will, when yours doth go
 You shall have still one to bestow;
For you shall mine, when yours doth part,
  Inherit.

Yet if you please I 'll find a better way
  Than change them;
 For so alone, dearest, we shall
 Be one and one another's all.

Let us so join our hearts that nothing may
            Estrange them.   *Anon.*

J. Dowland's *A Pilgrim's Solace*, 1612.*

THE SILVER SWAN

The silver swan, who living had no note,
When death approached, unlocked her silent throat,
Leaning her breast against the reedy shore,
Thus sung her first and last, and sung no more:
Farewell all joys! O death, come close mine eyes;
More geese than swans now live, more fools than wise.

                                                Anon.
O. Gibbons' *Madrigals and Motets*, 1612.

FAIR IS THE ROSE

Fair is the rose, yet fades with heat or cold.
Sweet are the violets, yet soon grow old.
The lily 's white, yet in one day 'tis done.
White is the snow, yet melts against the sun.
So white, so sweet was my fair mistress' face,
Yet altered quite in one short hoür's space.
So short-lived beauty a vain gloss doth borrow,
Breathing delight to-day, but none to-morrow.   *Anon.*

Ibid.

PRISONERS

Dainty fine bird, that art encagèd there,
Alas, how like thine and my fortunes are.
Both prisoners be, and both singing thus
Strive to please her, that hath imprisoned us.
Only thus we differ, thou and I,
Thou liv'st singing, but I sing and die.   *Anon.*

Ibid.

THE ANGLER'S SONG

Let me live harmlessly; and near the brink
Of Trent or Avon have a dwelling place,
Where I may see my quill or cork down sink
With eager bite of perch, or bleak, or dace;
And on the world and my Creator think,
Whilst some men strive ill-gotten goods to embrace,
   And others spend their time in base excess
    Of wine, or worse, in war and wantonness.

Let them that list these pastimes then pursue,
And on their pleasing fancies feed their fill;
So I the fields and meadows green may view,
And by the rivers fresh may walk at will
Among the daisies and the violets blue,
Red hyacinth and yellow daffodil,
   Purple narcissus like the morning rays,
    Pale ganderglass and azure culver-kays.

I count it better pleasure to behold
The goodly compass of the lofty sky,
And in the midst thereof, like burning gold,
The flaming chariot of the world's great eye,
The wat'ry clouds that in the air uprolled
With sundry kinds of painted colours fly;
   And fair Aurora lifting up her head,
    All blushing rise from old Tithonus' bed;

The hills and mountains raisèd from the plains,
The plains extended level with the ground,
The ground divided into sundry veins,
The veins inclosed with running rivers round,

The rivers making way through nature's chains
With headlong course into the sea profound,
   The surging sea beneath the valleys low,
   The valleys sweet, and lakes that lovely flow;

The lofty woods, the forests wide and long,
Adorned with leaves and branches fresh and green,
In whose cool bowers the birds with chaunting song
Do welcome with their quire the summer's Queen;
The meadows fair where Flora's gifts among
Are intermixed the verdant grass between;
   The silver-scaléd fish that softly swim
   Within the brooks and crystal wat'ry brim.

All these, and many more of his creation
That made the heavens, the angler oft doth see,
And takes therein no little delectation
To think how strange and wonderful they be;
Framing thereof an inward contemplation
To set his thoughts from other fancies free;
   And whiles he looks on these with joyful eye,
   His mind is rapt above the starry sky.   *Dennys.*

The Secrets of Angling, 1613. (Written before 1613. An excerpt. Stanza 1
from 1653.)*

PRAISE OF CERES

With fair Ceres, Queen of Grain,
   The reapéd fields we roam, roam, roam:
Each country peasant, nymph, and swain,
   Sing their harvest home, home, home;
Whilst the Queen of Plenty hallows
Growing fields as well as fallows.

Echo, double all our lays,
   Make the champians sound, sound, sound
To the Queen of Harvest praise,
   That sows and reaps our ground, ground, ground.
Ceres, Queen of Plenty, hallows
Growing fields as well as fallows.   *T. Heywood.*

The Silver Age, 1613. (Acted before 1613.)

BRIDAL SONG

Roses, their sharp spines being gone,
Not royal in their smells alone,
   But in their hue;
Maiden pinks, of odour faint,
Daisies smell-less, yet most quaint,
   And sweet thyme true;
Primrose, firstborn child of Ver,
Merry springtime's harbinger,
   With her bells dim;
Oxlips in their cradles growing,
Marigolds on death-beds blowing,
   Larks'-heels trim—
All dear Nature's children sweet,
Lie 'fore bride and bridegroom's feet
   Blessing their sense.
Not an angel of the air,
Bird melodious, or bird fair,
   Is absent hence.
The crow, the slanderous cuckoo, nor
The boding raven, nor chough hoar,
   Nor chattering pie,
May on our bride-house perch or sing,

---

champians] champaigns.   chough hoar] Seward, 1750; clough hee, 1634.

Or with them any discord bring,
     But from it fly.   *Shakespeare*(?)

The Two Noble Kinsmen, 1634. 'By Shakespeare and Fletcher.' (Written
1612–3 ?)

URNS AND ODOURS BRING AWAY!

Urns and odours bring away!
Vapours, sighs, darken the day!
Our dole more deadly looks than dying;
     Balms, and gums, and heavy cheers,
     Sacred vials filled with tears,
And clamours through the wild air flying!

Come, all sad and solemn shows,
That are quick-eyed Pleasure's foes!
We convènt nought else but woes,
We convènt nought else but woes.

Ibid.   *Shakespeare*(?)

ORPHEUS

Orpheus with his lute made trees,
And the mountain-tops that freeze,
     Bow themselves when he did sing:
To his music plants and flowers
Ever sprung; as sun and showers
     There had made a lasting spring.

Every thing that heard him play,
Even the billows of the sea,
     Hung their heads, and then lay by.
In sweet music is such art,

---

convènt] summon.

Killing care and grief of heart
Fall asleep, or, hearing, die.   *J. Fletcher*(?)

King Henry VIII., 1623. 'By Shakespeare and Fletcher' (?)* (Written 1612–3 ?)

SONG FOR A DANCE

Shake off your heavy trance!
And leap into a dance
Such as no mortals use to tread:
Fit only for Apollo
To play to, for the moon to lead,
And all the stars to follow!   *Beaumont.*

The Masque of the Inner Temple and Gray's Inn, [n.d.]. (Acted Feb. 20, 1612/3.)

GENTLE NYMPHS, BE NOT REFUSING

Gentle nymphs, be not refusing,
Love's neglect is time's abusing,
They and beauty are but lent you,
Take the one and keep the other:
Love keeps fresh what age doth smother:
Beauty gone you will repent you.

'Twill be said when ye have provëd,
Never swains more truly lovëd:
Oh, then fly all nice behaviour.
Pity fain would, as her duty,
Be attending still on beauty,
Let her not be out of favour.   *Browne.*

Britannia's Pastorals, Bk. i., 1613. (Text 1616.)

NEVER WEATHER-BEATEN SAIL

Never weather-beaten sail more willing bent to shore,
Never tired pilgrim's limbs affected slumber more,
Than my weary sprite now longs to fly out of my troubled
      breast.
Oh, come quickly, sweetest Lord, and take my soul to rest!

Ever blooming are the joys of heaven's high paradise,
Cold age deafs not there our ears nor vapour dims our eyes:
Glory there the sun outshines, whose beams the blessèd only
      see.
Oh, come quickly, glorious Lord, and raise my sprite to thee!

Campion.

Divine and Moral Songs, in *Two Books of Airs*, [c. 1613].

COME, CHEERFUL DAY!

Come, cheerful day, part of my life, to me;
    For while thou view'st me with thy fading light,
Part of my life doth still depart with thee,
    And I still onward haste to my last night.
Time's fatal wings do ever forward fly,
So every day we live a day we die.

But oh, ye nights, ordained for barren rest,
    How are my days deprived of life in you;
When heavy sleep my soul hath dispossessed
    By feignèd death life sweetly to renew!
Part of my life in that you life deny;
So every day we live a day we die.

Campion.

Ibid.

THERE IS NONE, OH, NONE BUT YOU

There is none, oh, none but you,
  That from me estrange your sight,
Whom mine eyes affect to view
  Or chainëd ears hear with delight.

Other beauties others move,
  In you I all graces find;
Such is the effect of love,
  To make them happy that are kind.

Women in frail beauty trust,
  Only seem you fair to me;
Yet prove truly kind and just,
  For that may not dissembled be.

Sweet, afford me then your sight,
  That, surveying all your looks,
Endless volumes I may write
  And fill the world with envied books:

Which when after-ages view,
  All shall wonder and despair—
Woman to find man so true,
  Or man a woman half so fair.   *Campion.*

Light Conceits of Lovers, in *Two Books of Airs,* [c. 1613].

DESCEND, FAIR SUN!

Descend, fair Sun, and sweetly rest
  In Thetis' crystal arms thy toil;
Fall burning on her marble breast,
  And make with love her billows boil.

Blow, blow, sweet winds, oh, blow away
   All vapours from the finëd air,
That to this golden head no ray
   May languish with the least impair.

Dance, Thetis, and thy Love's red beams
   Embrace with joy; he now descends,
Burns, burns with love to drink thy streams,
   And on him endless youth attends.   *Chapman.*

The Masque of the Middle Temple and Lincoln's Inn, [1613].

BRIDAL SONG

Now, Sleep, bind fast the flood of air,
   Strike all things dumb and deaf;
And, to disturb our nuptial pair,
   Let stir no aspen leaf.
Send flocks of golden dreams
   That all true joys presage,
Bring, in thy oily streams,
   The milk and honey age.
     Now close the world-round sphere of bliss,
     And fill it with a heavenly kiss.   *Chapman.*

Ibid.

OF BOOKS

Since honour from the honourer proceeds,
How well do they deserve, that memorize
And leave in books for all posterities
The names of worthies and their virtuous deeds;
When all their glory else, like water-weeds
Without their element, presèntly dies,

---

memorize] Mod. eds.; memorie, 1613 and 1632.

And all their greatness quite forgotten lies,
And when and how they flourished no man heeds.
How poor remembrances are statues, tombs
And other monuments that men erect
To princes, which remain in closëd rooms,
Where but a few behold them; in respect
  Of books, that to the universal eye
  Show how they lived; the other where they lie!

Florio (?)

The Essays . . . of Montaigne, 1613. (Not in 1st Ed. 1603.)

NUPTIAL HYMN

Nymphs of sea and land, away,
This, Eliza's wedding day,
Help to dress our gallant bride
With the treasures that ye hide:
Some bring flowery coronets,
Roses white and violets:
Doris, gather from thy shore
Coral, crystal, amber, store,
Which thy queen in bracelets twist
For her alabaster wrist,
While ye silver-footed girls
Plait her tresses with your pearls:
Others, from Pactolus' stream,
Greet her with a diademe:
Search in every rocky mount
For the gems of most account:
Bring ye rubies for her ear,
Diamonds to fill her hair,
Emerald green and chrysolite
Bind her neck more white than white;

On her breast depending be
The onyx, friend to chastity;
Take the rest without their place,
In borders, sleeves, her shoes, or lace:
Nymphs of Niger, offer plumes;
Some, your odours and perfumes:
Dian's maids, more white than milk,
Fit a robe of finest silk:
Dian's maids who wont to be
The honour of virginity.
  Heavens have bestowed their grace,
  Her chaste desires, and angel's face.   *Peacham.*

The Period of Mourning, 1613.

SONNET

Mockado, Fustian, and Motley

Sweet semi-circled Cynthia played at maw,
The whilst Endymion ran the wild-goose chase:
Great Bacchus with his cross-bow killed a daw,
And sullen Saturn smiled with pleasant face:
The ninefold Bugbears of the Caspian lake
Sat whistling ebon hornpipes to their ducks;
Madge-owlet straight for joy her girdle brake,
And rugged Satyrs frisked like stags and bucks:
The untamed tumbling fifteen-footed Goat
With promulgation of the Lesbian shores
Confronted Hydra in a sculler boat,
At which the mighty mountain Taurus roars:
  Meantime great Sultan Soliman was born,
  And Atlas blew his rustic rumbling horn.   *Taylor.*

Odcomb's Complaint, 1613.

HAVE I FOUND HER?

Have I found her? O rich finding!
  Goddess-like for to behold,
Her fair tresses seemly binding
  In a chain of pearl and gold.
Chain me, chain me, O most fair,
Chain me to thee with that hair!

Anon.

F. Pilkington's *Madrigals and Pastorals,* i., 1613.

SEE WHERE MY LOVE A-MAYING GOES

See where my Love a-maying goes,
  With sweet dame Flora sporting!
She most alone with nightingales
  In woods delights consorting.
Turn again, my dearest!
    The pleasant'st air 's in meadows:
Else by the rivers let us breathe,
    And kiss amongst the willows.

Anon.

Ibid.

SWEET PITY, WAKE

Sweet pity, wake, and tell my cruel sweet
  That if my death her honour might increase,
I would lay down my life at her proud feet,
  And willing die and, dying, hold my peace;
And only live and, living, mercy cry,
Because her glory in my death will die.

Anon.

J. Ward's *Madrigals,* 1613.

DIE NOT, FOND MAN

Die not, fond man, before thy day.
    Love's cold December
    Will surrender
To succeeding jocund May.
And then, oh, then, sorrow shall cease;
    Comforts abounding,
    Cares confounding,
Shall conclude a happy peace.   *Anon.*

Ibid.

MADRIGAL

I always loved to call my lady Rose,
For in her cheeks do roses sweetly glose;
And from her lips she such sweet odours threw,
As roses do 'gainst Phoebus' morning view.
But when I thought to pull 't, hope was bereft me,
My Rose was gone, and nought but prickles left me.

H. Lichfield's *Madrigals*, 1613.   *Anon.*

DRINKING SONG

Drink to-day, and drown all sorrow,
You shall perhaps not do it to-morrow:
Best, while you have it, use your breath;
There is no drinking after death.

Wine works the heart up, wakes the wit,
There is no cure 'gainst age but it:
It helps the head-ache, cough, and tisic,
And is for all diseases physic.

tisic] consumption.

Then let us swill, boys, for our health;
Who drinks well, loves the commonwealth.
And he that will to bed go sober
Falls with the leaf still in October.

J. Fletcher (?)

The Bloody Brother, 1639. (Written c. 1613–4, by Massinger, Field and Fletcher.) *

HARK, NOW EVERYTHING IS STILL

Hark, now everything is still,
The screech-owl and the whistler shrill,
Call upon our dame aloud,
And bid her quickly don her shroud!
Much you had of land and rent;
Your length in clay 's now competent:
A long war disturbed your mind;
Here your perfect peace is signed.
Of what is 't fools make such vain keeping?
Sin their conception, their birth weeping,
Their life a general mist of error,
Their death a hideous storm of terror.
Strew your hair with powders sweet,
Don clean linen, bathe your feet,
And (the foul fiend more to check)
A crucifix let bless your neck:
'Tis now full tide 'tween night and day;
End your groan, and come away.   *Webster.*

The Duchess of Malfi, 1623. (Written 1613–4.)

THE MADMAN'S SONG

Oh, let us howl some heavy note,
Some deadly doggèd howl,

Sounding, as from the threatening throat
  Of beasts and fatal fowl!
As ravens, screech-owls, bulls, and bears,
  We 'll bell and bawl our parts,
Till irksome noise have cloyed your ears,
  And còrrosived your hearts.
At last, whenas our quire wants breath,
  Our bodies being blessed,
We 'll sing, like swans, to welcome death,
  And die in love and rest.   *Webster.*

Ibid.

IN OBITUM M S, Xº MAIJ, 1614

May! Be thou never graced with birds that sing,
    Nor Flora's pride!
In thee all flowers and roses spring,
    Mine only died.   *Browne.*

B.M. Lansd. MS. 777.

DAWN OF DAY

Thomalin

Where is every piping lad
That the fields are not yclad
    With their milk-white sheep?
Tell me: is it holiday,
Or if in the month of May
    Use they long to sleep?

Piers

Thomalin, 'tis not too late,
For the turtle and her mate

---

bell] 1640; bill, 1623.

                    Sitten yet in nest:
          And the thrustle hath not been
          Gath'ring worms yet on the green,
                    But attends her rest.
          Not a bird hath taught her young,
          Nor her morning's lesson sung
                    In the shady grove:
          But the nightingale in dark
          Singing woke the mounting lark:
                    She records her love.
          Not the sun hath with his beams
          Gilded yet our crystal streams,
                    Rising from the sea;
          Mists do crown the mountains' tops,
          And each pretty myrtle drops:
                    'Tis but newly day.   *Browne.*

The Shepherd's Pipe, 1614. (The opening of the Third Eclogue.)

EYES, HIDE MY LOVE

          Eyes, hide my love, and do not show
                    To any but to her my notes,
          Who only doth that cipher know
                    Wherewith we pass our secret thoughts:
          Belie your looks in others' sight,
          And wrong yourselves to do her right.   *Daniel.*

Hymen's Triumph, 1623. (Written 1614.)

HAD SORROW EVER FITTER PLACE

          Had sorrow ever fitter place
                    To act his part
                    Than is my heart?

Where it takes up all the space,
    Where is no vein
    To entertain
A thought that wears another face.

Nor will I sorrow ever have
    Therein to be,
    But only thee
To whom I full possession gave:
    Thou in thy name
    Must hold the same
Until thou bring it to the grave.   *Daniel.*

Ibid.

LOVE

Love is a sickness full of woes,
    All remedies refusing;
A plant that with most cutting grows,
    Most barren with best using.
            Why so?
More we enjoy it, more it dies;
If not enjoyed, it sighing cries,
            Heigh ho!

Love is a torment of the mind,
    A tempest everlasting;
And Jove hath made it of a kind
    Not well, nor full, nor fasting.
            Why so?
More we enjoy it, more it dies;
If not enjoyed, it sighing cries,
            Heigh ho!   *Daniel.*

Ibid.

WOMAN'S INCONSTANCY

Who sows the seas, or ploughs the easy shore?
Yet I, fond I, more fond and senseless more:
Who strives in nets to prison in the wind?
Yet I in love a woman thought to bind:
   Fond, too fond thoughts, that thought in love to tie
   One more inconstant than inconstancy.

Look, as it is with some true April day,
The sun his glorious beams doth fair display,
And straight a cloud breaks into fluent showers,
Then shines, and rains, and clears, and straight it lours,
   And twenty changings in one hour do prove:
   So, and more changing, is a woman's love.

Fond then my thoughts, that thought a thing so vain;
Fond love, to love what could not love again;
Fond hopes, that anchor on so false a ground;
Fond thoughts that fired with love, in hope thus drowned:
   Fond thoughts, fond hope, fond heart, but fondest I
   To grasp the wind and love inconstancy.   *P. Fletcher.*

Sicelides, 1631. (Written 1614.)*

TEARS, FLOW NO MORE!

Tears, flow no more! or if you needs must flow,
      Fall yet more slow,
    Do not the world invade.
From smaller springs than yours rivers have grown,
     And they again a sea have made
Brackish like you, and which like you hath flown.

---

fond] foolish.

Ebb to my heart, and on the burning fires
        Of my desires
    Let your torrents fall.
From smaller sparks than theirs such sparks arise
      As into flame converting all,
This world might be but my love's sacrifice.

Yet if, the tempests of my sighs so slow,
        You both must flow
    And my desires still burn,
Since that in vain all help my love requires,
      Why may not yet their rages turn
To dry those tears and to blow out those fires?

Herbert of Cherbury.

Occasional Verses, 1665. (Poem dated 1614.)

THE CHARACTER OF A HAPPY LIFE

How happy is he born or taught,
That serveth not another's will;
Whose armour is his honest thought,
And simple truth his highest skill;

Whose passions not his masters are;
Whose soul is still prepared for death,
Untied unto the world with care
Of princes' grace or vulgar breath;

Who envies none whom chance doth raise,
Or vice; who never understood
The deepest wounds are given by praise,
By rule of state, but not of good;

Who hath his life from rumours freed;
Whose conscience is his strong retreat;

Whose state can neither flatterers feed,
Nor ruin make accusers great;

Who God doth late and early pray,
More of his grace than goods to send,
And entertains the harmless day
With a well-chosen book or friend,—

This man is free from servile bands
Of hope to rise or fear to fall;
Lord of himself, though not of lands;
And having nothing, yet hath all.   *Sir H. Wotton.*

Bodley MS. Rawl. Poet. 212.* (Poem written 1614?)

WHEN YOUTH AND BEAUTY MEET TOGITHER

When Youth and Beauty meet togither,
          There 's work for breath;
But when they both begin to wither,
          There 's work for Death.

When Love and Honour work togither,
          There 's work for fame;
But when they both begin to wither,
          There 's work for shame.

When Hope and Labour go togither,
          There 's work for gain;
But when they both begin to wither,
          There 's work for pain.

When Wit and Virtue work togither,
          Their work goes well;

ruin] Bodl. MSS. Mal. 13 and 19; ruins, MS. Rawl. Poet. 212.   bands] Mal.
MSS. as above; bonds, MS. Rawl. Poet, 212.

But when they both begin to wither,
      There 's work for Hell.

Let then perfections live togither,
      And work for praise;
For when their work begins to wither
      Their worth decays.   *Anon.*

Cobbe's Prophecies, 1614.

TO THE DETRACTED

Though wolves against the silver moon do bark,
   They blemish not her brightness; nor the spite
Of bawling curs, which she disdains to mark,
   Can any whit eclipse her of her light.
So may'st thou slight the railing of ill tongues
   If a clear shining conscience be thy guard,
Which, to defend thee from the worst of wrongs,
   Will, as a wall of brass, be found as hard.   *Andrews.*

The Anatomy of Baseness, 1615.*

OF MAIDS' INCONSTANCY

Foolish I, why should I grieve
   To sustain what others feel?
What! suppose frail women leave
   Those they loved, should I conceal
      Comfort's rest
      From my breast
For a fickle brittle woman?
      No, no, no!
      Let her go!
Such as these be true to no man.

Long retirèd hast thou been
  Sighing on these barren rocks,
Nor by sheep nor shepherd seen;
  Now return unto thy flocks;
      Shame, away!
      Do not stay
With these moving-loving women!
      They remove
      From their love:
Such as these do oft undo men.

Tender-tinder of affection,
  If I harbour thee again,
I will do it by direction
  Of some grave experienced swain.
      Nor will I
      Love by th' eÿe,
But where judgement first hath tried;
      If I live
      E'er to love,
It is she shall be my bride.   *Brathwaite.*

A Strappado for the Devil, 1615.

SONG OF THE SIRENS

Steer hither, steer your wingèd pines,
  All beaten mariners!
Here lie Love's undiscovered mines,
  A prey to passengers;
Perfumes far sweeter than the best
Which make the Phoenix' urn and nest.
      Fear not your ships,
Nor any to oppose you save our lips;

But come on shore
Where no joy dies till love hath gotten more.

For swelling waves, our panting breasts
    Where never storms arise,
Exchange; and be awhile our guests:
    For stars, gaze on our eyes.
The compass Love shall hourly sing,
And as he goes about the ring,
        We will not miss
To tell each point he nameth with a kiss.
        Then come on shore,
Where no joy dies till love hath gotten more.

Browne.

The Inner Temple Masque, [1615]. Emmanuel Coll. MS., I. 3.16.

SIR EGLAMOUR

Sir Eglamour, that worthy knight,
He took his sword and went to fight;
And as he rode both hill and dale,
Armëd upon his shirt of mail,
A dragon came out of his den,
Had slain, God knows how many men!

When he espied Sir Eglamour,
Oh, if you had but heard him roar,
And seen how all the trees did shake,
The knight did tremble, horse did quake,
The birds betake them all to peeping—
It would have made you fall a weeping!

But now it is in vain to fear,
Being come unto, 'fight dog! fight bear!'

To it they go and fiercely fight
A live-long day from morn till night.
The dragon had a plaguy hide,
And could the sharpest steel abide.

No sword will enter him with cuts,
Which vexed the knight unto the guts;
But, as in choler he did burn,
He watched the dragon a good turn;
And, as a yawning he did fall,
He thrust his sword in, hilts and all.

Then, like a coward, he to fly
Unto his den that was hard by;
And there he lay all night and roared.
The knight was sorry for his sword,
But, riding thence, said, 'I forsake it,
He that will fetch it, let him take it!'   *S. Rowlands.*

The Melancholy Knight, 1615.*

THE POETASTER

Rapier, lie there! and there, my hat and feather!
  Draw my silk curtain to obscure the light,
Goose-quill and I must join awhile together:
  Lady, forbear, I pray! keep out of sight!
Call Pearl away, let one remove him hence!
Your shrieking parrot will distract my sense.

Would I were near the rogue that crieth, 'Black!'
  'Buy a new almanac!' doth vex me too:
Forbid the maid she wind not up the jack!

---

turn] period of time, spell.

Take hence my watch, it makes too much ado!
Let none come at me, dearest friend or kin,
Whoe'er it be I am not now within.   *S. Rowlands.*

Ibid.*

SHALL I, WASTING IN DESPAIR

Shall I, wasting in despair,
Die because a woman 's fair?
Or make pale my cheeks with care
'Cause another's rosy are?
Be she fairer than the day,
Or the flowery meads in May,
  If she be not so to me,
  What care I how fair she be?

Should my heart be grieved or pined
'Cause I see a woman kind?
Or a well-disposèd nature
Joinèd with a lovely feature?
Be she meeker, kinder than
Turtle-dove, or pelican,
  If she be not so to me,
  What care I how kind she be?

Shall a woman's virtues move
Me to perish for her love?
Or her well-deserving, known,
Make me quite forget mine own?
Be she with that goodness blessed
Which may gain her name of best,
  If she be not such to me,
  What care I how good she be?

'Cause her fortune seems too high,
Shall I play the fool, and die?
Those that bear a noble mind,
Where they want of riches find,
Think what with them they would do
That without them dare to woo;
    And unless that mind I see,
     What care I though great she be?

Great, or good, or kind, or fair,
I will ne'er the more despair:
If she love me, this believe,
I will die ere she shall grieve:
If she slight me when I woo,
I can scorn and let her go;
    For if she be not for me,
     What care I for whom she be?

Wither.

Fidelia, 1615. (Text from *Fair Virtue*, 1622.)

THE INDIFFERENT

Never more will I protest
To love a woman, but in jest;
For as they can not be true,
So, to give each man his due,
    When the wooing fit is past
    Their affection cannot last.

Therefore, if I chance to meet
With a mistress fair and sweet,
She my service shall obtain,
Loving her for love again:

Thus much liberty I crave,
Not to be a constant slave.

But when we have tried each other,
If she better like another,
Let her quickly change for me;
Then to change am I as free.
  He or she that loves too long
  Sell their freedom for a song.   *Beaumont.*

Poems, 1640. (Written before 1616.)

TRUE BEAUTY

May I find a woman fair,
And her mind as clear as air:
If her beauty go alone,
'Tis to me, as if 'twere none.

May I find a woman rich,
And not of too high a pitch:
If that pride should cause disdain,
Tell me, lover, where 's thy gain?

May I find a woman wise,
And her falsehood not disguise:
Hath she wit as she hath will,
Double-armed she is to ill.

May I find a woman kind,
And not wavering like the wind:
How should I call that love mine,
When 'tis his, and his, and thine?

to ill] Mod. eds.; too ill, 1640.

May I find a woman true:
There is beauty's fairest hue!
There is beauty, love, and wit—
Happy he can compass it!   *Beaumont.*

Poems, 1640. (Written before 1616.)

ON MR. WM. SHAKESPEARE

Renownèd Spenser, lie a thought more nigh
To learnèd Chaucer; and rare Beaumont, lie
A little nearer Spenser; to make room
For Shakespeare in your three-fold four-fold tomb.
To lodge all four in one bed make a shift
Until Doomsday; for hardly will a fift,
Betwixt this day and that, by fate be slain,
For whom your curtains may be drawn again.

If your precedency in death doth bar
A fourth place in your sacred sepulchre,
Under this carvèd marble of thine own,
Sleep, rare tragedian, Shakespeare, sleep alone:
Thy unmolested peace, unsharèd cave,
Possess as lord, not tenant, of thy grave;
That unto us and others it may be
Honour hereafter to be laid by thee.   *Basse.*

B.M. Lansd. MS. 777. (Poem written c. 1616.)

VENUS AND ADONIS

Venus, by Adonis' side,
Crying kissed, and kissing cried,
Wrung her hands and tore her hair
For Adonis dying there.

'Stay!' quoth she, 'Oh, stay and live!
Nature surely doth not give
To the earth her sweetest flowers,
To be seen but some few hours.

On his face, still as he bled,
For each drop, a tear she shed,
Which she kissed, or wiped, away,
Else had drowned him where he lay.

'Fair Proserpina,' quoth she,
'Shall not have thee yet from me;
Nor thy soul to fly begin,
While my lips can keep it in.'

Here she ceased again. And some
Say Apollo would have come
To have cured his wounded limb,
But that she had smothered him.   *Browne.*

Britannia's Pastorals, Bk. ii., 1616.

SHALL I TELL YOU WHOM I LOVE?

Shall I tell you whom I love?
    Harken then awhile to me,
And, if such a woman move
    As I now shall versify,
Be assured 'tis she or none
That I love, and love alone.

Nature did her so much right
    As she scorns the help of art,
In as many virtues dight

As e'er yet embraced a heart.
So much good so truly tried,
Some for less were deified.

Wit she hath without desire
    To make known how much she hath;
And her anger flames no higher
    Than may fitly sweeten wrath;
Full of pity as may be,
Though perhaps not so to me.

Reason masters every sense,
    And her virtues grace her birth;
Lovely as all excellence,
    Modest in her most of mirth;
Likelihood enough to prove
Only worth could kindle love.

Such she is: and if you know
    Such a one as I have sung,
Be she brown, or fair, or so
    That she be but somewhile young,
Be assured 'tis she or none
That I love, and love alone.

Browne.

Britannia's Pastorals, Bk. ii., 1616.

GLIDE SOFT, YE SILVER FLOODS

Glide soft, ye silver floods,
    And every spring:
Within the shady woods
    Let no bird sing!
Nor from the grove a turtle-dove
Be seen to couple with her love;

But silence on each dale and mountain dwell,
Whilst Willy bids his friend and joy farewell.

But (of great Thetis' train)
Ye mermaids fair,
That on the shores do plain
Your sea-green hair,
As ye in trammels knit your locks,
Weep ye, and so enforce the rocks
In heavy murmurs through the broad shores tell
How Willy bade his friend and joy farewell.

Cease, cease, ye murd'ring winds,
To move a wave!
But if with troubled minds
You seek his grave;
Know 'tis as various as yourselves,
Now in the deep, then on the shelves,
His coffin tossed by fish and surges fell,
Whilst Willy weeps and bids all joy farewell.

Had he Arion-like
Been judged to drown,
He on his lute could strike
So rare a soun',
A thousand dolphins would have come
And jointly strive to bring him home.
But he on shipboard died, by sickness fell,
Since when his Willy bade all joy farewell.

Great Neptune, hear a swain!
His coffin take,
And with a golden chain

plain] make smooth.

                        For pity make
                    It fast unto a rock near land!
                Where every calmy morn I 'll stand,
            And ere one sheep out of my fold I tell,
            Sad Willy's pipe shall bid his friend farewell.   *Browne.*

Britannia's Pastorals, Bk. ii., 1616.

A KISS

                Hark, happy lovers, hark!
                This first and last of joys,
                This sweet'ner of annoys,
                This nectar of the gods
            Ye call a kiss, is with itself at odds;
                And half so sweet is not
                In equal measure got
                At light of sun, as it is in the dark:
                Hark, happy lovers, hark!   *Drummond.*

Poems, 1616.

OF PHYLLIS

            In petticoat of green,
            Her hair about her eyne,
            Phyllis beneath an oak
            Sat milking her fair flock:
            Among that strainëd moisture, rare delight!
            Her hand seemed milk in milk, it was so white.

Ibid.   *Drummond.*

SONNET

            How that vast heaven intitled First is rolled,
            If any other worlds beyond it lie,

And people living in eternity,
Or essence pure that doth this All uphold;
What motion have those fixëd sparks of gold,
The wand'ring carbuncles which shine from high,
By sprites, or bodies, contrare-ways in sky
If they be turned, and mortal things behold;
How sun posts heaven about, how night's pale queen
With borrowed beams looks on this hanging round,
What cause fair Iris hath, and monsters seen
In air's large fields of light, and seas profound—
    Did hold my wand'ring thoughts, when thy sweet eye
    Bade me leave all, and only think on thee.   *Drummond.*

Ibid.

MADRIGAL

Like the Idalian queen,
Her hair about her eyne,
With neck and breast's ripe apples to be seen,
At first glance of the morn
In Cyprus' gardens gathering those fair flowers
Which of her blood were born,
I saw, but fainting saw, my paramours.
The Graces naked danced about the place,
The winds and trees amazed
With silence on her gazed,
The flowers did smile, like those upon her face;
And as their aspen stalks those fingers band,
That she might read my case,
A hyacinth I wished me in her hand.   *Drummond.*

Ibid.

band] bound.

PHOEBUS, ARISE!

Phoebus, arise!
And paint the sable skies
With azure, white, and red;
Rouse Memnon's mother from her Tithon's bed,
That she thy càreer may with roses spread;
The nightingales thy coming each-where sing;
Make an eternal spring!
Give life to this dark world which lieth dead!
Spread forth thy golden hair
In larger locks than thou wast wont before,
And, emperor-like, decore
With diadem of pearl thy temples fair:
Chase hence the ugly night
Which serves but to make dear thy glorious light!
This is that happy morn,
That day, long-wishëd day,
Of all my life so dark
(If cruel stars have not my ruin sworn,
And fates not hope betray),
Which, only white, deserves
A diamond for ever should it mark:
This is the morn should bring unto this grove
My Love, to hear and recompense my love.
Fair king, who all preserves,
But show thy blushing beams,
And thou two sweeter eyes
Shalt see, than those which by Peneus' streams
Did once thy heart surprise—
Nay, suns, which shine as clear
As thou when two thou did to Rome appear.
Now, Flora, deck thyself in fairest guise:

---

càreer] course.   decore] decorate, adorn.

If that ye, winds, would hear
A voice surpassing far Amphion's lyre,
Your stormy chiding stay;
Let zephyr only breathe
And with her tresses play,
Kissing sometimes those purple ports of death.

The winds all silent are;
And Phoebus in his chair
Ensaffroning sea and air
Makes vanish every star:
Night like a drunkard reels
Beyond the hills to shun his flaming wheels;
The fields with flowers are decked in every hue,
The clouds bespangle with bright gold their blue:
Here is the pleasant place,
And every thing, save her, who all should grace.

Drummond.

Poems, 1616.

SONNET

Sleep, Silence' child, sweet father of soft rest,
Prince, whose approach peace to all mortals brings,
Indifferent host to shepherds and to kings,
Sole comforter of minds with grief oppressed;
Lo, by thy charming rod all breathing things
Lie slumb'ring, with forgetfulness possessed,
And yet o'er me to spread thy drowsy wings
Thou spares, alas! who cannot be thy guest.
Since I am thine, oh, come, but with that face
To inward light which thou art wont to show,
With feignèd solace ease a true-felt woe;
Or if, deaf god, thou do deny that grace,

Come as thou wilt, and what thou wilt bequeath,
I long to kiss the image of my death.   *Drummond.*
Poems, 1616.

MADRIGAL

The ivory, coral, gold,
Of breast, of lips, of hair,
So lively Sleep doth show to inward sight,
That, wake, I think I hold
No shadow, but my fair:
Myself so to deceive,
With long-shut eyes I shun the irksome light.
Such pleasure thus I have,
Delighting in false gleams,
If Death Sleep's brother be,
And souls relieved of sense have so sweet dreams,
That I would wish me thus to dream and die.
Ibid.   *Drummond.*

MADRIGAL

The beauty and the life
Of life's and beauty's fairest paragon—
O tears! O grief!—hung at a feeble thread,
To which pale Atropos had set her knife;
The soul with many a groan
Had left each outward part,
And now did take his last leave of the heart:
Nought else did want, save death, even to be dead.
When the afflicted band about her bed,
   Seeing so fair him come in lips, cheeks, eyes,
   Cried, 'Ah! and can Death enter Paradise?'
Ibid.   *Drummond.*
hung] Mod. eds.; hang, 1616.

MADRIGAL

My thoughts hold mortal strife;
I do detest my life,
And with lamenting cries,
Peace to my soul to bring,
Oft call that prince which here doth monarchise;
But he, grim-grinning king,
Who caitives scorns, and doth the blessed surprise,
    Late having decked with beauty's rose his tomb,
    Disdains to crop a weed, and will not come.

Ibid.   *Drummond.*

SONNETS

My lute, be as thou wast when thou didst grow
With thy green mother in some shady grove,
When immelodious winds but made thee move,
And birds on thee their ramage did bestow.
Sith that dear voice, which did thy sounds approve,
Which used in such harmonious strains to flow,
Is reft from earth to tune those spheres above,
What art thou but a harbinger of woe?
Thy pleasing notes be pleasing notes no more,
But orphan wailings to the fainting ear;
Each stop a sigh, each sound draws forth a tear,
Be therefore silent as in woods before:
    Or, if that any hand to touch thee deign,
    Like widowed turtle still her loss complain.

Ibid.   *Drummond.*

Sweet Spring, thou turn'st with all thy goodly train,
Thy head with flames, thy mantle bright with flowers:
The zephyrs curl the green locks of the plain,
The clouds for joy in pearls weep down their showers.

Thou turn'st, sweet youth, but, ah! my pleasant hours
And happy days with thee come not again;
The sad memorials only of my pain
Do with thee turn, which turn my sweets in sours.
Thou art the same which still thou wast before,
Delicious, wanton, amiable, fair;
But she, whose breath embalmed thy wholesome air,
Is gone; nor gold, nor gems, her can restore.
   Neglected virtue, seasons go and come,
   While thine forgot lie closëd in a tomb.   *Drummond.*

Poems, 1616.

Alexis, here she stayed; among these pines,
Sweet hermitress, she did alone repair;
Here did she spread the treasure of her hair,
More rich than that brought from the Colchian mines.
She set her by these muskëd eglantines,
The happy place the print seems yet to bear;
Her voice did sweeten here thy sugared lines,
To which winds, trees, beasts, birds, did lend their ear.
Me here she first perceived, and here a morn
Of bright carnations did o'erspread her face;
Here did she sigh; here first my hopes were born,
And I first got a pledge of promised grace:
   But ah! what served it to be happy so,
   Sith passëd pleasures double but new woe?   *Drummond.*

Ibid.

What doth it serve to see sun's burning face,
And skies enamelled with both the Indies' gold,
Or moon at night in jetty chariot rolled,
And all the glory of that starry place?
What doth it serve earth's beauty to behold,

The mountains' pride, the meadows' flowery grace,
The stately comeliness of forests old,
The sport of floods which would themselves embrace?
What doth it serve to hear the Sylvans' songs,
The wanton merle, the nightingale's sad strains
Which in dark shades seem to deplore my wrongs?
For what doth serve all that this world contains,
   Sith she for whom those once to me were dear,
   No part of them can have now with me here?

Ibid.   *Drummond.*

MADRIGAL

This life, which seems so fair,
Is like a bubble blown up in the air
By sporting children's breath,
Who chase it everywhere,
And strive who can most motion it bequeath:
And though it sometime seem of its own might,
Like to an eye of gold, to be fixed there,
And firm to hover in that empty height,
That only is because it is so light.
But in that pomp it doth not long appear;
   For even when most admired, it in a thought,
   As swelled from nothing, doth dissolve in nought.

Ibid.   *Drummond.*

HER TRIUMPH

See the chariot at hand here of Love,
   Wherein my lady rideth!
Each that draws is a swan or a dove,
   And well the car Love guideth.
As she goes, all hearts do duty

Unto her beauty;
And enamoured do wish, so they might
But enjoy such a sight,
That they still were to run by her side,
Through swords, through seas, whither she would ride.

Do but look on her eyes, they do light
All that Love's world compriseth!
Do but look on her hair, it is bright
As Love's star when it riseth!
Do but mark, her forehead 's smoother
Than words that soothe her;
And from her arched brows such a grace
Sheds itself through the face,
As alone there triumphs to the life
All the gain, all the good of the elements' strife.

Have you seen but a bright lily grow
Before rude hands have touched it?
Have you marked but the fall of the snow
Before the soil hath smutched it?
Have you felt the wool o' the beaver,
Or swan's down ever?
Or have smelt o' the bud o' the brier,
Or the nard i' the fire?
Or have tasted the bag o' the bee?
Oh so white, oh so soft, oh so sweet is she!   *Jonson.*

The Devil is an Ass, 1631, (Acted 1616); and *Underwoods*, 1640.*

THAT WOMEN ARE BUT MEN'S SHADOWS

Follow a shadow, it still flies you;
Seem to fly it, it will pursue:

So court a mistress, she denies you;
    Let her alone, she will court you.
Say, are not women truly, then,
Styled but the shadows of us men?

At morn and even, shades are longest,
    At noon they are or short, or none:
So, men at weakest, they are strongest;
    But grant us perfect, they 're not known.
Say are not women truly, then,
Styled but the shadows of us men?   *Jonson.*

The Forest, 1616.

SONG: TO CELIA

Drink to me only with thine eyes,
    And I will pledge with mine;
Or leave a kiss but in the cup,
    And I 'll not look for wine.
The thirst that from the soul doth rise
    Doth ask a drink divine:
But might I of Jove's nectar sup,
    I would not change for thine.

I sent thee late a rosy wreath,
    Not so much honouring thee,
As giving it a hope that there
    It could not withered be.
But thou thereon didst only breathe,
    And sent'st it back to me:
Since when it grows, and smells, I swear,
    Not of itself, but thee.   *Jonson.*

Ibid.

SONG: TO CELIA

Kiss me, sweet; the wary lover
Can your favours keep, and cover,
When the common courting jay
All your bounties will betray.
Kiss again; no creature comes.
Kiss, and score up wealthy sums
On my lips thus hardly sund'red
While you breathe. First give a hundred,
Then a thousand, then another
Hundred, then unto the tother
Add a thousand, and so more
Till you equal with the store
All the grass that Rumney yields,
Or the sands in Chelsea fields,
Or the drops in silver Thames,
Or the stars that gild his streams
In the silent summer nights
When youths ply their stol'n delights:
That the curious may not know
How to tell them as they flow;
And the envious, when they find
What their number is, be pined.   *Jonson.*

The Forest, 1616.

SHALL I COME, SWEET LOVE, TO THEE

Shall I come, sweet Love, to thee
    When the evening beams are set?
Shall I not excluded be,
    Will you find no feignëd let?

them] Mod. eds.; 'hem, 1616.

Let me not, for pity, more
Tell the long hours at your door.

Who can tell what thief or foe,
   In the covert of the night,
For his prey will work my woe,
   Or through wicked foul despite?
So may I die unredressed
Ere my long love be possessed.

But to let such dangers pass,
   Which a lover's thoughts disdain,
'Tis enough in such a place
   To attend love's joys in vain:
Do not mock me in thy bed,
While these cold nights freeze me dead.   *Campion.*

The Third Book of Airs, [c. 1617].

SLEEP, ANGRY BEAUTY

Sleep, angry beauty, sleep and fear not me!
   For who a sleeping lion dares provoke?
It shall suffice me here to sit and see
   Those lips shut up that never kindly spoke:
What sight can more content a lover's mind
Than beauty seeming harmless, if not kind?

My words have charmed her, for secure she sleeps,
   Though guilty much of wrong done to my love;
And in her slumber, see! she close-eyed weeps:
   Dreams often more than waking passions move.
Plead, Sleep, my cause, and make her soft like thee,
That she in peace may wake and pity me.   *Campion.*

Ibid.

NOW WINTER NIGHTS ENLARGE

Now winter nights enlarge
The number of their hours,
And clouds their storms discharge
Upon the airy towers.
Let now the chimneys blaze,
And cups o'erflow with wine;
Let well-tuned words amaze
With harmony divine.
Now yellow waxen lights
Shall wait on honey love,
While youthful revels, masques, and courtly sights
Sleep's leaden spells remove.

This time doth well dispense
With lovers' long discourse;
Much speech hath some defence,
Though beauty no remorse.
All do not all things well;
Some measures comely tread,
Some knotted riddles tell,
Some poems smoothly read.
The summer hath his joys
And winter his delights;
Though love and all his pleasures are but toys,
They shorten tedious nights.   *Campion.*

The Third Book of Airs, [c. 1617].

COME, OH, COME, MY LIFE'S DELIGHT

Come, oh, come, my life's delight,
    Let me not in languor pine!
Love loves no delay; thy sight
    The more enjoyed the more divine:

Oh, come, and take from me
The pain of being deprived of thee!

Thou all sweetness dost enclose
   Like a little world of bliss.
Beauty guards thy looks: the rose
   In them pure and eternal is.
Come then, and make thy flight
As swift to me as heavenly light!   *Campion.*

Ibid.

THRICE TOSS THESE OAKEN ASHES

Thrice toss these oaken ashes in the air,
Thrice sit thou mute in this enchanted chair;
Then thrice-three times tie up this true love's knot.
And murmur soft 'She will or she will not.'

Go burn these poisonous weeds in yon blue fire,
These screech-owl's feathers and this prickling brier,
This cypress gathered at a dead man's grave,
That all thy fears and cares an end may have.

Then come, you Fairies! dance with me a round!
Melt her hard heart with your melodious sound!—
In vain are all the charms I can devise:
She hath an art to break them with her eyes.   *Campion.*

Ibid.

NEVER LOVE UNLESS YOU CAN

Never love unless you can
Bear with all the faults of man:
Men sometimes will jealous be

Though but little cause they see,
And hang the head as discontent,
And speak what straight they will repent.

Men that but one saint adore
Make a show of love to more:
Beauty must be scorned in none,
Though but truly served in one.
For what is courtship but disguise?
True hearts may have dissembling eyes.

Men, when their affairs require,
Must awhile themselves retire;
Sometimes hunt, and sometimes hawk,
And not ever sit and talk.
If these and such like you can bear,
Then like and love and never fear!   *Campion.*

The Third Book of Airs, [c. 1617].

THERE IS A GARDEN IN HER FACE

There is a garden in her face
    Where roses and white lilies grow;
A heavenly paradise is that place
    Wherein all pleasant fruits do flow.
There cherries grow which none may buy,
Till 'cherry-ripe' themselves do cry.

Those cherries fairly do enclose
    Of orient pearl a double row,
Which when her lovely laughter shows,
    They look like rosebuds filled with snow.
Yet them nor peer nor prince can buy,
Till 'cherry-ripe' themselves do cry.

Her eyes like angels watch them still,
  Her brows like bended bows do stand,
Threatening with piercing frowns to kill
  All that attempt, with eye or hand,
Those sacred cherries to come nigh,
Till 'cherry-ripe' themselves do cry.   *Campion.*

The Fourth Book of Airs, [c. 1617].

LOVE ME OR NOT

Love me or not, love her I must, or die;
Leave me or not, follow her needs must I.
Oh, that her grace would my wished comforts give!
How rich in her, how happy should I live!

All my desire, all my delight should be
Her to enjoy, her to unite to me;
Envy should cease, her would I love alone:
Who loves by looks is seldom true to one.

Could I enchant, and that it lawful were,
Her would I charm softly that none should hear;
But love enforced rarely yields firm content:
So would I love that neither should repent.   *Campion.*

Ibid.

WEEP NO MORE

Weep no more, nor sigh, nor groan,
Sorrow calls no time that 's gone:
Violets plucked, the sweetest rain
Makes not fresh nor grow again;
Trim thy locks, look cheerfully;
Fate's hid ends eyes cannot see:

Joys as wingèd dreams fly fast,
Why should sadness longer last?
Grief is but a wound to woe;
Gentlest fair, mourn, mourn no moe.

J. Fletcher (?)

The Queen of Corinth, 1679. (Acted 1617? Song omitted, 1647.)*

ELEGY OVER A TOMB

Must I then see, alas, eternal night
    Sitting upon those fairest eyes,
And closing all those beams, which once did rise
    So radiant and bright,
That light and heat in them to us did prove
    Knowledge and love?

Oh, if you did delight no more to stay
    Upon this low and earthly stage,
But rather chose an endless heritage,
    Tell us at least, we pray,
Where all the beauties that those ashes owed
    Are now bestowed?

Doth the sun now his light with yours renew?
    Have waves the curling of your hair?
Did you restore unto the sky and air
    The red and white and blue?
Have you vouchsafed to flowers since your death
    That sweetest breath?

Had not heaven's lights else in their houses slept,
    Or to some private life retired?
Must not the sky and air have else conspired
    And in their regions wept?

owed] owned.

Must not each flower else the earth could breed
   Have been a weed?

But thus enriched may we not yield some cause
   Why they themselves lament no more,
That must have changèd course they held before
   And broke their proper laws,
Had not your beauties given this second birth
   To heaven and earth?

Tell us, for oracles must still ascend
   For those that crave them at your tomb,
Tell us, where are those beauties now become
   And what they now intend;
Tell us, alas! that cannot tell our grief,
   Or hope relief.   *Herbert of Cherbury.*

Occasional Verses, 1665. (Poem dated 1617.)

EVEN SUCH IS TIME

Even such is Time, which takes in trust
   Our youth, and joys, and all we have;
And pays us but with age and dust,
   Which, in the dark and silent grave,
When we have wandered all our ways,
Shuts up the story of our days:
   And from which earth, and grave, and dust,
   The Lord shall raise me up, I trust.   *Raleigh(?)*

The Prerogative of Parliaments, 1628. (For an earlier version, see Note.
Written before 1618.)

SONNET

They say that shadows of deceasèd ghosts
Do haunt the houses and the graves about,

Of such whose life's lamp went untimely out,
Delighting still in their forsaken hosts:
So, in the place where cruel Love doth shoot
The fatal shaft that slew my love's delight,
I stalk, and walk, and wander day and night,
Even like a ghost with unperceivëd foot.
But those light ghosts are happier far than I,
For, at their pleasure, they can come and go
Unto the place that hides their treasure so,
And see the same with their fantastic eye:
    Where I, alas, dare not approach the cruel
    Proud monument that doth enclose my jewel.

Posthumi, in *Du Bartas,* 1633. (Written before 1618.)   *Sylvester.*

GO, SILLY WORM

Go, silly worm, drudge, trudge, and travel,
    Despising pain,
    So thou may'st gain
Some honour, or some golden gravel;
But death the while, to fill his number,
    With sudden call
    Takes thee from all,
To prove thy days but dream and slumber.

Mottoes, in *Du Bartas,* 1621. (Written before 1618.)   *Sylvester.*

AUTUMNUS

When the leaves in autumn wither
    With a tawny tannëd face,
Warped and wrinkled up together,
    The year's late beauty to disgrace;

There thy life's glass may'st thou find thee:
  Green now, grey now, gone anon,
  Leaving, worldling, of thine own
Neither fruit nor leaf behind thee.   *Sylvester.*

Spectacles, in *Du Bartas,* 1621. (Written before 1618.)

A MEMENTO FOR MORTALITY

*Taken from the view of Sepulchres
of so many Kings and Nobles, as lie
interred in the Abbey of Westminster.*

Mortality, behold and fear!
What a change of flesh is here!
Think how many royal bones
Sleep within this heap of stones,
Hence removed from beds of ease,
Dainty fare, and what might please,
Fretted roofs, and costly shows,
To a roof that flats the nose:
Which proclaims all flesh is grass,
How the world's fair glories pass;
That there is no trust in health,
In youth, in age, in greatness, wealth:
For if such could have reprieved,
Those had been immortal lived.
Know from this the world a snare,
How that greatness is but care,
How all pleasures are but pain,
And how short they do remain:
For here they lie had realms and lands,
That now want strength to stir their hands;

Where from their pulpits seeled with dust
They preach, 'In greatness is no trust.'
Here 's an acre sown indeed
With the richest royal'st seed
That the earth did e'er suck in
Since the first man died for sin;
Here the bones of birth have cried
'Though Gods they were, as men they died.'
Here are sands, ignoble things,
Dropped from the ruined sides of Kings;
With whom the poor man's earth being shown,
The difference is not easily known.
Here 's a world of pomp and state
Forgotten, dead, disconsolate.
Think then, this scythe, that mows down kings,
Exempts no meaner mortal things.
Then bid the wanton lady tread
Amid these mazes of the dead;
And these, truly understood,
More shall cool and quench the blood
Than her many sports a-day,
And her nightly wanton play:
Bid her paint till day of doom,
To this favour she must come.
Bid the merchant gather wealth,
The usurer exact by stealth,
The proud man beat it from his thought—
Yet to this shape all must be brought.

Basse (?)

W. B. & E. P.'s *A Help to Discourse, or, A Miscellany of Merriment,* 1619.
(Registered 1618.)*

seeled] canopied; but possibly, sealed.   bones of birth] *i.e.* of high birth.

THE HOURS OF SLEEPY NIGHT

The hours of sleepy night decay apace,
And now warm beds are fitter than this place.
All time is long that is unwilling spent,
But hours are minutes when they yield content.
The gathered flowers we love that breathe sweet scent,
But loathe them, their sweet odour being spent.
     It is a life is never ill
     To lie and sleep in roses still.

The rarer pleasure is, it is more sweet;
And friends are kindest when they seldom meet.
Who would not hear the nightingale still sing,
Or who grew ever weary of the spring?
The day must have her night, the spring her fall,
All is divided, none is lord of all.
     It were a most delightful thing
     To live in a perpetual spring.   *Campion(?)*

The Mountebank's Masque. (Performed 1618.)* Bodley MS. Ashm. 36–7.

THE DANCE

Robin is a lovely lad,
No lass a smoother ever had.
Tommy hath a look as bright
As is the rosy morning light.
Tib is dark and brown of hue,
But like her colour firm and true.
Jinny hath a lip to kiss
Wherein a spring of nectar is.

Simkin well his mirth can place
And words to win a woman's grace.
Sib is all in all to me,
There is no queen of love but she.
Let us in a lovers' round
Circle all this hallowed ground.
Softly, softly trip and go,
The light-foot fairies jet it so.
Forward then and back again,
Here and there and everywhere,
Winding to and winding fro,
Skipping high and louting low.
And like lovers hand in hand
March around and make a stand.   *Campion(?)**

G. Mason and J. Earsden's *Airs*, 1618.

SONG

O harmless feast,
With mirth increased
  Where music and love do meet!
Where the piper does find
A more delicate wind
  To make his pipe sound more sweet;
    Whiles his stick does belabour
    The head of his tabor
        Amain:
  Where the wine in the bowls,
  And every tongue, rolls,
    Yet never disturbs the brain.

Jove's Trojan boy
Was no such joy,
  Nor all his heavenly whores:

> There's no such delight
> By day or by night
>   E'er felt by feigning wooers,
>   As is the soft pleasure
>   At such honest leisure
>   To sport:
>   When all are so merry,
>   They sing till they 're weary,
>   And trip it in comely sort.   *Holyday.*

Technogamia, 1618.*

ON TOBACCO

> Void, damnëd weed! that hell's dry sweetmeats art
> As molten lead is marmalade and tart:
> What cheating devil made our gallants think
> Thee physic, wenches, company, meat and drink,
> And money? for at this dear drug alone
> They catch, when for it all their gold is flown.
> 'Tis our artillery too, and armed this way
> Our English scorn Bucquoy and Spinola:
> Set but each man unto his mouth his pipe
> And—as the Jews gave Jericho a wipe,
> Raising a blast of rams' horns while it fell—
> Some ballad, on a time, the truth shall tell
> How it befell, when we our foes did choke
> Like bees, and put them pell-mell to the Smoke.   *Pestel.*

Bodley MS. Malone 14. (Poem dated 1618.)

SONG

> Silly Boy, there is no cause
> Why any lad, that will go love,

Curse or Cupid or his laws
 If that his lass inconstant prove:
Though she do sail with every wind,
Yet that 's no fault in womankind;
   That heinous sin
   Thou think'st her in
Thou shalt in thine own bosom find.

They that go to Cupid's mart
 To gain a heart, a heart do give;
Not thine own but hers thou art,
 Thy soul within her breast doth live.
Though she be then as bold and bad
As ever fame or story had,
   Do not exclaim
   'Tis thine own shame;
Her frailty to thy follies add.

Nor adventure thou to name
 The goodness thine thou hap'st to show;
Think but where thou hadst the same—
 The tree whereon such fruit does grow,
Which if thou cherish, prune and fence,
She cannot but in tender sense
   Do so for thine
   And strive to fine
Thy native ill, to innocence.

Here is then the only way
 To keep thy love for ever sure:
Keep her heart in thee does stay,
 And she will thine, for ever pure.
Happy turtles, heartening so
Each other's truth which both do show

>   And just alike,
>   On virtue strike,
>   As two true clocks together go.   *Pestel.*

Bodley MS. Malone 14. (Poem dated 1618.)

A LOVE SONNET

I loved a lass, a fair one,
   As fair as e'er was seen;
She was indeed a rare one,
   Another Sheba Queen:
But, fool as then I was,
   I thought she loved me too:
But now, alas! sh'as left me,
   Falero, lero, loo!

Her hair like gold did glister,
   Each eye was like a star, ·
She did surpass her sister,
   Which passed all others far;
She would me honey call,
   She 'd—oh, she 'd kiss me too!
But now, alas! sh'as left me,
   Falero, lero, loo!

In summer time to Medley
   My Love and I would go:
The boatmen there stood ready
   My Love and I to row;
For cream there would we call,
   For cakes and for prunes too:
But now, alas! sh'as left me,
   Falero, lero, loo!

Many a merry meeting
    My Love and I have had;
She was my only sweeting,
    She made my heart full glad;
The tears stood in her eyes
    Like to the morning dew:
But now, alas! sh'as left me,
    Falero, lero, loo!

And as abroad we walkëd,
    As lovers' fashion is,
Oft as we sweetly talkëd
    The sun would steal a kiss;
The wind upon her lips
    Likewise most sweetly blew:
But now, alas! sh'as left me,
    Falero, lero, loo!

Her cheeks were like the cherry,
    Her skin as white as snow;
When she was blithe and merry
    She angel-like did show;
Her waist exceeding small,
    The fives did fit her shoe:
But now, alas! sh'as left me,
    Falero, lero, loo!

In summer time or winter
    She had her heart's desire;
I still did scorn to stint her
    From sugar, sack, or fire:
The world went round about,

Oft as we] 1638; Oft we, 1629.   sun would] 1638; sun should, 1629.

No cares we ever knew:
But now, alas! sh'as left me,
 Falero, lero, loo!

As we walked home together,
 At midnight, through the town,
To keep away the weather
 O'er her I 'd cast my gown;
No cold my Love should feel,
 Whate'er the heavens could do:
But now, alas! sh'as left me,
 Falero, lero, loo!

Like doves we would be billing,
 And clip and kiss so fast,
Yet she would be unwilling
 That I should kiss the last:
They 're Judas kisses now,
 Since that they proved untrue:
For now, alas! sh'as left me,
 Falero, lero, loo!

To maidens' vows and swearing
 Henceforth no credit give;
You may give them the hearing,
 But never them believe;
They are as false as fair,
 Unconstant, frail, untrue:
For mine, alas! has left me,
 Falero, lero, loo!

'Twas I that paid for all things,
 'Twas others drank the wine;
I cannot now recall things,

Live but a fool to pine;
'Twas I that beat the bush,
    The bird to others flew:
For she alas! hath left me,
        Falero, lero, loo!

If ever that Dame Nature,
    For this false lover's sake,
Another pleasing creature
    Like unto her would make,
Let her remember this—
    To make the other true:
For this, alas! hath left me,
        Falero, lero, loo!

No riches now can raise me,
    No want make me despair,
No misery amaze me,
    Nor yet for want I care;
I have lost a world itself:
    My earthly heaven, adieu!
Since she, alas! hath left me,
        Falero, lero, loo!   *Wither(?)*

A Description of Love, 1618. (Text 1629.) (Registered June 1618.)*

CUPID IN A BED OF ROSES

Cupid, in a bed of roses
        Sleeping, chancéd to be stung
        Of a bee that lay among
The flowers where he himself reposes;
And thus to his mother weeping
        Told that he this wound did take

want make] Mod. eds.; want makes, 1625, 1629 and 1638.

Of a little wingëd snake,
As he lay securely sleeping.
Cytherea smiling said
That 'if so great sorrow spring
From a silly bee's weak sting
As should make thee thus dismayed,
What anguish feel they, think'st thou, and what pain,
Whom thy empoisoned arrows cause complain?'   *Anon.*

T. Bateson's *Madrigals*, ii., 1618.

ENJOY THY APRIL NOW

Enjoy thy April now,
Whilst it doth freely shine;
This lightning flash and show,
With that clear spirit of thine,
Will suddenly decline;
And thou, fair murdering eyes,
Shall be Love's tombs, where now his cradle lies.

Thy gold and scarlet shall
Pale silver colour be;
Thy row of pearls shall fall
Like withered leaves from tree;
And thou shall shortly see
Thy face and hair to grow
All ploughed with furrows, over-swoln with snow.

That which on Flora's breast,
All fresh and flourishing,
Aurora, newly dressed,
Saw in her dawning spring;
Quite dry and languishing,
Deprived of honour quite,
Day-closing Hesperus beholds at night.

Fair is the lily, fair
The rose, of flowers the eye;
Both wither in the air,
Their beauteous colours die:
And so at length shall lie
Deprived of former grace,
The lilies of thy breasts, the roses of thy face.

What then will it avail,
O youth, advisèd ill,
In lap of Beauty frail
To nurse a wayward will,
Like snake in sun-warm hill?
Pluck, pluck betime thy flower,
That springs and parcheth in one short hour!   *Daniel.*

Stanzas from *A Description of Beauty*,* *Works,* 1623. (Written before 1619.)

THE NIGHTINGALE

Jug, jug! Fair fall the nightingal,
    Whose tender breast
Chants out her merry madrigal,
    With hawthorn pressed:
Te'u, te'u! thus sings she even by even,
And represents the melody in heaven:
        Tis, tis,
    I am not as I wish.

Rape-defilèd Philomel
    In her sad mischance
Tells what she is forced to tell,
    While the satyrs dance:
'Unhappy I,' quoth she, 'unhappy I,

That am betrayed by Tereus' treachery;
    Tis, tis,
  I am not as I wish.

'Chaste-unchaste, deflowered, yet
    Spotless in heart,
Lust was all that he could get,
    For all his art:
For I ne'er attention lent
To his suit, nor gave consent;
    Tis, tis,
  I am not as I wish.'

Thus hath faithless Tereus made
    Heartless Philomele
Moan her in her forlorn shade,
    Where grief I feel—
Grief that wounds me to the heart,
Which though gone hath left her smart;
    Tis, tis,
  I am not as I wish.   *Brathwaite.*

Nature's Embassy, 1621. (Registered 1619.)

TO HIS COY LOVE

I pray thee leave, love me no more,
    Call home the heart you gave me!
I but in vain that saint adore
    That can but will not save me.
These poor half-kisses kill me quite;
    Was ever man thus servëd,
Amidst an ocean of delight,
    For pleasure to be stervëd?

Show me no more those snowy breasts
   With azure riverets branchëd,
Where, whilst mine eye with plenty feasts,
   Yet is my thirst not stanchëd.
O Tantalus, thy pains ne'er tell!
   By me thou art prevented:
'Tis nothing to be plagued in Hell,
   But thus in Heaven tormented!

Clip me no more in those dear arms,
   Nor thy life's comfort call me!
Oh, these are but too powerful charms,
   And do but more enthral me.
But see, how patient I am grown
   In all this coil about thee!
Come, nice thing, let thy heart alone!
   I cannot live without thee.   *Drayton.*

Odes, with other Lyric Poesies, in *Poems,* 1619.

THE CRIER

Good folk, for gold or hire,
   But help me to a Crier!
For my poor Heart is run astray
After two Eyes, that passed this way.
   O yes!   O yes!   O yes!
   If there be any man,
   In town or country, can
   Bring my Heart again,
   I 'll please him for his pain.
And by these marks, I will you show
That only I this Heart do owe:
   It is a wounded Heart,

owe] own.

Wherein yet sticks the dart;
Every piece sore hurt throughout it,
Faith and troth writ round about it;
It was a tame Heart, and a dear,
  And never used to roam:
But having got this haunt, I fear
  'Twill hardly stay at home.
For God's sake, walking by the way
  If you my Heart do see,
Either impound it for a stray,
  Or send it back to me!   *Drayton.*

Ibid.

SONNETS

Since there 's no help, come let us kiss and part—
Nay, I have done: you get no more of me;
And I am glad, yea, glad with all my heart,
That thus so cleanly I myself can free.
Shake hands for ever, cancel all our vows,
And when we meet at any time again,
Be it not seen in either of our brows
That we one jot of former love retain.
Now at the last gasp of love's latest breath,
When, his pulse failing, Passion speechless lies,
When Faith is kneeling by his bed of death,
And Innocence is closing up his eyes,—
 Now, if thou wouldst, when all have given him over,
 From death to life thou might'st him yet recover!

Drayton.

Idea, in *Poems*, 1619. (Sonnet first printed 1619.)

How many paltry, foolish, painted things,
That now in coaches trouble every street,
Shall be forgotten, whom no poet sings,

Ere they be well wrapped in their winding-sheet!
Where I to thee eternity shall give,
When nothing else remaineth of these days,
And queens hereafter shall be glad to live
Upon the alms of thy superfluous praise.
Virgins and matrons, reading these my rhymes,
Shall be so much delighted with thy story
That they shall grieve they lived not in these times,
To have seen thee, their sex's only glory:
 So shalt thou fly above the vulgar throng,
 Still to survive in my immortal song.   *Drayton.*

Idea, in *Poems*, 1619.

ARM, ARM, ARM, ARM!

Arm, arm, arm, arm! the scouts are all come in:
Keep your ranks close, and now your honours win.
Behold from yonder hill the foe appears;
Bows, bills, glaves, arrows, shields, and spears!
Like a dark wood he comes, or tempest pouring;
Oh, view the wings of horse the meadows scouring!
The van-guard marches bravely. Hark, the drums!
         Dub, dub!
They meet, they meet! Now the battle comes:
   See how the arrows fly,
   That darken all the sky!
   Hark how the trumpets sound,
   Hark how the hills rebound,
     Tara, tara, tara, tara, tara!
Hark how the horses charge! In, boys, boys, in!
The battle totters; now the wounds begin:
   Oh, how they cry
   Oh, how they die!

boys, boys] 1679; boys, in, boys, 1647.

Room for the valiant Memnon, armed with thunder!
   See how he breaks the ranks asunder!
They fly! they fly!   Eumenes has the chase,
And brave Polybius makes good his place.
        To the plains, to the woods,
        To the rocks, to the floods,
They fly for succour.   Follow, follow, follow!
Hark how the soldiers hollo!
                    Hey, hey!
        Brave Diocles is dead,
        And all his soldiers fled;
        That battle 's won, and lost,
        That many a life hath cost.   *J. Fletcher.*

The Mad Lover, 1647. (Acted before March 1618/9.)*

HYMN TO COMUS

Room! room! make room for the bouncing belly,
First father of sauce and deviser of jelly;
Prime master of arts, and the giver of wit,
That found out the excellent engine the spit,
The plough and the flail, the mill and the hopper,
The hutch and the bolter, the furnace and copper,
The oven, the bavin, the mawkin, the peel,
The hearth and the range, the dog and the wheel:
He, he first invented the hogshead and tun,
The gimlet and vice too, and taught 'em to run;
And since with the funnel and hippocras bag
He has made of himself, that he now cries swag!
Which shows, though the pleasure be but of four inches,
Yet he is a weasel, the gullet that pinches

---

bavin] bundle of brushwood as fuel for oven.   mawkin] oven mop.
peel] baker's shovel.   hippocras bag] conical bag used as filter.   He
has] N.A.; H'as, 1641.

Of any delight, and not spares from his back
Whatever to make of the belly a sack!
Hail, hail, plump paunch! O the founder of taste,
For fresh meats, or powdered, or pickle, or paste;
Devourer of broiled, baked, roasted, or sod,
And emptier of cups be they even or odd:
All which have now made thee so wide i' the waist,
As scarce with no pudding thou art to be laced;
But eating and drinking until thou dost nod,
Thou break'st all thy girdles, and break'st forth a god.

Pleasure reconciled to Virtue, 1641. (Acted 1619.)   *Jonson.*

HENCE, AWAY, YOU SIRENS!

Hence, away, you sirens! leave me,
And unclasp your wanton arms!
Sugared words shall ne'er deceive me,
Though thou prove a thousand charms.
     Fie, fie, forbear!
     No common snare
Could ever my affection chain:
     Your painted baits
     And poor deceits
Are all bestowed on me in vain.

I 'm no slave to such as you be;
Neither shall a snowy breast,
Wanton eye, or lip of ruby
Ever rob me of my rest.
     Go, go, display
     Your beauty's ray
To some o'ersoon enamoured swain!
     Those common wiles

---

his back] Nichols, 1828; this back, 1641.   powdered] salted.   sod] seethed.

>   Of sighs and smlies
>   Are all bestowed on me in vain.
>
>   I have elsewhere vowed a duty;
>   Turn away thy tempting eyes!
>   Show not me a naked beauty:
>   Those impostures I despise.
>   My spirit loathes
>   Where gaudy clothes
>   And feignëd oaths may love obtain.
>   I love her so,
>   Whose look swears 'No,'
>   That all your labours will be vain.   *Wither.*

Fidelia, 1619. (Text from *Fair Virtue*, 1622.)*

ON HIS MISTRESS, THE QUEEN OF BOHEMIA

> You meaner beauties of the night,
>   That poorly satisfy our eyes
> More by your number than your light;
>   You common people of the skies,
>   What are you when the sun shall rise?
>
> You curious chanters of the wood,
>   That warble forth Dame Nature's lays,
> Thinking your voices understood
>   By your weak accents; what 's your praise
>   When Philomel her voice shall raise?
>
> You violets that first appear,
>   By your pure purple mantles known,
> Like the proud virgins of the year,

---

sun shall] 1651; moon doth, 1624; (for other variants, see Note).

As if the spring were all your own;
What are you when the rose is blown?

So, when my Mistress shall be seen
  In form and beauty of her mind,
By virtue first, then choice, a Queen,
    Tell me, if she were not designed
    The eclipse and glory of her kind?   *Sir H. Wotton.*

Reliquiae Wottonianae, 1651. (Variant in M. East's *Sixth Set,* 1624. Poem written 1619.)

SWEET SUFFOLK OWL

Sweet Suffolk owl, so trimly dight
With feathers, like a lady bright,
Thou sing'st alone, sitting by night,
    Te whit, te whoo! Te whit, te whoo!

Thy note, that forth so freely rolls,
With shrill command the mouse controls;
And sings a dirge for dying souls,
    Te whit, te whoo! Te whit, te whoo!   *Anon.*

T. Vautor's *Songs of divers Airs and Natures,* 1619.

DING DONG

Whilst we sing the doleful knell
Of this princess' passing-bell,
Let the woods and valleys ring
Echoes to our sorrowing;
And the tenor of their song
Be ding dong, ding dong, dong,
    Ding dong, dong,
        Ding dong.

Nature now shall boast no more
Of the riches of her store,
Since in this her chiefest prize
All the stock of beauty dies:
Then what cruel heart can long
Forbear to sing this sad ding dong?
     This sad ding dong,
       Ding dong.

Fauns and sylvans of the woods,
Nymphs that haunt the crystal floods,
Savage beasts more milder then
The unrelenting hearts of men,
Be partakers of our moan,
And with us sing ding dong, ding dong,
     Ding dong, dong,
       Ding dong.   *Anon.*

Swetnam, the Woman-Hater, 1620. (Registered 1619.)

ON QUEEN ANNE'S DEATH
(*March 2, 1619*)

March with his wind hath struck a cedar tall,
And weeping April mourns the cedar's fall;
And May intends no flowers her month shall bring,
Since she must lose the flower of all the spring:
   Thus March's wind hath causëd April showers,
   And yet sad May must lose her flower of flowers.

                                           Anon.

Bodley MS. Ashm. 38.

ALL THE FLOWERS OF THE SPRING

   All the flowers of the spring
   Meet to perfume our burying;

---

milder then] milder than.   Queen Anne] *i.e.* Anne of Denmark, wife of
James I.

These have but their growing prime,
And man does flourish but his time:
Survey our progress from our birth—
We are set, we grow, we turn to earth.
Courts adieu, and all delights,
All bewitching appetites!
Sweetest breath and clearest eye
Like perfumes go out and die;
And consequently this is done
As shadows wait upon the sun.
Vain the ambition of kings
Who seek by trophies and dead things
To leave a living name behind,
And weave but nets to catch the wind.   *Webster.*

The Devil's Law-Case, 1623. (Written 1619–20?)*

SONG IN THE WOOD

This way, this way, come and hear,
You that hold these pleasures dear;
Fill your ears with our sweet sound,
Whilst we melt the frozen ground.
This way come; make haste, O fair!
Let your clear eyes gild the air;
Come, and bless us with your sight;
This way, this way, seek delight!   *J. Fletcher.*

The Little French Lawyer, 1647. (Acted c. 1620.)*

THE SPRING OF JOY IS DRY

The spring of joy is dry
    That ran into my heart;
And all my comforts fly:
    My Love and I must part.

Farewell, my Love, I go,
If fate will have it so.
Yet to content us both
Return again, as doth
The shadow to the hour,
The bee unto the flower,
The fish unto the hook,
The cattle to the brook,
That we may sport our fill,
And love continue still.   *Anon.*

M. Peerson's *Private Music*, 1620.

OPEN THE DOOR

'Open the door! Who 's there within?
The fairest of thy mother's kin,
        Oh, come, come, come abroad,
        And hear the shrill birds sing,
        The air with tunes that load.
It is too soon to go to rest,
The sun not midway yet to west.
        The day doth miss thee,
And will not part until it kiss thee.'

'Were I as fair as you pretend,
Yet to an unknown seld-seen friend
        I dare not ope the door:
        To hear the sweet birds sing
        Oft proves a dangerous thing.
The sun may run his wonted race
And yet not gaze on my poor face;
        The day may miss me.
Therefore depart, you shall not kiss me.'   *Anon.*

Ibid.

PRETTY WANTONS

Pretty wantons sweetly sing
In honour of the smiling spring;
Look how the light-winged chirping choir
With nimble skips the spring admire!
But oh, hark how the birds sing! mark that note—
Jug, jug, tereu, tereu!
Oh, prettily warbled from a sweet sweet throat!   *Anon.*

M. Peerson's *Private Music*, 1620.

OF HIS LADY

What flower is my lady like?
    You think the rose is my suppose;
But it doth not my fancy strike.
    The gaudy rose in summer blows,
In winter it is cold and dead:
    My lovely flower blooms most the hour
When days are dark, and summer fled.

My lady 's like no mortal flower
    That hath its birth upon this earth,
Though formed in nature's chosen hour:
    Albeit indeed it had the seed
In garden bright of Paradise,
    And endless bloom from thence hath come
To bless each other sense and eyes.

I ne'er shall think my lady old:
    I feel no fears of coming years;

I 'll love the more, a thousand fold.
   Time cannot vade what Virtue made:
Virtue puts back the hand of Time;
   And love like mine is so divine,
To think of failing is a crime.

Unworthy her I am, I know;
   And what is best in me and blessed
Is only that I love her so.
   There cannot be no worth in me,
Seeing I love so passing well:
   If me she loved, it would be proved
How much I did all men excel.

That cannot come within my scope;
   Yet service true I still will do,
And even hope in spite of hope.
   She is above my humble love
That but looks up in still delight:
   The stars are high within the sky;
I reach them not for they are bright.

Fair star, look down! and as a friend
   On me but think for one sweet wink,
And I am blessed sans sum or end.
   Stars never frown, but aye look down
On earth with smiling cheerful eyes.
   Ah me! but then they see all men:
Thy smiles are my monopolies.   *Anon.*

J. P. Collier's MS.* (*Temp*. Elizabeth or James I, probably not later than 1620.)

HEY NONNY NO!

Hey nonny no!
Men are fools that wish to die!
Is 't not fine to dance and sing
When the bells of death do ring?
Is 't not fine to swim in wine,
And turn upon the toe
And sing hey nonny no,
When the winds do blow,
And the seas do flow?
Hey nonny no!

Anon.

Christ Church MS. 439. (Song written not later than 1620.)*

ABBREVIATIONS,
NOTES TEXTUAL,
& BIOGRAPHICAL,
& INDEXES

ABBREVIATIONS AND REFERENCES

[n.d.] No date printed on title page or colophon of book.

[c. 1567] The approximate date of an undated book or MS.

[1567] Date, originally omitted, supplied by extraneous evidence.

(Registered 1567) Year of entry in Registers of Stationers' Company. The register year ran from July to July; hence, as the month and day were not entered in the early registers, the year of registration is sometimes shown thus, (Registered 1565–6).

(?) A Note of Interrogation implies a doubtful ascription of date or author, according to position.

* An Asterisk refers to a note dealing with authorship, date, or source, according to position, or, in a few instances, with details of excision or excerption. To save repetition, however, any question affecting several poems (e.g. the dates ascribed to the posthumously published work of Wyatt, and Donne, or to Shakespeare's *Sonnets*) is discussed in a note to the *first* included poem of the author, or of the particular work, as the case may be; and accordingly an asterisk is affixed to that poem only.

B.M.——British Museum.

Bodley——Bodleian Library.

Camb.——*Cambridge History of English Literature.*

D.N.B.——*Dictionary of National Biography.*

Eng. Hel.——*England's Helicon*, 1600.

P. of D.D.——*The Paradise of Dainty Devices*, 1576.

Times Lit. Sup.——*Times Literary Supplement.*

Tottel——Tottel's miscellany—*Songs and Sonnets*, 1557.

NOTES

(The references are to pages on which an asterisk, or 'See Note,' appears)

iv. Line 3, may, N.A.; word incomplete—'m' and a portion of 'a,' 1584. Arber wrongly conjectured 'might.' Eight lines, not applicable to this book, omitted after l. 4. Jones, the printer of the *Handful,* may have got some one to write this for him.

2. For dates, see A. K. Foxwell's *Poems of Sir Thomas Wiat,* 1913.

5. Said to have been written to Princess Mary when she was eighteen years of age. (See *D.N.B.*)

11. Ascribed to Rochford—on eve of execution—1536.

14. Date approximate. A prayer for the King and Queen, in MS., shows it to be *temp.* Hy.VIII. B.M. experts date script 'middle 16th cent., rather earlier than later.' Heywood was aged forty-eight in 1545; and the poem expresses the married love of middle age.

15. From the same MS. as 14. MS. l. 1, 'All a green willow willow w w'. MS. last l., 'For all'; as usual, the scribe leaves the reader to go on with the repeated burden. In stz. 4, l. 4, after 'steadfast,' and stz. 5, l. 2, after 'plant,' the word 'still' has been added above the line, but by a *later* hand; and this former editors have wrongly printed. Three poorer stanzas omitted after stz. 3.

20. I have followed *Brittons (Breton's) Bower of Delights,* 1597, in omitting the last 16 lines of this poem.

21. For date and ascription, see *Nugae Antiquae,* 1769.

23. *Nugae Antiquae* says the MS. of this is dated 1564; but Harington married Isabella early in 1554, and wrote other poems to her in 1549. Park suggested 1546 or 1549 as probable. I suspect some 18th cent. 'polish' here and there in the poem.

23. Note. Mid-16th cent. MS. L. 7, though thou, N.A.; thou y^t, MS.—'thou' being probably a contracted 'though,' intentional or not; and 'y^t' a scribal error for 'y^u.'

24. L. 12, even, N.A.; euy, MS. The scribe omitted to mark the contraction, euȳ, *i.e.* euyn, *i.e.* evyn—a usual spelling.

25. This is from the earliest edition (Vele's), which is undated, but contains a prayer for Ed. VI., who died 1553.

26. Wilson's *Rule of Reason,* 1553, quotes from this play.

27. *Nugae Antiquae,* 1769 (printed from Harington's papers), gives only these stzs., with title 'Elegy wrote in the Tower by John Harington, confined with the Princess Elizabeth, 1554.' Extra stzs. are found in Tottel, and the *P. of D.D.,* and MS. Ashm. 48. The text I print follows the MS., that being the earliest authority.

30. L. 6, knows, 1580; knoweth, 1576 and 1578. Ll. 12 and 18, knows, 1576, 1578, and 1580.

38. Failing to trace Collier's MS., I follow his reproduction in *Extracts from the Registers of the Stationers' Company*, 1848.

40. The attribution is not certain. In the MS. (late 16th cent.) the poem is headed: 'Verses made by the Queen when she was supposed to be in love with Montague.' Little is known of him, but he was apparently in favour in 1561, when the Queen chose him for a special mission to the court of Spain, as one 'whom she highly esteemed for his great prudence and wisdom.' (See *D.N.B.*)

41. The only known copy of the original was sold in 1907, and I have been unable to trace it. I am therefore dependent on the Malone Soc. reprint of it, ed. by Messrs. Greg and McKerrow, 1909. There, stz. 1. l. 2, runs—'Sing lulla by baby, lulla by baby'; but I believe l. 2 of stzs. 2 and 3 is what Phillip originally wrote, and so have followed it.

43. Authorship and date problematical. But this play, with 'Diccon the Bedlam' as an important character, was printed in 1575 by Colwell, to whom had been registered in 1562–3 a play entitled *Diccon of Bedlam*, thought by many to be the same. (See J. S. Farmer's *Gammer Gurton's Needle*, 1906.)

45. These are stzs. 1, 2, 3, and 8 of the *Induction*.

47. Note. L. 22 is supplied from a version in B.M. Add. MS. 26737. The *P. of D.D.*, 1576, 1578, and 1580 eds., reads 'That might before have lived their time and nature out'; which is both a foot short and, I believe, corrupt.

51. This seems to have been well known before 1566–7, when a ballad, entitled 'Ah, fain would I have a godly thing to show unto my lady,' was registered. Popular ballads were frequently thus moralized; and as there is some evidence that the 1584 collection was first published in 1566, the 1566–7 ballad was probably a 'conversion' of the text here given.

51. Note. L. 6, Their enemies, N.A.; These enemies, 1567. But a similar line in the second stz. reads 'Their enemies to tame.' Thus 'These' would seem to be a misprint for 'Their.'

54. This breathless dancing metre is, at this date, so unusual that I have selected stzs. 3, 4, 9, 10, and 11 of the lengthy original.

55. Originally in long lines of six and seven feet. A separate feeble 'posy' in two lines at the end is omitted.

57. Tobacco is thought to have been first brought into England by Sir John Hawkins in 1565. It is, however, certain that as early as 1573 the new custom had become popular enough for Harrison to comment on it that year, as follows: 'In these days, the taking-in of the smoke of the Indian herb called Tabaco . . . is greatly taken up and used in England.' It would therefore appear that, barely five years earlier, Wisdome had ample opportunity to observe the growing practice and moralize on it before he died.

57. These lines, with three slight alterations, were reprinted anonymously in J. Farmer's *Madrigals*, 1599. They are, however, the opening of a poem entitled 'The Lover deceived writes to his Lady.' I print the 1567–8 text, but in six short lines instead of the original three long ones.

58. Prof. Quiller-Couch printed a shortened version of this, omitting, without notice of excision, ll. 5 and 8, in his *Golden Pomp*, 1895, and mistakenly assigned it to *New Sonnets and Pretty Pamphlets*. Other editors, copying his text, have given further currency both to the abbreviation and to the mistaken attribution.

59. Last two stanzas omitted.

59. Originally printed in long alternate lines of six and seven feet.

61. Dated by a statement in the 1587 ed.

62. See note 38.

69. First printed 1575. A stanza omitted after stz. 2.

73. T. Newton, in some verses in Hunnis's *A Hive Full of Honey*, 1577, mentions among the titles of several poems written 'in prime of youth' by Hunnis, 'thy *Nosegay*.' No poem by Hunnis with this title is known. Mrs. C. C. Stopes conjectures (*Times Lit. Sup.*, May 1, 1924) that this anonymous 'Nosegay' from the *Handful*, 1584, may be the one. There is some evidence that this collection was first published in 1566.

79. Authorship not certain, but the poem seems to fall within the section headed, 'Pretie pamphlets, by T. Proctor.'

80. A variant, in ten lines, appeared in the *P. of D.D.* 1576.

80. 'By H. C.' Malone's conjecture, Henry Cheke, is probable.

89. This was apparently popular before it was registered to Jones (printer of the *Handful*): for the same day, Sept. 3, 'The Lady Greensleeve's Answer to Donkyn her friend' was licensed to another printer. References to ballad, in *Merry Wives of Windsor*, II. i.; V. v.

90. Sidney's dates are doubtful and controverted. These assigned to my selections have perhaps found most acceptance.

100. 'By R. W.'—generally attributed to Robert Wilson.

100. This 'Prayer' was reprinted in *Greenes Funerals* (c. 1597), where it states that Greene quoted it on his death-bed.

102. 'By R. P.'—generally attributed to Robert Parry.

103. Date of writing given in the preface of the book.

104. As often with the dramatists, the songs were not printed in the original eds. of the plays. They were first included in Blount's reprint, *Six Court Comedies*, 1632. Lyly's authorship of the songs in his plays has occasionally been disputed in the past; but they are still usually called his, and his right to them has recently been re-examined and reasserted by his editor, R. W. Bond (See R.E.S. VI, VII, 1930–1.)

105. I am glad to reinstate the original 'How at heaven's gates' with the rapture it suggests, in place of the dull and flat emendation 'Now at heaven's gates,' usually printed.

110. The first four and last two stzs. are omitted.

117. The title page of the poems says, 'Written in his Youth and familiar Exercise with Sir Philip Sidney.' Sidney died 1586.

120. Sidney, who died 1586, wrote an 'answer' to this.

121. These lines, with a slight alteration, were reprinted anonymously in W. Byrd's *Psalms, Songs, and Sonnets*, 1611. The *Emblems* has other stzs.

127. Anonymous both in Byrd's version (which has stzs. 1–4 only) and in the late 16th century MS. (which supplies stz. 5), this poem was later included in Deloney's *Garland of Good Will*, 1631, many years after his death, and also—but again anonymously—in *Le Prince d'Amour*, 1660. It was, however, ascribed to Raleigh in a lost MS., and the case for his authorship is argued by A. M. C. Latham in her edition of his *Works*, 1929.

135. Parodied in *The Jew of Malta* (c. 1589), iv., ll. 1812–16.

136. Author and date uncertain. 'Made by . . . Raleigh in his younger

days'—Walton. Probably written soon after Marlowe's lyric, it is placed next to it for convenience. Raleigh was aged 37 in 1589.

141. *D.N.B.* says the 1616 ed. is the oldest extant; and Dyce and Grosart both print from it. There is, however, a unique copy of the 1st ed., 1590, in Trin. Coll. Library, Camb., from which I have taken my texts. As regards my selections, however, the two eds. differ very little; though 'once folded' (stz. 2, l. 1), 1590, is much better than 'are folded,' 1616. In l. 7 of all stzs. except stz. 1, both eds. omit 'do'; and in last stz., l. 5, print 'when' for 'where.' Stz. 1, l. 1, 1590, misprints 'is it' for 'It is.'

141. The only conceivable meaning of 'taint,' in l. 18, is 'a successful hit' (metaphor), but this is out of key with the context; besides, 'taint' occurs earlier (l. 6) in another sense. 'Saint' was a favourite epithet of Elizabethan poets for their loves, and Greene himself uses it in *Perimedes* and *The Orpharion.*

143. I can nowhere find a copy of 1590 ed., so follow the text of 1592.

146. This poem, which was originally called 'A Sonnet,' has occasionally been ascribed to Sir Henry Lee (or Leigh), the Queen's 'Champion,' whose retirement on November 17, 1590, it records.

147. The opening stzs. of one of the Choruses.

150. A unique copy of *Brittons Bower of Delights*, 1591, is in the Huntingdon Library, U.S.A. Compare concluding lines with Sidney's 'To Stella' (p. 92). Also compare the first stz. with T. Heywood's 'Ye little birds' (p. 347), which is borrowed from this.

154. This play is lost, but a few fragments exist in MSS.

157. Ascribed to Essex in MS. Rawl. Poet. 112, and to Campion in R. Alison's *An Hour's Recreation*, 1606. Many versions exist, mostly anon., some with more stzs. There is also a 15th cent. ballad, commencing in much the same way, which is possibly the original source (see P. Vivian's *Campion's Works*, 1909). My text is, I believe, now printed for the first time; it is one of the earliest, and certainly the best of all I have seen. Apparently unknown to previous editors, it is not noticed in A. E. H. Swaen's bibliography and examination of the early texts of the song (*Modern Philology*, iv., 3, 1907; and v., 3, 1908).

172. Stzs. 1–6, and 15 (last), of one of the Choruses.

181. Poem of 36 stzs; I print stzs. 15–19, 26 and 27.

184. The composers of the Song Books sometimes took great liberties with the poems they were setting to music, adding, repeating, transposing, substituting, and omitting words at will. Morley being in this respect perhaps the most arbitrary, it is at times difficult to reconstruct the original text he used; and thus differences of opinion arise. My reconstruction of this song differs slightly both from Bullen's and from Dr. Fellowes'.

187. Variant also in *Eng. Hel.*, 1600. Last stz. is found in MS. only.

193. Authorship of *Avisa* is very doubtful. The 1594 and 1596 eds. contain contradictory prefaces by Hadrian Dorrell (an assumed name?). See *D.N.B.* Last three stzs. omitted.

198. Note. *Spring* and *Winter* are jointly entitled 'The Song' in the Quarto and the Folios, and obviously were meant to be either one song or twin songs in the same form; but in all the old texts the last three lines of their choruses differ in form:

Spring thus—   The cuckoo then on every tree
                    Mocks married men; for thus sings he,
                    Cuckoo.
                    Cuckoo, cuckoo: O word of fear,
                    Unpleasing to a married ear.

Winter thus—   When blood is nipped and ways be foul,
                    Then nightly sings the staring owl
                    Tu-whit to-who,
                        A merry note,
                        While greasy Joan doth keel the pot.

Editors have usually emended or rearranged *Winter* to make it conform to *Spring* but with little success. *Winter* is perfect in form—a regular stanza of eight lines, each of four feet, l. 7 being subdivided to give emphasis to the bird's call, and also to rhyme the two birds' notes. Yet it does not seem to have occurred to any one that the fault may not lie there. By a printer's error, a 'cuckoo' too many might easily be added (similar errors abound in Elizabethan printing); or else the Elizabethan obsession with the 'cuckoo joke' may have led the actors to over-emphasize it. But, however it happened, when this superfluous 'cuckoo' is removed, *Spring's* chorus takes the same form as *Winter's*; 'Cuckoo, cuckoo' balances and rhymes with 'Tu-whit to-who'; and 'O word of fear' balances and supplies an antithesis to 'A merry note.' Consequently I have ventured to emend *Spring* to this extent, and have left *Winter* untouched. (For dates assigned to Shakespeare's plays, see Sir E. K. Chambers' *William Shakespeare*.)

222. Stzs. 32, 33, and 38 of the concluding poem.

222. Set to music by G. de Wert (c. 1536–1596).

226. Details of conflation: Ll. 1–8, 13–14, 19–24, 29–31 from MS. Ll. 15–18, 27–28, 32–36 from 1597. Ll. 9–12, 25–26 from 1599. Title from 1600. But in l. 25, MS. reads 'Like thousand'; the 'a' in my text being supplied from 1597, 1599, and 1600. MS. ends abruptly with l. 32. L. 33, thy like, 1599 and 1600; the like, 1597. Last line reads thus in the Song Book (1597): *Cantus I,*—'other help for him there's none, other help for him I know there's none.' *Cantus II,*—'other help for him I know there's none there's none.' *Bassus,*—'other help for him I know there's none I know there's none, I &c.,' [repeated, except 'I &c.']. Thus the only rhyme to 'woe' is 'know,' which I believe Weelkes transposed from its original place at the end of the line (see note 184); I have replaced it accordingly.

226. The first of the *Gulling Sonnets*, parodies of the sonneteers and 'The bastard sonnets of these Rymers base,' (*Zepheria*, 1594, being mentioned in one). The most probable date is c. 1596.

239. Ascribed to Cumberland in Francis Davison's MS.

245. Walton says that the bulk of Donne's secular poetry was written before 'his twentieth year'; and Drummond notes that Jonson 'affirmeth Donne to have written all his best pieces ere he was 25 years old'; which statements taken literally would mean either before 1593 or before 1598. Students of Donne, while agreeing that much of his verse, including those lyrics marked by cynicism and lack of tenderness or passion, was most

probably written before 1598, relate the deeply felt, intenser, and more spiritual love poems to his love for Anne More, whom he married in 1601. This seems to me probable, and I have grouped most of my selections as 'Before 1598' or 'Before 1602' accordingly. Doubtful poems I have dated by first publication; and the sonnet on Death, by the 'Elegy on Mrs. Boulstred' (1609), which seems to refer to it. There is also evidence for connecting a 'Song' (p. 428) with his journey to France in 1611; which song, by the by, I have seen entitled in a Bodl. MS. 'To his Mistress when he went to travel.' (See E. K. Chambers' *Poems of John Donne* [c. 1891], and H. J. C. Grierson's *The Poems of John Donne*, 1912.)

248. For date, see H. J. C. Grierson's *The Poems of John Donne*, 1912.

249. Last two ll., 1600, take place of 30 moralizing lines, 1598. Except this and two words given in the footnotes, the texts are alike.

257. The only direct evidence of date is Meres' well-known reference (1598) to Shakespeare's 'sugared sonnets among his private friends,' and also that two of them were printed in *The Passionate Pilgrim*, 1599. They are usually dated c. 1595–8; but a few may be later.

270. In *The Shirburn Ballads*, 1907, ed. by A. Clark, stz. 2, l. 5, reads 'Thy woe, thy time, [and] thy downefall,' spoiling rhyme and rhythm alike. The 'too,' omitted by Clark, is pinched in the binding, but can be seen if MS. is opened wide. Stz. 4, l. 1, 'purge' is written 'purgd' in MS. I suspect the scribe omitted a stanza, or stanzas (between stzs. 4 and 5), referring to a 'willing love'; if not, 'a bird in hand' has little point. For stz. 5, l. 4, read 'Nor true nor constant are to me.'

270. Set to music by Luca Marenzio, who died 1599.

276. Late 16th cent. MS. Poem 'said to have been enclosed in a letter to the Queen from Ireland, in 1599.' (See J. Hannah's *Poems of Sir Walter Raleigh*, etc. 1875.)

277. Possibly a revision by Marston (about 1599) of an earlier play c. 1589? Date of this song uncertain.

278–280. Attribution is extremely doubtful; Jaggard printed as Shakespeare's this collection from many authors.

280. This excerpt was printed twice in *England's Parnassus*, 1600.

282. Late 16th cent. MS.

284. Late 16th cent. MS.

285. Such poems are rarely written after middle life. Raleigh was forty-eight in 1600. No other evidence for date. Early 17th cent. Ms.

286. Stz. 5, l. 4, carry, Bullen 1890; carryed, 1627. Stz. 2, l. 2, 'Tis pity, 1627; Bullen emends ''Tis a pity.' For date, see Bullen's *Poems . . . from the Romances*, etc. 1890.

287. For date, see Collier's 'Introduction' to *Robin Good-Fellow*, Percy Soc., vol. ii., 1840. While believing it derives from the 16th cent., I am doubtful of placing it as early as Collier's 'before 1588.'

289. Late 16th cent. MS.

291. Variants in 1623 are: l. 3, field; l. 4, In the springtime; l. 9, country folks; l. 19, And therefore take the present time; chorus, ding a ding, ding.

291. The music of a song entitled 'O mistress mine' was printed in T. Morley's *The First Book of Consort Lessons*, 1599.

293. Another stanza of this song appears in *King Lear*, III, iii, as follows:

He that has and a little tiny wit,
    With heigh-ho, the wind and the rain,
Must make content with his fortunes fit,
    Though the rain it raineth every day.

298. L. 6, Io, mod. eds.; Ioue, 1603. L. 9, Beauty arise, mod. eds.; Beauty arise, beauty arise, 1603. L. 11, Io to, mod. eds.; Io, Io to, 1603. I have followed mod. eds., taking ll. 5–8 as the correct form.

302. In these three poems the texts of 1601 and 1616 correspond.

312. Stz. 3, l. 3, also emended thus: 'But my heart *wherein* duty,' etc., Bullen; 'But my heart *lives* where duty,' etc., Dr. Fellowes. Both miss the meaning: 'Within this pack these things, but in my heart these very different things.' L. 4, there is little evidence of this use of 'court's' for 'courtship's' tentatively suggested to me by a friend; but it may be preferred to the alternative of reading 'court' and 'brood' as verbs, thus: 'Turtles and twins court, brood, a heavenly pair.'

324. Stzs. 1–4 of 24 stzs. These four were reprinted in Peerson's *Private Music*, 1620. My text follows 1601, with the exception noted.

328. The printed poem is anonymous, 1601; the MS. version ascribes it to F. B. P., which is thought to mean F. B., P[resbyter].

331. Stz. 2, law, N.A.; lone, 1601; loan, Bullen; love, Dr. Fellowes. 'Lawe' hastily written in Elizabethan script might easily have been mistaken for 'lone' by the printer. It does at least make sense.

337. L. 5, asked, many MSS.; ask, 1609, 1633, etc. L. 9, Or, 1635, etc.; Oh, 1609, 1633.

340. As the unique complete copy of 1602 (now in U.S.A.) reads 'mone' where 1611 and 1621 read 'moue,' 'moan' was probably intended originally, in spite of its lack of rhyme. Best frequently used assonance instead of rhyme, and sometimes not even that: for, in addition to this 'moon'–'moan' combination, he attempts to rhyme 'Mary' with 'marry' elsewhere in the two later editions. See note 343.

342. The first three of seven stzs.

343. This and Best's poem (p. 340) have vanished with the missing leaves from the (Bodleian) copy of 1602. I have failed to trace 1608.

346. Judging from Donne's and Hoskins' other poems, I believe, with Prof. Saintsbury and others, that Donne wrote this; in spite of Prof. Grierson's plea for Hoskins (*op. cit.* note 248). It was reprinted in *The Grove*, 1721, with these words–'Absence,/By Dr. J. Donne./This Poem was found in an old Manuscript of/Sir John Cotton's of Stratton/in Huntington-Shire.'

348. This song was freely borrowed from Breton (?), *cf.* p. 150.

349. Note. Every reprint I have seen of this sonnet reads 'done' (l. 12). But the collocation of heaven 'blind' (*i.e.* wanting light), and the world 'dun' (*i.e.* dark), shows the reading of 1602, 1611, and 1621 is correct. Authorship uncertain.

350. Stz. 3 is omitted.

357. Note. Other versions exist, but this, I believe, is the earliest; it is also the best, despite a few mistakes. MS. stz. 7, l. 4, reads 'weep and flock above me,' thus repeating l. 3. My emendation is taken from Rox. stz. 6, which, while otherwise unlike the MS. stz., compresses its theme into one line: 'Ne'er a girl in the town but fain would have me.' I omit an incomplete stz. after stz. 7. Minor points—Stz. 1, l. 4, saileth, Rox.; sealeth, MS. Stz. 4,

l. 7, thy dart, Clark 1907; the dart, MS.   Stz. 6, l. 1, not so coy, Rox.; not coy,
MS.   Stz. 7, l. 3, sheep, Clark; sleep, MS.   Stz. 8, l. 1, Maiden, Clark; Maide
(possibly Maidë) MS.; (Rox. reads 'Fair maiden, have a care, and in time
take me'). Stz. 8, l. 5, One, Rox.; The one, MS.   Stz. 8, l. 6, T'other, Rox.;
The other, MS.   Stz. 11, l. 3, cushnets, N.A. (*cf.* Greene's 'her cushnet,'
1592); cushings, MS. The MS. was written in short lines—

> I will give thee rush rings,
> Key knobs, and cushings,
> Pence, purse, and other things,
> Bells, beads, and bracelets—

and 'cushings' being a familiar spelling of 'cushions,' the '-ings' was probably
caught up from the lines above and below—a common mistake in transcrip-
tion. Also pin-cushions better suit with the other feminine trifles offered.
Finally, stz. 2, l. 6, At me, MS.; Clark misprints 'On me,' (*op. cit.* note 270).
Dated by a ballad on Q. Elizabeth's death 'to the tune of Phillida flouts me,'
in R. Johnson's *Crown Garland of Golden Roses*, 1612.
    358. Set to music by T. Morley (1557–1603).
    360. Texts of 1603 and 1616 correspond.
    362. For date see Hannah, *op. cit.* note 276.
    364. 1608 omits but alludes to this song.
    366. The continuation of this (44 lines) changes into a love poem.
    367. For date, see Hannah, *op. cit.* note 276.
    373. *Wit's Pilgrimage* [n.d.] was registered Sept. 27, 1605.
    393. The arrangement of 1665 vol. was apparently chronological; this and
the following poem are dated by their position in the book.
    400. In Ayton's poems is first heard the distinctive cadence which later
becomes typical of Caroline lyrics. His dated pieces range from 1603 to
1607, with none later except a sonnet in Craig's *Poetical Recreations*, 1609.
In this book Craig has a sonnet bidding Ayton 'Sing, and be not silent. . . .
Shall thy Muse no further fruits forth bring? . . . Tune thy string, be still
admired as thou hast been of yore,' etc. To which Ayton's sonnet replies,
'Fain would I force my silent Muse to please,' and goes on to imply the
vanity of song to relieve sorrow. Therefore, and because love songs like
his are seldom written after middle life (he was then in his 40th year), I
have dated his lyrics 'Before 1609.' My texts are taken from a MS. collec-
tion of his poems made by his nephew and successor after his death.
    403. Attribution doubtful, also date. Not in MS., see note 400.
    404. See note 245.
    406. Emendations: l. 9, low, 1679; lowde, 1609–10 and 1629; l. 27, watches,
1629; walkes, 1609–10.
    407. I cannot find Collier's MS., so follow his reproduction in *Inigo Jones*,
etc., Shakespeare Soc. 1848.
    410. The MS. has an additional, but poorer, stanza.
    412. Fletcher says these poems (1633) were the 'raw essays of my very
unripe years, and almost childhood.' He was aged 28 in 1610. (For date,
see Grosart's *The Poems of Phineas Fletcher*, 1869.) Last four of seven
stzs. entitled 'To my ever-honoured Cousin W. R. Esquire.'

413. Grosart's attribution, see (and for date also) *op. cit.* note 412.

414. Little is known of Fowler. He was in France, a grown man, in 1581; and was Secretary to Q. Anne from 1590 to c.1609, when he disappears from record. His dated pieces range from 1581 to 1603, with three poems in a gloomy moralizing strain in 1610. This poem is placed among 'Poems of doubtful authenticity' in the Scot. Text. Soc. reprint. My text is from the MS. Ll. 1–6 are set to music in Ch. Ch. MS. 87.

417. Variant (2 stzs.) in *The Knight of the Burning Pestle*, 1613.

428. This song was omitted in the 1st ed. 1619 included 1622, and exactly reprinted 1630. 'Gently' was misprinted 'gentle' in the 4th ed. 1638, (I have not seen 5th ed. 1641), and again in 1650, in 1661, in the folio 1679, and in the 10 vol. reprint 1711. Seward in 1750 (10 vols.) also prints 'gentle,' and changes 'lay' to 'lie'—'lie lightly, gentle earth'; and this reading Dyce repeats (1843) with a footnote: 'lie] Old eds. lay, and so perhaps the author wrote.' And since Dyce, all the editors, while varying between 'lay' and 'lie,' have *without exception* perpetuated the 1638 misprint 'gentle' with no reference to the original and correct reading. This is not a question of the common confusion of 'lay' and 'lie': for obviously the second 'lay' is related to the first: 'Lay a garland on my hearse, and lay earth lightly gently on my buried body.' The poem is here printed correctly for the first time for nearly 300 years.

433. Stz. 2, l. 5, rise, rise, rise, rise, 1611. Stz. 2, l. 7, 'and' is omitted, 1611. I have taken the reading of stz. 1 as correct.

434. The *Epigrams* were possibly written before 1600.

437. The poems of Pembroke and Ruddier (*i.e.* Rudyerd) were published jointly in 1660; but as the vol. contains poems by other persons, attribution to either author is sometimes doubtful; as are also the dates. This song was printed anonymously in 1612, at which date Pembroke was 32 years old. Wood says Rudyerd's 'youthful years were adorned with all kinds of polite learning'; and in 1612 he was aged 40. Jonson addressed to him three of his *Epigrams* (registered 1612), one of which begins, 'Writing thyself, or judging others writ,/I know not which th' hast most, candour or wit.' I have grouped the selections from both under 1612, that being the nearest definite date ascertainable.

439. See previous note.

441. Compare *Lovers' Infiniteness*, p. 332. Prof. Grierson says this is ascribed to Donne in one MS. (see note 248). Though differing in form, it follows Donne's thought very closely.

443. First excerpted by Walton, who altered it, chiefly to enable it to stand alone. His reason may perhaps excuse my printing stz. 1 from *The Complete Angler*, 1653. The 1613 text of it here follows:—

> O let me rather on the pleasant brink
> Of Tyne and Trent possess some dwelling place,
> Where I may see my quill and cork down sink
> With eager bit of barble, bleak, or dace,
> And on the world and his Creator think,
> While they proud Thais painted sheet embrace.
>   And with the fume of strong Tobacco's smoke,
>   All quaffing round are ready for to choke.

446. Song generally ascribed to Fletcher.

454. For authorship and date, see *D.N.B.*

458. For date, see *D.N.B.*

460. Several versions exist. Said to have been first printed with Overbury's *Wife*, 1614, but is in no known copy. It is in *Reliquiae Wottonianae* 1651, whence it is usually reprinted. My text is from an early 17th cent. MS., which is probably the oldest extant text and (because it clears up *Rel. Wott.'s* obscure stz. 3) the most authentic. I have, however, adopted *Rel. Wott.'s* order of stzs.; the MS. places stz. 4 last.

461. The opening lines of a long poem, *To the Detracted*.

464. This parody was written in ridicule of the old romances, and, I suspect, with a side glance at *The Faerie Queen*.

465. Original title is 'Melancholy Conceits.'

480. Stzs. 2 and 3 are from 1631, where they first appeared; stz. 1 from 1640, where the whole poem first was printed.

488. 'Written by Fletcher, Massinger, Middleton, and Rowley,' see *D.N.B.* for authorship and date. Song alluded to 1647, first printed 1679.

489. Note. This piece (with the possible exception of lines 7 and 8) was probably written by Raleigh, but *not* as an epitaph on himself. The question is discussed in my letter to the *Times Lit. Sup.*, Oct. 27, 1932, where the legend that Raleigh wrote these lines in his Bible on the eve of his execution is shown to be of late growth and therefore suspect. As Bullen pointed out in 1889, lines 1–6 form the last stz. of an undated poem in B.M. MS. Harl. 6917, entitled, 'A Poem of Sir Walter Rawleighs'; since when at least three anonymous transcripts of it, partial or complete, have been recorded in other MSS. The oldest known printed text of any part of the poem was formerly the so-called 'Epitaph' in *The Prerogative of Parliaments*, 1628, which is given in the text; but in the second edition of the present work, I was able to give a still earlier printed version of ll. 1–6, from *A Helpe to Memorie and Discourse*, 1621, a little-known book of which apparently only one copy has survived. This copy is imprinted 'Second Impression'; thus, as the book was registered Nov. 1619, the lines were probably printed that year or early in 1620. The introductory words seem to refer to the death of Raleigh, and, followed by the verse, run thus:

'The Court hath made few happy, it hath undone many: and those that it hath most favoured it hath undone, dealing with her favourites as Dalilah with Sampson, or as time with her minions, that still promiseth better and longer days, when in a moment she withdraweth the one, and performeth not the other, but falsifieth in both, as one lately to this purpose hath both experienced, and uttered as followeth.

> —Even such is time that takes in trust
>   Our youth, our joys and all we have
> And pays us but with age and dust,
>   Within the dark and silent grave,
> When we have wandred all our ways,
>   Shut[s] up the story of our days.'

492. The well-known short version of this poem, beginning 'Mortality, behold and fear,' formerly attributed to Francis Beaumont, consists (as I

showed in the first edition) of three excerpts from a long anonymous poem previously unknown. The original version was first printed in W. B. & E. P.'s *A Helpe to Discourse*, 1619, (registered 1618), with the title 'A Memento for Mortalitie./Taken from the view of Sepulchres of so many Kings and Nobles, as lye interred in the Abbey of Westminster'; and was reprinted in all the later editions I have been able to trace, viz.: 1620, 1621, 1627, 1628, 1635, 1636, 1638 and 1648; it also appears in Weever's *Ancient Funerall Monuments*, 1631. The familiar short version (which consists of lines 1–4, 19–30, and 33, of the longer poem, plus a meaningless last line) was first printed without attribution in *Wits Recreations*, 2nd ed., 1641, and entitled 'On the Tombes in Westminster'; it likewise was reprinted in all the later editions. Beaumont died in 1616; his collected *Poems*, published in 1640, includes neither version; but in 1653 this collection was enlarged by the addition of other pieces, such as songs from his and Fletcher's plays, together with a number of poems by other men (*e.g.* Sir John Beaumont, Donne, Basse, etc.) which were included as Beaumont's, and among these, a reprint (even repeating a misprint) of this short version from *Wits Recreations*. The facts may now be summarized thus—(*a*) the long version is the older by 22 years; (*b*) it had been printed at least 14 times both before Beaumont's *Poems*, 1640, was published (in which it was *not* included), and before the first appearance of the short version in 1641; (*c*) the short version had likewise been printed several times before it appeared in the 1653 vol. as Beaumont's along with other poems certainly not his; (*d*) the original poem has never been claimed for Beaumont, but only the late short version of it; and (*e*) there is no other evidence on record for the association of Beaumont's name with the poem earlier than the 1653 volume. From all of which it would appear that the attribution of the short version to Beaumont can no longer be seriously considered. On the other hand, there is much reason to believe the concealed author was William Basse, to whom it is here attributed with a query. For evidence and argument, see my letter in the *Times Lit. Sup.*, Jan. 12, 1933.

493. 'The Last Song' in *The Mountebank's Masque* was printed in the first edition of this work from the then oldest known text of the song, namely that in J. Nichols' *Progresses . . . of Queen Elizabeth*, 1788. The masque had not been printed before that date, and all trace has since been lost of the MS. from which Nichols took his text. J. P. Collier next printed the masque (Shakespeare Society, 1848) from a Devonshire MS. which omitted this 'Last Song'; and A. H. Bullen (Marston's *Works*, 1887), stating that the Devonshire MS. had likewise vanished, printed the masque from Collier's text, but inserted this song from Nichols' text. The only other recorded MS. of the masque is the B.M. Add. MS. 5956, but there again the song is omitted. While searching through Bodley MS. Ashm. 36–7 (a well-known collection of some 150 MSS. of various dates) I discovered on two closely written leaves—obviously a fragment of an early Seventeenth Century MS., but one which had remained unidentified—the latter part of *The Mountebank's Masque* containing 'The Last Song.' The MS. begins with the 'twenty neuter paradoxes' read by Paradox, but, towards the end, has an excision where these words occur; 'His [Paradox's] deciphering of them particularly and his after speeches are omitted because

tedious.' Happily the old transcriber, unlike the other two, cut the dull speeches rather than the charming song. The MS. fragment gives fuller stage directions than either the Nichols or Collier text, which suggests an earlier transcription from the original; the writing is 'probably not later than 1630,' and may very well be contemporary with the performance. It throws no light on the problem of authorship, but enables us to correct the 1788 text of the song, and some more recent emendations, in several places. Bullen attributed this song to Marston (*op. cit.*), but later (1889) to Campion; and with the latter, Mr. P. Vivian (*Campion's Works*, 1909) is inclined to agree.

494. The song is anonymous. For attribution to Campion see Vivian's *Campion's Works*, p. LI f.

495. The last two and best of four stzs.

500. The 5th ed. 1625, in the Bodleian, seems to be the oldest extant copy, but this has lost the leaves containing the poem except the last two stzs. The next oldest is the 6th ed. 1629, from which my text is taken, with collations from the 9th ed. 1638. If this is Wither's (Hearne quoted stz. 3 as Wither's), it was probably written either while he was still at Oxford (c. 1605–6) or shortly afterwards, though not published till some twelve years later.

502. These are stzs. 6 and 8–11 (the last).

507. For date, see *Camb*.

509. The first three of ten stzs.

509. Note. The 1624 variants are—l. 5, the moon doth rise; l. 6, you wandering chanters; l. 7, Who fill the ears with Nature's lays; l. 8, your passions understood; l. 9, By weaker accents; l. 10, voice doth raise; l. 11, violets which first; l. 12, By those your purple; l. 13, Much like proud; l. 16, my Princess shall; l. 17, In sweetness of her looks and mind; l. 18, Oh, tell if. Also stzs. 2 and 3 are transposed.

512. For date, see *The Jacobean Drama*, by U. M. Ellis-Fermor.

512. For date, see *Camb*.

515. Failing to trace Collier's MS., I have followed his reproduction in *Twenty-five Old Ballads and Songs*, 1869.

516. Bullen first discovered this song, but unfortunately published a faulty version of it in *More Lyrics from the Song Books*, 1888, which has since been followed by scores of editors, all of whom have apparently preferred to copy his text, rather than to examine the original MS. Bullen printed as l. 8, 'When the winds blow and the seas flow.' The MS. reads 'When the winds do blow'; and originally read 'And the seas do flow'; but this second 'do,' having been written at the edge of the page, was cut away when the edges of the MS. were trimmed—presumably by the binder,—for a fragment of the note of music to which 'do' must have been sung is still left on the extreme edge of the page. The music was composed by N. Giles, M.D., Chorister at Magdalen Coll., Oxford, 1559–61, and Clerk, 1577; later Master of the Children of St. George's, Windsor, and of the Chapel Royal; died 1633. In 1620 he must thus have been an old man of 70 or more; and it being very improbable that he was composing after that date, and as the lyric must have been written before he set it to music, I have dated it accordingly.

BIOGRAPHICAL NOTES

[The chief authority for the following notes is the D.N.B., though more recent 'Lives' have also been consulted when available]

Beaumont, Francis (1584–1616). Dramatist, descended from an old Leicestershire family, his father being a Justice of the Common Pleas. He was educated at Broadgates Hall (Pembroke College), Oxford; then went to London and entered the Inner Temple, 1600. He became an intimate friend of Drayton, Jonson, and Fletcher, most of the plays for which he is famous being written in conjunction with the last-named. As methods and details of their collaboration are not known, the authorship of the songs in those plays cannot be determined. He failed to collect and publish his poems in his lifetime, and the posthumous editions of them in 1640 and 1653 contain much verse by other people.

Breton, Nicholas (1545?–1626?). The son of a wealthy merchant, probably educated at Oriel College, Oxford. Little is known of his long life, or of his relations with his contemporaries, though the Countess of Pembroke was among his early patrons. He devoted himself to literature and was pre-eminently a poet, but was also a versatile and prolific writer of romances, dialogues, essays and tracts in prose, his numerous works being published throughout his life from 1577. He was a lover of nature, and his verse reflects much of the beauty and freshness of the countryside.

Browne, William (1591–1643?). A Devonshire man, born and educated at Tavistock, and later going on to Exeter College, Oxford, and the Inner Temple. He was for some time a member of the retinue of the Earl of Pembroke at Wilton, and his latter years were passed quietly in the country. He wrote eclogues and a masque, but his chief work was *Britannia's Pastorals*, in three books, though Book III was not printed until 1852. He greatly admired Spenser, and ranks next to him as a writer of pastoral poetry. Amongst later poets who have been influenced by his work are Milton, Keats, and Mrs. Browning.

Campion, Thomas (1567–1619?). Poet, musician, and physician; educated at Cambridge and Gray's Inn, he became a 'Doctor of Phisicke' not later than 1606. He was a musician as well as a poet; and after joining with his friend Rosseter in 1601 in producing a song book for which he wrote much of the verse and music, he published four *Books of Airs* which were all his own work, words and music. He was also the author of many masques which were performed at Court. In 1602 he wrote *Observations in the Art of English Poesy* in which he held forth against the use of rhyme in English verse; his contention was ably opposed by Samuel Daniel. As a poet he was forgotten for two and a half centuries until A. H. Bullen first collected and published his works in 1889; since when his songs have taken their rightful place amongst the most exquisite lyric poetry of all time.

Chettle, Henry (1562?–1607?). Dramatist and pamphleteer; the son of a dyer in London; became a printer and publisher; wrote satirical pamphlets, was author or joint author of over forty plays, and wrote an elegy on the death of Queen Elizabeth. He is said never to have been free from money troubles, and was at least once imprisoned for debt.

Constable, Henry (1562–1613). Son of Sir Robert Constable of Newark; was a graduate of St. John's College, Cambridge, and a friend of Sir Philip Sidney. He became a Roman Catholic and lived for many years, and died, on the continent. For a time he was a papal envoy to Edinburgh. He suffered a short term of imprisonment in the Tower after coming to London without permission in 1603. He is chiefly known for his sonnets, which were very typical of his time; the first edition of his book of sonnets, *Diana*, appeared in 1592.

Daniel, Samuel (1562–1619). A poet, born in Somerset, the son of a music master; educated at Magdalen Hall, Oxford, which he left without taking a degree; was tutor to William Herbert, the third Earl of Pembroke. He published a book of sonnets, *Delia*, in 1592, and in 1602 printed his *Defence of Rhyme*, attacking Campion's *Observations*. He also wrote a long historical epic on the Lancastrian civil wars, tragedies in the manner of Seneca, a *General Defence of Learning*, *Epistles* to persons of importance, and masques for production at Court, where he held office. His poems were criticised by Ben Jonson, but praised by other writers, including Drummond of Hawthornden. He frequently revised his poems, and rarely without improvement; and his sonnets fall—if at all—very little short of the finest in the language. On retirement he returned to Somerset, where he died.

Davison, Francis (1575?–1619). Was the son of a Privy Councillor and Secretary of State to Queen Elizabeth, educated at Gray's Inn, and afterwards travelled much abroad, chiefly in Italy. He is known for his *Poetical Rapsody*, a collection of poetry published in 1602, which was one of the best of the miscellanies then so popular, and was several times republished. He included many of his own poems in it, with much justification, for they are amongst the best in the collection.

Dekker, Thomas (1570?–1640?). A dramatist and pamphleteer of whom very little is known. He was born in London and gained his living by literary work; was familiar with the lowest haunts of the city and their dissolute and desperate inmates; and when engaged by Henslowe to write plays, he based them on the life around him; many being written in collaboration with other dramatists. He quarrelled with Ben Jonson, who ridiculed him in a play; Dekker soon retorted in like fashion. Besides numerous plays, he wrote satirical pamphlets, prose tracts and sketches, pageants, and lyric and other verse. The greatest of the many contemporary pamphleteers, he paints the most realistic pictures of the life of his time.

Donne, John (1572?–1631). Poet and cleric; the son of a London iron-monger, who died when he was three; he was brought up as a Roman Catholic by his mother, and entered Hart Hall, Oxford, when he was eleven, to avoid having to take the oath of supremacy. He was later ad-mitted at Lincoln's Inn. He went with Essex's expedition to Cadiz in 1596, and subsequently travelled in Italy and Spain. He was Secretary to Sir Thomas Egerton, Lord Keeper of the Great Seal; but having married secretly in 1601, was dismissed, and for a long time suffered real poverty. As a young man he had joined the Church of England, and he was urged by one of the King's chaplains to take orders, but refused on religious grounds, in 1607. With the passing years, however, his interest in religion increased, and, still lacking any secular advancement, he was ordained in 1615, and shortly afterwards appointed chaplain to James I; he was made divinity reader at Lincoln's Inn the following year, and in 1621 Dean of St. Paul's. He became the foremost preacher of his time, and his sermons are among the finest in our literature. His love poetry was written while he was a young man, his religious poetry later, as his interests changed; but hardly any verse was published in his lifetime, while many of his sermons were printed as soon as they were preached. He was the first of the metaphysical poets, his lyrics are personal, passionate and intellectual, in contrast with those of the earlier Elizabethan writers; and his preoccupation with the idea of death tinged much of his verse with strange sombre colors, from which even his love lyrics are not entirely free.

Drayton, Michael (1563–1631). Poet; a Warwickshire man by birth, and traditionally said to have been a friend of Shakespeare and Ben Jonson. He was a voluminous writer of poetry of all kinds, and of plays in collab-oration with others. He collected and issued many editions of his own works. Early religious and pastoral poetry was followed by numerous poems inspired by his love of England—*Legends* from historical chronicles; *The Barons' War* (1596), a historical epic; and *England's Heroical Epistles* (1597), love letters supposed to have been written by historical persons. He is perhaps best known to students for his *Poly-Olbion*, written in rhymed couplets and published in parts between 1613 and 1622, a description of Great Britain which, besides being geographical, deals with legendary his-tory, antiquities and local wonders of all kinds; but for most readers his fame rests on the well-known *Agincourt*, *Nymphidia*, and a handful of his early lyrics.

Drummond, William, of Hawthornden (1585–1649). Son of a Scottish landowner, educated at Edinburgh High School and Edinburgh University, later studied law in France. Succeeded to his father's property in 1610, and spent the rest of his life at Hawthornden as the laird. He was a writer, student (knowing many languages), and inventor of mechanical devices, taking no active part in public affairs, but enjoying the company of learned men, among whom was Ben Jonson who visited him in Scotland in 1618–19. He was the first Scottish poet to write in English as his mother tongue. His best-known works are his two books of poems, the first is dated in 1616, and contains sonnets and lyrics written for the most part in memory of his lost love (whether betrothed, young wife, or mistress—authorities differ) who had died the previous year; the second book, published in 1623, is chiefly religious in character and includes some of his finest verse.

Fletcher, John (1579–1625). Dramatist, born at Rye in Sussex, where his father—who later became Bishop of London—was officiating as minister; educated at Bene't (Corpus) College, Cambridge. He was probably living in London and already writing plays before 1607, for in that year he is known to have been working with Beaumont, which fruitful and famous collaboration lasted till Beaumont's death in 1616. Thereafter, till his own death, Fletcher continued to write plays both alone and with other dramatists. Of the sixteen that were entirely his own work *The Faithful Shepherdess,* a pastoral play, shows his lyrical power at its best, and is his greatest work. He excelled in comedy and romance, and his plays were still popular at the time of the Restoration.

Gascoigne, George (1525?–1577). Poet, born at Cardington, Bedfordshire, educated at Trinity College, Cambridge, and Gray's Inn; he was a member of Parliament; a soldier, who saw service in Holland, and a courtier, as well as a poet and dramatist. He adapted a comedy of Ariosto which was acted at Gray's Inn, wrote a book of tales, lyrics, one of the earliest English tragedies in blank verse, and an essay on the making of verse in English. His poems show the transition from the work of Wyatt and Surrey to that of Sidney and the younger Elizabethans, and he held a high place as a writer in the opinion of his contemporaries.

Greene, Robert (1560?–1592). Pamphleteer and poet; born in Norwich, educated at St. John's College, Cambridge; travelled abroad for a time, and on his return to England is thought by some to have been ordained and given a living in Essex. He lived a dissolute life, however, deserted his wife after spending her dowry, went to London and made a livelihood by writing, but died in poverty. Though he accused himself of many crimes he would seem, judging from his own works, to have been rather reckless than vicious. He wrote plays, the best known being *Friar Bacon and Friar Bungay;* romances, of which *Pandosto* was the source of Shakespeare's *The Winter's Tale;* and pamphlets. In the last of these, *A Groatsworth of Wit bought with a Million of Repentance,* which is autobiographical, he attacks Shakespeare (of whose popularity as a playwright he was jealous), as an 'upstart crow'. Though inclined to euphuism, his work is fresh and pleasant; his great gift being for lyrics, the best of which occur in his romances.

Jonson, Ben (1572?–1637). Born most probably in or near London, of Scottish descent, his father having died a month previously, leaving his mother in penury. He was educated at Westminster School, then apparently worked for a short time at his step-father's trade of bricklaying, which he 'could not endure', and from which he escaped by volunteering for military service with the English troops against the Spaniards in Flanders. On his return home he joined a company of actors, and began to write plays, sometimes in collaboration with other writers, working for Henslowe. His first great comedy, *Every Man in his Humour*, was acted in 1598, and his earliest extant tragedy, *Sejanus*, in 1603. He was in great favour at the Court of James I, wrote many Court masques, and was rewarded with a pension. Though the best of his plays were written between 1603 and 1615, he continued to write till almost the end of his life. In 1618 he set out on foot for a long visit to Scotland, saw the old home of his family, stayed with Drummond of Hawthornden, and was made a burgess of Edinburgh. In 1628 he became Chronologer to the City of London. Besides plays and masques, he wrote a volume of prose essays and three volumes of poems. He was successful, arrogant and didactic, and had very definite theories as to the writing of plays, which tended to make him contemptuous of other writers, rousing enmity which led to quarrels. He did not, however, lack for friends, amongst whom were many important people of the time and most of the best-known writers. Of the dramatists of his age, he ranks next to Shakespeare.

Lodge, Thomas (1558?–1625). Author, son of a Lord Mayor of London; was educated at Merchant Taylors' School, London, and Trinity College, Oxford, and entered Lincoln's Inn. He soon left law for literature; his first publication, *A Defence of Poetry, Music, and Stage Plays*, appeared in 1579. He wrote both prose and verse: pamphlets, romances and tracts, lyrics, satires and plays, and translations from the classics. After some years he began to travel and visited Italy, the Canary Isles and South America, continuing his writing during his voyages. His romance, *Rosalynde, Euphues Golden Legacy*, was the basis of Shakespeare's *As You Like It*. His collection of poems, *Phillis*, contains his pastoral lyrics, which are esteemed his best work. When aged about forty he became a Roman Catholic, took up the study of medicine and qualified in 1603 as a physician.

Lyly, John (1554?–1606). Born in Kent, graduated at Magdalen College, Oxford, and later studied at Cambridge. He then went to London, where he spent the rest of his life. He was popular at Court where he had a post producing the entertainments and training the actors, and for some years was a member of Parliament. He is chiefly known for his *Euphues, the Anatomy of Wit*, published in 1579, a very original work in content and style, which ran to many editions and was largely imitated, though ridiculed by Shakespeare and Ben Jonson, among others. He wrote many plays which were acted at Court, mostly comedies in prose, with artificial plots and little characterization, but depending for their effect on their literary qualities. They contain some excellent songs which though alluded to were not included in the original editions, but appeared in print for the first time in *Six Court Comedies*, 1632, in their proper positions in the plays. Their authenticity was questioned some time ago; but in R. W. Bond's review of the evidence for and against, in 1930–1, the traditional authorship is reaffirmed as the most probable. (See Note 104).

Nashe, Thomas (1567–1601). Author, born at Lowestoft, educated at St. John's College, Cambridge, visited France and Italy, then settled in London and earned his living by writing. He published several satires on contemporary subjects, took part in the Martin Marprelate controversy against the Puritans, and carried to great lengths a pamphlet warfare with Gabriel Harvey (who had attacked the memory of his friend Greene). The following year he was imprisoned for his attack on abuses of the time in a comedy, *The Isle of Dogs*. Of his works the best was *The Life of Jack Wilton*, a novel of low life and adventure; it was the first novel of adventure in English. Both his character and the style of his writing were independent and outspoken, original and audacious. His sombre lyrics in *Summer's Last Will and Testament* take their place amongst the best of the period.

Peele, George (1558?-1597). Son of a clerk of Christ's Hospital, he was educated there, at Broadgates Hall (Pembroke College), Oxford, and later, across the road, at Christ Church. He went to London, and began to write for the stage. His life is said, possibly with some exaggeration, to have been dissolute, and the Governors of Christ's Hospital forbade him his father's house in the precincts. Though he became successful as an actor and dramatist he died in distress. His numerous writings include pageants, many plays, the best being a pastoral, *The Arraignment of Paris*, and miscellaneous verse, his lyrics being deservedly popular amongst his contemporaries.

Raleigh, Sir Walter (1552?-1618). Soldier, sailor, and author; born in Devonshire, and educated at Oriel College, Oxford. He began his career as a soldier, first serving with the Huguenots in France, and later, after undertaking a 'voyage of discovery' with his half-brother, Sir Humphrey Gilbert, in 1578, served both in the Netherlands and in Ireland. While in Ireland he was sent home with despatches (1581), was noticed by Queen Elizabeth at Court, became a great favourite with her, remained at Court several years, and was knighted in 1584. Under a patent to colonize which he obtained, Virginia was settled, and several other expeditions undertaken, though with little success. He took a leading part in preparing the defence of England against the Spanish attack of 1588, and was present at the naval actions against Spain near the Azores and at Cadiz. On the accession of James I he was imprisoned on charges of conspiracy against the King and condemned to death. He was reprieved, but lived in the Tower with his family and wrote there his great work, *The History of the World*, which was published in 1614. Two years later he was allowed to take an expedition to the Orinoco to seek gold—a most ill-fated venture, as no gold was found, and, against express orders, a Spanish settlement was destroyed. Partly to appease Spain, he was beheaded in 1618 under the original death sentence. Besides his *History* he wrote poetry, much of which is lost, essays, and accounts of battles and discoveries.

Shakespeare, William (1564-1616). Born at Stratford-on-Avon, son of a farmer who was Alderman and Bailiff there. He was educated at the local Grammar School, worked for his father for a time, married early (1582), and left his family at home three years later. Arriving in London in

1586, he soon afterwards joined a company of actors and worked not only as player but also as playwright, training his prentice hand by revising or altering the plays of others for the stage. Such, for instance, is the accepted explanation of the obviously different hands in the three parts of *Henry VI*, which date from 1591–2; Shakespeare's own early plays like *Love's Labour's Lost*, *Two Gentlemen of Verona*, and *A Midsummer Night's Dream*, being now ascribed to the years 1594–6. In the meantime his long love poems, *Venus and Adonis*, and *Lucrece* (both dedicated to the Earl of Southampton), had been published, and many of the sonnets written. Also at Christmas, 1594, he had been one of the actors summoned to perform before the Queen at Court, which is said to have been the beginning of the great favour she showed him for the rest of her life—a royal patronage that was happily maintained by her successor, James I. Shakespeare prospered throughout his career; and continued to write plays steadily year by year until about 1611–2. Then, his last complete play, *The Tempest*, being finished, he returned to Stratford-on-Avon, where, years before, he had bought New Place—the largest house in the town—against his retirement. There, at Stratford, he settled down for the last years of his life, taking part in local affairs, but also making frequent journeys to his house in London to see his numerous friends—journeys which perforce were discontinued towards the end. And there, in 1616, fitly rounding off a life of the highest human achievement, he died where he was born, and was buried in the church in which he was baptized.

Sidney, Sir Philip (1554–1586). Soldier, statesman, and poet; born at Penshurst in Kent, educated at Shrewsbury and Christ Church, Oxford, afterwards travelling extensively on the continent. He was interested in literature, was a friend of Spenser who dedicated his first important poem, *The Shepherd's Calendar*, to him; began to write poetry himself, particularly sonnets addressed to 'Stella', whom he loved in vain. He was much at Court, and though for a time out of favour, because of his opposition to the marriage projected between the Queen and the Duke of Anjou, was soon forgiven and knighted. Other honours and offices followed, amongst which he was named Master of the Horse and later Master of Ordnance. He was interested in the colonization of America; attempted to join Drake's expedition, 1585, but was recalled to Court, subsequently becoming governor of Flushing. During an attack on the Spaniards near Zutphen he was wounded in the thigh, and died some days later at Arnhem. His chief work was his *Arcadia*, a romance written for his sister, the Countess of Pembroke, partly in prose and partly in verse, and never intended for publication. It was first printed in 1590; his other works being *Astrophel and Stella*, 1591, and *Apology for Poetry*, 1595; and all three, with other minor pieces, were collected in one volume in 1598. These works became extremely popular and were praised and imitated for a hundred years.

Spenser, Edmund (1552?–1599). The son of a Lancashire man who had settled in London; was educated at Merchant Taylors' School and Pembroke Hall, Cambridge. He made many friends among literary men, Sir Philip Sidney being one, and started early to write verse, both in sonnet form and in classical metres. *The Shepherd's Calendar*, a pastoral published in 1579, was at once acclaimed. In 1580, while in the household of the Earl of Leicester, he was appointed secretary to Lord Grey of Wilton, Lord Lieutenant of Ireland. For the next ten years he held offices in Ireland, finally settling at Kilcolman Castle near Cork, which was granted to him with a large estate. *The Faerie Queen*, Books I–III, was published in 1590; *Colin Clout's Come Home Again*, written after a visit to England, *Amoretti*, a collection of sonnets, and *Epithalamium*, written at the time of his marriage in 1594, appeared in 1595; Books IV, V, and VI of *The Faerie Queen* and the *Four Hymns* in 1596. He was appointed Sheriff of County Cork in September, 1598, and a month later during a sudden rising of the Irish his castle was burnt and he and his family escaped with only their lives. He was sent to London on official business and died while there, in poverty, in January, 1599. He was considered by contemporaries the greatest living poet, an opinion which (apart from Shakespeare) is still a true one.

Surrey, Henry Howard, Earl of (1517?–1547). Son of Thomas Howard, 3rd Duke of Norfolk; educated by John Clerk, his father's secretary. He served with his father in the army in England (1536), and Scotland (1542), and commanded the English Army on the continent in 1544–6. The King's brother, the Earl of Hertford, was jealous of him, he was recalled to England, groundlessly charged with high treason, condemned and beheaded. He translated two books of the *Aeneid* into blank verse in iambic pentameters (the first use of this metre in English), wrote lyrics, and with Wyatt introduced the sonnet into England. His verse was widely circulated in manuscript during his life; but, with one or two exceptions, was first printed in Tottel's miscellany ten years after his death.

Wyatt, Sir Thomas (1503?–1542). Poet, born in Kent, educated at St. John's College, Cambridge. He held office at the court of Henry VIII, was High Marshal of Calais and Ambassador to Spain. He was twice imprisoned for supposed treasonable activities. At the time of his death he was Knight of the Shire for Kent. He turned psalms into English metre (published 1549), wrote much poetry, was interested in foreign literature, and is noteworthy as having introduced the sonnet into England from Italy.

INDEX OF AUTHORS

(The references are to pages; but an italic figure in parentheses following a reference—e.g. 455(2), or 317–321(8),—denotes the number of the author's poems occurring on the page or pages indicated. The dates are taken, with a few exceptions, from the D.N.B. A double dagger ‡ placed in front of a name signifies that the poet was writing after 1620, and selections of his later work appear in the succeeding volume—'Seventeenth Century Lyrics.')

INDEX OF SUBJECTS

(The references are to pages on which the poems will be found)

545

[Note. Ordinarily the references are to complete poems on the theme indicated. There are, however, a few peculiarly interesting exceptions where only a portion of the poem is concerned with the particular subject. The indexing of incidental allusions could of course be indefinitely extended; for many poems (such as Spenser's *Epithalamion* and Shakespeare's *Sonnets*) reflect innumerable aspects of contemporary life and thought.]

INDEX OF FIRST LINES

(A dagger † denotes poems printed for the first time.)

547